Singing with the Mountains

Singing with the Mountains

The Language of God in the Afghan Highlands

William E. B. Sherman

Fordham University Press
New York 2024

Visit us online at www.fordhampress.com.

Library of Congress Cataloging-in-Publication Data available online at https://catalog.loc.gov.

Printed in the United States of America

26 25 24   5 4 3 2 1

First edition

Contents

Preface: First Words vii

Acknowledgments xi

Mountains and Messiahs: An Introduction 1

1 Bayazid's Doubles: Hagiography and History in the Messianic Community 29

2 The *Dhikr* of the Wretch: Text, Practice, and the Roshani Self 62

3 Revelation through Repetition: The Roshaniyya Write the Word of God 90

4 Vernacular Apocalypse: Poetic and Polemical Emergences of Pashto Literature 118

5 The Vanguard of Disbelief: Afghan Ethnicity and Temporality after the Roshaniyya 151

Ishmael's Daydream: A Conclusion 180

A Note on Sources 189

Notes 193

Bibliography 227

Index 253

Preface: First Words

This is the story of a religious community in the sixteenth and seventeenth centuries. Known as the Roshaniyya ("the people of light"), they lived in the mountainous regions that are currently divided by the border between Afghanistan and Pakistan. In these Afghan highlands, they sought to speak the language of God. What is the language of God? How can we describe the timbre of divine revelation and speak it anew? In posing these questions and seeking to develop a practice of revelation, this community followed the leadership of Bayazid Ansari, remembered by the epithet of *pir-i roshan*: the luminous master and messianic guide (*mahdi*) of the apocalyptic age in which they lived.

As this book relates, their efforts to bring God into language and to build a messianic community around their revelatory language earned them the hostility of Mughal emperors and Sunni polemicists. Though the Roshaniyya suffered defeat in battle and though their religious teachings were forgotten by later generations, this book argues that their story is one worth pondering today. Out of their pursuit of God's language, Pashto literature emerged in new modes. Out of their violent suppression, new forms of Afghan identity were developed and consolidated. In battling the Roshaniyya, the Mughal Empire consolidated its power throughout the Afghan highlands. The Roshaniyya's approach to Islam, the Qur'an, and the prophetic past challenges our assumptions of how Muslims situated themselves in time. Thus, as this book argues, their case invigorates our understanding of vernacularization, of Islamic history and the Mughal Empire, and of ethnic identity and belonging.

Above all else, though, this is a book about the language of the Roshaniyya and about their imagination of language as the connective tissue between the human, God, and a cosmos saturated with communicative potential all around. Furthermore, the practices and theories of language that we find among the Roshaniyya—however startling they may be—are precisely what connect this group to larger, transregional histories of linguistic experimentation throughout Central and South Asia. This is a crucial point. Despite nearly twenty years of military presence in Afghanistan, Americans frequently imagine Afghanistan as a timeless space. History has been shielded from this country ringed with foreboding mountains, and so it exists isolated, caught in some other time—or so the story is told in the soldiers' memoirs, Hollywood films, and sporadic news reports that shape the contours of the American conception of Afghanistan.

Given the importance of language to the Roshaniyya and the sprawling multilingualism of their texts, it is necessary to clarify the linguistic commitments of this book. As much as possible, I try to bring their words, practices, and ideas into contact with the reader. Thus, I use translations as much as possible and adopt a simple transliteration scheme in which transliterated words will appear initially with diacritical marks and subsequently without: *mahdī*, the "guided one" of many Islamic end-times narratives, will become mahdi for most of this book. I transliterate most names without diacritical marks, and I transliterate names according to a simplified Arabic transliteration scheme when the names appear in different sources and multiple languages (thus, Khidr instead of Khizr or Khiḍr, for instance). Moreover, the titles of texts are found here as *The Endeavor of the Believers* and *The Book of States* rather than as *Maqṣūd al-mu'minīn* and *Ḥāl-nāmah*, for example. Despite its precision, transliteration creates distance. *Maqṣūd al-mu'minīn* rests uneasily on the edge of most English-language readers' consciousness, forgotten quickly unless one already has a working understanding of Arabic, Persian, or Pashto. Similarly, *walī* keeps Bayazid Ansari as something foreign while *saint* does not. To put a spin on Walter Benjamin's famous argument, rather than turning "their" Arabic, Persian, and Pashto into "our" English, we should reshape our English through encounter with Arabic, Persian, and Pashto.[1] We should let *saint* turn into something different and something new as it bears the load of Roshani imaginations.

There is, of course, a grave risk in preferring *saint* to *walī*. As has happened far too often, a term such as *saint* threatens to consume and colonize *walī* by forcing a local understanding of a Sufi "friend of God" into a conceptual space dominated and shaped by European Christianity. I believe this risk is worth taking, however, as long as we grant these English terms a porousness that they already have. Saint can mean something new once seen through the story of the Roshaniyya. We in the twenty-first century can expose our minds to their imaginations. Given the aforementioned isolation of Afghanistan in American discourse, I have chosen the risk of translation with the hope that English may be transformed through the intimacy of translation.

There is another language to note here in the preface: the language of "theory." With some regularity in this book, I lean upon the concepts and vocabularies of scholars such as Saba Mahmood and Giorgio Agamben. I do not do so to "apply" their theory to premodern South Asia. Rather, I turn to Mahmood and Agamben (among many others) out of some desperation for that next word or that next turn of phrase that helps describe the elusive world of the Roshaniyya. The Roshaniyya's practice of revelation hinged on a conception of language that is quite different than the dominant "semiotic ideologies" of the twentieth and twenty-first centuries. The work of words was understood in ways different from the way we typically understand it today. The problem, therefore, is that our very habits of language prevent us from naming—and possibly even seeing—the Roshani imagination of language. Mahmood, Agamben, and others explore alternative understandings to dominant conceptions of language, and they have thus done the exceedingly difficult work of developing the vocabulary to name the limits of language. I draw upon their language not to offer a fully theorized explanation of the Roshaniyya but to express in different ways the critical lesson the Roshaniyya offer us: language is a wilder and more powerful thing than we often assume.

Acknowledgments

As I think back upon this project, an image of an hourglass comes to mind. A vast number of friends, colleagues, librarians, books, manuscripts, libraries, offices, cups of tea, keystrokes, notebooks, hard drives, fellowships, and hours all come to a single point—*this book*—and then, through a type of alchemy, I hope that the project proliferates once again, this time into readers and critics. Put more simply: there is no book without the constellation of supporters and mentors who have assisted me along the way.

To begin with, I am grateful to those institutions and sponsors that generously supported me financially, allowing me to pursue this project at all: the Abbasi Program for Islamic Studies at Stanford, the Institute for South Asia Studies at UC Berkeley, the American Institute of Pakistan Studies the American Council of Learned Societies, and the College of Liberal Arts and Sciences at UNC Charlotte. I am also grateful for the flexibility and support shown by my own Department of Religious Studies as I have completed this project. As this project has transformed from a set of questions into a something fashioned of ink, paper, and glue (or some buzzing lights on liquid crystal displays), I have been lucky to find myself working with Fordham University Press. While I have no doubt that this book has benefited from the efforts of a whole team at Fordham, I have had the pleasure of working most closely with Richard Morrison and Nancy Basmajian. Their support, enthusiasm, and edits have made this a far stronger book. I am so grateful to Nabila Horakhsh, who gave me permission to let a work of art known as "Moon's Yell" grace the cover. Nabila's paintings are where I would often turn my eyes when I needed to find some inspiration while writing this book.

Devoted librarians in Palo Alto, London, Islamabad, Lahore, Rampur, and Hyderabad have been essential to project. Ali Abu Turab was particularly helpful while I was in Islamabad. I would also like to thank faculty members and researchers at Lahore University of Management Sciences (LUMS) and Quaid-i-Azam University who not only guided me through the scholarly and archival networks of Pakistan, but were magnanimous and gracious while doing so. I owe an immense debt of gratitude to Athar Masood, Rifaqat Ali Shahid, Himayatullah Yaqoobi, Sikander Ahmed Shah, and Yasmeen Hameed among others.

I have found that sharing this work has been an intimate endeavor—I was startled by the vulnerability I felt in circulating and discussing ideas and words into which I have poured my intellectual energy and my time. Given this, it is with profound gratitude that I invoke those who so eagerly, rigorously, and warmly have responded to drafts and ideas related to this project: the two anonymous reviewers for Fordham University Press, Tanvir Ahmed, Kent Brintnall, Robert Crews, Jamal Elias, Munis Faruqui, Nasim Fekrat, Kathryn Gin Lum, Eric Hoenes del Pinal, Abbas Jaffer, Phil Kaffen, Ali Karjoo-Ravary, Alex Kaloyanides, Joanne Maguire, Ariela Marcus-Sells, Mejgan Massoumi, Sean McCloud, Naveena Naqvi, Noah Salomon, and many others. I owe an even greater debt to my dear friend Ahoo Najafian. She not only listened to my wild ideas and discussed book anxieties with me, but she patiently helped me read a number of perplexing Persian passages. As I began to learn from Shahzad Bashir, I came to see the world as more colorful and alive. Shahzad has been a ceaseless guide, inspiration, and mentor throughout my academic career. So, too, was Robert Gregg, who passed away during the production of this book. I miss him profoundly, and I feel immensely grateful that Bob was one of the very first readers of this book. I hope that an iota of the joyous curiosity that infused Bob's life finds its way into my own.

My parents and my older brothers have taught me that knowledge and love are fullest when bound together. My brothers, Jake and Nick, are my most enduring teachers. As my family has grown to include sisters-in-law, nephews, nieces, and parents-in-law, I have gained so much, and I am thankful for their unconditional support. My partner, Devyn, continues to show me how vast and brilliant the world can be, and how little a thing like my intellect can ever grasp what truly moves the sun and other stars. Her laughter, her presence, and her commitment to justice astound me daily. She has gifted me my own ignorance, and I am so much better for it. As this project concluded, my world was made new with the birth of Hayes: *un punto solo*, a single moment, that continues to cast an unmatched light.

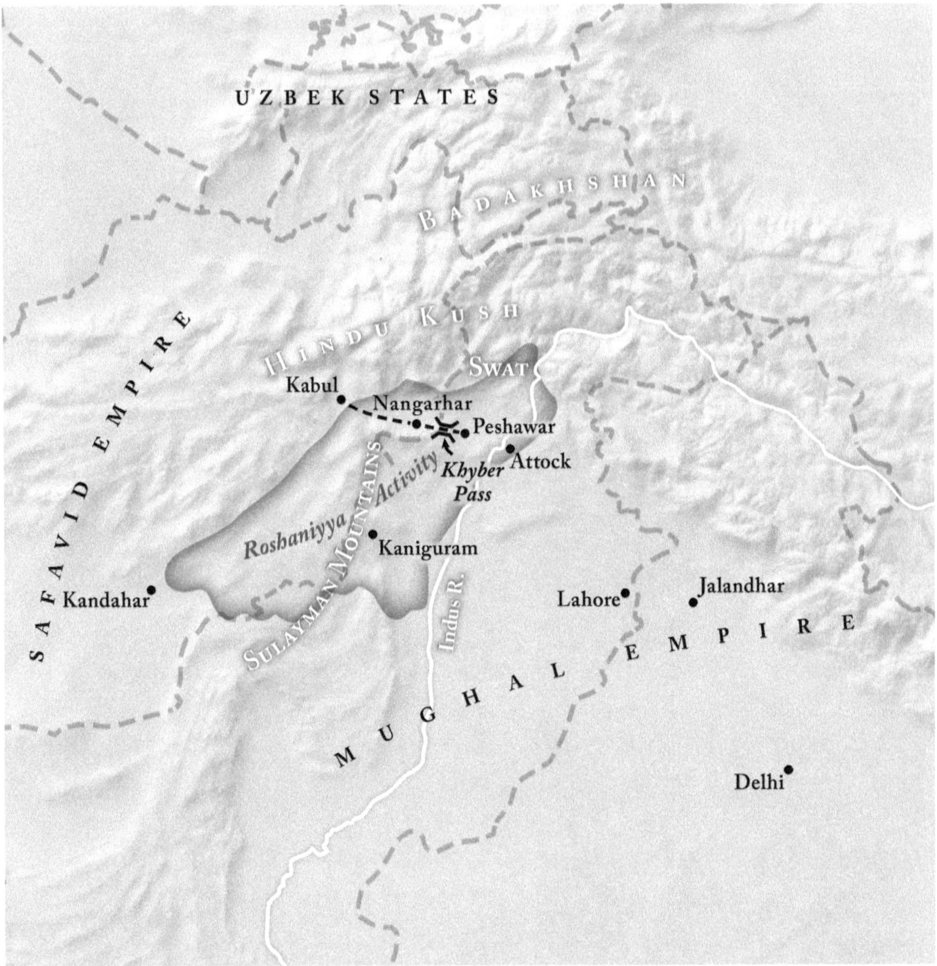

The world of the Roshaniyya, sixteenth and seventeenth centuries. Map by Daniel P. Huffman

Mountains and Messiahs: An Introduction

O the mind, mind has mountains.

—GERARD MANLEY HOPKINS, "No worst, there is none"

What does a failed messiah have to teach us? In the sixteenth century, a community in the Afghan highlands remembered as the Roshaniyya—"the people of light"—followed a Sufi Muslim teacher named Bayazid Ansari toward understandings of God and language that challenge many of the ways that we in the twenty-first tend to think about the history of Afghanistan, the boundaries of Islam, vernacular language, and messianic claims. This book is a story of their attempt to speak the word of God—and the new formations of literature, violence, and identity that followed in the wake of this effort. In many ways, the Roshaniyya failed: they fell into violent conflict with the Mughal Empire, which brutally suppressed them, while rival religious leaders detailed Roshani heresies and ridiculed them. And yet, for us to judge them as failures reflects back on us and our limited imaginations of how language might carry a divine charge or how a messianic community may find different paths through Islamic history and Afghan belonging. The possibilities that the Roshaniyya pursued—that God may be in Pashto, that our tongues might be remade as angelic, that Bayazid speaks new revelation, that our voices can join a cosmic chorus of praise in the creation of a new, sacred community—are worth our attention in their own right as intriguing examples of religious thought and practice, but this book considers also the consequences of the Roshaniyya's experiments with religion and language. Out of the violent fragmentation of the Roshaniyya, we see the emergence of a new Pashto literature, the transformation of Afghan identity, shifts in Mughal sovereignty, the dominance of a Pashto Sunni Islamic tradition among the early modern Afghan diaspora, and a template of "Afghan fanaticism" that British and American empires continued to use to understand the region, often to disastrous effect.

This is also a story of what we cannot know, and that is where we begin.

As the dawn drew near in the Afghan highlands, an elderly woman called Second Mary (Maryam-i thānī) began to fast. Her name, Second Mary, portended a Second Jesus ('Īsá-yi thānī), and, indeed, an infant by that name had just been born in Mary's village. Second Jesus's first tender sounds bore the name of God. They were a *dhikr*, a recitation and recollection of God, and Mary began to listen to the dhikr cries of this infant born to another woman. His dhikr satisfied all that Mary desired. She let the dhikr of God's name nourish her and carry her beyond sleep, beyond hunger, and beyond the fatigue of her aged body. The day stretched to the night, the night to the next day, day to night, and so it continued for forty days. Jesus's dhikr bore Mary past the impermanence of her flesh until this dhikr bound her to God as a friend.

Mary's forty days in devotion were not hers alone, and nor was her death a private matter. In these mountains on the edge of the Mughal Empire, as the Islamic *hijrī* calendar turned ever nearer to the year 1000 (1591 CE), Mary's community—identified as Afghans of the Tu'i tribe—understood the meaning of the infant's dhikr and the old woman's death. This was a time electric with apocalyptic possibility. Day and night, month and year: these markers no longer mattered as time bent and circled back on itself, saturated with possible pasts and remembered futures. Time became a matter of repetition and transformation. The world was spilling forth with a message: the End was near.

In another portent of the End, the cows of Mary's neighbor 'Abd al-Karim stretched their necks willingly to his knife until he had slaughtered twenty cows for the coming feast without the assistance of any other hand. The community had prepared themselves for this very moment. The Greater Resurrection must be near, and this meant too that the *mahdī*—the guide at the End—was coming.[1] They had been taught by their luminous teacher Bayazid, their *pīr-i roshan*, to prepare for these final events, to train their tongues to recite dhikr phrases, and to let these blessed words transform the community into one freed from shadows and brought into angelic and divine light. They were no longer just Tu'i Afghans; they were the Roshaniyya, the luminous people, the beings of light.

Shortly after the death of Second Mary and all it portended, a merchant caravan passed through this community on its way north and west through the mountains toward Kabul. The Roshaniyya of this Tu'i village seized the caravan's goods in an outburst of disgust at the crass materialism that stood in flagrant rejection of the immediacy of these apocalyptic times.[2] Gathering the goods in a central field, the Roshaniyya used their horses to trample and destroy the merchandise. The dispossessed caravanners fled to Kabul and told the governing Mughal authorities that "the luminous master had drawn his sword." Bayazid was at war, and the Roshaniyya had rebelled. Five hundred Mughal horsemen rode to this Tu'i community, slaughtered the inhabitants, and inaugurated some fifty years of violent clashes between the Roshaniyya and the Mughal Empire.[3]

Here is what I find so intriguing about that story: in all its mystery, this is the fullest and most detailed account of the immediate cause of the conflict between this group known as the Roshaniyya and the forces of the Mughal Empire. Despite the importance of this story as a hinge for an important conflict, I confess that there are aspects of this story that strike me as fundamentally unknowable and strange. What kind of names are "Second Mary" and "Second Jesus"? Did Second Mary begin her fast in response to some secret insight or was she, in her way, *causing* the events of end times through her practice? And perhaps most beguiling: Where is Bayazid in all this? The story implies that he is the mahdi—a term we will explore in a moment—but he is absent even as the distressed merchants pin the events in this Tu'i village on him. *Bayazid* drew his sword, according to the merchants, and *Bayazid* is the promised one, according to the Tu'i Roshaniyya. So where is he?

I begin with this story not to catch your attention with a bizarre tale but to set the tone of this book with a note of the *unknown*. There is much that we simply cannot answer about the Roshaniyya, and so we need an ethic of hermeneutic hesitation before we rush to fill the gaps and cracks in our account. This book is not just about the Roshaniyya and the cultural, political, and religious transformations left in their wake. Secondarily, this book is also about the way Mughal, British, and American agents of empire and Afghan and Pakistani nationalists have flooded the dark crevices of Roshani history with prior assumptions on the determinacy of ethnic identity, the "actual" nature of true Islam, stereotypes on the enduring recalcitrance of Afghans and their graveyard of empires, and the boundaries of sovereign power. Indeed, there are a number of confident histories of the Roshaniyya that look beyond the Roshani narrative that roots the origins of the Roshani-Mughal conflict in the death of a fasting woman named Second Mary, the prayers of a newborn named Second Jesus, the eschatological message seen in the cows' willingness to stretch their necks to the knives, and the decision of some caravanners to interpret the antimaterialism of a village's apocalyptic anticipation as a declaration of war from Bayazid Ansari. Excising the language of end times and those references to dhikr-fasts that unsettle us, the more common history of the Roshaniyya anesthetizes the mystery so that we may see patterns and explanations that are more familiar. I will use this book to largely reject the story that we typically relate of the Roshaniyya, but *that* story—the one I invite you to reject along with me—is nonetheless an informative one that is worth telling.

That is a story that does not begin with Second Mary nor with the precorporeal blessed light of the Prophet Muhammad nor with the story of Abu Ayyub al-Ansari, the Prophet's celebrated companion, from whom Bayazid's followers traced his descent. Those are how histories told by the Roshaniyya begin, but the confident history that we will seek to emend typically begins with a short biography of Bayazid Ansari, the teacher of the Roshaniyya. He was born in 1525 CE in the town of Jalandhar in the region of the Punjab (in present-day India). In 1526 CE, his family moved some 350 miles west of Jalandhar to Kaniguram, a town in Waziristan in what is now Pakistan. This was a significant year, for it was in 1526 that the Central Asian general Babur and his allies defeated King Ibrahim Lodi north of Delhi at the Battle of Panipat—and so began the Mughal dynasty that ruled much of South Asia until the era of British colonialism. According to one source, the infant Bayazid and his family passed the Mughal horsemen of Babur as they moved south from Kabul on their way to defeat the ruling Lodis and conquer India.

Bayazid grew up in the highlands of Kaniguram among people typically described as *Afghan* in early modern sources, though other words such as *Pashtun, Pukhtun*, and *Pathan* have been frequently used to name the communities in the mountainous regions between Kabul, Peshawar, Kaniguram, and Kandahar. As Bayazid grew, he began to preach to the Afghans and call them to renew their devotion to the one true God. His reputation grew, and he was recognized as a Sufi *pīr*—a master who taught his disciples the spiritual path. He taught his vision of Islam to Afghans primarily residing in a region that is now called Khyber Pakhutnkhwa, a province of Pakistan. He trained them in dhikr practices in which his disciples would recite pious phrases, and he led them in forty-day retreats called *chilla*s. His reputation grew further, and he was recognized by some as the messianic mahdi. The mahdi—or "guided one" in Arabic—is a common figure in Islamic discourses of the end times, and the mahdi is generally understood to be a descendant of the Prophet who will join the returning Jesus—the *masīḥ* (messiah)—to lead the world's Muslims in delivering peace and truth across the globe. As we will see, the Roshani celebration of Bayazid's messianic status did not conform with common Sunni or Shi'i descriptions of the mahdi, but the title was invoked (even if at times in denial) by the Roshaniyya.

As Scott Kugle's recent work on Sayyid 'Ali Mutaqqi and his complicated connection with the Mahdawi movement in India suggests, there were vibrant and diverse explorations of the idea of the mahdi that were contemporaneous with the Roshaniyya. Unlike the Roshaniyya, these Mahdawi claims did not emerge primarily from the "frontiers" of Islamic scholarly networks or royal courts but circulated within and through imperial courts, Sufi shrines, and scholarly madrassas (even while the Mahdawis strove to build a separate, utopian community).[4] While claims to being the mahdi are fairly common in Islamic history, however explosive they may be, less common is that Bayazid was considered to be the voice of God. He spoke and wrote the revelations of God, and, radically, he did so in *Pashto,* the language of the Afghans. A language now spoken by some sixty million people and with a rich literature first found its way into ink on paper with the Roshaniyya. The typical, scholarly story goes that the proto-nationalist leader Bayazid used claims of Pashto revelation to tether religious fervor—even millenarian fanaticism—to parochial Afghan virtues of self-governance and hostility to the Mughals. The result was that Bayazid's *roshani* teachings (his "teachings of light") sparked an ever-increasing ethnic self-consciousness and cultural self-awareness that temporarily cut across Afghan tribal divisions. In the light of Bayazid's messianic zeal, Afghans began to recognize themselves as Afghans. The ethnic self-consciousness, in fact, frequently serves as the *explanation* for the conflict between the Roshaniyya and the Mughals mentioned above. The Roshaniyya resisted the Mughals *because* they were Afghans. Bayazid "used" religion to temporarily unite the disorganized, fissiparous Afghan tribes of the highlands against the rule of the Mughal court.[5] Under Bayazid's leadership, many of the Afghan tribes rebelled, won some unlikely victories due to their advantages as locals in a treacherous, mountainous topography, and then were ultimately defeated by the far vaster Mughal armies. The sons and grandchildren of Bayazid continued to lead Roshani rebellions for some decades, but, by 1620 CE or so, the story of the Roshaniyya had ended.

I will suggest that this story fails in many regards, and that many of the terms and assumptions of this story (such as the invocation of "Afghan tribes") are anachronistic. For the moment, though, let me register my biggest complaint: how *familiar* this story feels. The Roshaniyya are likely not familiar to readers, and the names of these towns and regions may also be unknown. But is the story not one that we can easily grasp? A story of local, "tribal" people uniting around a dangerous, charismatic, and fanatical leader to fight in the name of their own ethnic self-determination using their own vernacular literature in the face of the mighty empire? Told in this way, we can process the history of the Roshaniyya and file them away as a somewhat interesting example of how an ethnic identity and a vernacular literature took shape around a popular religious movement before being domesticated as part of the fabric of early modern empires. The familiarity of *that* pattern perhaps explains the level of certainty that has characterized previous scholarship on the Roshaniyya despite the strangeness (in my eyes) of accounts characterized far more by stories of Second Mary's fast than by any notion of a collective Afghan spirit for rebellion.

Why did Bayazid go to war? A Roshani source tells us that it was because of Second Mary's fast and the response of some alarmed caravanners, while later British and American explanations emphasize the role of Afghan tribal recalcitrance and ethnic mobilization. It is here, in this gap that opens between the unfamiliarity of our sources and the familiarity of our explanations, that we find the real value of lending our imaginations to the Roshaniyya—or so I argue with this book. I do not want this book's sole aim to be a "correction" of the histories we record of the Roshaniyya, the Mughal Empire, and Afghanistan. Rather, I want us to seek that trembling space between the stories inked on manuscript and the histories printed in books, and I wager that it is in that space that the stories of the Roshaniyya turn back on *us* and confront *us* with our habits of relating to language, of thinking the relationships between religion and belonging, and of telling stories of the past. The philosopher Sara Ahmed has explored just how common and tempting it is to "straighten" experiences that crack us with their disorienting unfamiliarity. "To live out a politics of disorientation," Ahmed suggests, might be to sustain what Maurice Merleau-Ponty has called the "vital experience of giddiness and nausea, which is the awareness of our contingency."[6] While this introduction will discuss this book's methodological and theoretical commitments in more detail below, its first commitment is to maintaining as long as possible the twinned nausea and giddiness of the unfamiliar and how it unsettles our presumptions.

We will explore the reasons why stories such as that of the Tu'i village are transmuted into stories of ethnic self-determination and proto-nationalism against a horizon of presumptions of Islamic orthodoxy and heterodox messianism. But let me offer a simple, material reason why the peculiarities of the Tu'i village are so often lost: it is difficult to access the sprawling, lurching, revelatory linguistic messianism of the Roshaniyya we find in early sources. A personal example can clarify this. I first encountered the story of the Roshaniyya in a short chapter in an edited volume on Sufism. In this chapter, there is mention of a text attributed to Bayazid Ansari called "Khayr al-bayān," *The Best Exposition*, that conveyed the doctrines of the Roshaniyya in Pashto—and this work is considered the *first* prose text written in Pashto.[7] Intrigued, I requested through interlibrary loan an edition of *The Best Exposition* published in 1967 in Peshawar by Muhammad 'Abd al-Quddus Qasimi. In the decades since Partition and the emergence of the nations of India and Pakistan in 1947, there have been Pashtun activists, politicians, and scholars interested in the cultural and historical resources for theorizing a *Pashtunistan* that dissolves the infamous Durand Line dividing the Pashtun communities of Pakistan and Afghanistan. This partially explains why an edition of an early Pashto work (however beguiling) was published in the post-Partition period. In any case, I received my copy of *The Best Exposition* and was stunned by what I found. This was not a Pashto work of Sufi doctrine—as I had expected—but rather a cobweb of multiple, interpenetrating languages holding together the voices of God and Bayazid in revelatory dialogue.[8] In this text, Arabic was made to rhyme with Pashto while Persian and Hindawi flashed through *The Best Exposition* in a pattern I could not detect. Moreover, here, among the first pages of *The Best Exposition*, was God delivering the Arabic-Persian-Pashto alphabet—one letter at a time—to Bayazid so that he may tell the people of the oneness (*tawḥīd*) of God. And, here, among these first pages, was God telling Bayazid to deliver his messages according to the melodies (*alḥān*) of Surat al-Rahman of the Qur'an and to deliver this message to the peoples all over the world.

This was, in short, unlike any text that I had encountered in Islamic literary traditions, and it seemed shockingly ill-suited as a "manifesto" for a community ostensibly organized around ethnic Afghan self-consciousness and invested in Pashto as a proto-nationalist means of reaching a wider Afghan audience. *The Best Exposition* was not unique in its capacity to startle and elude. The other sources of the Roshaniyya are also in a mix of Arabic, Persian, Pashto, and Hindawi; they often rely on cross-linguistic models (e.g., Pashto poems based on Persian poetic rhythms); and they evince a reliance on previous literary traditions (e.g., the rich tradition of Persian narratives of saints) coupled in confounding ways with tropes and narrative patterns that seem distinctive (e.g., hagiographies that feature numerous doppelgängers of the saint). So here's that *gap* again—the gap that opens between a source that shakes free of our interpretative categories and the scholarly description of that source that seeks to wrestle it into something known, something familiar, something that does not challenge our definitions of "Islam," our notion of Afghanistan, and our relationship to the past.

Bayazid's failure to build an empire like other sword-drawn messiahs of the premodern Islamic world—such as Shah Isma'il of the Safavid Empire—leaves a historiographical record of aporia and absence. Even relative to the traces of other premodern Muslim movements, we have few details for an elaborate social history of the Roshaniyya.[9] But into this absence various actors have projected images of Bayazid and the Roshaniyya that disclose much about those doing the projecting. As representations of Bayazid pass through Roshani, Mughal, British, and scholarly histories, different Bayazids emerge. Indeed, according to the Roshaniyya, this was a miracle of Bayazid: "His heart could take the shape of all that appears in it."[10]

The indeterminacy of the historical Bayazid is at once a frustrating and a revealing conundrum. There is no way to fully grasp or to fully know the "Bayazid" to whom Sufi texts, multilingual revelations, and messianic stories are attributed. We will encounter multiple Bayazids: a Hindustani fanatic, an Afghan heretic, a Turkic preacher, a saint capable of doubling and dissolving his physical body, and a messiah granted dreams and words of God. There is no way to write his history without filling in the gaps, without implicating ourselves, and without irrevocably shaping the Bayazid of our projects according to present concerns and ideologies. This is true of all history writing, but both Bayazid's failures and his position on geographic, ideological, and categorical frontiers intensify our entanglement in telling his story.[11] Rather than striving to untangle these knots of complicity and construction, the approach of this book is to maintain their tension. As I argue, habits of representation and imaginations of language are intimately bound up with the social formations of the Roshaniyya and their historical fate. The revelatory words constitute the social worlds and cosmos imagined by the Roshaniyya.

The historiography of the Roshaniyya and, more generally, of religious cultures of the Afghan highlands has consistently sought to cut through the veils of religious language, miraculous narratives, apocalyptic urgency, and messianic timescapes.[12] With few exceptions (such as Sana Haroon's *Frontiers of Faith*),[13] histories of Afghanistan have striven to identify and relate—and, possibly, generate—accounts of ethnic groups and tribal societies that are alternatively motivated, inspired, burdened, and constrained in simple ways by a simple concept of religious "belief."[14] The implicit premise is that Afghan ethnicity, tribal society, and frontier geography are ontologically thicker, analytically richer, and historically more consequential than the religious ephemera described in texts of dhikr practice, hagiographies replete with dream visions and doubles, and eclectic imitations of the Qur'an. The premise in much of this literature is that "religious language" is an obstacle to overcome in the quest to understand the *really real*.[15] We often seek to look beyond the mirage of false messiahs and orient our scholarship with something more natural and more material: those enduring mountains of analysis such as ethnicity, tribe, and fanaticism that populate the writing on Afghan religion and history.

While I will argue that the analytical categories previously brought to a study of the Roshaniyya, Afghanistan, and religion in South Asia have tripped over unexamined metaphysical and ontological premises, we must be wary of replacing "ethnicity" with "Sufism" or "tribe" with "religion" as firmer footholds. In Euro-American studies of Islam, an idea of mysticism has been a tool to pry Sufism away from the rigidities spotted and posited in Islamic traditions of learning and practice—a procedure often performed according to the political interests of empires, both American and European.[16] This is, in fact, a central rhetorical move of John Leyden, an English doctor who, in 1812, wrote an early and influential analysis of Sufism—and he based his conclusions about Sufism on his study of the Roshaniyya. My motivation for this study emerges not from a commitment to "taking religion seriously." The issue is both stickier and more elemental. The issue is this: the revelatory, messianic language of the Roshaniyya does not primarily aim to relate some religious experience out there or describe a transcendent God up there or beatify an individual saint back then. This is not an account of *beyonds*, *aboves*, or *hidden withins*. Rather, the revelatory language of the Roshaniyya is the ground itself for the idealization, reflection, and—critically—constitution of Roshani social formations. In the Roshaniyya's religious imaginations, who they are and what the world is depends on how they speak. The Roshaniyya emerge from world-making words, and our analyses will stumble from their very beginnings if we force Roshani language to conform to our semiotic imaginations. And if language and the use, imagination, habits, genres, and structures of language are the very grounds through which the Roshaniyya understand their being and messianic becoming, then we cannot so easily unravel religious text and historical reality.

Back to the story of Second Mary and Second Jesus: despite my insistence on beginning with this story that confronts us with the unknowability of the Roshaniyya (in the face of an overly confident historiography), I nevertheless insist that there is much that we can learn from such narratives. The story of Second Mary among the Roshaniyya demonstrates the intersection of themes of language, temporality, and belonging that define this book. This story insists that the inciting event of the conflict that would spell the doom of the Roshaniyya began with an elderly woman fasting until death because a newborn was reciting God's name. To understand the ways in which this story and the other sources of the Roshaniyya function effectively and felicitously, we will attend to the Roshani imaginations of language and narrative that precede the specific stories they tell and revelations they preach. We find this particular story in a hagiography written about Bayazid Ansari, but this story of a Tu'i village's eschatological anticipation is not just a record of some local events. It is a declaration of messianic unveiling, or, better, it is a *performance* of the messianic claim rather than its representation. Animal domesticity, the presence of a Jesus (even a "second" one), the announcement of the imminent Resurrection, and the weight given to the dhikr all coincide to present Bayazid Ansari as the mahdi.[17] As noted, Bayazid is absent in this narrated declaration of his status as a messianic, world-changing figure who appears at the end of time—and his absence is an indication that we are dealing with a relationship between history, text, and language different from the one we have often assumed in the study of religion. We are studying not how a person made religious claims but how religious claims made the person. Bayazid's messianism is not merely a matter of a historical personage's claim for authority, nor is his revelation a matter of new laws or predictions of the future. Rather, the messianism of Bayazid circulates in the language of the dhikrs practiced by his disciples, and his revelation emerges from the complex temporality that Roshani language seeks to create. Bayazid does not need to be present for his revelatory language to shape the worlds and times of his disciples. It is through the very act of storytelling—of language use—that the messianic qualities of Bayazid manifest. Uncomfortable as it may be at times, we begin to understand the Roshaniyya only in the realm of revelatory language and its ability to shape the very stuff of self, time, and cosmos.

I have already related the story as it is typically told, in which the Roshaniyya primarily appear as exemplars of *Afghan* unruliness and excess. The expanse of this book will be necessary to relate a different story. In summary, though, this is the story I see in the sources of the Roshaniyya: an attempt to speak the language of God, though critics would deem this effort a failure. In the Afghan highlands of the sixteenth century, the Roshaniyya sought revelation. This was a Sufi community that not only desired to abide by the true understanding of God's revelation but also attempted to develop techniques of language intended to render their own tongues the organs of continuous revelation. Though the Roshaniyya flourished in a particular region of the Afghan highlands, they were active on either side of the contemporary border between Afghanistan and Pakistan that weaves throughout these frontier highlands. Moreover, they understood their role as calling the *world*—not just "Afghans"—to the light of the truth. They followed the messianic Bayazid Ansari in dhikr practices, in spiritual retreats, in war with the soldiers of the Mughal Empire, and in the first use of Pashto as a written language. While they have often been described simply as "Afghans," this term masks the social complexity of this group. The Roshaniyya consisted of orphans, blacksmiths, poets, women, merchants, visionaries, nomads, and wandering ascetics. Upon receiving the dhikr phrases from Bayazid and letting these words shape their tongues, many of the Roshaniyya disavowed the term "Afghan" and their local identification to receive a new name: *Roshani*. They sent epistles and missionaries to governors, princes, and emperors throughout South and Central Asia. Bayazid—and his sons, his wife, and his disciples—spoke to God and heard God *in and as language*; from this linguistic encounter, a number of Persian, Arabic, and Pashto texts emerged that sought not to convey a theological lesson but to find divine presence in the letter. Some of these texts were attributed to Bayazid, some to his followers, and others directly to God—but all of them attest to a bid to find God upon human tongues and through the ink of pens in human hands.

As their critics would contend, however, the Roshaniyya attempted to make language do something that language *should not and could not do*; there is a heretical immediacy in the way the Roshaniyya sought to infuse the semiotic with the divine. While the practices and beliefs of the Roshaniyya were legible and familiar in the religious landscapes of a sixteenth-century Islamic world remade by the proliferation of Sufi networks in the preceding centuries, the Roshaniyya had enemies who claimed that the Roshaniyya had stepped off the precipice into outright disbelief. In this way, the Roshaniyya's is a story of the conditions of impossibility in the cultural and religious worlds of the sixteenth century. We learn where Muslim scholars backed by Mughal force drew the line between belief and unbelief.

A central figure in this regard was Akhund Darweza—a Sunni theologian who inhabited the town of Nangrahar (near present-day Jalalabad, Afghanistan) and debated the Roshaniyya circa 1600 CE and detailed their sins. As we find him in his own texts, he often seems terrified, even debilitated, by the unstable semiotic imagination of the Roshaniyya. In response to Roshani efforts to warp time with language and bring God into Pashto, Akhund Darweza wrote a series of texts that became central to Afghan traditions of Islam throughout South Asia. Despite his absence from Euro-American scholarship, his vision of Afghan belonging and religion is arguably more foundational than that of the celebrated poet Khushhal Khan Khatak.[18] Akhund Darweza penned an immensely popular summary of Islamic theology that reads much like an "Introduction to Islam" textbook today; he condemned the Roshaniyya in unrelenting heresiographies; and he inscribed one of the first written genealogies of the descent of the Afghans from King Saul (*Malik Ṭālūt*), of the shared Biblical-Qur'anic heritage. The debate between Akhund Darweza and the Roshaniyya—despite its intensity and the frequency with which *damnation!* was hurled—speaks to a shared appreciation of the stakes of language in a religio-cultural moment alive with eschatological anticipation of the End. It was only later nineteenth-century British readers of Akhund Darweza who began to interpret this debate between Akhund Darweza and the Roshaniyya as something confined to the timeless disorder of a *race* or *ethnicity* known as the Afghans.

One way to approach this book is as a history of the debate between the Roshaniyya and Akhund Darweza. Sympathetic to Mughal rule and well-sponsored by local rulers, Akhund Darweza "won" this debate. The Roshaniyya's revelatory pursuit ended in a tower of their own skulls and the proliferation of heresiographies that detailed the linguistic sins of the Roshaniyya. Bayazid's career was short. His texts were rejected. His sons and Roshani followers were slaughtered, enslaved, displaced, and, if lucky, incorporated into the Mughal Empire. His ideas were condemned as heresy, and his messianic claims ridiculed as delusion and entombed as the bizarre prehistory of an emerging Afghanness.

For the remainder of this introductory chapter, I want to share the *whats*, *whys*, and *hows* of this book. What does a failed messiah have to teach us? First and foremost, the ostensible failure of Bayazid offers us an important glimpse of a stranger story of the Afghan past than is typically told. His is a story centered on a pursuit of revelation that ended in ruin but offers a glimpse of a larger regional concern for finding gods and messiahs in language and *as language*. The first use of Pashto (or "Afghan," as the language is called in our sources), to name an example that we will revisit in some detail, speaks not to a Roshani concern for Afghan independence but to a larger regional pattern of expanding the repertoire of God's communication through an expanded alphabet. Rather than condemning them to heterodox isolation, the intersection of language and messianic revelation is precisely where the Roshaniyya form their identities and make a bid for a universality that exceeds the limits of ethnic particularism and historiographical marginalization. The Roshaniyya represent a compelling example of messianic, Sufi experimentation with language as embedded in transregional networks of religion and literature. These Roshani experiments and especially the *rejection* of these Roshani experiments had significant consequences for formations of Afghan identity, Pashto literature, and the consolidation of Mughal sovereignty in the Afghan highlands.

Given the dearth of literature on histories of religion and culture in Afghanistan and among Afghan communities, the failures of Bayazid teach us much about a region that US audiences have viewed through frames of violence and warfare—almost exclusively so.[19] As its primary aim, this book draws into relief the theoretical challenges posed by the literature of the Roshaniyya to our habits of imagining language, finding ourselves in time and history, and connecting religion, rhetoric, and belonging. Despite the conceptual richness of encountering Roshani texts and worlds, we should not lose focus on a simple historical point—how unusual the story of the Roshaniyya looks when placed within American discourses on Afghanistan and Afghans. As I wrote most of this manuscript, the United States' war in Afghanistan was in its eighteenth and nineteenth years.[20] As I edit this, the United States military has recently evacuated Afghanistan in a way that has left many Afghans dangerously exposed to Taliban violence and famine. As this book entered production, a profound silence on Afghanistan has settled upon popular US media. These recent decades of US military adventure have not witnessed the emergence in popular American media of sympathetic, textured, and historical accounts of the lives of Afghans.[21] To the cruel contrary, we mostly find neglect punctuated, perhaps, by an annual Hollywood movie celebrating US military might and violence.[22] Even in the hasty retreat of the US military, the lesson learned has not been one of American failure but of the stubborn, unfixable savagery of Afghanistan. As Shahzad Bashir and Robert Crews have noted, framed through Washington's security concerns, the inhabitants of this region "are portrayed as living without any sense of change, eternally wallowing in a world of barbarity."[23] This image of timelessness largely serves to mask the American (and, previously, Soviet and British) entanglement in the violence of the region. Quite clearly, the Afghan highlands are a crossroads and lie on the well-traveled paths between India and Iran and Central Asia. As Bashir and Crews note, "Contrary to its stereotypical portrayal as a land forgotten by time . . . there is hardly any modern idea or weapon that has not had a significant impact on the region."[24] Indeed, as Waleed Ziad's recent work demonstrates, Sufi groups such as that of the Naqshbandi-Mujaddidis in the eighteenth and nineteenth centuries sustained a network of Islam that reached across much of Central Asia and South Asia, including Afghanistan.[25] Our historical attention will be given to the sixteenth and seventeenth centuries, but the story of the Roshaniyya echoes the points of Bashir, Crews, and Ziad. Not only does this account of messiahs and divine languages and visionary dreams given to women and doppelgängers roaming the Afghan highlands represent a *different* story, but it is also a story that attests to Afghan participation in transregional cultural and religious phenomena flourishing in the early modern period—a story of *connection* and *change.*[26] When written by Mughal, British, and American scholars, the history of the Roshaniyya has been a *cause of* (and not a *remedy for*) the amnesia, timelessness, and isolation that characterize the current, warped imagination of Afghanistan. This book offers a different story.

So to pose the question again: What does a failed messiah have to teach us? In this book, I argue that the story of the Roshaniyya offers a perspective on the religious cultures and literatures of premodern South and Central Asia different from the one we often encounter, and this perspective is one that will benefit those interested in questions of language, religion, and belonging—regardless of their geographic focus. If we lend our imaginations to the world conjured by the Roshaniyya, we find that the Afghans are not isolated among timeless mountains, that language moves and functions in powerful, material ways, that the anticipated apocalypse allows for new potentialities of self and semiosis, and that vernacularization can also be a process of divinization. In attempting to reconstruct this vision of language, self, and belonging that we find in the Roshani texts, moreover, we are confronted with the strangeness of our own conceptions of language and time—strange in that our language comes ripe with ethical, ontological, and epistemological stakes that we rarely consider.

Mountains and Messiahs (A Note on the Past)

Much of the work of this book lies in examining *what* the Roshaniyya tell us about a broader religio-cultural moment (that we might label as early modern Persianate) and in tracing the process by which the very markers of transregional participation were reinterpreted to be markers of parochialism, nativism, and isolation among a timeless Afghan people. *How* and *why* did we become so confident that a term such as "tribe" or a concept such as "vernacular" speaks to local concerns among Afghans?[27] And *how* and *why* do we pursue a different approach?

To start more simply, why call this chapter "Mountains and Messiahs"? On one level, it merely names elements of our story, set among the Spin Ghar and Hindu Kush mountains. Roshani devotees recognized Bayazid as the mahdi, a messianic figure of Islamic eschatology. As chapter 1 will explore, however, the narratives of Bayazid center on the multiplicity of this messianic figure. In these hagiographic accounts, there are multiple Bayazids, proliferating Bayazids, and disciples who seem to become Bayazid—and, thus, multiple messiahs. The archcritic of the Roshaniyya, Akhund Darweza, also relates stories of multiple (would-be) messiahs. Bayazid is only one of many messianic claimants that Akhund Darweza must debate, defuse, and castigate.

More significantly, this book finds itself caught between two approaches to temporality and the past. As noted, previous scholarship on the Roshaniyya has focused upon their importance (or unimportant failures) in the history of Afghan ethnic mobilization. The Roshaniyya are but a chapter in an enduring tale of Afghans, ever pulled apart by the centripetal force of tribal society, failing to unite except in rare and brief moments. Or perhaps their use of Pashto attests to a burgeoning nationalist sentiment, an early stirring on the frontier of political organization along the lines of ethnicity. As Olaf Caroe wrote in his influential 1958 history of Afghans: "Rather are [the tribes] like the waters of the sea; the storm-waves pass and disturb the surface, bringing flotsam and jetsam with the wind and sending the froth flying; the water, the essential element, mixes and turns around, but in itself remains the same."[28] Tribe, ethnicity, and frontier have become naturalized in the historiography of Afghanistan and are laden with greater ontological weight and explanatory heft than the miracles, dreams, and recitations of the Roshaniyya.

Joining this naturalization of ethnicity and tribe in histories of Afghan religion are naturalized visions of Islamic history. As Saba Mahmood, Shahzad Bashir, and Anand Vivek Taneja have argued, the "homogenous, empty time" of the modern, secular state has converged with specific sectarian visions of Islamic history.[29] There is overwhelming acceptance of the idea that Islam has "a single timeline" beginning with the Prophet Muhammad and continuing until today.[30] And so it is that we frequently speak of Islam's emergence at the time of the Prophet, Islam's consolidation in the ninth and tenth centuries, a medieval period for Islam, and globalization of Islam in modernity—a tree growing upward from seventh-century soil with a solid trunk.[31] As instinctual as this timeline may appear, it is a nakedly theological and sectarian argument emerging from particular formations of being Muslim in the modern world.[32] In this book alone, we find multiple alternative textures to time: pasts that can be repeated, futures lived in the present, and Islams that begin with the precorporeal prophetic light of Muhammad descending into the loins of an Adam freshly given flesh. If pegged to the linear time of hegemonic narratives of Islam, the Roshaniyya represent a blip in which local practices formed a temporary "hybrid" with Islam before giving way to the preordained Islamization of the Afghans.[33] Critically, this conception of Islam's single, linear timeline reinforces (and relies upon) what Mahmood calls a "secular conception of temporality" characterized by "the positivity of events as they occur in linear time."[34] There is, in other words, an entanglement of secular approaches to history and specific, sectarian visions of Islam.

Ethnicity, tribe, "Islamic history"—such are the mountains marking the landscapes of our scholarship. The Qur'an hints that even the might of mountains may be an illusion: "A day when the earth and the mountains will tremble, and the mountains become heaps of flowing sand."[35] And as Walter Benjamin suggests, even a "weak messianism" can interrupt the natural(ized) order of things.[36] The changes brought by a transformative messiah need not be large to shake dramatically a foundation that is seen as eternal.

In contrast to the mountains, we find the radical contingency that messianic thinking acknowledges. A messiah who dwells in the weak, often failed, reclamation of the past still promises cessation and rupture. Benjamin's "weak messianism" does not need to involve extravagant prophecies delivered by unsettling preachers. Rather, it is a fragile *historical* project in which the "past flits by" and is "seized only as an image which flashes up at the instant when it can be recognized and is never seen again."[37] Benjamin continues: "For every image of the past that is not recognized by the present as one of its own concerns threatens to disappear irretrievably." In Giorgio Agamben's formulation, the messianic is not the future promise of transformation but is the relationship between our "time of the end" and the pasts we reclaim and fulfill in those fragile, flitting moments.[38] The result is a messianic "tiny displacement" in which "everything will be as it is now, just a little different."[39] This tiny displacement does not "refer simply to real circumstances, in the sense that the nose of the blessed one will become a littler shorter . . . or that the dog outside will stop barking." For Agamben, the "tiny displacement does not refer to the state of things, but to their sense and their limits."[40] This "messianic" approach is, in short, a practice of history in which an untold story opens a small crack in ways of thinking that we believed to be settled and complete. The tiny displacement of the messianic rests in an "imperceptible trembling of the finite" that makes the limits—the categories, frames, words that we hang upon our objects of study—indeterminate and mobile.

Bayazid's project involved the (re)articulation of the Qur'an and a (re)living of Muhammad's prophetic career. Though the Mughals defeated the Roshaniyya, the texts of the Roshaniyya nevertheless demonstrate tiny displacements which can result in a transubstantiation of our own historical vision. To label him a failed messiah is to misunderstand how the messianic can operate. The messianic involves an act of historical recognition and historiographical hesitation that questions the determinacy of our own tools of analysis; the messianic is an awareness of an interruptive and rapturous repetition that—with a finite trembling—suspends the naturalized order of a "linear" Islamic history and the determinacy of tribe and ethnicity. It is a relationship of exposing the present to the past, a posture of humility to *what could have been different*. It is a relationship that the Roshaniyya strike up and sustain through distinctive linguistic practices. It is in this sense of alternative historical possibilities and their linguistic instantiation that I use the term "messianic," though it is equally suitable in its more common usage. The Roshaniyya indeed celebrated Bayazid as a messianic deliverer of truth and spiritual liberator in a moment of millenarian expectation, the intensity of which was heightened by the approaching year 1000 of the hijri calendar. In more specifically Islamic terminology, Roshani sources disagree on whether Bayazid claimed the title of the mahdi (the guided one); despite the disagreement, however, all Roshani sources agreed that Bayazid's teachings ushered in a period of transformation through which Bayazid would guide the Roshaniyya into the light. More relevant than adjudicating the labels for Bayazid himself as "millenarian preacher," "messianic teacher," or "mahdi," however, is the messianic historicity of the Roshaniyya as a whole. They imagined the past as something to grab, crack open, and let spill forth for meaning in the immediacy of their lives as reiterations of Muhammad's blessed community.

Bayazid once dreamt of a scrap of paper with the "Greatest Name" of God written upon it; similarly, the Roshaniyya grasped at the scraps of the past and pursued in them a shimmering articulation of divine language born by their very own tongues trained by dhikr recitations. The Roshaniyya, therefore, practiced a "weak messianism" not because Bayazid was (or was not) a failed messiah; rather theirs was a weak messianism that involved a historical and linguistic fulfillment of the past. Through its trembling, the ostensibly fixed and singular moment of God's revelation to Muhammad became unmoored in time, cracked away from the seventh century, and left open to respoken reclamation through the ambiguity of its temporal limits.

What happens to those mountains of ethnicity, tribe, and "Islamic history" when we lend our imaginations to the Roshaniyya's messianism? We find a history of Islam that does not unfold in "empty, homogenous" time as a scroll being unraveled with linear inevitability or a sentence read in one single direction. For the Roshaniyya, Islam did not emanate outward from seventh-century Mecca, and they did not find themselves on some frontier between the local and the Islamic. The phenomena of seventh-century Mecca became the phenomena of the sixteenth-century Afghan highlands—and they were rendered such through the dhikr remembrances and Qur'anic rhymes of Bayazid Ansari. The Roshaniyya were not alone in such theo-semiotic play with time. Alongside groups in South Asia mentioned later in this book (such as Hurufis, Nurbakhshis, Nuqtavis, Sikhs, Zoroastrians, and others), we can see language and messianism intersect in Muslim communities far from the Roshaniyya. Consider, for example, the Morisco networks of apocalyptic exchange in the sixteenth-century Mediterranean which have been so vividly traced in Mayte Green-Mercado's recent work. Such Morisco apocalyptic *jofor* texts had a profound effect in Spain and beyond on the ways that Muslims oriented themselves to remembered pasts and potential futures through complex but prevalent linguistic acts. The messianic linguistics of Islam were a global pursuit in the early modern world.[41]

This is not a perspective that accords with the common histories of Islam nor with some of the common practices in the discipline of history more generally. The historical "problem" posed by the Roshaniyya is both a theoretical and a practical one—and Kathryn Gin Lum's article on the "historyless heathen" in American historiography captures the stakes of this issue despite the distance of its topic from this book's own. As I read Gin Lum's work, she is suggesting that there is an affinity between the *form* of common US habits of history writing (from the eighteenth century until the contemporary period) and *ideologies* of providence, expansionism, liberalism, and the rugged individuals who dragged the wild into history in the name of God and nation. When "change over time" defines *what* the discipline of history studies, Gin Lum suggests that this concords with (and perhaps serves) the ways in which American settlers and Protestant missionaries understood their work of civilizing: witness the baptism in history of the Hawaiian heathen *changed* into the Christian farmworker. As Gin Lum suggests, the affinity between such a providentialist historical ideology and the formal contours of the discipline of history often masks their continued (accidental?) alignment. Or, to give an example from the context of this book, we might say this: there are Mughal chronicles that write about the Roshaniyya in year-by-year chronological fashion—thereby reiterating an ever-growing temporal distance between the prophetic past and the present horizon—and rely on "Afghan ethnicity" in explaining the Roshaniyya. For many scholars, these chronicles resemble historical sources in a way that the Roshaniyya texts of doppelgänger saints and tetralingual revelations do not. That *resemblance*, however, hides that these Mughal chronicles themselves were often textual displays of the emperor's messianic unveiling and sovereign force, displays that were no less powerful than a war elephant.

So how can we better balance these sources, all of which are efforts to shape and mold the past despite their different rhythms and timescapes? I am not insisting that we adopt the Roshaniyya's messianic vision of time, history, and language as our own model for narrating Islamic history. Rather, the point is to maintain the tension between mountains and messiahs so that the hidden metaphysics of our world and our time become clearer. Roshani worlds will shake free of easy interpretative efforts as messiahs turn some of our hermeneutic mountains to dust, and it will become clear that the mountains of our scholarship could have been different.[42] As Shahzad Bashir has argued, the past of Islam is "a matter forever in the process of being made and unmade through the agency of the authors who invoke it in specific sociohistorical circumstances."[43]

Revelation and Its Practice (A Note on the Vernacular)

Though it is difficult to prove definitively, the Roshaniyya's *The Best Exposition* is often described as the first text using Pashto as a written language—and, thus, the Roshaniyya have been cast as central to a process sometimes called "vernacularization."[44] Etymologically, "vernacular" suggests a space of the home and domesticity, and literary vernacularization involves a process by which the shared, public space of the written word comes to include the everyday life of the home. Scholars such as Farina Mir, Sheldon Pollock, Anne Murphy, Francesca Orsini, and Christian Novetzke have offered different models for understanding the process of literary vernacularization in South Asia whereby the dominance of Sanskrit and Persian gave way to diverse, multilingual, local and regional literary cultures.[45] Was it a matter of regional princes and governors sponsoring new literatures for their own political distinction? Or did the use of vernacular literatures represent a larger shift in the gravitational center of society toward the political and cultural importance of everyday life? Or, as some scholars have suggested with the Roshaniyya's use of Pashto, was the development of vernacular literature the result of an emergent ethnic self-consciousness?[46]

To varying degrees, these models hinge on an idea of *Pashtuns* (or Afghans, as premodern sources prefer) using *Pashto*, whether those Afghans were princes, mystics, or cyphers of ethnic identity.[47] But are we sure Pashto is a language of the Pashtuns? We might instinctually answer in the affirmative, but, as will be explored throughout this book (with special attention in chapter 4), this is not the answer that we find in the literature of the Roshaniyya. Pashto is *God's* language in these sources—or, more accurately, Pashto is *part* of God's language. If we accept these first emergences of Pashto literature as a vernacular transformation, then the Roshaniyya do not conceive of vernacular literature as an expansion of literature to include more voices and more communities. In these texts, we find the turn to vernacular literature as an exclusionary process that raises Roshani language to divine status through the use of Pashto in concert with other linguistic practices. The exclusions, however, are not in service of the social hierarchies that shaped the backgrounds of Roshani disciples. It was the elder widow Second Mary, after all, who first read the signs of the end and began a dhikr-fast that heralded the mahdi.

Pashto is part of a repertoire of techniques to close the gap between God's language and the language of humans. Revelation—God's language—becomes a matter of practice, discipline, and performance. As chapter 2 will examine, dhikr practices (and the writing about dhikr practices) are tools for linguistic divinization. The Roshaniyya's approach to revelation as something to be achieved and practiced departs sharply from the images of "mad messiahs" struck by lightning bolts of divine inspiration.[48] Bayazid's revelation was a matter of training the tongue, and thus it was not confined to Bayazid alone—as will be examined in the poetry of Mulla Arzani. Vernacular literature, in this case, was bound up with messiahs and apocalypses and revelations. Given that this book includes the first non-Pashto analysis of Mulla Arzani's poetry (and select translations), it affords a chance to see different patterns of emergent vernacular literatures in South Asia.

It is here, again, that Roshani revelation offers another instance of a "weak messianism." When we gaze through the literature of the Roshaniyya onto vernacularization in the Islamic world at large, the presumption of Arabic's privileged and sanctified place is not to be found. There is a slight trembling in the order of things as the Roshaniyya offer an alternative understanding of Islam and language. To more capably articulate the Roshani imagination and use of language, I rely upon the concept of semiotic ideology, as the next section explains.

Between Us and the Roshaniyya (A Note on Method)

According to the stories of *The Book of States*, as Bayazid transformed his tongue into an instrument of God's language, the revelation he uttered was not his alone. Revelation and worship preceded Bayazid's own utterances. Mountains, rivers, trees, musical instruments, and even the flesh of his own body praised God, singing the ineffable "greatest name" (*ism-i a'ẓam*) and beckoning Bayazid's words to join the chorus of revelation echoing around him. More than a charming passage in the hagiography of Bayazid, this story offers us a glimpse of how the Roshaniyya imagined words and language as sutured to the very stuff of the world. Language worked *not* by pointing beyond itself, as if a linguistic world hovered above our material one or as if signifiers skim virtually and arbitrarily upon the thicker realities of the signified. Rather, the Roshaniyya practices of language and revelation suggest that they imagined words as working metonymically: the "work" of words was as parts connected to wholes. The entire Roshani cosmos was saturated with communicative meaning, and so Bayazid's dreams, songs, and verses were continuous with the universe itself. Bayazid did not speak "about" the world; he sang with the world.

We can label this imagination of language as the *semiotic ideology* of the Roshaniyya. In this section, I discuss the reasoning behind this book's focus on semiotic ideology and, more generally, questions of language, and I argue that these are valuable entry points into our attempt to understand the Roshaniyya. Before that, however, it is worth pausing and asking: Who is this "us" and this "we" that I invoke?

Imagine that these words that you're reading were spray-painted on a brick wall or tattooed on a body. Or, better yet, that they were whispered in your ear by your mother or father when you were a child—or that each and every sentence of this book were delivered in rhyming verse. The words in front of you are not whispered, tattooed, etched, painted, or anything of the sort, of course. Likely they are black ink stamped on a white page, or perhaps they are a play of light created on a laptop screen. In such cases, we are dealing with a medium that seeks to obscure its own materiality.[49] And if I am deft enough, my rhetoric will have a similar effect: in most of this book, I seek to remove myself from your encounter with the story of the Roshaniyya and the academic arguments carried therein. There is something self-effacing and self-denying about the words that connect us, as should be clearer when these words before you are contrasted with loving whispers and graffiti. As recent works in the philosophy and anthropology of language have suggested, this approach to language is not simply the way of the world; rather, it is a stance taken toward language that emerges from a host of contingent and intersecting projects. This self-effacing language of black ink on white page and of a tone of academic detachment enables certain types of relationships to the world and forecloses other relationships. This particular language *here* before you is particularly well suited to facilitating a relationship of subject to object. I know the world, capture that knowing with my clear words, and convey that knowledge to you through these words without interference. That we reckon this to be possible suggests that we not only share some cultural background; this possibility is also *created* by the very way we communicate in form, style, and material. In other words, the "we" that I invoke is a "we" that emerges—at least in part—from the characteristics of the language that marks our communication, however one-sided.

Dragged in the wake of our shared language (black and white, as it is, and full of the tics of twenty-first-century American academic prose), there are a host of ethical, ontological, epistemological, and even theological stakes and valorizations. This draws near to what Webb Keane and others mean by *semiotic ideology*.[50] Keane intends something quite simple by semiotic ideologies: they are the modes of a culture's communication in practice and as ideally imagined.[51] How do we, in a particular semiotic ideology, understand the functioning of language and signs? And in what ways do we valorize certain communicative practices and semiotic forms over others? Keane's project draws into relief the formation and effect of an instrumentalist semiotic ideology that has become naturalized in a modern, liberal era. As Keane writes, "The modern West is a world in which representation produces the effect of there being a world of objects that exist external to it, and of subjects that stand outside the world, which is made available for them by means of those representations."[52] Modern Westerners frequently approach language as an arbitrary set of symbols open to instrumental use, and this approach comes laden with presumptions about what counts as subjectivity, sincerity, and truth. The semio-ontological distinction between world and representation that characterizes modern semiotic ideology has specific roots in Protestant anxieties about Catholic ritual, according to Keane—and Keane's work traces the development and consolidation of these Protestant concerns for fetishes and material signs in colonial encounters and conflicts.[53]

Beyond this genealogy of modern semiotic ideologies, Keane's conclusion is a simple but striking one: language is irrevocably shot through with moral stakes and norms. Language is always a matter of distributing who has agency and who and what deserve recognition as subject or object.[54] Even before we consider rhetoric or semantic meaning, the materiality of this book makes an ethical claim through black ink and white paper—or the digital buzz of a screen—and implicitly establishes a preference for an instrumentalist stance to a world of objects distinct from *me*, the subject. The intimacy of a whisper, the brute form of a painted wall, narrative structures, rhyme—these become distractions according to the epistemological and moral stance that *this* language is taking (a stance adopted with regret).

Keane is certainly not the first to explore this line of thinking, even if I find his account and his lexicon particularly compelling.[55] As other scholars have demonstrated, questions similar to semiotic ideology are fruitful for gaining some analytical leverage on tensions, paradoxes, and exclusions of modernity and secularism. Saba Mahmood, for instance, has examined the inability of contemporary liberal commentators to understand the affective force of blasphemous comments on the Prophet Muhammad.[56] Karmen MacKendrick has meditated on the importance of voice—of the sonic waves produced by contracting and relaxing vocal cords—to philosophical and theological discourses in the medieval Christian tradition.[57] Rowan Williams has described the way that the "edges of language" seem to hint at metaphysical commitments, no matter to what use our language is brought.[58] In a different vein, Noah Salomon's ethnography of Sudan gives sustained attention to the importance of aesthetics in projects of state-making, suggesting that aesthetic acts are not a separate or *superficial* concern relative to other semiotic acts of organizing the political world.[59] And Charles Taylor has discussed in great detail the failures of current linguistic ideologies (rooted in the works of Hobbes, Locke, and Condillac)—failures to account for the "constitutive" aspect of language.[60] In Taylor's perspective, language does not merely represent the world; in diverse ways, it is ceaselessly shaping the world.

These constitutive, affective, ethical, embodied, material dimensions of language are often shunted aside as we inhabit a world shaped by a hegemonic semiotic ideology that idealizes language at its most instrumental, transparent, and arbitrary—as free-floating signs that do not get caught in the muck of the world. Indeed, as Keane describes, Calvinist missionaries in nineteenth-century Indonesia deemed the improper valorization of words and prayer books as acts of fetishism.[61] The words of modernity are meant to do their work and then dissolve; to linger on them is to slip into enchantment.

So what of the Roshaniyya? As we will see, the literature of the Roshaniyya evinces a persistent consciousness of its linguistic nature. At times, it is explicitly metalinguistic: letters are revealed, dhikr phrases are exchanged as icons of sheer language, acts of communication and speaking are discussed, and creation beckons with a voice. At other times, this linguistic reflexivity characterizes the structure of a Roshani text. The frequent use of chiasmus to structure the conversations of Bayazid and God, for instance, models how an idealized conversation should unfold; other lessons are presented as if a child were questioning a parent. Given the centrality of language about language in the literature of the Roshaniyya, these texts are sites for the expression, performance, and constitution of semiotic ideology.

There are ways in which the semiotic ideology of the Roshaniyya resonates with the alternative approaches to language that the aforementioned scholars uncover within the folds of our modern world. Mahmood's attention to the nonsemantic, communicative work of the body, for instance, compares to the nonsemantic communicative work of some Roshani texts.[62] Though I do not seek to equate the semiotic ideologies of the Roshaniyya with these comparative examples, contemporary thinkers nevertheless offer us a vocabulary for naming the attitudes and potentialities that we find in Roshani imaginations of language. The theorists invoked in this book—Mahmood, Keane, Agamben, and others—provide a lexical next step in our attempts to describe what we see in Roshani texts. Importantly, they attune us to a particular obstacle that we face as we turn to the semiotic ideology of the Roshaniyya. Given the investments of our semiotic ideology (constantly being willed into effect through communicative practices such as this book), it is too easy to think of the affective, material, or ethical weight of language as an *addition*—as something draped on top of the representative function that is centered in our instrumentalist approach to language.[63] Importantly, the semiotic ideology of the "modern West" (as described by Keane) works in concert with the ideological work of the category of "religion" in modern Euro-American societies. As "religion" has emerged in the modern era as a conceptual category with preference to certain ways of "being religious" (loosely: white, Protestant or post-Protestant secular, not-too-poor, patriarchal, cisgendered, heteronormative, capitalist),[64] so too has the Saussurean semiotic ideology of contemporary Euro-American societies given preference to certain ways of being. How we communicate and how we imagine the workings of our communication are inherently raced, gendered, sexed, and classed.[65] The hegemonic semiotic ideology of modernity, however, is one predicated on its own disavowal, its own obliteration—a denial of this racing, gendering, and so on. Our aesthetic is the aesthetic of no-aesthetic: black ink and white paper intended to let us forget that our communicating carries matter, form, color, heat, time, weight, and shape.[66] As such, it is always shaped with preference toward certain ways of being and certain performances of personhood—and this is especially true when language seeks to hide its own materiality. As we approach the language of the Roshaniyya, therefore, we are not describing *their religious language* with a language that is free of moral and metaphysical commitments. Rather, we must admit the tension between the visions of the world inherent to *this language* and the worlds constituted by the words of the Roshaniyya. It is this gap again, however, that renders the story of the Roshaniyya a story in which we too are cast as actors and shapers of the narrative as it unfolds. When Second Mary understands the words of Second Jesus's dhikr to be nourishment and offers her body in all its impermanence to the dhikr; and when the Roshaniyya of this Tu'i village imagine these events to be a linguistic act in which God's word has folded the time of the End into their present moment; and when, even further, stories of this village, these narrated repetitions of Mary and Jesus, and the revelatory Pashto, Persian, Arabic, and Hindawi written by Bayazid circulate and constitute the messianic sainthood of Bayazid Ansari—it is then that we see that our habits of representation and language use cannot skate across these historical events free of their own metaphysical conceptions. This is a sticky process and one in which we find our own relationship to language (as used and conceived) implicated.[67]

All of this is to argue for the value of *semiotic ideology* for the study of the Roshaniyya and their interlocutors. This is our entry point into understanding the intense debate spurred by the Roshani pursuit of God's language because this was, as I argue, a debate primarily concerned with the capacity of language and its saturation with the divine. An attention to semiotic ideology does not simply mirror the projects and anxieties of the Roshaniyya; it is a valuable means to understanding a host of other ontological, ethical, and cosmological commitments dragged in the wake of imagining language. Language constitutes ways of relating to other people and the world. Through the semiotic ideology of the Roshaniyya, we gain a sense of the sociality and sense of belonging that they idealized and *performed* through their language. *How* they wrote tells us *who* they strove to be—and, perhaps, were.

The theoretical challenge before us lies in understanding the communities of belonging that emerge from Roshani sources and from the dim glimpses of Roshani social formations found in their use and imagination of language. This requires a recursive process: interpreting Roshani texts to find their metapragmatic implications (that is, embedded instructions for how a text "should" be read), theorizing how the Roshani imagine language, and then asking how this imagination of language should inform interpretations of Roshani texts.[68] We can only do this successfully in light of our reflection on our own semiotic ideology, even though this aspect of reflection and theorization will remain largely in the background of this book. Through this process, we can, however dimly, begin to understand "the Roshaniyya" even if "we" only hold books and manuscripts in our hands.

So what do a "failed" messiah and his followers have to teach us? The Roshaniyya offer us a rarely told history of Afghans and Afghanistan, and this is a history that sheds light on an early modern moment in which religious imaginations throughout South and Central Asia and across "religious" difference were animated by semiotic dreams and apocalyptic pursuits of God in language. As disputed, condemned, and later remembered, the history of the Roshaniyya is also one in which we see the workings of imperial logics by which *ethnicity* and *vernacular—Afghan* and *Pashto*—become the conceptual categories of containing messianic experimentation to a parochial, localized space. In this way, the story of the Roshaniyya's practice of revelation transforms into a story of the production of an image of Afghan timelessness and isolation.

The failed messiah also teaches something of our own habits of language, however secular, modern, and distant we may imagine our language to be from the seething semio-theologies of the Roshaniyya. Through an encounter with the words of the Roshaniyya, we can let our semiotic ideologies be dragged into the light. The story of Bayazid and his revelation offers a glimpse of some past that flits by and reminds us that we do not possess the words of others nor the imaginations from which they emerge.[69]

A Brief Outline

As noted, our story is of an attempt to speak the word of God—and the new formations of literature, violence, history, and ethnicity that followed in the wake of this effort. We begin in chapter 1 with the life of our main actor, Bayazid Ansari, and how that life may or may not enter the gaze we call history. The hagiography of Bayazid, known as *The Book of States*, offers stories of a Bayazid whose blessedness emerges from the way his body and his dreams scatter and fragment. Paradoxically, his power emerges from his dissolution. The following chapters (2 and 3) then turn fully to the practice of revelation and its achievement, tracing the dhikr performances that transform a human tongue into a vehicle for divine language. Chapter 2 examines the architecture of the Roshani Sufi path and the importance of dhikr practice in guiding disciples up a spiritual hierarchy that culminates in being a blessed, revelatory "wretch." Chapter 3 turns directly to *The Best Exposition*: the multilingual imitation of the Qur'an that inaugurates Pashto literature and earned the Roshaniyya the condemnation of Sunni theologians. What does it mean to inscribe the very voice of God? The next chapters (4 and 5) turn to the aftermath and the inheritances that the Roshaniyya left behind to both devotees and critics. In chapter 4, we compare the Pashto poetry of a Roshani disciple named Mulla Arzani to the Pashto prose of an anti-Roshani polemicist named Akhund Darweza. In many regards, it is Arzani and Akhund Darweza—the poet and the polemicist—who consolidate the lurching, inchoate Pashto of Bayazid Ansari. Chapter 5 stays with Akhund Darweza, a figure whose importance in Afghan religiosity is difficult to overstate. In his response to the Roshaniyya (whom he deemed the very worst of heretics), Akhund Darweza wrote a genealogy of the Afghans. In rejecting the heresies of a false messiah, why does Akhund Darweza find it useful to tell a story of Afghan descent from King Saul? In what ways do ethnicity and orthodoxy intersect?

Singing with the Mountains is the story of a community of Sufis, orphans, widows, nomads, menial laborers, and itinerant poets who gathered around a pursuit of the very language of God. In their efforts, they drew upon a transregional repertoire of cultural and religious practices and cosmologies: Persianate concepts of sainthood, hurufi-lettrist notions of a world built from letters, Qur'anic vocabularies, and Mughal forms of sovereignty among much else. The resultant practices and literatures of the Roshaniyya were unpredictable. As the Gerard Manley Hopkins verse that began this chapter suggested, "O the mind, mind has mountains." There are vaster, wilder, "no-man-fathomed" topographies to Islam, South Asia, and Afghan identity than English-language scholarship has mapped. Hopkins's poem, however, is not a poem on the thrilling expanses of the mind. It is a poem of death and despair. As the concluding sestet reads:

> O the mind, mind has mountains; cliffs of fall
> Frightful, sheer, no-man-fathomed. Hold them cheap
> May who ne'er hung there. Nor does long our small
> Durance deal with that steep or deep. Here! Creep,

> Wretch, under a comfort serves in a whirlwind: all
> Life death does end and each day dies with sleep.[70]

There is a darkness to the story of the people of light. Mughal generals stacked their skulls in towers along the Khyber as a reminder of Mughal power. British scholars read their history as proof of the inborn recalcitrance of Sufi masters to the civilizing project and as emblems of inherent Afghan unruliness. This judgment of Afghans as eternally wild and violent has carried over into American imperial discourses. The cliffs of fall frightful and sheer endure.

There are other curious resonances in this poem with the Roshaniyya, however. In teaching about the fragility of life and the human dependence on God's ceaseless creative and communicative presence, Bayazid quotes a verse from the Qur'an, "[God] is the one who reaps you at night."[71] As Bayazid explains, each day dies with sleep—but each morning God resurrects all the world anew. Moreover, as we will see, the highest stage of spiritual advancement is that of becoming the *miskīn*, the "wretch." It is the wretch whose tongue most fully speaks the whirlwind powers of God and creeps toward the possible death found in sleep and dreams at each day's end.

Whatever Hopkins's harrowing poem on depression and futility has meant in the arc of Catholic poetry or Victorian aesthetics, I want to suggest that we can reread it as we lend our minds to the Roshaniyya. This is no doubt a reach across considerable time and space, but my point is that one way to understand the Roshaniyya is not to make them the objects of the theories, frameworks, and lexicons that have prevailed in the academy. Rather, their imaginations might shade our own, their words might sink into ours, and their theories might render our conventions the object of study. In the literary and temporal gestures of the Roshaniyya, we find an imagination of language in which words have power, might, material weight, and meaning that endure beyond their speaker's intention or their propositional signification. Words slip their contexts and spill into the world in unpredictable ways: "wretch" and "death of sleep" offer new resonances when filtered through the revelations of this premodern band of Sufis. To examine the Roshaniyya—I hope—is to learn how little we possess of the past and how it cannot be fixed within our monographs. There is a chance that our own words slip their contexts and that new ways of understanding the history of religion in Afghanistan become possible.

1 / Bayazid's Doubles: Hagiography and History in the Messianic Community

"This Bayazid and that Bayazid are one Bayazid!"

—MUKHLIS, *The Book of States*

"Tell Balgeary that Balgury is dead!"

—ERIC CROSS, *The Tailor and Ansty*[1]

The moon sliver hid behind the early spring clouds. Bayazid Ansari—the guide, the protector, the holy wretch of Kaniguram, the speaker of God's blessed language—lay asleep in a guest room of a home belonging to Payanda Khan, a *malik* (or leader) living in one of Tirah's dales. Payanda Khan was a rich man, one of Bayazid's few wealthy devotees. Payanda Khan's pride still needed to be broken by the recitation of the dhikr phrases Bayazid had given to him, but Payanda Khan's generosity flowed like the streams of melting snow descending from the slopes of the Sulaiman Mountains. He lent his homes and land to Bayazid for whatever the master needed: pasture for the Roshani nomads of the highlands, rest for the Roshani merchants having recently crossed through the Khyber's defiles, food for the orphans and widows embraced by the Roshaniyya, room for Bayazid's instruction in prayer and recitation, and privacy for when the Roshani devotees could face each other, man and woman, as servants and wretches before the might of God with no veils between them.[2] Payanda Khan was generous enough that he could offer Bayazid, the master of light—*God bless his innermost heart!*—a room of his own.

At the night's darkest, the four assassins crept toward Bayazid's room. They had waited in the obscurity of the hawthorn shadows for hours, and only now did the heretic Bayazid finally extinguish the lamp of his vigil. They slipped through the outer door left ajar by a bribed servant, crossed the threshold of Bayazid's room, and took their positions. One clasped a hand over Bayazid's mouth, two pinned his arms to the floor, and the fourth cut his throat. As instructed by Payanda Khan's rival Masum Khan, the malik who had paid for this grim work, the assassins began the task of dismembering Bayazid. Their work completed, they crept outside bearing sacks dripping and sagging with their damp weight. As the first light of dawn climbed the eastern crags, they scattered Bayazid's organs, head, and limbs in four directions as a macabre sign of what awaited those whose words and practices threatened the chiefs and scholars of this Mughal frontier. Bayazid had been broken, dissected, and scattered.

In the morning, 'Ali Shir woke late and with regret. In his sloth, he had surely missed the chance to pray the dawn prayers with his beloved illuminated master, Bayazid. 'Ali Shir crossed the courtyard of Payanda Khan and knocked on his master's door. He heard no answer, so he cautiously opened the door. He saw Bayazid sitting and gently rocking with the rhythm of the dhikr. Whole, powerful, aglow: Bayazid smiled and invited 'Ali Shir to remember God.[3]

This is a version of a story found in the Persian hagiography of Bayazid Ansari known as *The Book of States.* While I have participated in this storytelling by adding some small details, the central point—the dismemberment and reconstitution of Bayazid—is what we find in *The Book of States.*[4] It is a story that illustrates the elusive quality of Bayazid's sainthood and memory: the more Bayazid is diffused, fragmented, and doubled, the more Bayazid's authority and blessedness as a messianic and Sufi master increase. The narratives of Bayazid seek the dissolution of Bayazid as a discrete individual in the hagiographic performance of Bayazid's sainthood. This chapter examines both the texture of Bayazid's sainthood and the challenge posed to contemporary historical practice by the narrative and linguistic performances of *The Book of States* and other stories of Sufi saints and friends of God.

We obscure the social work and logic of *The Book of States* when we approach this hagiography as a text—however fanciful or symbolic—*about* Bayazid Ansari. The "about" of that approach drags in its wake a host of assumptions on the fundamentally representational nature of language and a preference for history writing that centers on agential, individual subjects. In *The Book of States*, however, we confront a text emerging from alternative semiotic ideologies and guided by relationships to time and personhood which are anchored in doubling, recursion, and anticipation. In simpler terms, our question is: What do we do when the "individual" in our archives gains his life and power through stories of doppelgängers, dreams, and dismemberments? What do we do when the individual is remembered and shattered in the same instance?

Through an exploration of Bayazid and his doubles in *The Book of States*,

I suggest that we must release our search for the historical Bayazid and instead focus on the sociality made possible through a hagiography: What is the nature of the connective tissue of belonging that is presented in the hallowing stories of Bayazid? I make a counterintuitive argument: *The Book of States* is not about a historical figure named Bayazid. Rather, as we attend to internal literary qualities of *The Book of States*, we see this text create "Bayazid the Saint": a narrated, recollected figure open to the participation of others in a messianic community. With the doubling of Bayazid and other narrative techniques, *The Book of States* widens the *historical* Bayazid Ansari into a hallowed, plural saint whose recollection is expansive enough to stage and shape the very social relationships of the Roshaniyya. As we spot the doppelgängers of Bayazid, we spot the "social logic" of texts such as *The Book of States*; that is, we spot the way a text like this works in and through the community around it.[5] Hagiographies are texts in which literature and social life overlap at the point of miracles, dreams, saints, and doubles. The miraculous material is precisely where the text works to instill "a habitus," "a form-of-life," and a way of participating and belonging among the Roshaniyya.[6] This is a literature beckoning a community into being. *The Book of States* serves as a mold into which the Roshaniyya poured their social relationships, and so these accounts of doubled Bayazids shape and mold the idealized social relationships of a messianic community. In this chapter, I call that model of social relationships *participatory messianism*: the community constitutes the messianic nature of "Bayazid the Saint" through these practices of narration and memory.

Spotting the doppelgängers of Bayazid, we also understand the futility of our efforts to find the "real" Bayazid Ansari and to reduce these doubles to a single. In *The Book of States*, we find notions of self, time, and literature tethered to one another in such a way that our hermeneutic techniques begin to crack. This is ultimately the promise of a study of this hagiography for those readers without a particular interest in the Roshaniyya and Bayazid Ansari. Emerging out of the intersection of commitments to messianic interruption, notions of Sufi sainthood and hagiography, and the experimentation with theo-linguistics, the doppelgängers of Mukhlis's account surround us and outpace our typical efforts to render the "religious language" of hagiography into contemporary notions of *history* and *biography*.

The Death of Bayazid and the Question of Hagiography

A story of Bayazid's death illustrates the historical challenges of Mukhlis's hagiography. While staying in an Urakzai village outside Peshawar,

Bayazid heard news of the imminent arrival of hostile Mughal horsemen. Bayazid insisted that the villagers seek shelter in the relative safety of the hillsides, but God had told Bayazid to stay and be delivered to the rank of martyr. And so Bayazid waited to face down his Mughal persecutors until the enemy army delivered his death while the "morning sun exhaled."[7] As much as the Roshani story is a story of death and suppression by the forces of the Mughal Empire, it is also a story of doubling and of the literary and linguistic manipulation of time so that futures and pasts anticipate and consummate one another. This Bayazid who died in a small Urakzai village was not *the* Bayazid. If Bayazid Ansari was the revered messiah, saint, leader, and prophet of the Roshaniyya as we find him in their manuscript memories such as Mukhlis's *The Book of States*, then the Bayazid who died outside a dawn-lit Peshawar was not that Bayazid. As Mukhlis's hagiography continues, we find Bayazid Ansari mourning and commemorating the other Bayazid martyred in an abandoned village.[8] It was his beloved disciple about whom Bayazid Ansari commented, "This Bayazid and that Bayazid are one Bayazid!"[9] *That* Bayazid—the disciple who died outside Peshawar—mirrored *this* Bayazid Ansari in other ways as well. In the presence of Bayazid the martyred disciple, Roshani members witnessed miracles such as Bayazid's ability to discern precisely the contents of individual pages selected randomly from a book he had not read or his ability to make limited quantities of food abound and proliferate to feed a crowd. Like Bayazid Ansari, this martyred Bayazid visited villages in Tirah and Bangash and initiated numerous men and women as disciples of the pir-i roshan, the illuminated master.[10]

There are many Bayazids in *The Book of States*: some are dreamt, some wander as dervishes, some are disciples, and some are whispers of a Bayazid yet to appear or a memory of a Bayazid that has already come and gone in another form. How can we approach these Bayazids?

To begin with, we can attend to the genre of *The Book of States*. Composed in the mid-seventeenth century, *The Book of States* is what we now call "hagiography": an umbrella term that refers to the genre for writing the biographies of saints ("friends of God") and similar blessed figures.[11] The attributed author of *The Book of States* is 'Ali Muhammad Qandahari, who bore the pen-name of Mukhlis. In his introduction to *The Book of States*, Mukhlis claims to have merely compiled the autobiographical writings and sayings of Bayazid, and we'll return to this claim below. There are peculiar features of *The Book of States* that demand our attention; the claim of an autobiographical source and the proliferation of Bayazid's doubles are two examples that mark *The Book of States* as a distinctive work in the hagiographic literature of the premodern period. But let's be clear: even the distinctive features of *The Book of States* would be eminently recognizable and legible for a Persian-literate audience familiar with hagiographies—an audience such as Mukhlis's Mughal nobles in India in the 1640s.[12] Persian hagiographies—in various forms such as *tadhkiras*, *malfūẓāts*, *manāqib*, and so on—are among the most common texts produced in the thirteenth to eighteenth centuries in the eastern Islamic world, and Arabic hagiographies were similarly widespread throughout West Asia, North Africa, and West Africa.[13]

Moreover, in Persian-language contexts, hagiographies and courtly chronicles were co-constitutive genres.[14] Frequently, to write about Sufi saints was to draw upon the royal language of thrones, kings, and their subjects. And to write about kings and queens was to use the language of blessedness, sanctity, and Sufi belonging. The porousness of the line between "hagiography" and "court chronicle" becomes immediately apparent through a comparison of the introductory sections of *The Book of States* and Abu Fazl's history of the emperor Akbar found in the *Akbar-Namah* (or *The Book of Akbar*). Akbar's birth was marked by visionary dreams, a miraculous and revelatory light descending upon his mother, and the deliberate use of the name Maryam to plot Akbar's mother in a prophetic history that includes Jesus and his mother.[15] Akbar receives the kisses of disciples, he bestows cloaks and titles on those who submit to his will, and he claims to uphold a cosmic order in much the same way Sufi saints do.

The rhetorical and literary techniques of *The Book of Akbar*, moreover, aim to make Akbar's sovereignty manifest in the text itself. Abu Fazl offers us a glimpse of the stakes of *The Book of Akbar* in his introduction. The courtier begins by narrating his own confused frustration, even despair, at being unable to capably praise God because of the insufficiency of human language relative to divine sublimity. In this narrative, an epiphanic "message of awareness" commands Abu Fazl to write a history of the events of the empire, and it is through such an exercise that Abu Fazl's speech can bend toward the exaltation of God:

> You will write the history of the ruler of the earth, the jewel of the crown of monarchs, and praise of God can be included. Praise does not need praise, for the perfect creator's creatures are themselves praise of the giver expressed in a tongueless language, comprehension of which makes those with enlightened minds receptive to absolute light, and it causes one to reach a high level of praising, which is essentially the exalted rank of necessary existence.[16]

The solution becomes clear: to write the actions of Akbar's reign *is* to praise God. Through its focus on Akbar—in all his cosmic, embodied power—*The Book of Akbar* becomes the vehicle for transforming language itself. Devotion to Akbar is precisely what lifts the very language of this account from insufficient and hollow cyphers into praise of God—into action. Symbolic representation and proposition transmute into linguistic performance and world-making.

> In olden practice, praise of the worshipped one consisted of speech, while in this new court of wisdom, to praise the king consists of action; previously words were resorted to for divine praise, but in this innovative preface refuge is taken in the perfect man, who is the reality-worshipping emperor, the lord of the world who has lifted the veil from external and internal by his act of searching for and finding God.[17]

Given its subject matter and the locus of its devotion, *The Book of Akbar* is hardly "language" as we understand it at all. Refracted through descriptions of the perfection of Akbar, language becomes an extension of empire, a performance of divine praise, and the marker of cosmic reality.

The *Book of Akbar* is a throne, a war elephant, a shrine—it seeks to be a direct index of power as much as it is an observed account of a political figure. Hagiographies often aim for a similar immediacy of presence and power—even if that power is not planted firmly in the domain of courtly politics and military conquest. These genres inform one another in expression, execution, and purpose; they are co-constitutive genres. Thus, we should hesitate before we assume the chronicles of Akbar's court to be "more historical" according to our habits of historical thinking than the stories of Bayazid.

Despite the ubiquity of hagiographies, they remain a beguiling source for historians and other scholars of religion. Hagiographies tether together types of events that contemporary scholars tend to sort into different ontological categories. In *The Book of States*, Mukhlis tells us who Bayazid's parents were, where he lived, where he traveled, whom he loved, what he said, what battles he fought, and how he died. Mukhlis also tells us what Bayazid dreamt, what Bayazid heard from God, what vows Bayazid exchanged with the mysterious prophetic figure Khidr, what miracles Bayazid's body made manifest, what desires and whims Bayazid managed in his disciples, and how Bayazid encountered other Bayazids.

Hagiographies do not pose a *problem*, though Euro-American scholars have often approached them as if they were a body of literature in need of solving and being unlocked for its historical value.[18] Rather, the problem emerges when we assume that our history telling is free of its own generic constraints, free of its own ideologies of language and cause, and free of its own metaphysics of time and agency.[19] If a search for the "history" hidden in a hagiography is not accompanied by a reflection on the intersecting manners in which life and literature—semiotics and sociality—co-constitute one another, then we risk entering into efforts to forcefully translate the untranslatable. These hagiographies cannot become histories in any narrow sense. I write this not because these hagiographies are condemned to the realm of fantasy nor because they have nothing to teach us of the lives and imaginations of those in the past. Instead, we can reconsider Kathryn Gin Lum's argument that *history* is not a "native category."[20] As noted in the introduction, contemporary and widely shared practices of history emerge from the prevalence of "secularity," according to Saba Mahmood, in which *history* is a calendrical sequence of events with agential subjects as the focus.[21] In Gin Lum's argument, *history*—as a discipline and method of writing the past in Euro-American institutional settings of the nineteenth to twenty-first centuries—has gained its commitment to "change over time" as part of an imperial project of distinguishing the drivers of progress and history from the "historyless" and "stagnant" other. While Gin Lum's discussion of American historical narratives is quite clearly working in a different context than that of Persian hagiography, we can identify a similar risk in the context of reading hagiographies. To uncritically approach hagiographies as sources of *potential history*—as sources that "need us" to translate their claims into history—is to reify particular metaphysical stances toward the past and toward agency that Mahmood and Gin Lum associate with modern ideologies of empire and secularity.

Previous scholarly approaches to *The Book of States* are indicative of such larger historiographical patterns. When confronted with a text shot through with happenings that are alternatively mundane, miraculous, messianic, and mystical, a common approach has been to perform some metaphysical surgery.[22] By sloughing the miraculous and the oneiric into an inaccessible realm of "religious belief," scholars have sought to tease out a plausible "calendrical history," as Mahmood has labeled that form of historical thinking that represents time as a linear sequence of events.[23] While Bayazid's meeting with a Mughal governor in Kabul enters our histories, the dreams and revelations that inspired his visit to Kabul are set aside. While Bayazid's childhood is rendered "disturbed" in a recent assessment, the devilish whispers that incited these troubles are not mentioned.[24] In making this division between the events and beliefs of the Roshaniyya, we, as scholars of religion and historians, distribute judgments of what counts as *real*. We are casting substance. Or, to paraphrase Felice Lifshitz's memorable assessment, we are bobbing for apples of the real.[25]

The death of "the other Bayazid" illustrates this problem. In S. A. A. Rizvi's article that meticulously reconstructs the life of Bayazid Ansari based on *The Book of States*, the martyrdom of "the other Bayazid" finds no mention in the discussion of Bayazid's disciples.[26] Our first option in reading *The Book of States*, therefore, is to excise what is implausible and unsuitably miraculous for a historical narrative. A man named Bayazid died, and we ignore that the dead Bayazid is somehow a double of the living Bayazid. Another option would be to focus on the discursive, representative, and symbolic function of these stories of dreams, doubles, and miracles. This story of Bayazid's martyrdom *represents* the threat facing the "real" Bayazid or perhaps *symbolizes* the "real" Bayazid's letting go of worldly concerns. This symbolic option is certainly valuable but ultimately unsatisfying, as it replicates the metaphysical surgery of the previous approach by corralling the extraordinary into a purely symbolic space where miracles, dreams, and other strange happenings can be decoded and interpreted.[27]

As I understand both Mahmood and Gin Lum, the challenge for the scholar is to call attention to the specific ideologies of contemporary history writing when engaging sources of the past; the aim is *not* to abandon a historical project altogether. It is, rather, to let the rhythms and features of our sources articulate a sense of the past, of temporality, and of a form of life that may be quite different from the contemporary dominant ideologies of time, subjectivity, and sociality.[28] *The Book of States* presents a stark example. The hagiography upholds Bayazid as a saint insofar as Bayazid Ansari dissolves and fragments as a historical individual. *The Book of States* is the story of Bayazid's doppelgängers and his dissolution that allow for the Roshaniyya to *become* Bayazid and share in his blessedness.

In this chapter, therefore, I wager on the worth of pursuing the doubles and dreams of *The Book of States*; I wager that the miraculous and uncanny of this particular hagiography will allow our sense of history to be generatively reshaped by the genre of hagiography. What I will attempt to demonstrate in this chapter is that an alternative approach to apple-bobbing for the real can focus on the social relationships made possible and given form and shape through the doubling narratives of "Bayazid the Saint." What we can see in the rhetorical and narrative patterns of *The Book of States* is the cultivation of a "form of life."[29] As a "form of life," *The Book of States* is not *about* Bayazid Ansari, be he positive historical individual or a symbol pointing to something beyond. Rather, *The*

Book of States is the form of the relationship that the Roshaniyya have to each other and to their master; such hagiographic stories are the medium through which their sociality comes to exist. The nature of this sociality is marked in equal parts by submission and equal participation: a messianic status is extended to all who submit to the master as modeled by the narrative acts of hallowing Bayazid. In the example of the martyred "other" Bayazid, we find a model of sainthood that simultaneously reifies the blessedness of Bayazid, the *illuminated master*, while casting this saintly master as someone for others to become. "Bayazid" is constituted through the participation of others in his blessedness, his actions, his words, and his very name. While I will readily confess my skepticism that *The Book of States* can offer us a glimpse of the "real" Bayazid Ansari, *The Book of States* nevertheless offers a striking vision of how literature can facilitate particular engagements with the past, particular forms of life, and particular socialities. A single story does not suffice to reveal *The Book of States* as a form of life and as the staging of a particular sociality. Over the remainder of this chapter, we will pursue the doubles and dreams of Bayazid insofar as they narratively mold Roshani devotees into men and women who constitute and participate in their messiah-saint.

Before turning to the doubled and dispersed lives of Bayazid as he is remembered in *The Book of States*, is it worth reconstructing the "historical Bayazid" at all? The Bayazid who was an individual making subjective and agential choices that shaped the arcs of history? I doubt it, but I offer a brief reconstruction of the "historical Bayazid" as a counterpoint to the other Bayazids we will meet—and as a demonstration that even the historical individual is a product of genre and is fashioned from the narrative lives of those who preceded him. In finding this "historical Bayazid" within Mukhlis's *The Book of States*, I follow the cues of S. A. A. Rizvi, who performed the metaphysical surgery of separating the fanciful and miraculous from those events considered plausible, real, and ontologically thick enough to make it into our *history* books. Rizvi's articles are meticulous and careful, and they guide us to the following glimpse of a "historical" Bayazid.[30]

The Life of a Bayazid

Bayazid was born in 1525 CE in Jalandhar, a town in present-day Punjab in India, to a man named ʿAbd Allah from the mountainous regions (*kohistān*) around Kaniguram in present-day Waziristan, Pakistan.[31] ʿAbd Allah's father was the *khān* of two mountain towns near Kaniguram who traced his lineage to Abu Ayyub al-Ansari—the revered companion of the Prophet Muhammad whose home in Yathrib (Medina) was chosen as the temporary abode of Muhammad following the *hijra*. 'Abd Allah married Bayazid's mother in Jalandhar, and she was the daughter of a wealthy Punjabi merchant. Shortly after Bayazid's birth, 'Abd Allah agreed to leave his "Hindustānī wife" in Jalandhar as he returned to Kaniguram.[32]

The young Bayazid remained in Jalandhar with his mother until his uncle Khudadad came to them bringing news of the impending arrival of Babur's armies. Khudadad recounted the terrible cruelty of Babur's armies in burning, pillaging, and murdering those that resisted them. In fear of such violence, Khudadad, his sister, and his nephew Bayazid fled to Kaniguram. Eventually, Bayazid found his father in Kaniguram, only to be disappointed by his father's clear affection for his new wife and their child, Fatima and Ya'qub. On account of "her jealousy," Fatima pressured 'Abd Allah to send his first wife away. He acquiesced, and Bayazid's mother returned to Jalandhar while Bayazid remained with his father, stepmother, and half brother.

Bayazid struggled to receive his due from his father, be that in terms of affection, respect, or material support. Fatima and Ya'qub rejected Bayazid and treated him cruelly. As he grew older, Bayazid displayed a yearning for spiritual and religious education. 'Abd Allah frustrated Bayazid in this regard as well, denying him the ability to pursue his own religious teachers. Despite his familial struggles, he continued to perform his duties as a member of a merchant family.[33]

As Bayazid grew older, he devoted himself to dhikr practices. In his youth, he had shown a propensity for ecstatic experiences, and his father expressed occasional concern that Bayazid was crazy or *majnūn* (possessed by the jinn). When Bayazid was forty years old, he felt the urge to go on an extended retreat (chilla). During this retreat, he received the knowledge of secrets (*'ilm al-asrār*), and Bayazid claimed that everyone in Kaniguram was participating in some form of polytheistic "associating" of God and the nondivine (*shirk*).[34]

Bayazid journeyed to Kandahar as part of a trading caravan. He arrived hoping to find spiritual guidance in a city renowned for its piety, but he was disappointed by the pirs and qalandars (wandering ascetics) he encountered. Moreover, he was disturbed by the rapaciousness of the Mughal authorities. They demanded two-thirds of all profits as compensation for their protection. As Bayazid returned to Kaniguram, his desire to devote himself fully to the spiritual life had only increased.[35]

Bayazid's reputation as a man of spiritual insight grew. He began to share his critiques of the traditional religious leaders, decrying their propensity to ground their authority in lineage, cloaks, and officially granted positions to the exclusion of insight and learning. He put aside his initial reluctance to train disciples and began to accept whomsoever came to his door. Among his first disciples were 'Ali Shir—a blacksmith identified as part of the Barki tribe—and his own wife, Bibi Shamsu. These initial disciples were representative of those who would come later. Bayazid seemed to hold a special attraction as a religious leader for the poor, the orphaned, and women.[36]

The fame of his effective spiritual teachings and the renown of his unsparing polemics dragged him into numerous conflicts, and he began to face trials and inquisitions. He fluctuated between attempts to assuage his critics—especially his father—and renewed commitments to his aggressive preaching, alternately dropping assertions of Muslim hypocrisy and reiterating such accusations. While Bayazid was under the protection of his father, he was spared from the direct persecution of others. His relationship with his father, though, was a tenuous one that finally broke after Bayazid criticized his father and half brother for their habit of severely taxing nomadic Afghans who pastured on their lands. Exposed without his father's protection, Bayazid fled Kaniguram.[37]

The pace of *The Book of States* changes quite suddenly after Bayazid's departure from Kaniguram. While he continued to recruit and teach in the city of Tirah and among the Lohani Afghans and others, Mukhlis's account focuses on spare descriptions of Bayazid's growing conflict with his various rivals. As we read in the beginning of this chapter, Bayazid's disciple (also named Bayazid) was killed outside Peshawar.[38] Shortly after this martyrdom, Mukhlis relates the story of a small village populated by the Tu'i tribe that began this book.[39] The Tu'i Afghan residents of this village claimed to recognize a series of portents such as the birth of Second Jesus and the death of Second Mary. After these occurrences, the Tu'i villagers trampled the goods of a caravan en route to Kabul in denunciation of the materialism of merchants. The caravan merchants reported the incident to the governing authorities in Kabul, who subsequently sent mounted soldiers to slaughter the men and imprison the women and children of the Tu'i village. Though Bayazid reportedly denounced the actions of the Tu'i villagers, the Mughal authorities in Kabul interpreted these events as an act of hostility by Bayazid and the Roshaniyya. After a stunning victory over the Mughal forces in the Battle of Aghazpur (discussed below), Bayazid and his modest band of disciples wandered between the various regions of the Afghan highlands in an attempt to avoid capture and defeat.[40]

Mukhlis's narrative dramatically hastens once again. Bayazid made his way to Tirah through the Khyber Pass. In *The Book of States*, he condemned an Afridi and Urakzai raid on the caravan of Mirza Sulayman (governor of Badakhshan) as it crossed the Khyber on the way to Akbar's court.[41] The Afridi-Urakzai raid brought forth a renewed and intensified wrath from the Mughal armies, while some accounts also claim that it was Mirza Hakim's armies that pursued Bayazid. Abiding in Kabul, Mirza Hakim was the brother of Emperor Akbar whose own challenge to Akbar's sovereignty eventually brought the nomadic Mughal court of Akbar to the banks of the Indus in 1581, where the emperor would meet with a young man known as Jalala-yi Tariki—Bayazid's son remembered as "Jalala of the Dark."[42]

Returning to Bayazid's life: whether fleeing Mughal forces of Akbar or Mirza Hakim's own armies, Bayazid fled again to the Yusufzai domains in the region of Swat. And then the story abruptly ends. "Many times during his journeys over two and a half years, [Bayazid] had to draw his sword and fight. 980 years after the hijra of the Messenger [Muhammad], Bayazid was reunited with his friend [in death in the year 1572/73 CE]."[43]

So we can read the life of Bayazid in *The Book of States* as it may be stripped of the miraculous and the bizarre, following Rizvi's lead on what counts as historical. A local religious leader by the name of Bayazid with eccentric ideas recruited those who fell outside the traditional structures of social power (women, poor men such as blacksmiths, orphans, "Afghan nomads"), and he consolidated his influence through scathing critiques of ineffectual religious leaders. As Bayazid grew in reputation, different "tribal" leaders attempted to use either their partnerships with Bayazid (e.g., the leaders in Tirah) or their antipathy to Bayazid (e.g., the Urakzai in Kaniguram) as a wedge to gain power over tribal rivals. This dispute unfolded in a context of a Mughal interest in expanding and securing the trade routes between Kabul and Peshawar. Fearing the safety of this caravan route, the Mughal authorities engaged in a number of political projects, including the savvy manipulation of the local factionalism. Though the Roshaniyya were able to leverage their familiarity of the highlands to control these mountain passes despite the vastly superior Mughal army, they could not overcome Mughal alliances with local leaders.[44] Thus, when promised access to land for cultivation, Bayazid's allies betrayed his location to the Mughal armies who eventually defeated him.

Even the life of Bayazid Ansari described above—sanded down as it is of all dreams, visions, and miracles—reflects the tropes and rhythms of Persian hagiography and Qur'anic narrative: an itinerant merchant teaches his community the oneness of God, is compelled to migrate to another region, faces the trials and inquisitions of an oppressive regime, and leads his small collection of righteous followers into victories over larger armies.[45] We cannot cast off the weight of genre and literary tradition from *The Book of States.*

And so to reiterate my argument: *The Book of States* is not about the historical Bayazid but is a text that stages the constitution and creation of an idealized and intentional community—a community that we might even call "Bayazid the Saint." Through the unfolding of narratives and the literary qualities, *The Book of States* opens a "threshold of indistinction" and indeterminacy between life and literature, between the "saint" remembered in narrative and the hallowing community itself.[46] The work of the text, as it were, is to pluralize Bayazid, to transform the singular "he" of Bayazid to a collective "we" that emerges from these narratives and their circulation.

How Many Bayazids?

The Book of States seeks to cultivate and shape the sociality of the Roshaniyya, and it is in the narratives of Bayazid as someone dispersed, pluralized, and participated in that we find evidence for *The Book of States* as a "form of life" and as a mold into which the Roshaniyya poured their social relationships. These accounts of Bayazids shape and mold the social relationships of a messianic community. Bayazids proliferate, multiply, fragment, and coalesce. We can find Bayazids doubling in three principal sites in *The Book of States*: in dreams and their reception, in the prophetic and saintly tropes that find resonance in Bayazid's life, and in the repetition of initiation and inquisition. Collectively, these doubles "stage a relationality," as Dimitris Vardoulakis has written about the role of doppelgängers in European philosophical literature.[47] The doubled Bayazid—as narrated in *The Book of States*—becomes a clearing for the emergence of an idealized Roshani community.

Dreaming Bayazid

Dreams and visions punctuate Bayazid's life with such regularity that we cannot explore more than a few representative examples. In approaching these dreams, I am attempting to gauge their literary effect; these are reported narratives of dreams and *not* dream experiences in and of themselves.[48] The rhythms of the dream narratives we find in *The Book of States* are common to Persian hagiographies (and related genres), such as the collective dream of a glowing light in the house of 'Abd Allah just before Bayazid's conception.[49] Like many prophets and saints before him, dreams herald Bayazid's imminent and blessed birth. Other dreams are predictive in nature, such as when Bayazid received a vision that some of his family's goods would be consumed in a fire.[50] Many of the dreams serve as a confirmation of Bayazid's spiritual advancement in moments of moral ambiguity. Bayazid sees visions of the mysterious prophetic figure Khidr, for instance, in which Khidr acknowledges the righteousness of Bayazid's behavior toward his father.[51] Another key function of the dreams is to differentiate the levels of mediation between Bayazid and God's communication. In some dreams, Bayazid sees Khidr while in others he sees a saint deliver a goblet of wine from God or he finds God's words (such as the *ism-i aʿzam* or "the Greatest Name") written in a book.[52] In still others, Bayazid dreams that he "hears" an inner voice calling to him, and the voice communicates the word of God. Finally, after seeing some dreams, Bayazid receives the interpretation of the dream from "a calling voice" (*hātif*), an inner voice, or another human.[53] These dreams work as a theorization of divine communication through narrative, and they thus stand in a productive tension with the direct, ostensibly unmediated communication between Bayazid and God apparent in *The Best Exposition* (to be discussed in chapter 3). While these dream narratives provide an unsystematic theorization of divine communication, they emphatically perform one of the central arguments of Roshaniyya sources: God communicates through all aspects of creation, and this communication is *linguistic* even when transpiring in dreams, in the songs of birds, or in the rush of a flowing river.[54]

In understanding Bayazid as a saint, however, there are some dreams that we should consider in further detail: those that double and pluralize Bayazid. One particularly perplexing dream begins when a doppelgänger figure visits Bayazid at his home. This visitor, we read, was also named Bayazid and stayed as a guest in Bayazid Ansari's home *in waking life*. It is the *guest* who saw the following dream and narrated it:

> Two people came to me. One was a white-bearded man and the other black-bearded. White Beard asked, "Where is Bayazid? I intend to fight him." The guest said, "No one should fight him without a sufficient cause. Reveal the reason to fight." He said, "I intend to fight without cause." The guest asked, "Explain the cause of your hostility!" White Beard said again, "I will fight him without cause." Three times they discussed this, but White Beard did not reveal the source of his hostility. He said, "Show me where Bayazid is so that I can fight with him." The guest said, "He is not present, but, in his place, I am here. Come! Fight me! Perhaps it is for this reason that God has made me

> a guest in his house." White Beard then fought with the guest. In the end, the guest lifted White Beard and threw him on the ground. Then White Beard said, "Let me pass one time so that I may fight with Bayazid, even if you go far away on his boat [*kashtī*]." I [the guest] had thought that there was neither boat nor sea in this area. So I raised my head, and a vision of the boat and sea came to me. I said, "The boat is far from here. Look elsewhere until you no longer can see this person." The rage of that old man calmed.
>
> The guest awoke, performed his ablutions and then described his dream to a servant boy. The servant boy interpreted the dream. White Beard was ʿAbd Allah, father of Bayazid. Black Beard was Yaʿqub, his brother. These two were hostile towards him.
>
> The guest said, "This dream of mine must not be without effect. It is better that this young man reconciles with his father. He should slaughter a sheep and give it to the poor. He should behave in such a way with his father and brother that his father will be pleased with him, and thus he may obtain the benefit of religion and the world. Tell Bayazid of this conversation so that he will order the slaughtering of a sheep and its distribution to the poor so that he may reconcile with his father and be free of rumors of the people, so that he may obtain religious and worldly benefit, and so that my dream will not be without effect."[55]

The servant boy then delivered the guest's message to Bayazid Ansari:

> Bayazid the Benevolent Master (*may God sanctify his heart!*) said, "I always have peace for ʿAbd Allah and Yaʿqub, and I have never behaved poorly with them. But I have promised to my family to be halal, and I will not envy the possessions of ʿAbd Allah."
>
> The guest said, "A hundred mercies be upon you since this is righteous practice." Then the guest said, "I am a qalandar. I bid you farewell. The recompense for every sweet thought is a good thing to come." The guest took his leave and departed.[56]

Upon completing his dawn prayers, Bayazid Ansari went to ʿAbd Allah, kissed his feet, and sought his blessing. Mukhlis, however, specifies that Bayazid "did not reveal the guest's dream to [ʿAbd Allah]."[57]

Is it not strange that the saint of our hagiography has his dreams intercepted by a visiting qalandar and interpreted by a servant boy? How should we make sense of such a dream narrative?

We can begin by noticing that this is an intervention in the life of

Bayazid Ansari which spares him the disturbances of that which may distract Bayazid from God: conflict with his family and commercial interests (seemingly referenced by the boat). As Shahzad Bashir has described, Sufi masters often change their physical appearance in order to instill, defer, fulfill, and transfer a disciple's desires for the sake of spiritual education.[58] In this instance, we see a qalandar adopt the position of Bayazid Ansari in a dream in order to intervene on God's behalf. This dream thus inverts the usual master-disciple dream narratives found in Bashir's descriptions. The ostensible master (Bayazid) is delivered by a doppelgänger with no specificity to his own identity or ability. The qalandar merely "intercepts" the dream figures of White Beard and Black Beard who intended to encounter the "real" Bayazid. The qalandar is a cypher through which God manages the spiritual education of Bayazid the master by using the manifestation of an alternative Bayazid. The ethics of submission that characterize a Sufi master-disciple social relationship do not cease with the putative messiah-master. Rather, he becomes as a disciple to the master who is God mediated by a dream-catching doppelgänger.

More importantly, this story reveals that Bayazid's presence is a catalyst for visionary dreams in others. It is a central example that Bayazid's sainthood is a *staging of relationality*. "Bayazid the Saint" is a fragmented and distributed process in which others participate. The blessedness of Bayazid is found in between Bayazid and those around him. In this particular instance, it is the mysterious guest who saw the dream, and it was the servant boy who interpreted the dream. Elsewhere in *The Book of States*, Bayazid's disciples collectively saw a dream in which they are commanded to call Bayazid the "illuminated master" (pir-i roshan). Bayazid's son Shaykh 'Umar received his name from a dream bestowed to the sister of Bayazid's wife, Bibi Shamsu. Bayazid's initial appeal to disciples was that he would guide them to the vision of "secrets" (asrar) through the disciplinary program of dhikr recitation and chilla retreat.[59] The hagiographical narratives demonstrate the quality of Bayazid's teachings by recording moments in which Bayazid's companions and disciples see visionary dreams.

Moreover, the social status of the dreamers is yet another challenge to traditional markers of authority. Throughout *The Book of States* and *The Endeavor of the Believers* (a text discussed in the next chapter), Bayazid chastises those whose spiritual authority relies on family pedigree, sartorial demonstration, and hierarchies of gender. Servants, blacksmiths, orphans, married women, and widows all have significant dream narratives or interpret the dream narratives of others in Mukhlis's hagiography. The diffusion of dream narratives among a diverse group of actors in *The*

Book of States creates an imaginative space for disciples and sympathizers to participate in and *extend* the saintliness of Bayazid in their own dream worlds. There is not a delimiting of visionary dreams to the figure of a single master; to the contrary, the master is narrated *as master* by the dispersion of visionary dreams to those around him.

We find the most direct use of a dream narrative for the establishment of Bayazid as an authoritative saint in Bayazid's dreams of Khidr: a mysterious prophet who typically alights in the dream worlds of Sufis who exist apart from or on the edges of an institutionalized pious community. The introduction to the dream narratives mentions that Bayazid's "flowing spirit" (*rūḥ-i jārī*) went into the realm of the imaginal (*ʿālam-i mithāl*), and this language situates Bayazid's dream within the onto-cosmologies associated with the teachings of Ibn Sina and Ibn ʿArabi.[60] In *The Book of States*, Bayazid personally narrated the dream but recounts it from a third-person perspective:

> There was a man with his face toward the qibla. Bayazid passed by him and the man said, "O Bayazid! Do not fruitlessly pass by me." Bayazid said, "Who are you?" That great one said, "I am the blessed Khidr." Then Bayazid said, "Had I had known that you were the great Khidr (*peace be upon him!*), I would have come and kissed your feet and asked for a blessing from you."
>
> When Bayazid arose from kissing the feet of Khidr, Bayazid said, "Say a prayer for me."
>
> Khidr said, "I will not say a prayer for you, but I want you to become my brother in religion [*dīn*], and I want you to become a partner in religion with me, and I will become your brother in religion."
>
> Bayazid said, "Say a prayer for me since your prayer is sufficient for me."
>
> Then Khidr said, "Why do you not become my brother in religion and share your religion with me?"
>
> Bayazid said, "You are pure and your religion is pure. I am a sinner! For this reason, I will not share my religion with you, and I will not become your brother in religion lest the shame of my sins fall upon you and ruin comes to you."
>
> Khidr said, "What is the point of this speech? My wish is that you share your religion with my religion and that you become a brother in religion."

At this point in the dream narrative, Bayazid and Khidr exchanged vows with each other as "brothers in religion." Still within the dream world, Bayazid became suspicious of the true identity of Khidr:

> Bayazid wondered if it truly was Khidr [who accompanied him], but then they arrived at a town and the people of the town all kissed Khidr's feet. It was difficult to go anywhere because of the enthusiasm of all the people. They reached the center of the city and there was a fountain—the fountain of life. There were two angels, like two maiden girls, who were drawing water from the fountain.
>
> Khidr sat at the corner of the fountain with that group. They were all thirsty, and Khidr ordered the maidens, "Give water to these people." They gave water to each person, and they gave some to Bayazid as well, but he was not quenched. The maidens took more water from the well.
>
> In his heart, Bayazid thought, "I am not quenched from this water." Khidr heard the thoughts in Bayazid's heart and arose. He took a pitcher from a maiden. He said, "O Bayazid! Drink this water of life!" Bayazid took mouthful after mouthful from the pitcher, and, certainly, he drank much. When he raised his head from the pitcher, Khidr said, "Drink more water if you yearn to do so." Bayazid said, "There was not a need for this much water. When you gave it from your own hand, I drank much and my thirst was quenched." Then the great Khidr said, "Praise be to God, Lord of the World! Your thirst has been quenched by the water of life from my hand."[61]

This dream bids for Bayazid's spiritual eminence by explicitly binding Bayazid and Khidr together. Beyond this, however, it represents an additional critique of the conventional means for spiritual education and authorization. Bayazid sought a spiritual master in Kaniguram and in the much larger city of Kandahar, but he found no one whose knowledge ably matched the authority of their vestments, lineages, or professions. Bayazid's disappointment extended to his own father's role as a religious leader. This dream, therefore, demonstrates that it was only Khidr who could fully initiate Bayazid into the spiritual life. Any other mediating figure between Bayazid and the "water of life" failed to quench his thirst; his spiritual capacity—as represented in this particular dream—was simply too great.

Even as this dream distinguishes Bayazid as a particularly authoritative saint, it continues the diffusion of participatory dream visions that we saw in the dream of White Beard and Black Beard. As the "water of life" dream narrative makes quite clear, Bayazid enters into a brotherhood in faith with Khidr—among the most peripatetic and elusive prophetic figures in Islamic traditions. This is an "Uvaysi" initiation, in which Bayazid's incorporation among a community of the prophetic and saintly occurs by the hand of Khidr via a dream rather than by a Sufi master in the waking flesh. Uvaysi initiations recur throughout Persianate hagiographies, and the narrative of Bayazid's initiation works to cut out and displace religious authority from the usual structures of religious education in Bayazid's social milieu.[62] This dream serves as a critique, once again, of the reliance upon family pedigree, hypocritical scholars, and bribable judges. Paradoxically, even as these narratives offer forth a Bayazid who transcends the authority of rival masters and scholars in Kaniguram and elsewhere, "Bayazid the Saint" is more accessible to readers and listeners than other religious figures such as his criticized rivals ensconced in hierarchies of sartorial and genealogical distinction. As the reflection in the mirror of Khidr, Bayazid is doubled—and lifted beyond the specificities of a single historical body. The doubled saint is the social model: the staging of a way of life marked by the repetition of prophetic communication and full participation in the ongoing revelations of God. His blessedness and authority emerge out of the narrative dissolution of an individual, discrete subject.

Bayazid as the Prophet Repeated

The theme of doubling and repetition that we are chasing in *The Book of States* is not merely found in the proliferation of Bayazids, as if there were an "original" and then a series of "copies." The "original" himself repeats prophetic others, and so Bayazid is himself the double of prophets and saints that preceded him.

One of the more startling chapters in *The Book of States* relates Bayazid's desire to murder his half brother, Ya'qub. As mentioned above, Bayazid's father 'Abd Allah repeatedly denied Bayazid his share of the family's wealth from trading expeditions to India and Central Asia. Instead, 'Abd Allah lavished his wealth upon Bayazid's stepmother, Bibi Fatima, and half brother Ya'qub. In one particular dispute, after insistently arguing that he had a right to the family's increasing wealth, Bayazid received an enslaved boy (*ghulām*) from his family. When Bayazid attempted to send the ghulam away to do some long-distance trading as a proxy, a weeping 'Abd Allah forbade Bayazid this action because 'Abd Allah "would be lost without him."[63] Though Mukhlis's account does not reveal more on the nature of 'Abd Allah's relationship with the ghulam, Bayazid relented to his father's wishes in order to avoid shaming him before the elders of Kaniguram. Despite Bayazid's effort to preserve his father's social standing, 'Abd Allah quickly sold the ghulam after an argument with the ghulam and kept the money for himself. Bayazid's consideration for his father's honor and affection resulted in yet another example of material dispossession while demonstrating the pettiness of 'Abd Allah.[64]

In this state, Bayazid became increasingly frustrated, and so he beseeched God. Mukhlis writes:

> Bayazid called out to God, asking, "What is it that you want?" As he was thinking this, Satan cast a whisper into his heart. Satan said, "O Bayazid! Look what 'Abd Allah did with your rights. First, he divorced your mother. And he placed you under the control of Bibi Fatima, still in tender age, and he separated you from your mother."[65]

Satan proceeded to list the numerous ways in which 'Abd Allah, Bibi Fatima, and Ya'qub had wronged Bayazid, and Satan then concluded, "It is better for you to kill Ya'qub so that the goods and possessions of 'Abd Allah can fall into your hands."

The opportunity for fratricide soon appeared:

> Bayazid (*may God sanctify his inner heart!*) then set out to follow Ya'qub in order to kill him. One day, 'Abd Allah commanded some servants to bring wood and he appointed Bayazid and Ya'qub as their escorts. When they reached the forest, the slaves busied themselves with the cutting of wood. Bayazid and Ya'qub went to the summit of a mountain. There was a massive tree at the summit which gave shade. They stretched out under the tree, and Ya'qub fell asleep. Then Satan whispered, "Now is the time to kill Ya'qub. Throw him from the peak of the mountain to the depth below. If anyone asks, [say] that he was asleep, and, due to the height of negligence, he fell from the side of the mountain. No one will blame you." Bayazid (*may God sanctify his inner heart!*) raised a knife, saying, "I will strike him."[66]

Bayazid did not bring the blade down upon his brother, however, for in that moment "angelic voices" entered Bayazid's heart. He heard the angels tell him of the torments of hell, and he reflected, "If one hand or one foot falls in the fire, there is no strength that can bear it, for all the fire of this world is but one drop's worth of the fire of Hell, and this fire is washed by the mercy of God seventy times over." Bayazid meditated upon the shame that this deed would bring his family: "If it becomes known, I will have a bad name, and the people of God will say that the son of 'Abd Allah—who is from the people of Ibrahim, Siraj al-Din Ansari, and Chiragh al-Din

Ansari—unjustly killed his own brother for the sake of worldly interest."[67] Though Ibrahim was the name of one of Bayazid's ancestors, the mention of the name without the modifier *Ansari* is intriguing for its prophetic resonances. Elsewhere in *The Book of States*, the prophet Ibrahim stands alongside Muhammad as a referenced model of emigration (*hijra*), and the image of Bayazid with blade in hand ready to slay a family member is certainly suggestive of Ibrahim, father of Isma'il and Ishaq. Curiously, the appearance of the knife in this narrative directly contradicts the plan whispered by Satan into Bayazid's heart, which was to push the sleeping Ya'qub off a cliff, thereby framing his death as a plausible accident. The knife appears in this account *against* the immediate, criminal logic of covering up a murder, and this contradiction potentially calls attention to the knife as resonant with the prophetic logics at work in this narrative. Finally, like Ibrahim at his moment of angelic intervention, Bayazid recognized this temptation to commit murder as a trial delivered by God and meant to "reveal the states of men."[68] He then recalled the words of the Prophet Muhammad, "God tests the believers with trial just as one tests gold in a fire."[69]

Bayazid's near-fratricide is a transformational moment for him. Though he had studied the Qur'an as a child and been given to ecstasies and trances caused both by the Qur'an and by ritual music, this is the first instance of direct communication between Bayazid and a heavenly being. Subsequently, Bayazid's conversations with God, angels, and Khidr become the narrative engine for Bayazid's development in *The Book of States*. In this moment, Bayazid's visceral reaction to the fear of Hell and the disgrace of fratricide spur him to complete reliance upon God (*tawwakul*):

> Then, in his heart, Bayazid thought that God has created many people, and none of them eats from the home, property, and possessions of 'Abd Allah, for the Provider delivers them their daily bread from elsewhere. "If I do not eat from the property and possessions of 'Abd Allah, God Most High will not let me pass without my daily bread, and He will deliver in eternity what has been promised as my share."[70]

Yet again, *The Book of States* offers us a Bayazid who may elude our initial expectations. Not only do his dreams fall to his followers, one of the most crucial moments in his life pivots on his desire for murder. How do we make sense of this story?

The narrative identifies the family as a possible source of corruption and distraction from the blessed, revelatory path that Bayazid was to pursue. Bayazid harshly critiqued scholars of religion and spiritual masters who held their positions of authority solely through inheritance and family name. Before rejecting his familial connections to seek a religious life and rely upon God, Bayazid considered the murder of his own brother for the sake of material gain. This account attempts to reveal the glaring tension between lineage, economic ethics, and the religious life. There seems to be no balance among them; a choice is necessary. Bayazid's eventual break with his family occurred when he criticized Yaʿqub and ʿAbd Allah for their unjust exploitation of Afghan nomads. Through some of its most dramatic moments, *The Book of States* suggests that a truly ethical and pious life necessitates a suspicion of lineage, genealogy, and family. The near fratricide of Bayazid models and perhaps even encourages the emergence of idealized social relationships between master and disciple, even (or especially) when the cost of such a master-disciple sociality is the rejection of alternative frames of belonging. Join the cause, no matter the cost.

More importantly, though, is the narrative's reliance upon prophetic and Sufi models. As noted, there are resonances with Ibrahim's near-sacrifice of his son. This story's theme also falls within the shadow of the Qabil and Habil (Cain and Abel) story found in the Qur'an and Qur'anic interpretation where the jealous brother's murder is not stayed by angelic voices. The more significant resonances lie with Sufi narratives of repentance, however. From the earliest collected biographies of Sufis—such as those found in al-Sulami's *Sufi Generations* ("Ṭabaqāt al-ṣufiyya") or Farid al-Din ʿAttar's *The Remembrance of the Saints* ("Tadhkirat al-awlīyā'")—we can find the most pious saints and exemplars of beatitude with backgrounds of temptation, trial, and sin.[71] The narrative of Fudayl ibn ʿIyad, for instance, typically begins with Fudayl as a criminal brigand before his chance hearing of the recited Qur'an and subsequent repentance.[72] Bishr al-Hafi, in ʿAttar's iteration of the story, was a drunken degenerate before stumbling upon a scrap of paper with the *basmalah* ("In the name of God . . .") written upon it.[73] Alternatively, according to a fifteenth-century Central Asian hagiography entitled *The Eight Gardens* ("Hasht hadīqa"), Shaykh Ahmad Bashiri nearly threw himself to his death out of despair over his distance from God, just as—so the story goes—the prophet Muhammad nearly did centuries before.[74] In these cases, heavenly intervention at the last moment spared Shaykh Ahmad and Muhammad, just as Bayazid was spared before his great error. Bayazid's intended fratricide, the dramatic intervention, and Bayazid's subsequent repentance and reliance upon God would be readily legible in the religio-cultural world in which such Sufi hagiographies circulated.

As an echo of previous blessed lives, we can see in this narrative the dissolution of the particularity of an individual, "historical" Bayazid Ansari. These tropes of sin and repentance perforate the boundaries we might seek to draw between Bayazid and the prophetic exemplars before him. This becomes especially true as we turn to the model of Muhammad that structures this narrative of Bayazid's life.

Though Bayazid was not an orphan, his father was cruel to him and expelled his mother from Kaniguram. Bayazid thus grew up under the care of a protective uncle, much like Muhammad and his uncle Abu Talib.[75] From an early age, Bayazid had a contemplative and spiritual disposition, finding solace in retreats in the mountains. He was a merchant, but he was an ethical one troubled by the rapaciousness of the Mughal tax collectors and the exploitation of poor nomads by his wealthier relatives. At age forty, Bayazid began to devote himself with greater seriousness to extended spiritual retreats and receive the secret teachings of the ʻilm al-asrar, just as Muhammad received his first revelation from Gabriel at age forty.[76] In one of the most repeated comparisons drawn between Bayazid and Muhammad, Bayazid in *The Book of States* often quoted Qur'an 68:51 when accused by his father and rival religious leaders of insanity or possession: "Those who disbelieve—they would all but strike you down with their eyes when they hear the dhikr. And they say, 'Surely, he is truly possessed!'"[77] Just as Muhammad faced the criticisms of the suspicious while articulating the dhikr, so too did Bayazid.

The most intriguing comparison to Muhammad lies in Bayazid's actions around the Battle of Aghazpur. In *The Book of States,* we read of a leader named Shaykh Uriya whose hostility toward the Roshaniyya forced Bayazid to leave the hills of Kaniguram.[78] Bayazid referred to his departure as a hijra (emigration), describing hijra as a common experience for prophets and saints such as Muhammad, Ibrahim, and Bayazid Bistami.[79] After Bayazid's own emigration, the Mughal armies sought to capture and kill him. Bayazid met in counsel with his supporters about the imminent assault of the Mughal army. With no possibility of escape from the mountain upon which they had sought shelter, Bayazid's companions insisted upon battle: "Let us attack the enemy, relying upon God." Bayazid then performed his ablutions, prayed two *rakʻas*, made a supplicatory prayer (*duʻā*), and read the Surat al-Faitha to his companions.

> Then the companions all took up arms. Those who did not have a weapon grabbed stones and wood. All of those who were there numbered 313 people. . . . [Bayazid the] Benevolent Master read the Surat al-Faitha with his friends and sons, and then set out to meet the vanguard of the Mughal army. When they faced each other, the friends

> shouted *ho!* and attacked. God Most High shattered the Mughal army. Many were killed while the rest decamped and fled toward Peshawar. God Most High kept the Benevolent Master and his friends safe from the hands of the oppressors. He granted victory and success.[80]

Like Muhammad's 313 companions at Badr, Bayazid's small but sanctified army of 313 companions succeeds with God's assistance. The verses that follow the account of Aghazpur emphasize the similarities to Muhammad, drawing into relief the significance of renaming and epithets:

> He who followed the journey of the Master becomes God's beloved.
>
> O my son! He foreswore the infidels and from women he abstained.
>
> God named him Muhajir and amongst the Pure his honor increased.
>
> And like the Muhajirs, those in Yathrib are the princes and the respected.
>
> God has chosen them, and they are the Ansar—by God so named.
>
> He who aided the Perfect One and in his noble wake journeyed,
>
> His rank is near to God and his heavenly recompense is doubled.[81]

Just as some of Muhammad's followers became remembered as the *anṣār* ("the helpers") following their support of Muhammad's prophetic cause, so too Bayazid's were initiated through a transformative experience into new named identities. Bayazid's own Ansari family claims lineage to the ansar. The historical conditions that had produced a new title for the followers of Muhammad and Bayazid's own family occurred again for Bayazid's followers who were given the name *Aghazpuri*. Renaming follows desperation, emigration, and a miraculous battle in which those present emerge blessed (anew) by God. In this aspect of Bayazid's narrative, we see the gravitational pull held by the story of Muhammad in the construction of sainthood. As Bashir has argued about other late medieval Sufis:

> The appeal to Muhammad would have little rhetorical force were it not for Muslims' investment in Islam's originary period as a source of authority. But equally significant, the impact of the historical figure would not be as widespread were it not for the fact that Persianate Sufis appropriated him for the way they constructed their models of religious authority in this period.[82]

The construction of Bayazid's authority, therefore, both depends on the narrative models of Muhammad and perpetuates those narratives through their creative re-instantiation and alteration. In this way, Bayazid joins a long tradition of Persianate saints such as Sayyid Muhammad Nurbakhsh, Shaykh Ahmad Bashiri, and Khwaja Ahrar whose authority simultaneously drew upon and expanded the authority of the Prophet Muhammad.

To represent Bayazid's life as a series of events that coincide with the prophetic life of Muhammad is to bid for Bayazid's own prophetic authority while erasing the very particularity of Bayazid as an individual saint. In the mimetic subsumption of Bayazid's life under the arcs of Muhammad's own, we are finding the reiteration of one life being lived in multiple spaces and times. But whose life is it? Is it Muhammad's or Bayazid's? Ultimately, it is the very tension between these two possibilities that sustains the ability of literary acts of imitation to be meaningful texts for disciples and readers. In chapter 3, as we turn to a consideration of the messianic timescapes of Bayazid's revelatory *The Best Exposition*, we will revisit the polychronic registers of Bayazid's religious imagination. Bayazid and the Roshaniyya do not aim to *return* to a past age of prophetic greatness. Rather, the Roshaniyya strive to *fulfill* the past through a performance that is both imitative and expansive. Bayazid and his 313 companions come to be both themselves and instantiations of Muhammad and the first believers. It is this *surplus* presence—the coincidence of two identities in one, two Bayazids in one, two chronotopes in one—that forms the central component of the *messianic revelation* pursued by the Roshaniyya.[83] Though we will continue to explore this notion of surplus and revelation beyond this chapter, I seek here to draw our attention to "Bayazid the Saint," a figure that emerges from a constellation of text, of reader, of disciple, of imitation and fulfillment of Muhammad, of historical personage, and of his many doubles.

The Bayazid of Inquisition and Initiation

Among the most frequently recurring scenarios in the narrated life of Bayazid is Bayazid's questioning at the hands of a skeptic. Critics accuse him of insanity on numerous occasions, but Bayazid frequently parries such accusations with a demonstration of his similarity with Muhammad. The issue of madness (*majnūn shudan*) typically accompanies charges of heresy. The following encounter is a brief but representative instance of such inquisitions:

> An elder said to [Bayazid], "You should not say three things. You should not say that Gabriel comes to you. You should not say that you are the mahdi. And you should not say that the people are hypocrites." [Bayazid] the Benevolent Master said, "I do not say that Gabriel comes to me; rather, I say that inspiration [*ilhām*] is coming to me. I do not say that I am the mahdi; rather, I say that I am the guide [*hādī*]. Finally, I do not say that all the people are hypocrites and infidels; rather, I say that whomever God has made a hypocrite is a hypocrite. And whosever is an infidel is an infidel."[84]

We will revisit the distinction between inspiration (ilham) and revelation (*waḥy*) as well as Gabriel's role in later chapters, paying special attention to Bayazid's later statement in *The Book of States* that he has *stopped* making such claims about revelation (wahy)—an ostensible admission in an apologetic hagiography that Bayazid did indeed claim revelation at points in his life.[85] The denial of being the mahdi also finds contradiction in other Roshani sources. Our purpose here, however, is with the literary effect of Bayazid's self-defense.

The three accusations made against Bayazid reiterate the polemics of Akhund Darweza—the Sunni theologian who took it as his career's purpose to refute the heresies he perceived among the Roshaniyya.[86] The compactness of this event in *The Book of States*, moreover, suggests that this event is carefully crafted by the compiler of this hagiography, Mukhlis (or his sources), to counter the project of Akhund Darweza and similar polemicists. Whether convincing or otherwise, Bayazid's response to the elder's injunctions directly countered the accusations. While claims to being the mahdi were by nature political and potentially explosive in the premodern period, the Bayazid we encounter in such trials seems to believe that self-identification as a "guide" (hadi) was less troubling to rivals and enemies, despite its etymological connection to mahdi. In passages such as these, *The Book of States*' intended audience sharpens into focus as Mukhlis assures potential heirs and sympathizers of the Roshaniyya that Bayazid's teaching were not as transgressive of normative Islam as the polemics of Akhund Darweza would claim. These inquisitions are intertextually motivated even as the rival texts haunt *The Book of States* only in their absence.

More important than the intertextuality of these moments, the frequency of near-identical trials and inquisitions throughout *The Book of States* suggests that they too serve the purpose of using narrative to conjure a Bayazid the Saint in whom readers and listeners participate and constitute—thus granting the readers or listeners space to *become the doubles* of Bayazid. There are at least six such moments in which Bayazid faces the same set of questions, doubts, and accusations from a rival—including one inquisition in the court of Mirza Hakim in Kabul.[87] Each trial is an additional opportunity for the devout reader to stand with Bayazid and bear witness in the face of a critic.

Moreover, a particular initiatory practice confirms the significance of a broader participation in Bayazid—the significance of doubling him up and diffusing him through the lives and words of those who come after. In both *The Book of States* and Akhund Darweza's polemical account of the Roshaniyya, we find Bayazid breaking away from popular models of Sufi initiation. Saturated as the Roshaniyya are with the models and lexicons of Sufi networks and practices that came before them, we may expect that Bayazid would initiate Roshani "vicegerents" or "deputies" (*khalīfa*) who then would go and spread the Roshani network beyond the Afghan highlands. Indeed, Bayazid initiated the poet Mulla Arzani and sent him south with an epistle of Bayazid's revelations. In conventional networks of Sufi initiation, Mulla Arzani would then initiate new disciples into the Roshaniyya, and Mulla Arzani would become the master (pir) to these newly initiated disciples (*murīd*s). According to our sources, however, Arzani and other deputies of Bayazid initiated new disciples so that they were directly disciples of Bayazid, the master.[88] In other words, Mulla Arzani was the conduit through which new disciples entered into an immediate and intimate relationship with "Bayazid the Saint" if not Bayazid the historical personage.

Finally, we can treat Mukhlis's claim that he is merely collecting the autobiographical writings of Bayazid Ansari, a claim made at the very introduction of *The Book of States*.[89] It is unsurprising for a hagiographer to present himself or herself as a mere channel for the authentic or original sayings of a saint who came generations before, but Mukhlis's statement is partially corroborated by the extant manuscripts of the Roshaniyya. There are multiple copies of a manuscript titled *The Path of Oneness* ("Ṣirāṭ al-tawḥīd"), which is told from the perspective of an author identified as Bayazid. In copies of *The Path of Oneness*, the identified narrator Bayazid describes his dreams and trials in language nearly identical to that quoted above and found in Mukhlis's *The Book of States*.[90] While *The Book of States* is more extensive, the existence of manuscript copies of *The Path of Oneness* suggests that narratives of Bayazid circulated in different ways from different perspectives. Moreover, *The Path of Oneness* is the title of the epistle that Mukhlis claims was carried by Mulla Arzani into the regions of India. Though our sources are limited and later, we can find in the evidence a pattern of a *participatory messiah*. Arzani and other disciples of Bayazid were initiating in the name of Bayazid, reciting epistles from the perspective of Bayazid, and narrating a Bayazid whose own dreams land in the dreamscapes of his community to be interpreted by servants, orphans, widows, and others, whose own life and death echo and model the lives of others, whose own name is shared by disciples. All of this, I argue, shows a saint constellated and constituted by the relationships of the Roshaniyya among themselves.

Bayazid as the Community

We can conclude with one more miracle of a sleeping Bayazid that attests to the porousness of this narrated saint and his cultivation of the participation of others in his sainthood. One night, as a group of Roshaniyya and Bayazid slept in a single room, a disciple desired to touch and feel the body of his master. He reached over and attempted to caress the sleeping Bayazid, but his hand simply slid through empty space. Bayazid's body dissolved in that moment to spare the disciple from a violation of Roshani social and sexual norms. As the disciple pulled his hand back, Bayazid's body took shape again—and Bayazid then instructed the disciple on channeling his desire into proper devotion, recitation of the dhikr, and meditative attention to God.[91] Like the bodies of so many Sufi masters narrated before his own, Bayazid's body modulates, shifts, dissolves, and fragments to manage and cultivate the behavior of his disciples.

Stories such as this render it difficult to speak of Bayazid the Saint as "he" or "him," for the very ontology of Bayazid the Saint as imagined in *The Book of States* is plural and constituted by relationships. Moreover, he is *porous*, and his very blessedness depends on the participation of others: their dreams, their interpretations, their miracles, their role in saturating the name Bayazid with a sense of collectivity and sociality. Even after Bayazid Ansari's death, the reader may become a disciple to the master for the master is the dispersed, multiple, even fragmented literary life of Bayazid the Saint. The body of Bayazid Ansari is only part of this constellation of sainthood and sociality; it is the texts and narratives in circulation among disciples and readers that instantiate the presence of Bayazid the Saint—as well as the additional dreams, performances, and narratives that would compound this participatory sainthood among Roshani communities following Bayazid's death.

The doubles of Bayazid—the doppelgänger who intercepted a dream, the disciple of the same name who died before his master, the deputies who stood as Bayazid when they initiated members into the Roshaniyya, and the prophets whose lives Bayazid repeated through his own life—

reveal to us a point similar to these miracles of a permeable body. Bayazid is most powerful—is most "saintly"—in those moments of trembling indistinction between him and the world. As Bayazid meets his double, a gap opens between a historical Bayazid Ansari and this narrated figure, Bayazid the Saint. Bayazid the individual is dismembered and his limbs scattered; Bayazid the Saint becomes whole, if unstably so and always vibrating in relation to other bodies and concepts around him.

The gap between the two is not to be overcome, for we find the full performance of *The Book of States* precisely suspended between this Bayazid and that Bayazid. It is the gap itself—the clearing created—in which we can find the molding and staging of the idealized sociality of the Roshaniyya. The reader or listener of these narratives may walk between Bayazid and his double and participate in the sainthood and messianic potential of the Roshaniyya. In short, I suggest that these stories of doubling and dispersion appear in *The Book of States* because they express a *communal* attempt to form relationships of blessedness and belonging. We have few details about this Roshani community, and many of the details are conventional in hagiographies. They resist the tired trappings of formalized religion in which authority rests with mere cloaks and parentage. They include rich and poor devotees, men and women, orphans and widows, the illiterate and the poets. The Roshaniyya commit themselves to the importance of dhikr practice, to affirmations of God's unity, and to the defense of their community in the face of Mughal hostility. According to their critics, they "heretically" devoted themselves to Bayazid as a messianic mahdi and to *The Best Exposition* as the direct revelation of God. According to later chroniclers, they were motivated by their *Afghan*-ness.

More important than Mukhlis's direct descriptions of the Roshaniyya, however, are what we learn of them from their narrative techniques—from the type of relationality made possible through the narration of Bayazid and his doubles. So who were the Roshaniyya? If we follow *The Book of States*, they appear as a community bound together by a commitment to God's ongoing and ubiquitous communication with God's people. There is a striking surplus to God's communication: divine and blessed messages are bountiful and spill into the lives of all the Roshaniyya, no matter their social status. Servants, nomads, and widows share in Bayazid's revelations. The narrative imagination of *The Book of States* likewise suggests that the common Sufi ethic of absolute submission to the Sufi master extended to the master, Bayazid, who paradoxically had no physical master. In place of submission to the instructions of a living being, Bayazid's submission was *via* (if not *to*) the mysterious Khidr. Primarily, though, Bayazid's submission rested in a process of dissolving the notion of a discrete Bayazid—submission by Bayazid to the messianic "Bayazid" lying at the center of the Roshaniyya's perception of temporal renewal and possibility. This is most clearly seen in the anecdote that began this book: Second Mary and Second Jesus *lived* the declaration that "Bayazid" was the messianic mahdi without the presence of the historical Bayazid Ansari. Finally, we can see the beginning of a theme that will be developed throughout the remainder of this book: the Roshaniyya were a community tethered together by their collective reiteration of the rhythms of prophetic revelation. Theirs was a world not of *reference* to the past but of *fulfillment* of the past through its doubling: a prophet professing his illiteracy, a band of 313 soldiers, a Mary, a Jesus, and, as we'll see in chapter 3, an imitated Qur'an. *The Book of States* opens the possibility to readers and listeners to enter into these moments and roles and ethics and submissions.

Critically, the Roshaniyya as we find them beckoned into being by *The Book of States* were not *Afghan*. The descriptor "Afghan" allows us in the twenty-first century to locate and quickly catalogue the Roshaniyya, but the term is either absent or outright rejected in *The Book of States* (as will be explored in chapter 5). The social bonds cultivated in this hagiography make no appeal to a collective fate based on descent, geography, or tribe; the bonds are woven from shared practices of dhikr, shared commitments to the miracles of a saint and messiah, shared concern for language as a medium of immediate divine presence, and shared participation in the imagining of time and history as something awakened and graspable in the present. By attending to the constellated figure of Bayazid the Saint in *The Book of States*, the relevant comparisons to Bayazid become Sufis such as Shaykh Ahmad Bashiri, the Naqshbandis of *Drops from the Fountain of Life* ("Rashaḥāt ʿayn al-ḥāya") or *Breaths of Intimacy* ("Nafaḥāt al-'uns"), the Qadiri and Naqshbandi Sufis of Kabul and Peshawar found in sources such as *The Distinguishing Gift* ("Tuḥfa-yi qāsimī") and *The Finest Waystations* ("Zubdat al-maqāmāt"), Emperor Akbar of *The Book of Akbar*, or the countless Sufi saints of South Asia whose lives emerge as a configuration of text, disciple, and shrine.[92]

While *The Book of States* evokes the literature of Persianate hagiography, the other works attributed to Bayazid, such as *The Best Exposition*, *The Endeavor of the Believers*, and *The Path of Oneness*, similarly evince a cosmopolitan world that expands beyond the region of the Afghan highlands. *The Best Exposition*, as we will explore in greater detail in chapter 3, is a tetralingual dialogue between Bayazid and God that draws upon well-circulated tropes and techniques of lettrist discourse. It is partially composed in Pashto, and, indeed, it suggests that Pashto is a new language of revelation, but *The Best Exposition* expresses this claim in Arabic, Persian, and Hindawi as well. *The Endeavor of the Believers* is an Arabic description of the spiritual path and a careful meditation on the connection between dhikr and divine communication. *The Path of Oneness* is a Persian and Arabic epistle on Bayazid's teaching addressed to "kings and princes" and reportedly sent to Emperor Akbar and Mirza Sulayman Badakhshani, among others. In short, the internal literature of the Roshaniyya reveals an imagination of Bayazid as a spiritual leader on the eve of the new millennium who would be the guide for Muslims throughout Central Asia and South Asia, from Bukhara to the Deccan—a guide, moreover, whose imagined ontology necessitated the participation of a blessed community fulfilling a prophetic past through their present actions.

Given the expansiveness of this Roshani imagination that sought a community from Bukhara to the Deccan, *The Book of States* adopts a grammar of blessedness and belonging that was pervasive and legible throughout much of the Persianate cultural world. This should be no surprise, given that the Afghan highlands of the Roshaniyya were the site of numerous routes that stitched India to Central Asia and Iran. Nevertheless, the historiography of the Roshaniyya—and Afghanistan, more broadly—has habitually cast this region as one that is isolated and timeless. This is a topic that will be explored in chapter 5, but we can see the question take shape here. If the Roshaniyya fashioned their sociality through participation in the doubles and dreams of Bayazid and according to a cultural grammar common throughout Central and South Asia, then when and how did the horizons of our understanding become limited to Afghan ethnic identity? How do we move from the messianic imaginations of belonging found in *The Book of States* to the domination of proto-nationalist and ethno-tribal explanations in later histories?

The argument of this chapter has been that we obscure the social work and logic of *The Book of States* when we approach it as a text—however fanciful or symbolic—*about* Bayazid Ansari. The "about" of that approach drags in its wake a host of assumptions on the fundamentally representational nature of language and a preference for history writing that centers on agential, individual subjects. In *The Book of States*, however, we confront a text emerging from alternative semiotic ideologies and guided by relationships to time and personhood which are anchored in recursion and anticipation. And so we must adjust our hermeneutics to account for the way that history is not "a native category," to borrow again the line of inquiry pursued by Kathryn Gin Lum and Saba Mahmood, among others.

Rather, the past is something much more flexible than we typically allow, and it bends and curves in accordance with the models we establish with our habits of language. The doubles of Bayazid assist us in the necessary work of doubting our own sense of who and what may act in the past, how and why texts emerge as they do, and against what horizons of time we see change and repetition. We are left not with a text containing a core of Bayazid Ansari, his teachings, and a record of Roshani practices. Rather, the "decisive core" of a hagiography such as *The Book of States* is "a habitus or a form"—a patterned and framed way of relating to others via the collective participation in a saint and his revelations.[93] The ostensibly firmer ontological path of finding the life of a historical Bayazid dims our glimpses of the sociality of the Roshaniyya found in Bayazid's doubles—a sociality marked by a communal participation of the lightness of Bayazid, the pir-i roshan, a saint born from the very stories and dreams shared about him.

And even if we could parse the putatively probable and positivist of Bayazid's story from the miraculous, our hermeneutics would still spin within a semiotic ideology of representation and instrumentation. This book has wagered that the semiotic ideology of the Roshaniyya—their imagination of language and how it builds and binds humans, God, and the world—is worth exploring both in its own right and for how it permits us to recognize and name "our" semiotic ideology. Our hermeneutic habit has been to approach hagiographies as being *about* saints and blessed figures. It is in the *about* of that sentence that we can find the gap between our imaginations of language and the work performed by the dreams and doppelgängers of a hagiography such as *The Book of States*. The representational and propositional nature of a language anchored in the *about*—the assumption that *The Book of States* is *about* Bayazid—suggests that language is a tool, an instrument, a set of codes that permit us to master the world and coordinate our mastery with others. The more transparent the sign is (and the less stubbornly material it is), the more effective this instrument becomes and the more capably we can stand as discrete agents acting upon rather than *within* and *as part of* the world. But now we confront a fundamental question that will be examined in future chapters: if Bayazid, his followers, and his critics all believed that the very stuff of the cosmos is linguistic—that the very stuff of our worlds and selves are made of letters and phonemes of God—then how are we to think of language? Can there be any boundary between word and world? Are writing, speaking, listening, and reading irreducibly bound to matter, flesh, community, and God alike? The irreducibly linguistic nature of the Roshani cosmos invites us *not* to adopt their world as our own but to consider how language is bound to world-making. Our words—and their warp and weave—constitute, mold, and shape the social as much as they reflect it.

I struggle with these doubles. In presentations on this material and in conversations with colleagues and friends, I find it easy to slip into a language *about Bayazid*, a historical individual. I have few doubts that *a* Bayazid existed, given that a diverse range of sources attests to his existence: *The Book of States*, the chronicles of Akbar's court, the memoirs of the Jesuit Monserrate, and the polemics of the anti-Roshani theologian Akhund Darweza. Beyond this confidence *that* Bayazid existed, what else can we say about Bayazid? Not much at all. More importantly, it is that urge to talk *about Bayazid* that drives us to see the hagiographies as a "problem" to be solved, drives us to rely upon the logics of ethnicity and nation in describing the Roshaniyya, and drives us away from a fuller understanding of the intimacy of time, language, and belonging in the imaginations of the Roshaniyya. It is not Bayazid but the narratives of his doubling, his dreaming, and his dissolving that call the Roshaniyya into being as a community that participates in messianic sainthood, becomes Bayazid, submits to the shapeshifting master, and brings the prophetic past into the words and lives of the Roshaniyya's present world.

2 / The *Dhikr* of the Wretch: Text, Practice, and the Roshani Self

"There is no god but God.
There is no I but You."

—BAYAZID ANSARI, *The Endeavor of the Believers*

In the apocalyptic imagination of the Roshaniyya, the End is a time when the earth shakes and mountains shatter. Heralded by cosmic trumpet blasts, the dust of ruined mountains bears witness to the power of God. But the eschatological drama does not unfold solely upon the rent landscapes of creation. According to Bayazid Ansari's description of the Sufi path, the time of the End acts upon the human body with the performance of the *dhikr*—the recollection of God and the recitation of God's language. In Bayazid's account, as the pious disciple gives her tongue to the utterance of God's name, her body quivers, her lower-soul fragments into nothingness, and her spirit rises.[1] The End is an anticipated moment that will be the summation of God's story of creation, but the language of the End characterizes the description of Sufi dhikr. Earthquakes and dhikrs inhabit similar spaces in the symphonic manifestation of the God of the End.

This chapter examines the critical role of dhikr in the practices and imaginations of the Roshaniyya with particular attention to the power of the dhikr to make and unmake, create and decreate, the human self. We can trace the descriptions of dhikr in a central work of the Roshaniyya attributed to Bayazid Ansari: *The Endeavor of the Believers* ("Maqṣūd al-mu'minīn"). In *The Endeavor*, the striking polysemy of the term dhikr dashes the divisions we like to draw between linguistic description and ritual performance, between present moment and eschatological expectation, and between the text and the self. The story we are telling in this book is of the Roshaniyya's pursuit of God's language—and the violent rejection of this project that left in its wake heresiographies, towers of skulls, and new formations of Afghan identity and Pashto language. As the preceding chapter suggested, this story involved the emergence of a messianic community around Bayazid, the saint born of doppelgängers and dreams. The next chapter will query the very idea of divine language as it will attempt to excavate the Roshani understanding of revelation. This chapter joins the story here: how the Roshaniyya attempted to elevate their language to the level of the divine by forming Roshani selves capable of bearing the divine on their tongues. But how did dhikr shape the Roshani wayfarer? In what conceptual world and according to what semiotic ideologies is dhikr able to transform the Roshani wayfarer into a speaker of revelation? And, broader still, how do we understand the relationship between linguistic performance and the formation of the self?

It is to these questions that we turn by delving into *The Endeavor* and its imagination of dhikr as a polysemous concept that stitches together the self, the cosmos, and the text. I argue that we must understand *The Endeavor* as itself a "spiritual exercise," to borrow Pierre Hadot's term for those exercises which bring a self into "conformation" with the cosmos and God.[2] Dhikr offers a model of self that is formed in its exposure to being *acted upon*.[3] And *The Endeavor* is about dhikr and is itself a dhikr. Which is to say: Contrary to our historiographical habit of separating descriptions of dhikr found in Sufi literature from their effective "performance" through ritual acts, we can make no such separation here. *The Endeavor* renders grammar, structure, syntax, and wordplay as the theater of spiritual transformation. For this reason, our focus must remain tightly on *The Endeavor*; its literary and textual qualities are central to our argument, and we cannot, therefore, cobble together a theory of dhikr from an array of Roshani texts. Dhikr lifts the self to higher spiritual states by indexing the self to the language of dhikr found in *The Endeavor*. It is but a small exaggeration to say that the Roshani wayfarer becomes the dhikr, becomes *The Endeavor*.

Revelatory Wretches

Before all else, let me spoil a twist ending. Throughout the works attributed to Bayazid Ansari, we find him bearing titles and sobriquets that flit from the common honorifics bestowed upon a Sufi master to bolder claims of messianic authority. He is Bayazid *al-Hadi* ("The Guide"), *al-Mahdi* (the messianic "Guided One"), *al-Shaykh* ("The Elder"), and *al-Miskin* ("The Wretch"). According to his devotees and rivals alike, it is this last one—miskin—that Bayazid used when signing his epistles and entreating emperors, governors, and scholars to heed his teachings.[4]

In the lush history of Sufi literature, it is an unsurprising title. Miskin resonates with ascetic and poetic discourses of abjection: I am a humble *wretch* before the majesty of God, I am a desperate *wretch* begging for the (divine) beloved's attention, and I am a starving *wretch* renouncing my ravenous body's desires.[5] But here is the twist for Bayazid's title of miskin. When embedded in the religious imagination of the Roshaniyya, *miskin* holds a second set of meanings, reaching beyond a demonstration of humility (false or otherwise). Miskin is the title of the spiritual wayfarer who has ascended to the highest possible spiritual stage in which the *wretch* speaks with revelatory power and discerns with apocalyptic clarity the true nature of others. The surprise here is that Bayazid's signature of humility is an open declaration of Bayazid's messianic ascent, at least for those who know the rules of Bayazid's lexicon—rules which we will learn in this chapter.

This is more than a clever bit of wordplay. The tension between the apparent meaning of miskin and the additional meanings draped upon it—the tension between "wretch" and "speaker of revelation"—opens us precisely to the challenges of studying Roshani discourse on dhikr. The surprise punch of miskin, in other words, tells us quite a bit about the Roshani relationship to language as something to be molded, hammered, and wrought for immanent and powerful disclosure and self-fashioning—and *our* frequent inability to see this in our own language, which is cast as a series of arbitrary cyphers untethered to the material world.

The punchline of miskin's doubled meanings is especially evident in the concluding sections of *The Endeavor of the Believers*. Written as a series of lessons given in Arabic to a Roshani disciple, *The Endeavor* maps the Roshani vision of the Sufi spiritual path and details the dhikr phrases that push a disciple to ever more advanced spiritual stages entitled Law, Path, Truth, Knowledge, Intimacy, Union, Oneness, and Stillness. While much of *The Endeavor*'s spiritual mapping would be legible and familiar to Sufis from the eleventh century until today, the final spiritual stage of *The Endeavor* is unique to Bayazid and the Roshaniyya.[6] (And here I offer a reminder of one of the historiographical rules governing this book: often what seems *unique* and *extreme* in the Roshaniyya is useful in that it renders pervasive religious trends of the period more visible to us.)

The final stage is the stage of *sukūna*—a word we might variously translate as "silence," "tranquility," "dwelling," "inhabiting," or, per my preference, "stillness." Upon ascension into the stage of Stillness, the spiritual wayfarer experiences a disentanglement of spirit (*rūḥ*) and body (*jism*) that marks the apotheosis of the pious believer and an assumption of "lordship" (*rubūbiyya*). As Bayazid describes the "knower of Stillness" (*'ālim al-sukūna*):

> In body, he eats, drinks, dresses, arises, walks, moves, and rests. But in spirit, he does not eat, drink, dress, arise, walk, sit, nor move. His body busies itself with worship while his spirit attends to lordship. His body is perceived as a created-being and a servant, but his spirit possesses the trait of the Creator who is served. In body he is weak and impotent, but spiritually he is strong and able. The life of the body falls to death and annihilation, but the life of the spirit abides without death. The body is ruined and pathetic, but the spirit is prosperous and noble. The body has both a beginning and an end, but the spirit sees neither. There is an equal, an opposite, and a rival for the body, but the spirit is unique, unopposed, and unrivaled. The body is bound to fate and destiny, but the spirit has no limit, no fate, and no end.[7]

At this stage of spiritual apotheosis, the "knower of Stillness" realizes a dissolution of the boundaries between self and other. The spirit is limitless and unbound; there is no longer a haunting distance between the spirit and the Creator. The body is left, however, in a world still marked by distinction and separation.

The Endeavor reveals the name for those wayfarers brought into Stillness: miskin. The guiding voice of the text—attributed to Bayazid—calls out:

> O my son! There is no stage greater or higher than the stage of Stillness. The prophets seek the rank with the people of Muhammad, but Muhammad (*peace be upon him!*) seeks the rank of the wretches. As [Muhammad] said, "O God! Give me life as wretch, bring me to death as a wretch, and resurrect me as one in the fellowship of wretches!" Bayazid the Wretch has said, "Whosoever finds the Stillness of God becomes prosperous and everlasting. Outwardly his body continues to move but his spirit remains still."[8]

And there it is: a description of the miskin as a station to which Muhammad himself aspires.[9]

While the inclusion of Muhammad's prayer to be resurrected among the "wretches" offers evidence of the wretch's spiritual position based in the traditions of hadith, the logic of *The Endeavor* rests more fully upon the semiotic potential of the term miskin. According to the trilateral root system of Arabic language, words with shared roots frequently draw from a shared well of meaning. By way of example, the ***k-t-b*** root—suggesting something like "writing"—is the gravitational center for a host of orbiting words such as ***kitāb*** ("book"), *maktaba* ("library"), and ***kātib*** ("writer"). In *The Endeavor*, the recurrent juxtaposition of *miskīn* ("wretch") and ***sukūna*** ("stillness") activates the formal connection between the two words, infusing the title miskin with the stillness and ascendancy of sukuna: not just a wretch, but a "wretch who is still."

Before any Arabic-speakers throw this book away, we must recognize the problem this presents. According to grammarians and lexicographers of Arabic, the word ***miskin*** derives from the relatively rare class of Arabic words with quadrilateral roots: ***m-s-k-n***. In other words, there *should be no* substantive connection between miskin and words derived from ***s-k-n*** such as stillness; this is folly and transgression, according to conventional Arabic morphology.[10] Perhaps *The Endeavor*'s linguistic playfulness is merely a sign that Bayazid is an unskilled Arabist fumbling toward a formal resemblance and conjuring his own meanings therein. *The Endeavor* pushes this linguistic logic still further, though, suggesting that the wretches in Stillness possess their own manner of language:

> The scholar of monotheistic unity identifies idolaters by their language of associating things with God [*shirk*] and breaking away parts of God [*tafrīq*]. But in such a way, the wretch identifies the scholars of unity by their language filled with error and humanity. . . . The wretches speak a God-fearing language in Stillness, as God Most High said, "God sent down His sakina upon His messenger, and upon the believers, and He fastened them to the word of the God-fearing."[11]

This hierarchy of language and learning positions the wretch above the scholar who is above the idolater. As Bayazid's language breaks away from the linguistic conventions of the scholar, we are left to wonder whether grammatical transgression—the "erroneous" linking of miskin and sukuna—is proof itself that Bayazid has become a wretch. *The Endeavor* punctuates this passage with verse 26 of the 48th sura of the Qur'an to braid another word to miskin. While I leave ***sakina*** untranslated in the quoted passage above, A. J. Arberry translates the word as "tranquility." Arberry would have us read 48:26 as a demonstration that God rewards God's believers with an ease and calmness of mind.[12] The term *sakina*, though, scintillates with a divine presence and revelatory sense that is lost in a term such as "tranquility." As the not-so-distant cousin of the Hebrew term *shekhina*, the word *sakina* has been used in Qur'anic commentaries and hadiths to refer to all manner of theophanic manifestations: angelic armies, blessed clouds, and the presence that enveloped Muhammad upon the revelation of the Qur'an.[13] *The Endeavor* asks us to read miskin in the shadow of these linguistic histories and formal connections: not just a wretch, but a wretch in the stage of Stillness speaking a theophanic, revelatory language.

The arc of meaning that we have traced in the word *miskin* is representative of the active, performative quality of *The Endeavor*. The entire text is replete with mentions of "Bayazid the Wretch," and, as noted, Bayazid signed his letters to princes and emperors with the ostensibly humble sobriquet of "al-miskin." As we move through *The Endeavor* and read its description of the stage of Stillness, our understanding of the word and its meaning transforms in the process. In the theater of the text is a model for linguistic disclosure—a performance of signs progressively offering bolder and richer self-revelations.[14] Consonant with our exploration of semiotic ideology throughout this book, the crux of this textual performance rests in the formal, even material, aspect of language. It is the visually and aurally shared ***s-k-n*** of miskin, sukuna, and sakina that initially hides and then lays bare the promise of Bayazid's title.

All of this returns us to a recurring argument of this book: we miss something important about the Roshaniyya (and the Sufi cultures from which they emerge) if we begin with the premise that "their" language *means* in the same way as "our" language *means*—that the Roshani imagination of words, letters, and signs overlaps fully with our own in a twenty-first-century context. Rather, there is something substantial, something constitutive, and even something *ontological* about the language imagined by the Roshaniyya. For example, in the waning pages of *The Endeavor*, Bayazid cryptically discusses the realms that exist within a human being:

> O my son! Some of the realms in the human being have the form of the realm of the human, [while others have the form of] the realm of jinn, the realm of Satan, the realm of angels [*malakūt*], or the realm of divinity [*lāhūt*]. . . . In [each realm of the human being], if the character of the realm of jinn predominates, then [the human] becomes a jinn with the character of the jinn. He becomes a jinn with his tongue and language, but the [other] human beings consider him to be human.[15]

The Endeavor repeats the same point for each of these separate realms. When the character of Satan, the angels, or the divine predominates, the human being speaks the language of Satan, the angels, or divinity. She is Satan, she is an angel, and she is one from the realm of divinity with her tongue, even though her peers consider her still to be human. The true character of the human being lies veiled in her language, for there is an inherent connection between signs and self.

While most humans might fail to recognize the true character of one another's tongues, God does not. As Bayazid writes: "God recognizes them by their characteristics and not by descent. As in God Most High's speech, 'Then when the trumpet is blown, there will be no more relationships between them that Last Day, nor will one ask after another!'"[16] This verse on the eschatological trumpet is the last Qur'anic citation to appear in *The Endeavor*, and Bayazid uses it to illustrate that the self is not a product of lineage, social position, or appearance. The self is a matter of language, and one's language will be laid bare to all with frightening clarity as the apocalyptic trumpet blares. Before the end times, however, the wretch joins God and achieves an eschatological ability of semiosis and a way with words at world's end. The wretch perceives what God perceives and what the End promises to reveal.

Through *The Endeavor*, we can trace the particular semiotic ideology of the Roshaniyya in order to understand the worlds of sixteenth-century Afghanistan: religious texts, prayers, and descriptions of Sufi paths are all filtered through a pulsing and material sense of words as things to be molded, shaped, braided together, and transgressed. Doing so, moreover, is to play with the very stuff of time, of the cosmos, and of the self. Language is ultimately where the substance of a person's self lies. Speak to me, and I'll discern whether your tongue is that of Satan's, a jinn's, a human's, an angel's—or if it is a tongue touched by the divine.

While the games of miskin and the musings on jinn-tongues offer us a glimpse of Roshani semiotic ideology, it is in the rest of *The Endeavor* that we witness the process by which this "wretched" semiosis is achieved. Words are the entry points into *achieving* an eschatological clarity for the present.

With the remainder of this chapter, we will explore *how* this is so—how the convergence of text, language, and self-transformation is possible within the religious imagination of the Roshaniyya. *The Endeavor* seeks to tie a wayfarer's self to the discussion of dhikr that we find in *The Endeavor*. By developing an indexical relationship between interior self and text, the Roshani chart a path to speaking one's way into divinization. Map *is* territory if we live inside an atlas; and the linguistic cosmos of Persianate Sufis (described below) opens onto vertiginous possibilities for using language and texts to execute projects of self-formation, discipline, and apotheosis.

In this indexing of self and text—this tethering together of transformation and language—the literature of the Roshaniyya represents a challenge to our habits of understanding dhikr practice and "mystical" language. Far from being ineffable, spiritual development is shot through with words, grammar, and textuality regulated by and specific to Arabo-Persian discourses on Sufism and orthodoxy. And to reverse the equation, manuals on dhikr ritual and explanations of the Sufi path do not refer to practices *out there*. These texts strive to enact the very transformations they describe.

As Bruno Latour has suggested, "Angels do not convey messages; they change those they address."[17] The transformative speech of Latour's angels is the exception to his larger point about the modern world: that so much of what we might call religious language is bleached away in the search for a transcendent referent. Is it that language cannot reach the spiritual heights of our experiences? Or, as Latour suggests, is it that we have fallen into a trap by pressing performative, nonreferential language into conveying some message, signifying some higher meaning, and referring to some transcendent being or state?

It may seem as if I am propping up some straw-person, but the historiographical habit in Islamic studies has been to approach Sufi texts as, principally, mystical texts oriented at an experience, meaning, or divinity beyond the language of the text. Ian Netton's analysis of Naqshbandi dhikr is a representative example. In what is a rich and sympathetic treatment of Sufi rituals, Netton insists that rituals are "signs"; rituals "are not practised or undertaken for their own sake but always mirror, or are directed towards, a deeper reality."[18] Netton's line of thinking echoes the Western fascination with Sufism as, primarily, a matter of mysticism, and his presentation resonates with many contemporary Sufis' self-theorization.[19] He approaches Sufi dhikr with sophistication and subtlety, and he does not romantically gesture toward the essential compatibility of all mystical traditions. But as Richard King and Rosemary Corbett (among others) have argued, it is precisely by trivializing formal specificity that modern commentators have sought to sever the deeper reality of Sufism from the barren legalism of "normal" Islam while subsuming Sufi thinkers and poets into a lineage of mystical antimodernists.[20] As Sufism is broken away as a phenomenon distinct from "Islam," it becomes an ideological chisel—a means to split the world into camps of "good Muslims" and "bad Muslims," to borrow Mahmood Mamdani's memorable framing of the matter.[21] As I am trying to suggest with this chapter, there is a direct line to be drawn from semiotic ideology to the classificatory schemes we bring to the world.

When texts such as *The Endeavor* become sheer windows onto dhikr ritual practice or when they become the hollowed-out shells of a transcendent meaning, we are left with a library of coffined thoughts.[22] *The Endeavor*, however, holds an immanent attention on grammar, structure, form, and language. This attention, moreover, was developed within the semiotic conditions of the early-modern Persianate world—and we need to understand more of this moment to understand why and how *The Endeavor* places its wagers upon the possibilities of textuality, immanent language, and formal features.

Akhund Darweza levels numerous critiques against the Roshaniyya, and among the most often repeated of them is the accusation that they are *ḥurūfīs* ("lettrists"). The accuracy of Akhund Darweza's comment is beside the point, for he is indeed identifying a cultural inheritance of immense importance on both sides of the Khyber, including among the Roshaniyya: "lettrism," or the science of letters (*'ilm al-ḥurūf*). Closely braided to forms of apocalypticism and messianism, lettrism refers to a diverse range of practices and intellectual traditions that circulated widely throughout the Islamic world. Despite the diversity of lettrist traditions, a common vision of a "semiotic cosmology" connects many of them. As the Qur'an suggests, God spoke the world into existence with the command of *kun!* "When God wills a thing, God says to it: Be! [*kun!*] And it is."[23] The substance of the cosmos—its ontological stuffness—is thus irrevocably linguistic. In such a vision, letters are more akin to atoms than to symbols, and they thus have the power to directly index truths of the world. And, inversely, the time and space of creation may be approached "as language," as letters to be read. Within such a cosmos, a cascade of practices becomes possible: divination, the production of apotropaic amulets, astrology, and the manipulation of signs in contests of violence and power.

In the Roshaniyya's pursuit of followers and converts, they emphasized the radical break of Bayazid Ansari from corrupted traditions of knowing. As the previous chapter noted, hagiographies of Bayazid claimed that the mysterious, pan-temporal prophetic figure Khidr was his only true instructor and master. The rupture between the Roshaniyya and their predecessors was certainly exaggerated by both the Roshaniyya and their critics. Nevertheless, the insistence upon this rupture leaves us with few hard clues regarding who shaped the Roshani imagination of language. While we cannot name precisely the lineage of Roshani lettrism, it is clear that lettrism was a tradition of knowledge being pursued and expanded across South and Central Asia at the time of the Roshaniyya.

A community of Zoroastrian scholars active in sixteenth-century

Iran and India may provide the closest analogue to the Roshaniyya. As will be explored in the coming chapters, the Roshaniyya hitched their conception of language to an apocalyptic temporality. The time of the resurrection—the *qiyāma*—would be a time in which signs would coincide with the signed. This is not an infinite deferral in which signs are always in the wake of some meaning they can never fully catch until the (equally deferred) arrival of the messiah. Rather, the Roshaniyya suggested that language could become apocalyptic and could achieve its apocalyptic clarity through proper usage. That is to say: yes, language reaches its full potential only at the apocalypse, but language can also cause the apocalypse. The Zoroastrian community associated with Azar Kayvan similarly stretched language across a cosmological schema so that certain practices and forms of language were affixed to the afterlife and to heaven.[24] As Daniel Sheffield has argued, Azari Zoroastrian texts such as *The Heavenly Regulations* ("Dasātīr-i āsmānī") envisioned an ontology of letters and sketched a cosmogony in which "all of the languages of the world were descended from a single, otherworldly language, which they referred to as the celestial language (*zabān-i āsmānī*)." This celestial language is both a primordial cosmogonic-revelatory language and a messianic language: it is both pre- and post-history, both a human effort and more. Like the Roshaniyya's pursuit of God's language, the Azari Zoroastrians inscribed *The Heavenly Regulations* in a language claimed to be this celestial language. As Sheffield notes, "This celestial language . . . does not resemble any known language. Instead, the constructed language of the *Dasātīr*, though apparently unsystematically, appears to have incorporated elements from Arabic, Persian, Turkish, and Hindi."[25] Temporality, cosmology, and language practice mutually shaped and informed one another—and a wide array of actors from different religious traditions experimented with the possibilities of writing an apocalyptic, cosmic, meta-language.

Alongside the Zoroastrians associated with Azar Kayvan, the most intriguing comparison of this Persianate "lettrist" experimentation in language and cosmos is with Fazlallah Astarabadi and the Hurufis ("the people of letters"). Fazlallah Astarabadi (d. 1394) and the Hurufis exemplify and systematize a much broader intellectual current in the Islamic world: an approach to creation—and time, space, and the End—as a linguistic phenomenon. As Orkhan Mir-Kasimov writes in his recent examination of Fazlallah's *The Great Book of Eternity* ("Jāvidān-nāmah-yi kabīr"), "All objects and beings contained in the universe, at any scale, from the heavenly spheres down to the tiniest atoms, are essentially the manifestations of the ontological names derived from the Word."[26] The component parts of the cosmos are thus linguistic—we have a universe uttered into itself. According to Fazlallah, true knowledge is thus a matter of perceiving this cosmogonic meta-language and meta-alphabet that constitutes creations and our very existence. These types of semio-cosmological claims were by no means confined to the Hurufi followers of Fazlallah Astarabadi, and they represent just one aspect of a much more general intellectual and religious exploration of the power of letters to act, to reveal, to form, and to *be* the world.

Semiotics and etymology—in such a world as that of Roshaniyya, Hurufis, and Azar Kayvani Zoroastrians and others such as Nuqtavis, Sikhs, and more—were sciences of flesh, materiality, and cosmos.[27]

Beyond Ritual: The Many Meanings of Dhikr

But how do we get there? How do the Roshaniyya understand dhikr and how do they understand the spiritual path in such a way that allows these collisions of text, ritual, wordplay, self, and transformation?

The answer, laid bare over the sprawling spiritual mappings of *The Endeavor*, is dhikr—the "remembrance" or "recollection" of God. By presenting dhikr as the engine of spiritual transformation, *The Endeavor* joins the most conventional of Sufi discourses. Before Bayazid's plunge into the idiosyncratic stage of Stillness, *The Endeavor*'s vision of the Sufi path and the place of dhikr is strikingly familiar. The very familiarity of Sufi dhikr as a "ritual" of remembrance threatens to eclipse the semiotic imaginations of the Roshaniyya. Our task, therefore, is to identify the multiple meanings of the term *dhikr* as found in *The Endeavor*, thereby cracking open the term and letting it rupture our common explanations of Sufi ritual and language.

Beyond the general sense of "remembrance," dhikr is ritual. It is the Sufi ritual of chanting the names of God. This, at least, is how we find the term defined in most Western descriptions of Sufism.[28] The identification of the term *dhikr* as a distinctively *Sufi* practice dates to the early generations of the systematizers of the Sufi path. Even if we limit ourselves to a definition of dhikr as ritual chanting, there is a spectacular diversity in its practice. The Sufi can shout the dhikr, whisper it, or utter it silently in the depths of her heart. The Sufi may join his community in the collective performance of the dhikr under the leadership of a master—or he may perform it in absolute solitude. The dhikr can be a practice of complete bodily stillness, or the Sufi may rock her seated body back and forth to the rhythm of her chant. Chishti Sufis have extended dhikr into musical sessions, and the whirling dances of Mevlevi dhikrs have become the stuff of tourist attractions and garnered invitations to concert halls throughout the world. Thursday nights may be a popular time for dhikr sessions, but Sufis commonly teach the importance of perpetual dhikr—a perfuming of God's names into each and every breath of the Sufi.[29]

While Sufi networks have developed "proprietary" dhikr techniques, the remarkable diversity of dhikr practices is frequently found within a single Sufi network. The Naqshbandis, for example, have a reputation as the sober proponents of the silent dhikr, but eminent Naqshbandi scholars have vigorously defended the place of music, dance, and loud vocalization in its practice.[30] The plasticity of the term *dhikr* stabilizes only in local contexts and only for contingent periods.

And what of the local context of the Roshaniyya? Despite the distance of the Afghan highlands from imperial centers in the Mughal and Safavid empires, the Roshani heartland was a region of cosmopolitanism.[31] Horse traders, poets, and saints traveled from cities such as Bukhara, Samarqand, and Isfahan through Kabul, across the Khyber, and into Peshawar before continuing to Lahore, Delhi, and beyond—and the same routes were followed in the other direction.[32] Routes between Delhi and Bukhara, between India and the Central Asian steppes, continued to be well-trodden paths of religious networks such as the Mujaddidi-Naqshbandi Sufis into the twentieth century, as Waleed Ziad has demonstrated.[33] There is no question, therefore, of Bayazid's exposure to a range of dhikr practices and discourses. Bayazid would likely have known of a whole spectrum of styles, ranging from individual silent dhikrs to jubilant dhikrs performed in groups with musical instruments. Indeed, though *The Endeavor* emphasizes the silent dhikr as the central practice of the Roshaniyya, *The Book of States* describes Bayazid as an accomplished and creative musician who put Roshani religious texts into metric form.[34]

We could attempt to locate the specific influences of Roshani dhikr teachings in the prevalent Sufi communities of the time—there are good reasons to identify the Roshani dhikr as adapted from Qadiri teachings. Without denying the value of such a historical inquiry, *The Endeavor* allows us to ask different questions, questions less familiar in the historiography of Sufism. Given the generative tensions between the textuality of *The Endeavor* and the dhikr practices described therein, this work recasts dhikr as something *more* that "ritual." As Talal Asad has noted, the category of "ritual" establishes a division between the *ritual act* and descriptions of it. "Ritual" may allow us to focus on practices and embodied performances, but it frequently numbs the very language used to describe those rituals and the power structures in which that language gains traction. If dhikr is ritual, then *The Endeavor* becomes an instruction book of cues for some experience beyond the text.[35]

The polysemy of dhikr in *The Endeavor*, however, renders *The Endeavor* pulsing and performative, a text that spurs and enacts the transformations it describes. We might think of the difference between "dhikr-talk" and "dhikr-ritual" in *The Endeavor*. This chapter is concerned with "dhikr-talk": the discourse of dhikr in *The Endeavor*. Before we turn it into an abstraction such as "ritual" or "mystical experience," dhikr-talk is embedded in literary conventions, genre norms, and the linguistic regimes that regulate and authorize its shape. Most importantly, the dhikr-talk of *The Endeavor* both models and molds the semiotic ideology that we have been describing throughout this book: language engaged as a system of icons and indexes brought to immediate and immanent effect, language as constitutive of the self and social relations, and language ineluctably bound to cosmological and chronological imaginations.

There are aspects peculiar to Bayazid's effort to speak a divine language that situate *The Endeavor* as an especially useful text for examining the role of dhikr-talk and semiotic ideology in Sufi imaginations, but *The Endeavor* is by no means unique in its performative dhikr-talk. For example, Najm al-Din al-Kubra's *The Fragrances of Beauty and the Openings of Majesty* ("Fawā'iḥ al-jamāl wa fawātiḥ al-jalāl") includes extensive discussion of visions, dispositions, and sensual experiences that the Sufi disciple will witness in the process of dhikr practice and retreat. The extensive use of colors distinguishes Kubra's dhikr-talk. Addressing directly his imagined Sufi disciple undergoing the spiritual transformations and convulsions of a committed dhikr practice, Kubra writes, "When you witness *green*, you sense your heart beat with ease and your chest expand in comfort."[36] Does a flash of green not leap into ourselves as we read this? Can this be mere description when the "vision" cascades instantaneously from the description itself? I use the term dhikr-talk to name that space of indistinction between text, practice, and experience—the collapsing together of reading and seeing "green." In that space of indistinction, there is a different posture toward ethical and spiritual transformation. There is no self that is acting with various technologies to fashion itself anew. Rather, in the logic of dhikr-talk, the self exposes itself to the transformative potentialities that *act upon* the self.[37]

The dance of colors in Kubra's text is a simple example of the larger process we are seeking to understand: dhikr-talk as an immanent performance of the spiritual transformations that lift a disciple from her base human qualities and permit her to speak the "wretched" revelation touched with divine presence. Presented in abstraction, the Roshani logic of spiritual transformation is straightforward:

1. A self is constituted by language: it may be jinn-like, angelic, divine, etc.
2. One's language can be disciplined, shaped, and purified by dhikr.
3. Thus, dhikr can transform the self.

The complexity of this process lies with the term dhikr. As ritual practice, it is astoundingly flexible. Within ritual, the term refers both to the practice of reciting God's name (or other pious phrases) and the linguistic phrase uttered in this practice. Dhikr is also one of the many terms used for the Qur'an—including in *The Endeavor*. Elsewhere in *The Endeavor*, dhikr simply refers to the abstract habit of remembering God. Given the thorough entwinement of Qur'anic passages throughout *The Endeavor*, this text is itself a re-collection of the Qur'an. Another of Bayazid's titles confirms that *The Endeavor* is itself dhikr. Bayazid—a wretch, a guide, a master—is also "the bearer of dhikr." The dhikr is thus the Qur'an, *The Endeavor*, a state of remembrance, a practice of recollection, and the language of this practice. And as I argue in this chapter, the purpose of *The Endeavor* is to fashion the wayfarer into yet another translation of the dhikr.

The Qur'an of *The Endeavor*

We might summarize the aims of *The Endeavor* this way: it offers both a map and a performance of the spiritual path by which the disciple may advance beyond her human characteristics and realize the trait of "lordship" through both the recognition and achievement of the essential congruency between her existence and God's own. The preamble of *The Endeavor* follows conventional encomium, and we then find a voice attributed to Bayazid:

> My son Shaykh 'Umar (*may God show favor upon him!*) said, "May it please you to write some counsel [*naṣīḥa*] for all of your sons and your people, drawn from the verses of the Qur'an, the prophetic hadith, and the sayings of the friends of God." I accepted his words, and I decided to write [this counsel] in twenty parts to the extent of my knowledge and with the help, aid, and assistance of God Most High. I have called it *The Endeavor of the Believers*.[38]

Each of these twenty chapters gathers relevant Qur'anic verses and prophetic hadith to describe a particular aspect of Bayazid's imagined spiritual path and offer the resources necessary for the reader to begin to achieve spiritual stages in the theater of the text. Nearly half of the text consists of Qur'anic citations and hadith, but this is not a commentary in the tradition of *tafsīr* exegesis. It is instead a coordinated constellation of Qur'anic verses, hadith, saintly sayings (including Bayazid's own), and the rather sparse accompanying words of the imagined narrator, Bayazid. This constellation offers the disciple a path to ethical refinement and the elevation of the spirit over Satan (*al-shayṭan*), the lower-soul, and base human traits.

The first thirteen chapters discuss organs of the human being, this world and the Hereafter, techniques of spiritual refinement (preaching and counsel, reliance upon God, and repentance), and religious dispositions of faith, fear, and hope. There is a chapter on Satan that treats Satan in a way similar to Bayazid's discussion of the lower-soul: both as a nefarious force and as synecdoche referring to an entire realm contained within the human being. There are multiple worlds found within the believer, and the realm of Satan threatens to eclipse the emergence of the nobler topographies. The final eight chapters map the different stages of the spiritual journey: ascending from the Law to the Path, upward to Truth, Knowledge, Intimacy, Union, Oneness, and finally to Stillness.

The Endeavor is a self-identified act of counsel (*naṣīḥa*) between father and son. So what is Bayazid's advice? We are given no clear answers, and instead Bayazid refocuses on the nature of counsel itself by offering the following Qur'anic verse as an explanation of counsel: "Surely this is a dhikr! And whoever desires may set upon a way to his Lord."[39] Here, Bayazid defines *The Endeavor* as an act of counsel and then defines counsel using a deictic phrase. *What is counsel? "This reminder" is counsel.* The deictic *this* is a cited verse, however, and we thus have an immediate contradiction—a deixis that has slipped its context. What happens when I quote you saying "I"?[40]

With this citation, Bayazid shifts from counsel to dhikr. He subsequently offers more Qur'anic verses in which dhikr "alights" and "is sent down." His style of interpretation is to key in on a specific word in one verse (*counsel, remembrance, exhortation*, etc.) and pursue it to another, widening the semantic field of all words involved, with little to no commentary provided. In an ever-growing chain of correspondences, the "bearer of dhikr" becomes a "bearer of guidance," "a perfect guide, and a "teacher." The term *teacher* (*mu'allam*) becomes the bridge to another verse of the Qur'an: "Fear God and God will *teach* you." With a hadith on Adam's own fear of God, Bayazid links pious fear to the role of humans as the vicegerents and deputies of God on earth. Following another hadith, we see that deputies are also "proselytizers":

> The Prophet said, "The deputy manifests the proselytization of truth. The manifestation of God is in the character of the proselytizer. The guide calls the people to the Realm of Islam, and he is the guide and the proselytizer by way of his tongue."[41]

Bayazid's logic is dizzying in its peripatetic wandering from verse to verse. Through an extended chain of correspondences, we have seemingly arrived at the coincidence of "giving counsel" and "manifesting God through language."

More important than the theological content of Bayazid's explanation, however, is the semiotic ideology shaping his exegetical impulses. What I have translated as "bearer of guidance" (*ṣāḥib al-hidāya*) and "perfect guide" (*al-murshid al-kāmil*) are semantically similar. Bayazid's textual nomadism, however, pursues each word as an object of importance in and of itself. Any connection between hidaya and murshid is wrought through their relation in the Qur'an, hadith, and *The Endeavor*—and not primarily based upon a similar meaning of "guidance." These are beacons upon a surface, calling attention to themselves as emblems of divine truth rather than pointing to a signified sense shared in the depths.

In Bayazid's hermeneutics, he arranges careful constellations of meaning. Bayazid takes it as his task to use his sources to disclose—and forge—the connections between guidance and proselytizer. The "primary source" material for *The Endeavor* is therefore of central importance. Bayazid is not simply using the text of *The Endeavor* to explain and interpret the meaning of the Qur'an, hadith, and sayings of the saints of the God. Nor is he using this source material as proof of metaphysical or doctrinal axioms. Quite to the contrary, he is stitching Qur'an, hadith, and saintly sayings together to bind the language of *The Endeavor* into emergent meaning. *The Endeavor* arises from these blessed sources, and the emergence of *The Endeavor* in turn proves that the sources are capable of continued disclosure. "The guide . . . is the proselytizer by way of his tongue" results from such a constellation of guidance, proselytizer, and other terms that abut one another in Qur'an, hadith, saintly sayings—and, notably, the saintly sayings of "Bayazid the Wretch" (who is thus quoted by a narrator who is also identified as Bayazid). What we have in *The Endeavor* is a language-making machine that generates and proves the possibilities of words to disclose.

This language-making machine does not run on linguistic *symbols*, however. Rather, *The Endeavor* binds its own language to that of the Qur'an through a semiotic logic of icon and index, of resemblance and proximity. A word does not gain its meaning solely by pointing arbitrarily to a meaning (as we typically understand the action of a symbol), but, rather, a word also becomes meaningful through the way it shares sonic or visual resemblance to other words or how it is juxtaposed to other words in the Qur'an. We might consider *The Endeavor* as offering a model for how one should engage language, especially the classes of blessed language we see here: divine Qur'anic language, the exemplary language of Muhammad, the language of the Sufi saints cited throughout *The Endeavor,* and the language of Bayazid. According to this model, the thrust of language lies in its iconic and indexical abundance—the formal connections found and forged with a repeated term (hidaya or "guidance," for example) or with a repeated Arabic root (sakina and miskin, for example, however "wrong" that may be). In simpler terms, the Qur'anic logic of *The Endeavor* teaches us that words refer to words, as formal "things" with visual and aural substance. Language *means* itself. What matters for the Roshaniyya is *that* language communicates and not *what* it communicates.

We glimpse here the entanglement of semiotic ideology, text, and Bayazid's own bid for blessed authority. Central to Bayazid's authority is the coordination and metamorphosis of the relationship between implied-narrator, implied-reader, and the intertextuality of *The Endeavor*. Given that each chapter frequently begins different thematic sections with the implied-narrator addressing the implied-reader with the call *O my son!*, the implied-reader is immediately brought into a familial and hierarchical relationship. Moreover, as just noted, the language of "Bayazid the Wretch" serves as one of the sources for the constellational hermeneutics of the narrator. The Wretch's cited sayings become a raw material of sorts from which the language of the narrator emerges. Given the attribution of the text to Bayazid, the function of Bayazid as *source* thus reflects constantly back upon the language of Bayazid as narrator. Bayazid cites himself. The narrator guides the disciple to the founts of spiritual progress, and the path leads directly back to *The Endeavor*. The work is thus both a description of the path and an artifact from the path. While there is an undeniable circularity to this, we see again the structure and use of language in *The Endeavor* drawing our eyes to a familiar conclusion. More than *what*, it is *that* this text means. Language comes to sanctify language.

On a Cricket's Chirp

We might pause and note that there is something extraordinary about *The Endeavor*'s approach to "religious language." By shifting away from the *intended message* of religious language and toward the very presence of language itself, *The Endeavor* casts the power of language as a matter of letter shapes, sounds, grammar, narrative structures, genre, and perspective. The power of language becomes a matter of the materiality of language rather than lying solely in its conveyance of truth.

As startling as this approach was for some contemporaneous critics of the Roshaniyya (and as startling as it may be for many contemporary approaches to religious language), *The Endeavor*'s semiotic ideology here draws near to enduring philosophical projects. Is there a way, as humans, to speak simply, innocently, and immediately, just as a cricket may chirp or a bird may sing? Or is *sheer language* impossible for us, and so our language remains forever shattered by a fundamental "scission" between symbol and idea, sign and content? Though we remain under the sign of dichotomous, representational ideologies of language, certain theorists have argued that our human language draws closer to the chirping of a cricket in "poetry's emphasis on the material effects of language."[42] The effects of rhyme, rhythm, structure, stanza, grammar, and so on draw our attention to language *as language,* innocent and sheer.[43] The potential of revelation resides in these "material" aspects of language, for it is in these material and formal aspects of language that we find what Agamben has called the *aletheia*—or "un-forgetting"—of our ability to speak just as a cricket might chirp.[44] Or we might say more simply that through dhikr we remember the creative potentiality of human voice and communication as sheer voice.

I raise the resonance between this philosophical project and the religious language of *The Endeavor* because it helpfully directs our attention away from individual *intention* and toward the "depersonalizing" or "desubjectivizing" power of language as language.[45] As the cricket chirps, there is no striking up of subject and object; there is, rather, a naming without anything named. Theorists such Mikhail Bakhtin (and his carnivalesque socialities) and Giorgio Agamben (and his "profane community") tightly bind their visions of redeemed societies to their semiotics. In contrast to redemptive profanity or the carnivalesque, the Roshaniyya envision a path to divinization through language practices. Nevertheless, in resonance with this modern philosophical project, the Roshaniyya appeal to language-as-language and to the stripping away of the human subject that is found in giving one's self to the materiality of language. There is an annihilation of subject in the suspension of language's representative capacity. In short, language can make and unmake a self, but it does so not through the conveyance of knowledge; language dissolves a subject at the level of syllable, image, reverberation, and grammar. If Bayazid were to weigh directly in on this concern for the "scission" of representational language, he might write that our sense of selves as *distinct* from God relies upon an act of forgetting our original language—and the spiritual path to revelatory wretchedness is one of an aletheic unforgetting of the self, of using dhikr to transformatively remember the divine, and of indexing one's identity to God's language as it is found in the Qur'an, in *The Endeavor*, and in the very cosmos.

The Weight of Dhikr

In this system of thought, the dhikr becomes the propulsive force of spiritual transformation. We can see this unfold in narratives of Bayazid's life as found in the massive hagiography of his life, *The Book of States*. In these stories, the language of dhikr phrases has heft enough to bear designation as the agent, as the cause, and as the spark that catches in the realms of Bayazid's self. We find a recurring pattern in *The Book of States*: God, the angel Gabriel, or the extraworldly Khidr give Bayazid a particular phrase to silently recite, and only after years of devotion to such a phrase does Bayazid transcend to a higher plane and manifest the spiritual benefits of a particular dhikr. These transmissions of dhikrs are strikingly material: the dhikr is written on a piece of paper and shown to him in a dream, for instance. Or the dhikr is placed by the hand of an angel in the heart of Bayazid, and he can feel its weight.

A particular chapter of *The Book of States* illustrates this dynamic well. Bayazid is denied permission by his father to go study with a Sufi master in Ḳaniguram, and so he begins to orally recite the *shahāda* ("There is no god but God and Muhammad is the messenger of God"). God, as a calling voice (hatif), then informs Bayazid that it is better to recite it silently. Through years of practice and multiple dhikr phrases, Bayazid reaches the stage of Intimacy, but he strives for something still higher. God delivers the next dhikr phrase: the Great Name (al-Ism al-A'zam), a name for God that escapes the human capacity of articulation and inscription. As Bayazid struggles with the preponderance of the Great Name, Khidr twice re-reveals the Great Name to Bayazid. The narrative of this sublime dhikr emphasizes that a dreaming Bayazid possessed the dhikr on a heavy piece of paper upon which were written words of golden ink. The paper is so heavy, however, that he sets it down and loses it. God intervenes and offers Bayazid a dhikr of the stage of Union as a half-step to the Great Name:

> [Bayazid] could not begin the Great Name for eleven years due to the heaviness of the Great Name. It was more ponderous than both of the worlds because that Great Name is the Remembered Name

> [*madhkūr*], and if the name is not a remembering name [*dhākir*], then the rememberer [*dhākir*] does not take the trait of the remembered [*madhkūr*]. This means: if he is not erased in the remembered [*madhkūr*], the remembrance [*dhikr*] of the remembered [*madhkūr*] is not possible. Bayazid could not begin the Great Name. And so God Transcendent and Most High cast down upon his heart the *dhikr* of Union.[46]

The Great Name is a paradox—a name that can only be used when the separation between namer and named has collapsed. It is as if God is saying, "Only call me by my true name when that name refers to you as well." To work through this paradox, God gives the dhikr of Union to Bayazid as a ladder to a greater dhikr phrase. According to *The Endeavor*, the dhikr of Union is identified as the phrase: *There is no I but You.* Indeed, in *The Book of States*, this is the moment in which Bayazid begins to deny his own independent existence as a rememberer.

The dhikr of Union does not initially empower Bayazid to bear the Great Name; rather, the dhikr of Union first exposes Bayazid to the humming of the Great Name in all aspects of the cosmos around him:

> Although Bayazid had not begun [to recite] Great Name, he began to hear the dhikr of the Great Name in everything: from guitars, lutes, whistles, oboes, and other instruments, as well as from the earth, the sky, the trees, and from hands and feet, and the rest of the body. He thought: *I am hearing the dhikr of the Great Name from everything, including my own limbs. My own limbs recite the Great Name, but my heart and soul do not. I must compel my heart and soul to recite the Great Name!* Then Bayazid left the city. In the desert, a great stone had fallen, and there was a cave under that rock. He sat in that cave, and on Friday night he began the Great Name of the Remembered [*madhkūr*] until at midnight there was no longer a single breath during which he was not reciting the Great Name. After midnight, he placed his head upon the pillow of the earth for an hour. He awoke to recite the Great Name. When the time of prayer arrived, he went toward running water. He did his ablutions. He prayed the dawn prayers. Until the afternoon, he remained busy with the dhikr of the Name. [Bayazid] intended to do the full Friday ablutions. He went toward the edge of the water and began washing. He had not even stripped his cloak when he heard a call from God.[47]

God then explains that external washing is no longer necessary. The recitation of this Great Name has the effect of manifesting ritual purity in the body. The words or word of the Great Name—unable to be conveyed in our human languages—have direct material and spiritual power.

Throughout these stories of Bayazid, there is no anxiety or suspicion over a perceived disjunction between sincere intention and outward practice. The Roshani vision of sincerity here draws close to recent works in the anthropology of Islam, especially those of Saba Mahmood on piety. In her study of Egyptian women's prayer, Mahmood directs us away from questions of what the female body means and toward *how* the body is the theater upon which self-formation occurs. As she notes, "Disparity between one's intention and bodily gestures is not interpreted as a disjunction between outward social performance and one's 'genuine' inner feelings—rather, it is considered to be a sign of an inadequately formed self that requires further discipline and training to bring the two into harmony."[48] While Mahmood's work focuses upon bodies, we can see a similar dynamic unfold in the texts of the Roshaniyya through narrative and semiotics. At every step in the stories of *The Book of States* and the theories of *The Endeavor*, dhikr phrases raise the wayfarer through the spiritual stages of the Sufi path, eventually reaching a place of wretched Stillness. Language precedes epiphany.[49]

Throughout *The Endeavor*, when the polysemy of dhikr stabilizes as a form of "practice," it exists as the most righteous form of language among a range of choices that includes prayer and worship as well as a host of poor practices such as frivolity, obscenity, hypocrisy, and lying. Just as in the narratives of *The Book of States*, the theorization of *The Endeavor* offers a dhikr that lifts the disciple to increasingly lofty spiritual stages. It is a practice of spiritual and ethical refinement that both alerts the practitioner to her inherent immersion in divine existence and also—if paradoxically—intensifies and actualizes this immersion in divine existence. It is through dhikr that the disciple has a "vision of the essence of God Most High," and it is "through dhikr that he destroys all that is other than God and it is through the dhikr that he is established in His Essence."[50] Dhikr is the means to "salvation from the shadows" and "admission into the light of deliverance."[51] This process entails the sublimation of the disciple's own sense of action and deliberation as activity comes to rest in dhikr itself. The dhikr, as a given, inspired formula for recitation, demands repetition regardless of the reciter's individual self. As the disciple practices the dhikr with greater devotion, he casts off the baser traits of humanity (*bashariyya*) and assumes the traits of angelhood (*malakūt*), mightiness (*jabarūt*), and the lordship (*rubūbiyya*) of God.[52]

In stories of Bayazid considered above, we see God offering each dhikr phrase as if it were a rung on a ladder to a higher stage, and *The Endeavor* offers a fuller account of these dhikr phrases. Each phrase belongs to an aspect of the human being and corresponds to a particular stage. The expression "There is no god but God," for instance, is the dhikr of the heart and marks the stage of the Path. Here is Bayazid's full schema:

§ Dhikr Phrase	**§ Dhikr Description**	**§ Dhikr Stage**
Lā ilah illā Allāh wa Muḥammad rasūl allāh (There is no god but God and Muhammad is the messenger of God)	*Lisān* (Tongue)	*Sharī'a* (Law)
Lā ilah illā Allāh (There is no god but God)	*Qalb* (Heart)	*Ṭarīqa* (Path)
Illā Allāh (But God)	*Rūḥ* (Spirit)	*Ḥaqīqa* (Reality/Truth)
Allāh (God)	*Sirr* (Inner Heart)	*Ma'rifa* (Knowledge)
Huwā (He)	*al-Ghayba* (The Unseen/Absent)	*Qurba* (Intimacy)
Lā anā illā antā (There is no "I" but "You")	*Ghaybat al-Ghayba* (The Most Unseen)	*Wuṣla* (Union)
al-Ism al-A'ẓam (The Great Name)	*al-Madhkūr* (The Remembered)	*Sukūna* (Stillness)

Notice the movement from "There is no god but God and Muhammad is the Messenger of God" to a simple "God" and "He," and then finally to the unspecified "Great Name." This movement models this imagined spiritual journey, shifting from kataphatic assertions of divine presence and apophatic negations of all that is distinct from God. While the central proclamation of faith—the shahada—begins Bayazid's program, the following dhikrs trim this phrase until the *He!* is a remaining kernel, standing simply as a brute declaration of presence. The next phrases echo the shahada: just as there is no god but God, there is no I but You. The apophatic unsaying of the dhikr is directed inwardly to the Sufi disciple, and it negates her independent existence.[53] This appropriately results in the final dhikr that escapes our language but is still clearly a word or name (*ism*, in Arabic). It is a word that belongs to the Remembered One—the "dhikr-ed One," *al-Madhkūr*—and not to us lest we rise into the traits of the Remembered One.

This is more than a pedagogical manual; this is a map of the cosmos. The initial phrases belong to or are performed in various parts of the body: the tongue, the heart, the spirit, and the inner heart. The more advanced phrases leave the human body as typically conceived and belong to deeper cosmological structures: the Unseen, the Most Unseen, and, ultimately, God the Remembered One. As the dhikr penetrates deeper layers of the human being, it also escapes the confines of a single self. Depth yields expanse; in the fathoms of the self lies the vastness of the unseen realms.

The Givenness of Dhikr

This movement from a dhikr of the tongue to a dhikr of the Remembered One reflects the progressive dissolution of the disciple's own existence within the existence of God. Bayazid's spiritual journey is one in which the disciple grasps the increasing givenness of her own existence. She comes to understand that her existence is itself an act of reception. As a malleable organ, the tongue is disciplined until it conforms with the cosmos and God, shedding the baser traits of human language along the way. Called *thabt al-lisān* ("disciplining of the tongue") by Bayazid, this transformation of the tongue unfolds through repetition of given dhikr phrases. Subsequently, the transformation of the tongue then resonates through other parts of the human body—and so the "interior" of human being is rethought as a process of repeated, given utterances. The direction of this transformation is important, for it indicates yet again that spiritual transformation involves an *exposure* to the potentiality of language; as the self is laid bare to the work of the dhikr, the dhikr acts upon the entirety of the self by first shaping the habits of the tongue.

Elsewhere in *The Endeavor*, Bayazid offers an alternative mapping of the first five dhikr phrases by introducing the site of transformation (the fourth column below). While the dhikr of the stage of the Path persists as "There is no god but God," Bayazid introduces the notion that it transforms the body (rather than the heart, as in the previous schema).[54]

§ *Dhikr* Phrase	§ *Dhikr* Description	§ *Dhikr* Stage	§ Site of Transformation
Lā ilah illā Allāh wa Muḥammad rasūl Allāh (There is no god but God and Muhammad is the messenger of God)	*Lisān* (Tongue)	*Sharīʿa* (Law)	*Lisān* (Tongue)

Lā ilah illā Allāh (There is no god but God)	*Qalb* (Heart)	*Ṭarīqa* (Path)	*Jasad* (Body)
Illā Allāh (But God)	*Rūḥ* (Spirit)	*Ḥaqīqa* (Reality/ Truth)	*Qalb* (Heart)
Allāh (God)	*Sirr* (Inner Heart)	*Maʿrifa* (Knowledge)	*Baṣīra* (Sight)
Huwā (He)	*al-Ghayba* (The Unseen/ Absent)	*Qurba* (Intimacy)	*Ṣawt* (Sound)

There is certainly an ad hoc quality to all of this, but we should not mistake the shifting schemas of *The Endeavor* for incoherence. Like the relinquishment of independent subjectivity staged in the move from *tongue* and *heart* to *Unseen* and *Most Unseen*, we see a shift from *tongue, heart*, and *body* to *sight* and *sound*. The *activity* of earlier stages evaporates into a *receptivity* of sensation, just as the ostensible interiority of a dhikr gives way to cosmic expansion. The disciple no longer speaks praise with the tongue but, rather—and paradoxically—hears the praise spoken by the world around her through the uttered dhikr. As Bayazid's imagined disciple rises higher in the spiritual hierarchy and the dhikr penetrates deeper, the entanglement of self and cosmos becomes manifest. What we initially witnessed as the individual utterances of a disciple becomes ever more thoroughly a response to the cosmos. The "inner voice" collapses into the "ecstasy of voice that resounds in the world" (to borrow Jean-Louis Chrétien's stirring language).[55] Bayazid's voice joins the dhikr emerging from his limbs, the trees, and the world around.

We could conceive of a hierarchy incorporating "eyes" or "ears" that preserves a focus on individualized subjectivities, but Bayazid's movement is one toward "sights" and "sounds." Such a movement attests to an anthropological imagination in which the human comes to exist in the relationship between world and response-to-the-world.[56] The cultivated self of *The Endeavor* does not emerge as a self-sustaining formation; there is no self in a vacuum. Rather, the self takes shape relationally and in *conformation* with divine and cosmological realities through linguistic practice (and if not in conformation with divine realities, it will take shape in relation to carnal and Satanic realities). It is in this sense that the disciple, upon entrance into the stage of Oneness, sheds "humanity" (bashariyya) and enables the traits of "lordship" (rububiyya) to grow through the reckoning of existence as one and united. The stuff of the self is a matter of the in-between and the relational. And it is in this way that we may understand ethical refinement and ascension toward an indwelling in God as birthing receptivity, cultivating givenness, and disciplining a form of passivity that culminates in the stage of Stillness.

Our focus, however, remains on the convergence of this way of thinking—these propositional statements on cosmology and theology—with the textuality of *The Endeavor*. Structurally, as noted, the movement from topics of the tongue, body, and heart to sight and sound reflects an ecstatic transfer of activity from human to world. We can see a similar shift in grammatical form. As Bayazid describes the dhikr, his language shifts from utterances of "God" (*Allāh*) or "He" (*Huwā*) to repeated mention of the "remembered one" (*Madhkūr*). Bayazid, too, declares that the disciple must recite the dhikr as a "remembered one" (*madhkūr*) and not as a "rememberer" (*dhākir*). Outside of an ontology of givenness, this is an unresolvable paradox; the possibility of doing remembrance as the "remembered" is only possible if the "remembered" and the "rememberer" are one and the same. Moreover, this is another linguistic performance of Bayazid's central argument. Language itself reflects the disciple's journey as he becomes characterized by a passive participle of the *maf'ūl* form (*al-madhkūr*, "the remembered") rather than by an active participle of the *fā'il* form (*dhākir*, "the rememberer").

The hierarchy of dhikr phrases that we have been exploring suggests that the interior organs of the human being lie on a spectrum that includes unseen layers of reality, and thus we see that Bayazid conceptualizes the dhikr as a medium between the cosmological and the human. Linguistic repetition begets expansion as given words come to shape a disciple's being in conformity with creation.

As language braids cosmos to self, there is a temporal quality to this—a leap to the eschatological moment through the right kind of relationship to language. At the height of Bayazid's hierarchy, the Roshani disciple enters the stage of Stillness (sukuna) to become a wretch (miskin). As explored above, the very term *miskin* serves as a microcosm for the language performances of *The Endeavor*. The word trembles, taking shape with different meanings for different audiences. Through transgression of conventional grammatical norms, a humble sobriquet transforms into the title for one who abides in stillness and speaks with a theophanic, revelatory language. And in this ascension to Stillness, language reaches its eschatological potential. The dhikr has become an earthquake:

> The earth will shake twice, and all created beings will die in the first tremor. And just so, the dhikr-reciter shakes the heart and the body two times with the two dhikrs. Everything that is not God is annihilated in the first dhikr, until he sees the sign of the intimate angels in his own existence. With the second blow [of the trumpet], all the created beings become alive again, as God Most High said, "Then it shall be blown again, and lo, they shall stand, beholding."[57] Then the dhikr-reciter establishes the essence of God with a second dhikr.[58]

Having been laid bare and exposed to the transformative work of the dhikr words, the wretch's own tongue becomes a bearer of revelation. The wretch speaks revelation and hears the qualities of jinn, angels, satans, and God as they infuse the speech of those around her.

The aim of this chapter lay primarily in sounding out the imaginative architecture of the Roshaniyya—and I have argued that theirs is an imagination saturated with linguistic consciousness. There is no escaping grammar, wordplay, intertextuality, verbal root structure, the coordination of internal and imagined voices, and the subtle shifts away from active language to language of givenness throughout the hierarchies of dhikr. If we remove ourselves from the immanence of the text, we create something familiar and easy to digest: a Sufi path involving conventional spiritual stages and ubiquitous ritual practices. Gazing from this place of removal, however, we do not see the word-drunk world of the Roshaniyya. In this Roshani imagination of words and language—in this *semiotic ideology*—notions of selfhood, cosmos, and textuality have become irrevocably entangled.

We can be more precise in sounding out this semiotic ideology. (1) As seen in the play of Arabic letter and the polyvalence of the term *wretch*, language is not idealized and abstracted but can be a tool manipulated by those of sufficient authority. (2) In the care given to specific terms rather than shared meanings (e.g., hadi vs. murshid vs. shaykh), language is not, primarily, symbolic and semantic—there is an iconicity to Bayazid's language in which the formal and material qualities matter immensely. (3) As attested to in the concern for specific dhikr phrases, words, letters, and phrases themselves are immanently effective. Though intention, purity, and other qualities might make conditions more felicitous, there dwells a power in words. (4) Language and imaginations of language are temporally dependent; in *The Endeavor*, language *means* differently and more *clearly* in the time of the End. (5) Finally, as Bayazid's cryptic words regarding the language of Satan, the jinn, and the divine realm suggest, language marks the human being's true nature and belonging.

Beyond this immediate aim of understanding Roshani concepts of the self and divine language, this chapter has attempted to model an alternative approach to our understanding of dhikr, ritual, and text within Sufi networks. Since the earliest Orientalist writings on Sufism, Euro-American scholars have been drawn (like moths to the flame?) to a vision of Sufism that was, variously, cast as mystical, ethereal, transcendent, non-Muslim, non-Semitic, and apolitical. These early studies tended to discount or ignore "ritual practice." They understood dhikr recitation as a mere shell that could be cracked open and discarded so that we might hold in our hands an eternal truth or pure unitive experience.[59] This vision of Sufism was one conjured from manuscripts and translations that had left their communities of inscription to be catalogued in the offices and archives of one empire or another. More recent scholars have rightfully pushed back against these stock images of a "mystical" Sufism, and we have seen a remarkable and generative focus given to communities of practice and performance—to the breath, sweat, flesh, and voice of dhikr reciters and to the stone, dust, flower petals, and tombs where we find their performance.[60]

With these interventions, however, we must be careful not to expand or create an artificial distance between text and practice.[61] Descriptions of dhikr are more than instruction manuals or scripts. For the Roshaniyya, these descriptions of dhikr are artifacts of that blessed language they claim to describe. Dhikr-talk maps the dhikr, does the dhikr, is the dhikr. What I have done in this chapter is bring the abiding concern for semiotic ideology to a consideration of the central text on ritual and spiritual development for the Roshaniyya. When read in the light of Roshani imaginations of the word, *The Endeavor of the Believers* becomes a performative text in which aspects of the transformations it describes *happen* in the theater of its own language.[62]

In asserting that the words and texts of the Roshaniyya must be understood in the light of Roshani semiotic ideology, there is a danger in casting the Roshaniyya as foreign, strange, and exotic. Even worse is the possibility that I am suggesting that the Roshaniyya are *not* interested in developing propositional, theological content. Theirs is a system of subtle metaphysics that draws upon the sophisticated traditions of Ibn 'Arabi and lettrist theorists, as noted above.

I point to the nonsemantic, "material" work of a text such as *The Endeavor* not to deny the Roshaniyya the ability to engage in propositional, theoretical work. Rather, I hope to shake our own confidence in the language regimes and semiotic ideologies which organize our communicative habits and relationships to words and letters. The Roshaniyya insist that the use and imagination of language in all its materiality has irreducible moral stakes. How one speaks and writes, reads and listens, is bound up with the Roshani vision of the cosmos, of the End Times, and of the proper Sufi wretch. How we imagine our language to work is part of how we distribute value, ontology, and subjectivity throughout the world.[63] Our present moment has witnessed a general distrust of rhetoric and a heightened confidence in our ability to boil off the distracting materiality of signs. As explored in the introduction, our contemporary ideologies engage signs as arbitrary and disposable. Signs are the necessary, if regrettable, vehicles to transmit ideas. And the more transparent they become, the better. We have attended to the semiotic ideology of the Roshaniyya—and its disjuncture from our own semiotic ideologies. The words of the Roshaniyya do not *mean* in the way that our words *mean*. In this gap, however, there is an ethics to be found. As Rowan Williams writes:

> The ritual of suspending action and response declares that we must regularly and consciously acknowledge together that we live by incompleteness of understanding, that we are not transparent to each other; and that this, so far from being a handicap, is how we begin to get some grasp of the meanings of love, or attention or respect—or whatever we want to say about that *hesitation* before each other which stops us eating one another up, in one mode of fantasy or another.[64]

3 / Revelation through Repetition: The Roshaniyya Write the Word of God

In the name of Annah the Allmaziful,
the Everliving, the Bringer of Plurabilities!

—JAMES JOYCE, *Finnegans Wake*

Our story thus far has been one of formation and practice. The Roshaniyya emerged as a messianic community in the sixteenth century through the circulation and exchange of stories of Bayazid Ansari—stories full of dreams, doppelgängers, and inquisitions. They did this, moreover, in a cosmos composed of letters, as described in the previous chapter. To use stories, texts, words, and phrases as they did was to play with the stuff of creation. Staking out a religious vision of the world that falls under the larger canopy of "lettrism" ('ilm al-huruf), the Roshaniyya inhabited a world not of atoms and molecules but of letters and names. As we saw in the previous chapter, the Roshaniyya sought to fashion a "Roshani self" suitable for the messianic community through dhikr practices. In the theater of the text itself, dhikr transformed the Roshani disciple into a "wretch" whose language was touched with the divine. We turn now, however, to that very artifact of divine language that anchored the Roshani community: the language of God.

The Roshaniyya effort to speak the language of God culminated in a work known as *The Best Exposition* ("Khayr al-bayān"). In accounts both favorable and hostile to the Roshaniyya, *The Best Exposition* emerges as a clear manifestation of what marked the Roshaniyya as distinct, strange, and startling: this text evinces a seething imagination that brought the divine to the semiotic and collapsed cosmos and language together.[1] Later chroniclers who were sympathetic to the Roshaniyya described *The Best Exposition* as an exemplary work on the "unity of existence" (*waḥdat al-wujūd*), thus positioning *The Best Exposition* as well within familiar, albeit contested, Sufi intellectual traditions.[2] Detractors described this work as nothing but naked heresy and an absurd attempt to replace the Qur'an. Recent scholars have tended to ignore the perplexing multilingualism of *The Best Exposition* and instead have emphasized its centrality to a Pashto literature for Pashtuns. *The Best Exposition* is generally considered the first known work of written Pashto, and *The Best Exposition* presents itself as an innovative literary experiment (though not a *Pashto* one). With attention so tightly focused on this text as a Pashto text for Pashtuns, previous scholars have confined this text to a narrow logic of proto-nationalism and ethnic self-consciousness.[3] The poetics of *The Best Exposition*, however, offer us a wandering text that does not lie motionless within the categories to which we have confined it.

By looking at the poetics of *The Best Exposition*—by looking at grammar, structure, rhetoric, rhyme, and so on—we can trace a metapragmatic argument. That is to say: the text teaches us how we *should* use and imagine the language found in the text. By my interpretation, the internal logics and gestures of *The Best Exposition* suggest that the detractors had it partially right: this is indeed an attempt at revelation that tramples across the borders that enclose common understandings of Islamic orthodoxy, of ethnic vernaculars, and of the power of language. The poetics of *The Best Exposition* make a bid for divinity and train our eyes to see this as revelation. Without joining our voices to those levying accusations of heresy, we can nevertheless allow the ostensible transgressions of *The Best Exposition* to guide us to stranger conceptions of religious language and "sacred literature" than we typically hold. *The Best Exposition* sustains a relationship with the Qur'an that eludes conventional patterns in Islamic traditions: this is not a text that turns to the Qur'an as holy truth to be interpreted nor as an ultimate authority that grounds or proves a legal, philosophical, or political commitment. Rather, *The Best Exposition* imitates the Qur'an through rhyme and rhetoric, unfolding as a record of divine communication to a self-proclaimed illiterate merchant. Like James Joyce's *Finnegans Wake* quoted above, *The Best Exposition* wagers on the power of Qur'anic imitation as a way to erase the notion of a single "author." Through imitation (and a host of other literary techniques), *Finnegans Wake* strives to become a text written by the very reader.[4] Through imitation (and a host of other literary techniques), *The Best Exposition* strives to become a text written by God.

But is imitation an act of rivalry or devotion? This is a tension that we will not be able to resolve. Rather, our attention will be directed toward how and why *imitation* of the Qur'an alongside other literary gestures serves as the means by which *The Best Exposition* attempts to bring God into language. What is it about imitation that strikes the Roshaniyya as divine? In pursuing this, we begin to understand the Roshaniyya and their pursuit of God's language, but, more importantly, we gain new perspectives into the place of continuous revelation and vernacular language in Islamic cultures. Indeed, our very conception of the Qur'an may change. The strange Pashto-Persian-Arabic-Hindawi rhymes of *The Best Exposition* do not displace the Qur'an through Qur'anic imitation, but *The Best Exposition* might recast the Qur'an and frame it in new ways.[5] If we follow Gilles Deleuze and Felix Guattari, perhaps *imitation* is not so imitative: "At the same time something else entirely is going on: not imitation at all but a capture of code, surplus value of code, an increase in the valence, a veritable becoming, a becoming-wasp of the orchid and becoming-orchid of the wasp."[6]

Our task for this chapter is to trace the "becoming-Qur'an" of *The Best Exposition* and to acknowledge that this necessarily involves a "becoming–*The Best Exposition*" of the Qur'an. In this process of mutual code capturing, we can witness a shifting and elusive linguistic topography in Islamic history. From the mimetic perspectives of *The Best Exposition*, Arabic and the Qur'an do not persist as rigidly stable centers of Islamic tradition. Instead, the turn to Pashto as a language of writing comes to involve a pursuit of God's language and God's presence—and the creation of new centers of Islam spoken into being with new sacred languages.

At the Edges of the Qur'an

The argument of this chapter hinges on a challenge to some widely held conceptions of the Qur'an and its place in Islamic traditions. *The Best Exposition* tries to perform revelation through its imitation of the Qur'an. This might strike us as an odd notion. The doctrine of the *inimitability* of the Qur'an (*i'jāz*) was a widely held and well-defended position within Sunni intellectual traditions hundreds of years before Bayazid Ansari's dialogue with God, and Muhammad was the revered "seal of the prophets" (*khatm al-anbīyyā'*).[7] The possibility of continuous revelation—let alone in the form of an imitation—seems nakedly heretical, doesn't it? While imitation has long been a literary strategy within religious traditions across the globe, scholars of Islam have hardly considered the possibility of Qur'anic imitation within Islamic literary history.[8] Quite to the contrary, the academic reiteration of a standard narrative of Islamic history—a history found in monographs, textbooks, and Wikipedia alike, a history that unfolds in a linear fashion from Muhammad and the Qur'an—has tended to reinforce the unquestioned centrality of the Qur'an as inimitable scripture.[9]

As we attend to the finer brush strokes of Islamic traditions, however, the picture becomes more complicated, and *The Best Exposition* emerges as representative of larger patterns within Islam (albeit in a particularly bold and strange fashion). To begin with, as Daniel Madigan has argued, we should be open to reconsidering what we mean by "the Qur'an." In his careful analysis of the Qur'an's "self-image" and its lexicon of self-reference, Madigan notes the importance of the Qur'an's self-description as a *kitāb* (book). Crucially, Madigan emphasizes that "the *kitâb* is understood by the Qur'ân itself more in terms of process than of fixed content." As he continues:

> The central concepts in the Qurân's description of this *kitâb*—mercy, recitation, sending down, and communicating—are all terms describing divine-human engagement. They are not merely the mechanisms for delivering a preexistent canon. This motive of mercy and the processes of engagement between God and humanity together actually constitute and define the *kitâb* far more than any content.[10]

Madigan's presentation of Qur'anic self-image does not subsume the Qur'an into modern notions of the "book" and "scripture" as a stable collection of divinely revealed or inspired information—even if this is how both Muslims and non-Muslims alike often approach the Qur'an today.[11] The Roshaniyya might agree with Madigan. *The Best Exposition* frequently cites Sura 55 of the Qur'an (Surat al-Rahman), and this sura points to the continuities between God's revelation of the Qur'an and other processes of revelation that perhaps continue alongside and beyond the Qur'an. In Arberry's translation, we read:

> The All-Merciful has taught the Qur'an.
>
> He Created man and He has taught him the explanation [*bayān*].
>
> The Sun and the moon to a reckoning, and the stars and the trees bow themselves; And heaven—He raised it up and set the Balance.[12]

The sura continues by invoking other "bounties" and signs of God in the created world that all attest to God's engagement with humankind. Notably, we see that God teaches the Qur'an alongside the *bayān*. Arberry translates this as "explanation," but many Muslim interpreters consider *bayān* as referring to the human being's God-given capacity for speech.[13] It is also the word used to name Bayazid's imitative dialogue with God: "Khayr al-bayān": *The Best Exposition* or *The Best Explanation*.

It is not simply through Madigan's consideration of the Qur'an's self-image that we see possibilities of continuous revelation. Walid Saleh has demonstrated that certain "classical" Muslim exegetes staked out an analogous position. Al-Tha'labi, for instance, brought an "encyclopedic spirit" to his scriptural interpretation, and he turned to poetry and accounts of historical events as relevant tools for unfolding the Qur'an and understanding God's engagement with humankind. As Saleh writes, "That God spoke his word in history meant to the exegete that history was in the word of God."[14] Moreover, without the exegete's efforts to link history, poetry, grammar, and other fields to the Qur'an, al-Tha'labi suggested that the salvific potential of the Qur'an will be inaccessible.[15] The Qur'an becomes fully realized through exegetical engagement. The Qur'an becomes fully *the Qur'an* when conceptualized as threaded into the unfurling of time, event, and human society.

We can shift away from "the Qur'an" to more abstract concepts and find similar ambiguity. The archcritic of the Roshaniyya—Akhund Darweza of Nangrahar—excoriated Bayazid Ansari for presenting *The Best Exposition* as *waḥy* rather than as *ilhām*. This is a binary that we often find translated as "revelation" and "inspiration." Wahy, in Akhund Darweza's rendering, requires the mediating presence of the angel Gabriel to guarantee that an act of communication from God is more than personal.[16] Gabriel becomes a witness to something grander than an individual act of ilham, of inspiration. While Muslim scholars have drawn important lines between wahy and ilham since the emergence of Islamic theological traditions, any distinction between wahy and ilham is porous and contingent. As Diana Lobel has demonstrated, various scholars and Qur'anic interpreters, including figures such as al-Zamakhshari and al-Ghazali, consistently "blended" wahy and ilham, using the concept of inspiration (ilham) to describe the mechanism of revelation (wahy).[17] In Ibn Sina's theorizing of prophecy, moreover, he used "wahy" and "ilham" interchangeably. As Lobel summarizes, "For Avicenna [Ibn Sina] too, prophecy is the natural development of a gifted intellect and imagination. Avicenna does not seem to preserve any remnants of the distinction between *waḥy* and *ilhām*."[18] There is, in short, no stable referent for wahy and its consequent contrast of ilham that operates continuously in Islamic traditions. The distinction, rather, serves a polemical purpose for figures such as Akhund Darweza. A claim of ilham can, for instance, protect a medieval Sufi dialogue with God from potential critics by denying the applicability of the dialogue to a larger public, or a claim to wahy may elevate the Qur'an to a position of unrivaled authority in a textualist modern period.

All of this is to suggest that there is greater fluidity in Islamic notions of the Qur'an and revelation than scholars of religion have typically assumed. In some respects, this should be obvious. Do not the voluminous writings on the inimitability of the Qu'ran (i'jaz) speak precisely to the need to defend and clarify this point?[19] *The Best Exposition* may be unusual in the nakedness of its Qur'anic imitation, but it is not unique in its engagement with the Qur'an as merely one aspect of God's ceaseless communication with humankind. Revelation was a recurring literary practice in the medieval and early modern Islamic world, even in forms that occasionally skated close to challenging the doctrine of the inimitability of the Qur'an. The Qur'an suggests that God can speak the world into existence with the command of *kun!* "When God wills a thing, God says to it: Be! [*kun!*] And it is."[20] For many Muslim theorists in the premodern period, the substance of the cosmos—its ontological stuffness—is thus irrevocably linguistic. Under the larger canopy of 'ilm al-huruf (lettrism), letters themselves mattered and not primarily for their ability to combine into arbitrary combinations to enable the exchange of symbolized information between humans. In such a vision, letters are more akin to atoms than to symbols, and they thus have the power to directly index truths of the world. And, inversely, the time and space of creation may be approached "as language," as letters to be read. Used in the right ways, letters could reveal, protect, and empower those who wrote and spoke them. And what better model of using letters in the right way than the Qur'an?

In this vein, a fourteenth-century messianic group known as the Musha'sha'iyya (the shimmering ones) produced a text known as *The Speech of the Guided One* ("Kalām al-mahdī"), which included sections that formally imitated the Qur'an.[21] Like *The Best Exposition*, other mimetic acts of revelation were frequently connected to vernacular languages. Fazlallah Astarabadi (d. 1394 CE) wrote his longest work, *The Great Book of Eternity* ("Jāvidān-nāmah-yi kabīr"), in the Persian dialect of Astarabad. As Shahzad Bashir has suggested, Fazlallah's choice for this dialect "resonates with his general theory about languages superseding each other through newer scriptures."[22] It was the local language of Astarabadi rather than Persian that best served as the vehicle for renewed divine knowledge. Moreover, as Mir-Kasimov summarizes Fazlallah's thinking: "All objects and beings contained in the universe, at any scale, from the heavenly spheres down to the tiniest atoms, are essentially the manifestations of the ontological names derived from the Word."[23] The component parts of the cosmos are thus linguistic—we have a universe spoken into itself. According to Fazlallah, true knowledge is thus a matter of perceiving this cosmogonic metalanguage and meta-alphabet that constitute creation and our very existence. These types of semio-cosmological claims were by no means confined to the Hurufi followers of Fazlallah Astarabadi, and they represent just one aspect of a much more general intellectual and religious exploration of the power of letters to act, to reveal, to form, and to *be* the world. Semiotics and etymology, in such a world, were sciences of flesh, materiality, and cosmos.[24]

Another messiah from the regions around the Caspian Sea, Shah Isma'il Safavi of Ardabil, wrote his poetic verses in a Turcoman dialect similar to Azeri, as Vladmir Minorsky has described. These poems were the direct words of the "Godhead" and "reincarnation of the divine substance" that Isma'il manifested in his own bodily existence.[25] According to the narratives of Sultan Sahak's reception of *The Final Words* ("Kalām-i saranjām") from the angel Pir Musi, written Gurani likewise emerged as a divine artifact for the Kurdish Ahl-i Haqq.[26] Much later, in the nineteenth century, Soulaymane Kanté introduced the N'ko alphabet as a crucial component of the divinely inspired moral reformation of Mande-speaking people.[27] A similar story is told regarding the disclosure of the Vai script to Doalu Bukele in nineteenth-century Liberia.[28] Outside of traditions not typically studied under the label "Islamic," we find Sikhs and Zoroastrians of sixteenth-, seventeenth-, and eighteenth-century South Asia developing ideologies and literary practices of divine, sacred, and given letters.[29]

Before turning to the Qur'anic imitation found in *The Best Exposition*, another Roshani text efficiently demonstrates their participation in this lettrist, Qur'anic, and revelatory inheritance of South and Central Asia. According to the hagiography of Bayazid Ansari in *The Book of States*, Bayazid sent disciples to princely and imperial courts found north and south of the Afghan highlands: to Kabul, to Badakhshan in northern Afghanistan, to Delhi, to the Deccan of southern India. They bore with them an epistle (*risāla*) calling on the world to recognize the immensity of God's oneness (tawhid), to commit to the path of knowledge as mapped by Bayazid, and to give their tongues to the recitations of the dhikr as taught by Bayazid. We have no record from these courts that such letters were received, but there are extant manuscripts in archives in Bukhara, Islamabad, and Hyderabad that include an epistle attributed to Bayazid Ansari and named *The Path of Oneness* ("Ṣirāṭ al-tawḥīd").[30] Composed in Arabic and Persian, this letter is a series of calls to "kings and commanders" that they may learn and know the truth of God's oneness, the path to reaching this oneness, and the stages along the way. "Know, o kings and commanders, that the path of oneness is not to the east or the west, to the right or the left, above or below, or in any direction. It is the Straight Path upon the heart!"[31] While this epistle repeats many common Roshani themes, three significant aspects distinguish *The Path of One-*

ness: its description of previous scripture, its signature and attribution, and its addressees.

Early in the epistle, Bayazid (the attributed author) notes that each of the "four revelations" has been delivered in a specific language. The Torah was given to Moses in Hebrew, the Psalms (*Zabūr*) were given to David in Greek (*yūnānī*), the Gospel (*Injīl*) was given to Jesus in Syriac (*sūriyānī*), and the Qur'an was given to Muhammad in Arabic.[32] It is curious that Bayazid identified Greek as the language of David's Psalms, and this perhaps attests to the perduring legacy of Alexander the Great in the Afghan highlands. As will be discussed in chapter 5, Alexander held a place of prominence as a forefather for certain ethnic communities that emerged in the wake of his extensive conquests. Our focus, however, falls on Bayazid's careful association of each scripture with a single language. What are we to make of this scriptural monolingualism, given that this epistle will proceed to alternate between Persian and Arabic? Even more startlingly, *The Best Exposition*—Bayazid's own revelation discussed below—entangles four languages, grafting Arabic onto Persian onto Pashto onto Hindawi in different permutations. Is Bayazid's discussion of the language of past revelation born from a frustration that there is no common language emerging from the words and letters that form the cosmos and spoke being out of nonbeing? Is there a hint of a promise here that some fuller, more complete linguistic revelation might exist beyond a single language?

Moreover, Bayazid "signs" these counsels as "Bayazid the Wretch"—Bayazid al-Miskin.[33] As explored in the previous chapter, this term miskin operates at first blush as nothing more than a humble sobriquet. Internal to Roshani discourse, however, miskin anoints those who have come to speak God's language and abide in theophanic stillness (Sukuna)—a spiritual state discussed in chapter 2. It is a declaration of ultimate spiritual authority and revelatory capacity, though the boldness of this declaration is hidden from the "kings and commanders" receiving this epistle. This is not the only signature used by the Roshaniyya, according to Akhund Darweza. With characteristic vitriol, the polemical akhund also decries their use of the following: "Glory be to you, the King and Creator. He separated the world of light from fire. Bayazid Ansari."[34] In Akhund Darweza's interpretation, this second signature is evidence of the Roshani heretical equation of Bayazid and God because, by one reading, it attributes to Bayazid the cosmogonic capacity of separating the light of knowledge from the tortures of hellfire. That is far too facile a reduction of Roshani theo-linguistics.[35] Nevertheless, we can simply note that both signatures strike a balance: they initially appear as humble declarations of God's greatness and Bayazid's smallness even as they imply bolder claims. These signatures thus establish a hierarchy between a Roshani metalinguistic language and the language of the uninitiated.

Addressed to leaders and scholars across Asia, *The Path of Oneness* demonstrates that the Roshaniyya understood their theo-semiotic ideas as intelligible and effective beyond the immediate circle of Roshani devotees. This epistle *expects* the readers to sense and know the consequence of a metalinguistic claim of revelation, whether those readers were familiar with the precise cosmology that we find in Fazlallah's *The Great Book of Eternity* or any other lettrist tradition. Framed as a proto-nationalist or ethnic nativist reaction, the strangeness of Roshani linguistic practices serves to sever them from the histories and cultures of the world around them. And yet, as startling as the texts of the Roshaniyya might seem, there are patterns within Islamic intellectual history that speak to the possibility of just such a text as *The Best Exposition* and *The Path of Oneness*—patterns that position God's engagement with humankind as a continuously unfolding process, patterns that cast the Qur'an as open rather than closed, and patterns of reaching for new alphabets, dialects, and vernaculars as a way to renew the inscription of God's language. *The Best Exposition* exemplifies a particular relationship between local textual practices of Islam and the concept of the Qur'an. This is a relationship of imitation, participation, and "code capturing" that is exceptionally *visible* in Bayazid's text but is representative of a widespread gesture within the traditions of Islam. Framed differently, *The Best Exposition* invites us to rethink how we understand the stakes of turning to a vernacular literature.[36] This text reverses the vectors of the vernacular and reframes the turn to Pashto as *revelation* and *ascension* to the language of God rather than as *popularization* or *simplification* traveling downward to earth.

From Vernacular to Revelation

Hanging as an albatross around the neck of *The Best Exposition* is its innovative use of Pashto. This is the first example of written Pashto literature that we have, and *The Best Exposition* has been cursed by this firstness. Collectively, previous scholarship has focused on the question of ethnic identity; this is a text interesting only as it speaks to the emergence of the "cultural self-awareness of the Pashtuns."[37] According to such logic, Pashto *vernacular* literature bears an inherent and naturalized link with Pashtun identity—what Judith Irvine and Susan Gal describe as "linguistic iconization."[38] Linguistic features reflect an ethnic image, and we come to recognize "greatness" within the history of literature as a matter of "nationalist sentiment."[39] And so it is that a figure such as Khushhal Khan Khatak appears as the apotheosis of Pashto literature given that he "wrote consciously as a national poet, the first to express nationalist sentiment for uniting all Pashtuns."[40] As *The Best Exposition* is not solely in Pashto (as we will see) and has nothing to say of Pashtun people or Pashtun culture, it occupies a troubled and paradoxical place in histories of Pashto literature. Despite its innovation, it stands as a mere and stuttering prefiguration for the "Pashto vernacular" found in the brilliance of Khushhal Khan's patriotic cries for Pashtun unity and honor. Bayazid's Pashto thus appears in two hierarchical relationships simultaneously. Although commonly framed as "vernacular," it is nonetheless imitative of Persian and Arabic; and, secondly, as the starting point on a vector of ethnic "self-consciousness," Bayazid's Pashto is unrealized relative to later Pashto literature.

By approaching *The Best Exposition* in this way, we allow our encounter with the text to be shaped principally by what follows and only partially by the texture of the work itself. And what if we turn to the work itself and let our analytical models be transformed by Bayazid's words? What we find, I want to suggest, is something like an effort to write God's language: revelation.

My proposed usage of "revelation" turns on *genre* rather than *theology*, though they are intricately bound together. Simply as a way of framing a genre-based literary approach to revelatory language, we can appeal to works by Rowan Williams and Giorgio Agamben for a working definition of revelation. In Williams's presentation, revelation is a form of language that "think[s] through the universality of dependence."[41] This is not a definition of revelation as *heteronomy*, as the deliverance of a new law from outside. Nor is this "a matter of the dictation of propositional truths or divine laws that instruct us how to act in particular situations."[42] In the landscapes of Roshani thought—and, indeed, in Muslim cultures more generally—language comes as *given* from God. Revelation names a genre and a mode of semiosis that draw specific attention to the edges of language, to how language eludes our human control, and to how we chase after truth in language with particular intensity in certain rhetorical forms. The attribution of language to God is just one specific revelatory gesture that casts into relief the givenness of language.

We might also say that language has already come as given from God. As Agamben helps us understand, it is this very tension between the *present* disclosure and its *previous* antecedent that animates the text—the tension between *The Best Exposition* and the Qur'an. It is worth spending some time with Agamben because his inquiry provocatively models how we might connect rhetoric, temporality, and potential in a single analysis. It is chronology—and linguistic play with chronology—that characterizes the "messianic language" at the heart of Agamben's discussion (and is, I suggest, a fair guidepost for the revelatory language of the messianic Bayazid that we explore here). The complex intimacy of time and text shapes a messianic, revelatory language which comes to elude our representations of linear chronology. It is not possible to be a spectator and gaze at steady temporal progression after the messianic language event, for it is in that time that "we take hold of and achieve our representations of time."[43] Agamben is excavating the Epistles of Paul and their efforts to find a special remnant of time in which our experience of time cannot be divided between a past, present, and future. Nor can our experience be divided between "this worldly life" and the "afterlife." We are in that sliver of time that remains *after* such divisions have failed to fully classify the experience of time. We are not in the past, and yet the forms of the past coincide with their fulfillment in the present. We are not in the future and nor have we witnessed the "end of time," and yet the messiah has *already* come—and so we exist in the time of the end. Usefully for our purposes, Agamben places particular emphasis on the transposition of the past into the present. As the promises of the past have begun their fulfillment in the messianic event, so the past exists again.

By this model, writing revelation thus involves the performance of a complex chronology in the theater of language itself. It is not, after all, a lifeless reiteration of the past that is occurring. Agamben's Paul respeaks the words of the Hebrew prophets; he does not cite them. In order to achieve this messianic discourse, there must be a constant tension between past and present language. Messianic language is thus *not* a statement "about" the messiah. It is messianic through particular types of rhetoric, forms, and styles that activate and sustain a relationship between past and present: "The messianic is not just one of two terms in this typological relation, *it is the relation itself*."[44]

Building upon the analyses of Williams and Agamben, we may heuristically identify three aspects of revelation to track as we turn to *The Best Exposition*. To begin with, (1) there is the braiding together of meaning and medium, content and container. Revelation involves a collapse of the distance between divine meaning and the language used to convey it. Beyond that, (2) there is an effort to model a messianic, remnant time with language by letting past words inhabit present language. Finally, (3) this is language that attempts to speak from the edge of human capacity, rooting itself in claims of divine origin. The language of *The Best Exposition* comes as *given*. Such a claim ruptures assumed frames of reference and perforates boundaries drawn between language and cosmos. I offer these characteristics of *revelation* heuristically, asking that we see their full implications and stakes as they orient our eyes to aspects of *The Best Exposition* that have long been ignored.

Gestures of Revelation

Voices of the Divine

There are multiple manuscript copies of *The Best Exposition*, and, from the very beginning of the text, a copyist faces a conundrum. Contrary to the near-universal practice in the Islamic world of beginning a text in the name of God, the Berlin manuscript of *The Best Exposition* begins with a command to *write* the name of God: "O Bayazid! Write the basmalah in grand letters at the beginning of this book! I will not deprive the reward for those who write, perhaps make an error in letter or point, and then write for the sake of correcting the expression."[45] It is only after this command that we find the anticipated invocation, "In the name of God, the Compassionate, the Merciful." In contrast to the Berlin manuscript, the Hyderabad copy of *The Best Exposition* begins with the expected basmalah, but we thus find that God's command to inscribe the basmalah paradoxically appears after the written basmalah itself. In the example of the Berlin manuscript, there is a departure from Islamic literary convention that seeks to represent the presence of God's voice in text. In the Hyderabad manuscript, the text commences with a temporal displacement in which the performance of God's command precedes the command itself.

We should sympathize with the copyists of these manuscripts. They are reproducing a text that seeks to bend and rupture the constraints of its own composition. Though bound to the linear movement of language, the text stages the complex temporality of God's revelatory word. The challenge is one of immediacy and immanence. *The Best Exposition* is not presented as a record of Bayazid's inspired thoughts later put into written form such as we find in *The Endeavor of the Believers*. Rather, *The Best Exposition* strives for the direct production of God's voice in the written word, and, in this section, we will consider the techniques and gestures brought to this task.

God's command—"O Bayazid! Write the basmalah in grand letters at the beginning of this book!"—repeats four times in the manuscript copies we are considering. It is first in Arabic, but we find it reiterated in Persian, Pashto, and an early form of Urdu that is typically referred to as Hindawi.

Ya Bayazid! Uktub! ...

Ya Bayazid! Bi-navis! ...

Aw Bayazid! Wakasha! ...

Rey Bayazid! Likh! . . .[46]

The speaker—God, it would seem—develops the command further with reference to both prophetic hadith and the Qur'an, and God then issues another fourfold command: "Write the letters that explain in every language in order to benefit humankind!"[47] Bayazid responds to these declarations by lamenting his own inability to fulfill God's command: "You are the All-Knowing, and truly I know nothing but the letters of the Qur'an, o Glorious One!"[48]

In this first instance of dialogue, *The Best Exposition* introduces us to the voices that constitute this work of revelation. Our central figures are God and Bayazid, and their exchanges constitute the majority of *The Best Exposition*. The call of "O Bayazid!" functions in the text as an initiating marker of new sections. As God transitions from topic to topic, he beckons Bayazid to pay attention, and Bayazid concludes sections with the exclamation, "*Yā Subḥān*!" (O Glorious One!). *The Best Exposition* primarily alternates between God's entreatments to Bayazid (to write, to teach, to remember, and so forth) and Bayazid's responses affirming his reliance upon God, his willingness to declare God's oneness, and his explanations of God's exhortations.

Though the larger literary structure might unfold principally as a dialogue, other voices are consistently present. God directs Bayazid's attention to specific verses of the Qur'an ("there is a demonstration of this in the Qu'ran"), and Bayazid cites the Qur'an in his elaborations. The Prophet Muhammad's voice likewise participates in this exchange, as hadith (without a chain of transmission) punctuate the entire text. Additionally, we find frequent inclusion of the sayings of the hadi (an epithet of Bayazid's meaning "the guide"), who offers pithy summations in Arabic of the themes of *The Best Exposition*.

Given that *The Best Exposition* simply begins with a declaration from God to Bayazid, it is difficult to attribute "authorship" of the text by any internal criteria. We are privy to an inscribed exchange between God and Bayazid and their invocations of the presence of Muhammad through hadith citation. *The Best Exposition* therefore departs quite dramatically from a text such as *The Endeavor*, which follows a more conventional path in Islamic theological works of introducing the text, offering praise and gratitude to God and Muhammad, and explaining the genesis of the work before moving to the themes at hand. *The Best Exposition* offers us no such formalized entrances into the text. This very ambiguity of perspective and voice has led some scholars to mistakenly identify the hadi as an unmentioned scholar from Bayazid's childhood or some other figure.[49] The hadi, however, is certainly Bayazid. Indeed, the generation of multiple Bayazids in a carnivalesque dialogue is a recurrent strategy throughout the hagiography of Bayazid's life, *The Book of States*—and we see a similar literary strategy at work in *The Best Exposition*.

This is a *multicentered, polyvocal, tetraglossic* text. By *multicentered*, I intend the shifting perspectives of a text that is spoken by Bayazid in one line and by God in the next—shifts that lack any third-person scaffolding such as "God said" or "Bayazid responded." By *polyvocal*, I simply intend the symphony of voices: Bayazid, God, Muhammad, and Bayazid the hadi.[50] And by *tetraglossic*, I intend the use of Arabic, Persian, Pashto, and Hindawi all bound together in this eclectic discourse. These aspects of *The Best Exposition*—that it is *multicentered, polyvocal*, and *tetraglossic*—work together to generate an ineluctable ambiguity about *who* is speaking *when*. The result is that Bayazid's voice is grafted onto God's.

Frequently, it is not possible to parse when God's initial declaration ceases, when the "narrator" begins their commentary, when the narrator or God cites the prophet Muhammad and the hadi, and when (the internal literary character) Bayazid responds by concluding "O Glorious One!" God's insistence that Bayazid "write the letters" is immediately followed by the inclusion of the Qur'anic verse: "Recite! And thy Lord is the Most Generous who taught by the pen, taught the human that he knew not"—an Arabic verse that is itself punctuated by the Pashto expression *pah qurān kaṣh dī bayān* (And in the Qur'an there is explanation).[51] What is happening here? Is God citing the Qur'an to demonstrate that God previously has implored prophets in just such a manner? Is God respeaking (and re-revealing) this moment of communication to address Bayazid in Bayazid's present moment? Or is this the narrator connecting God's address to Bayazid (*write!*) with a previous moment in the history of God and God's prophets (*recite!*)?

The use of a rise-and-fall pattern known as chiasmus intensifies this entanglement of divine and human voices. *The Best Exposition* includes discussion of numerous topics: the capacity of letters to communicate the truth, the insistence upon eschatological anticipation, the description of ritual requirements, and a mapping of the eight stages of the spiritual path (which we considered in the previous chapter). Most of these topics, however, find elaboration in other works of the Roshaniyya, and so it is their presentation that distinguishes *The Best Exposition*. The cry of

"O Bayazid" marks the beginning of most new sections throughout *The Best Exposition*, and the exclamation of "O Subhan" (O Glorious One!) typically draws the section to its conclusion. These declarations bracket each topic to create the distinctive structure of chiasmus.

After God beckons Bayazid, the text then swiftly transitions to a Qur'anic verse followed by an aphorism of the hadi that echoes closely the themes of the Qur'anic verse. We then encounter the words of Muhammad. We next find unattributed passages that continue the discussion initiated by God. These passages primarily consist of Pashto explanations of the words of the prophet, the hadi, and the Qur'an—and they represent the foremost sites of propositional content in *The Best Exposition*. This is the meat of the text, we might say. After a sufficient discussion of the topic at hand, *The Best Exposition* reverses the polyvocal unfolding. A saying of the prophet, an aphorism of the hadi, and a verse of the Qur'an follow one after the other before we reach Bayazid's final word on the subject and his conclusive "O Glorious One!"

Let us consider a brief example:

> [Pashto] O Bayazid! It is upon you to fear our torment and to love and recollect our repose for all people. . . .
>
> [Arabic verse of the Qur'an] Surely in that is a sign for him who fears the chastisement in the world to come; that is a day mankind are to be gathered to, a day to witness, and We shall not postpone it, save to a term reckoned.
>
> [Persian translation of the verse]
>
> [Pashto] In the Qur'an there is evident manifestation.
>
> [Arabic] It is necessary for the human being to be between fear and hope.
>
> [Pashto] The hadi (*may the mercy of God be upon him!*) has said these words. . . .
>
> [Arabic] "The seeking of God is a duty prior to all other duties."
>
> [Pashto] The prophet (*peace be upon him!*) has said this.[52]

At this point, the text continues into a Pashto discussion of the value of the intellect in actualizing these two states of hope and fear through the recollection (dhikr) of the different possibilities of the afterworld. As the section concludes, we read another saying of the Prophet and an aphorism of the hadi (both in Arabic), a citation of the Qur'an in Arabic and often with accompanying Persian translation, and, in Pashto, Bayazid's final address to God on "the necessity of [following] your command, o Glorious One!"

With relative consistency, this pattern repeats throughout *The Best Exposition*. Schematically, we might represent it as such:

God: O Bayazid! — Qur'an — Hadi —Muhammad

Central Discussion

Muhammad — Hadi — Qur'an — Bayazid: O Glorious One!

In an even sparser schema, this pattern unfolds as: A1-B-C-D-E-D-C-B-A2.

Why the repetition of these chiastic arrangements? Given the repeated arrangements of chiasmus, the order of the nesting of the sources establishes lines of reciprocity. The chiasmus draws our attention to the relationship between A1 and A2, between God calling "O Bayazid!" and Bayazid responding "O Glorious One!" In this structural reciprocity, *The Best Exposition* shows us the call of Bayazid and God's response as echoes of one another. And, in such a way, *The Best Exposition* seeks to achieve in word the entanglement of divine and human voices that characterizes Bayazid's anthropological imagination of the capacity of the human being.[53]

Through chiastic structures and the ambiguity of voice and perspective, we begin to draw near to an understanding of *The Best Exposition* as an "imitation of the Qur'an"—an imitation of a foundational moment of divine communication and utterance. The mimetic features of *The Best Exposition* can be striking in their audacity. For instance, Surat Luqman includes one of the beloved images in the Qur'an: "Though all the trees in the earth were pens, and the sea—seven seas after it to replenish it—yet would the Words of God not be spent. God is All-mighty, All-wise."[54] Situating this Arabic verse amid Pashto and Persian comments, we find a similar sentiment expressed in *The Best Exposition*:

> [Pashto]: If the number of seas were equal to the number of creatures, and if all the seas were ink, or even if there were more, and if there were seventy thousand writers, or even if there were more, and if each writer had seventy thousands pens, yet would the words of praise for You not be written or spent, even if all pens should be broken and all ink exhausted in writing.
>
> [Arabic] Though all the trees in the earth were pens, and the sea ink, with seven seas after it to replenish it, yet would the Words of God not be spent. God is All-mighty, All-wise.

> [Persian] Though all that is on the earth became a type of pen, and the sea ink, and if beyond this there were seventy thousand other seas, yet would the writing of the attributes of Speech of God Most High not be spent. God is the All-Mighty, All-Wise.[55]

This is a daring passage. Following Bayazid's protestations that he is but an illiterate man, God assures Bayazid that he is capable of the task at hand—of praising God and teaching the people. Bayazid then responds with the passage above in which the Qur'anic hypothetical serves as a comparison point for the bolder images presented by Bayazid. While the Qur'an invokes a sea of ink and seven more beyond, the Pashto passage calls upon seventy thousand pens shattered from use.

We will return to this idea of "imitation" throughout this chapter. For now, we can simply note that it joins chiasmus and the symphonic coordination of multiple voices as a gesture of revelation. *Imitation, chiasmus,* and the symphonic coordination of a *polyvocal, multicentered,* and *tetralingual* text all call attention to the recursive nature of *The Best Exposition.* Portrayed in the structure of the language is an exemplary act of communication in which Bayazid successfully receives and acknowledges the disclosures of God. Multiple voices combine to imitate one another and stage a chiasmatic unfolding and reincorporation. As this happens, each section draws the reader into a drama.[56] There is not a single point to grasp in these sections nor the introduction of a single law to follow. The reader comes to understand the philosophical, theological, or legal propositions (the E-term of our chiasmus scheme) as embedded in dialogic call and response modeled upon the Qur'an. *The Best Exposition* is always communicating two ideas simultaneously. The message of the E-term offers a lesson—whatever the particular topic—while the structures, voices, and imitations formally index the section to a revelatory exchange between divine and human realms.

These structural, rhetorical, and stylistic gestures of revelation are at the heart of *The Best Exposition*'s engagement of the Qur'an, and the source for its later critique as blasphemy and heresy. There are scant new lessons or new messages offered in *The Best Exposition.* The project of this text lies with these acts of unrelenting self-consciousness and concern for the very act of communication between God and creation.

Of Time Machines and Rhyme Schemes

As God tells Bayazid to teach the people about the oneness of the divine, God gives Bayazid a cryptic command: "O Bayazid! Write *The Best*

Exposition according to the melodies (*alḥān*) that are in the writing of Surat al-Rahman!"[57] What is God asking of Bayazid?

We will consider later the theological and cosmological resonances between *The Best Exposition* and the fifty-fifth sura of the Qur'an, called Surat al-Rahman. For the moment, I want to suggest something quite simple. God is asking Bayazid to rhyme.

Though scholars of both Islamic theological and Arabic literary traditions have vigorously debated how we should characterize the style of the Qur'an, there are many sections of the Qur'an in rhymed prose (*saj*ʿ). Surat al-Rahman provides just such an example. Let us consider the first five verses:

The Most-Merciful	al-raḥm**ān**
taught the Qur'an.	ʿallama al-qur'**ān**
He created the human being.	khalaqa al-ins**ān**
He taught him the explanation.	ʿallama-hu al-bay**ān**
The sun and moon are in a reckoning.	al-shams wa-ʿl-qamar bi-ḥusb**ān**

While the length and meter of the verses vary, they share a common rhyme: **-ān**. This rhyme persists throughout the entirety of Surat al-Rahman, save for verses that end with the slight variation of **-ām**. Now, an excerpt from *The Best Exposition*:

§ ***Translation***	§ ***Translation that Simulates the Syntax of the Pashto Original***	§ ***Transliteration***
O Bayazid! Write much in description of Me, for I become happy when humans describe me.	O Bayazid! Write many descriptions of Me, for I become happy when many descriptions speak humans.	Aw Bāyazīd! Dzmā ḍayr stir ṣifat wakaṣha, khūṣ hī yem payda shī cheh dzmā ḍayr stir ṣifat wā'ī ādamiy**ān**
Behold! That which is on earth and that which is in heaven praise me.	Behold! Praise says that on my earth or in sky.	Gora! Dzmā tasbīḥ wā'ī cheh dzmā pah mazkah kaṣh dī yā pah āsm**ān**
There is nothing which does not praise me. May you believe this explanation.[58]	There is nothing outside that does not praise me, this explanation may you believe.	Na-shtah hayts bīrūn cheh dzmā tasbīḥ wā'ī, tah bāvar kaṛah pah da bay**ān**[59]

Just as in *Sūrat al-Raḥmān*, this **-ān** rhyme persists throughout the entirety of *The Best Exposition*. Some have interpreted the rhymed prose as a marker of its unrealized Pashto-ness. According to common narratives of Pashto vernacular literature (which are explored in the next chapter), it is only later with the works of poets such as Khushhal Khan Khatak and Rahman Baba that Pashto literature fully achieves a style of writing that accords with the internal patterns of a discrete Pashto language more suited to systems of emphasis than to meter and rhyme.[60] Indeed, in the excerpt above, we find prepositional phrases and sentence subjects in unconventional places to allow for the endurance of the rhyme. *The Best Exposition* has long struck Pashto litterateurs and scholars as convoluted, and this excerpt demonstrates the twists and bends taken to end Pashto sentences with **-ān** sounds.[61]

Stilted or not, might this be exemplary of what God reportedly asked of Bayazid?

But why rhyme? A common explanation—especially when we consider vernacular texts—is to describe rhyme as a mnemonic technique. As rhyme facilitates memory, poetic works can more widely circulate and spread. In its thematic sprawl and eclectic multilingualism, however, *The Best Exposition* seems an exceptionally difficult work to memorize. Absent, moreover, are other mnemonic features; there is no consistent meter, for instance.

We find the meaning of these rhymes in their chronotopic work—in the way they play with our sense of time.[62] As noted above, Agamben argues that rhyme is a powerful technique in the creation of messianic language. Rhyme is a time machine. It breaks the linear chronological time that characterizes much of our language and ignites a cycle of recapitulation and anticipation. The first term of a rhymed pair finds renewed presence in the second term, while the second term comes to hold multiple meanings that spill over the bounds of its "original" significance. As "the Most-Merciful," "the Qur'an," and "the human being" are stitched together through the rhyming of Surat al-Rahman (*al-raḥmān, al-qur'ān, al-insān*, respectively), we hear the "human being" through its resonances with "the Most-Merciful" and "the Qur'an." It is perfumed and saturated with the past terms, and "human being" is cast as fundamental to God's merciful revelation. This accumulation of rhymed endings instills an anticipation of what comes next. As Williams has commented, rhyme "is a reminder that we are always seeing 'through the other.'"[63]

I have been referring to *The Best Exposition*, but this is, of course, a translation—and a translation, moreover, that breaks an important rhyme. As *Khayr al-bay**ān***, we see this text "through the other" that is

Surat al-Rahmān of the Qur'**ān**. *The Best Exposition* does not introduce new laws, nor does it promise future events. Rather, in *The Best Exposition*, we find God transfiguring the past communication of the Qur'an into one point of a polyvocal constellation. *The Best Exposition* thus refers to itself but also to the Qur'an and the relationship between the Qur'an and *The Best Exposition*. Just as the term *qur'***ān** reverberates in the word *bay***ān** when they are presented in a rhyme scheme, so too does the Qur'an come to inhabit *The Best Exposition* because of the mimetic techniques that sustain their relation. Imitation renders *The Best Exposition* the second term in a grand prosodic couplet with the Qur'an. *The Best Exposition* is itself, and it is the excess that is *more than itself*. As *The Best Exposition* rhymes with the Qur'an, so *The Best Exposition* contains, extends, envelops, and reiterates the Qur'an. When assessing *The Best Exposition* alongside the other gestures of revelation already considered, we must pause before we say that *The Best Exposition* "cites" the Qur'an; rather, *The Best Exposition* seeks to lift the Qur'anic moment into the chronotope of its own manuscript leaves.

As rhyme schemes come to do the work of time machines, we can see that other aspects of *The Best Exposition* and the Roshani project contribute to this play with time. Early in *The Best Exposition*, God tells Bayazid to teach the people. Bayazid insists that he is illiterate (*ummī*) and ignorant (*'āmī*), and that he knows letters only by way of the Qur'an. Through this claim of illiteracy, Bayazid becomes an embodied repetition of Muhammad—or perhaps Muhammad is a prefiguration of Bayazid.[64] In either case, a claim of illiteracy extends beyond a mere bid for authority. The claim of illiteracy frees the text from temporal specificity, rendering the "author" of this text nothing more than the second in a pair of rhymed conduits of divine language. The author's self dissolves as he or she becomes the simple conduit for a message that annihilates the self. And as we saw in chapter 2's assessment of the hagiographic *Book of States*, the career of Bayazid reiterates Muhammad's own in a number of ways—most obviously in the events of the Battle of Aghazpuri. Just as Muhammad's 313 followers joined him at Badr, so too did Bayazid's 313 followers join him at his first battle. Bayazid's status as messiah lies not in his prediction of future events, but rather in the repetition of the life of Muhammad. He transforms the past in the process, recasting Muhammad's activities as fulfilled through Bayazid's participation.

Bayazid's role is not as a messenger to follow Muhammad in offering a new prophecy that is distinct and other from that which came before. His role is something else—a messianic revealer becoming Muhammad, rhyming Muhammad, nonidentically repeating Muhammad, and rendering the prophetic past something to be grasped, reenacted, and spoken anew for the Roshaniyya. *The Best Exposition* thus iconically and indexically inscribes the temporal and theological vision of the Roshaniyya. Revelation—like Bruno Latour's description of religious language—does not "distance us from passing time, from this world below, in order to sweep us away towards another realm, another time, but on the contrary, in order to bring us closer to this particular time, which is then fulfilled."[65] In the religious imaginations of the Roshaniyya, *this particular time* finds its fulfillment through the coincidental opening of the past.

A Saturated World

We have been working our way through our heuristic definition of *revelation* as genre and mode of semiosis. Gestures such as chiasmus, ambiguity of voice and language, and imitation evince a self-consciousness of language and communication. These examples extend our discussion in the previous chapter by drawing our attention to the fact *that* language means rather than *what* language means. Rhyme and the resonances of Roshani history with narratives of Muhammad's life converge in creating complex and multilayered chronotopes in which past prophetic moments abide in the present—and anticipate the future. We now turn to a third quality of revelation: that it "think[s] through the universality of dependence."

Revelation is a class of language that denies its origins in human creativity, and, in doing so, draws attention to the givenness of all language. As Karmen MacKendrick, Paolo Virno, and Jean-Louis Chrétien have all explored, we are always speaking in the wake of those words and letters that precede us, fashioning linguistic selves in dialogic response to what has been given.[66] In exploring the deliverance of language, revelation embeds language in the soil of a world that also comes as given and created. As we've referenced throughout this book, the Roshaniyya emerged in a cultural moment that frequently cast the cosmos as composed of letters, words, and divine names. This aspect of their religious imagination becomes especially clear in *The Best Exposition*, as this section explores.

We have largely explored the rhetoric and style of *The Best Exposition*, but the content of God's revelation in this text reflects upon divine communication as well. The themes of this work are common to much Sufi literature of the early modern period. Alongside emphatic declarations of the oneness of God, insistence upon an imminent eschatological moment, and description of the stages of the spiritual journey, there are many sections in *The Best Exposition* that discuss central tenets of Islam such as "the five pillars." The work includes presentations of the necessity and the means of completing the ritual acts of pilgrimage, fasting, prayer, almsgiving, and bearing witness to God's oneness (shahada). Where *The Best Exposition* offers some distinctive commentary on these topics or expands beyond their conventional presentation, it is to elaborate on the communicative potential of these topics. The "five pillars," the Sufi path, the imminence of the End, God's oneness, and other topics point toward a similar cosmological conclusion: the entirety of the created world is saturated with God's communication and, thus, coherent with continuous linguistic revelation.

A representative example is the exploration of ablutions in the absence of water, an aspect of *The Best Exposition*'s discussion of prayer. God cries out "O Bayazid!" and explains to Bayazid that the *tayammum* (non-water ablutions, typically performed with sand) become an obligation (*farḍ*) for people (*saṛey*) when there is not sufficient water.[67] In *The Best Exposition*, God (or an unspecified narrator) details conditions for proper tayammum. Unsurprisingly, the Qur'an passages quoted in this brief section include one of the two Qur'anic discussions on tayammum,[68] but we also find the following verse, "God has appointed a *qadr* for everything." Arberry translates *qadr* as "measure," but, given the context for this citation, the narrator of *The Best Exposition* likely intends "purpose" or *telos* (final goal). Indeed, in Pashto, we then find the narrator expanding upon tayammum as a moment for recollection (*yād kawal*) and for remembrance (dhikr) of the extension of God's creative power and being into the stone and sand of God's creation.[69] The discussion on tayammum reveals an important point about ritual prescriptions in *The Best Exposition*: even the legalistic, prescriptive, and practical work of this text drives toward the unveiling of God's existence as enveloping the cosmos and saturating it with meaning.

Among the persistent themes in *The Best Exposition* is that individual aspects of creation are sites of disclosure for cosmic and human truths. In one of the earliest articles on *The Best Exposition* in Euro-American scholarship, Georg Morgenstierne directs us to a perplexing passage in which we find a description of the *nakhṣha* (a term to be translated below) of wolves and grazing animals. Like many scholars who would follow him, Morgenstierne's interest lay solely in *The Best Exposition*'s role as "the first Pashto text," and he thus cut the Qur'anic verses, Arabic aphorisms of the hadi, and Persian translations from this Pashto passage on wolves and livestock. His translation is:

> The proof [*nakhṣha*] of a wolf . . . is that it wanders much about at night in the lust of its desires, in search of carrion or of animals

> (i.e. prey), or of other things which are their food. Demonstration: I was in torment on account of the lust of desire, of theft, of adultery, or of other things. Men are in the torment of w'č (?) on account of the voice (?) of the lust of Satan.[70]

Morgenstierne then includes a similar passage on grazing animals and their daily habits. There are aspects of this translation upon which I cannot improve, and I do not include it in order to critique Morgenstierne's groundbreaking philology. Rather, from the incoherence of this passage, we starkly confront the need to embed this "Pashto" text back in its multilingual, symphonic context as well as in the religious imagination of the Roshaniyya. I suggest we read *nakhṣha* as something like "signature" or "marker" rather than "proof."[71] A fuller translation of this section might look like this:

> [Pashto] Behold! It is upon human beings to [follow] the shariʿa, the sayings of the messengers, and the five pillars of the Muslims. Sin is obedience to the lower-soul and that which Satan sends forth, . . . and the one without shariʿa is like the wolf. And the one residing in shariʿa is like a grazing animal.
>
> [Arabic] They are but as the grazing animals; nay, they are further astray from the way. Those—they are the heedless. [Persian translation of the Arabic text follows]
>
> [Pashto] An explanation is in the Qur'an!
>
> [Arabic] The one residing in shariʿa does not reach the Path of Reality, and without Reality he does not reach the stage in which there is faith. [Persian translation] [Pashto] The hadi (*may the mercy of God be upon him!*) has said these words.
>
> [Pashto] Behold! The mark [*nakhṣha*] of the wolf is that it wanders at night by the desires of its lower-soul, seeking carrion, prey, and food. Here is a witnessing! In such a way does he wander in accordance with the orders of Satan. A witnessing! The desires of the lower-soul, theft, adultery, and other forbidden deeds—so will a heart be tormented. Humans under the command of Satan [will] be in the torment of burning in the fire![72]

The Best Exposition continues in its eclectic linguistic blend, declaring that the ones who "reside" in shariʿa become heedless like grazing animals with full bellies. With more clues at our disposal—with the Arabic and Persian statements and a familiarity of Bayazid Ansari's multistage Sufi path—we begin to understand that this is a familiar, yet stinging, critique of those who cease their spiritual journeys at the stage of shari'a ("Law"), the first stage of Bayazid's path. Though benign compared to the wolfish servants of Satan, those concerned with shari'a alone pass their lives in heedlessness and in abidance to the lower-soul. Theirs is a pathetic spiritual impoverishment (*muhān*) that contrasts with the righteous humility of the wretch (miskin) whom we met last chapter. More importantly, the wolf and the grazing animal—due to their "signatures"—disclose the multiple modalities of heedlessness in the cosmos.

Wolves and grazers are not allegories here. Like the stone and sand of waterless ablutions, the wolf and the grazing animal reveal the order of things—an order that is found in the natural world as well as in the realm of human capacities. Replete with references to fish, wolves, sand, and trees, *The Best Exposition* presents, frames, and amplifies the revelations found in a cosmos saturated with communicative purpose.

Language and the stuff of creation are co-constitutive, co-manifesting, and pertain to the same end. The deliverance of revelatory language does not represent a rupture with a sign-filled world. The melodies of Surat al-Rahman, as the designated model of *The Best Exposition*, gain particular significance in an immanentist ideology of revelation. Perhaps Surat al-Rahman models more than a rhyme scheme:

> The All-Merciful (1) has taught the Qur'an. (2) He created man (3) and He has taught him the explanation [*bayān*]. (4) The sun and the moon to a reckoning, (5) and the stars and the trees bow themselves; (6) and heaven—He raised it up, and set the Balance. (7) Transgress not in the Balance, (8) and weigh with justice, and skimp not in the Balance. (9) And earth—He set it down for all beings, (10) therein fruits, and palm-trees with sheaths, (11) and grain in the blade, and fragrant herbs. (12) O which of your Lord's bounties will you and you deny? (13)[73]

Here we find another form of capturing the code of the Qur'an. Surat al-Rahman provides the theological vision of the immanentist ideology of revelation in *The Best Exposition*. In this sura, God situates the Qu'ran among a multitude of avenues through which God communicates: the Qur'an, the creation of the human being, the sun and the moon, the judgment of the "balance," and the gifts of a verdant planet. These are all *ālā'*—the blessings or bounties of God—by which the human confronts the immediacy of divine presence and divine communication. There is a paradox at the heart of *The Best Exposition*. God calls to Bayazid and offers Bayazid a revelatory text with new, Pashto letters. The message, however, unspeaks its own radical newness by embedding linguistic revelation into a cosmos that has always and ever been saturated with semiotic potential.[74]

The Deliverance of Letters

We have been skirting the very feature of *The Best Exposition* that has drawn the attention of previous scholars: its status as the first text of Pashto. My hope is that we can see past the allure of being *first* and see the use of Pashto within its tetralingual context and alongside other gestures of revelation.

Early in the text, God commands that Bayazid teach the people, and Bayazid cries out that he does not know the way to do so. God responds:

> O Bayazid! Write the letters that are manifest for you, and the knowledge of the names of the letters is with me. By my command, write letters like those of the Qur'an, and place on some of the letters points, apocopes, and other marks in order that people may know. Write some of the letters four times over and in fours as explication. They will learn when they recite them. They exhale the breath with some of them.[75]

In a cascade of fourfold schemes and repetitions, *The Best Exposition* reveals the letters. Presumably still inscribing God's voice, *The Best Exposition* introduces first the *alif* before proceeding to fourfold demonstrations of the remaining letters.

> [Arabic] *Alif* is one, manifest. [Persian] *Alif* is one, manifest.
> [Pashto] *Alif* is one, manifest. [Hindawi] *Alif* is one, manifest.
>
> *B bā bā bah. P pā pā pah. Ṭ ṭā ṭā ṭah. Th thā thā thah.*
>
> [Arabic] This is explanation. [Persian] Meaning: This is explanation.
> [Pashto] This is explanation. [Hindawi] This is explanation.
>
> *J jā jā jah. Ch chā chā chah. Ts tsā tsā tsah. Ḥ ḥā ḥā ḥah. Dz dzā dzā dzah.*
>
> [Arabic] People recite. [Persian] Meaning: People recite.
>
> [Pashto] People recite. [Hindawi] People recite.[76]

Four by four, *The Best Exposition* reveals the entirety of the Pashto alphabet.

Notably, the letters delivered to Bayazid include letters such as *dzīm* and *tseh* which are common in Pashto but not found in Arabic, Persian, or Hindawi. *The Best Exposition* is our earliest extant source for the orthography of these distinct Pashto letters.[77] Even if *firstness* is a difficult thing to prove, it should not surprise us that among the earliest of Pashto texts is a work of revelation. The appeal is clear: Pashto letters are not mere derivatives of a "foreign" language. The Pashto letters themselves shimmer with divine purpose. These letters, moreover, are not simply written symbols. These letters are inescapably material. *The Best Exposition* stretches and pulls upon the letters, extending a "*b*" to "*bā*" and "*beh*." They are sounded out, recited, and exhaled. This is language-revealing language.

And we might ask: Is this even Pashto?[78] In all three extant manuscripts of *The Best Exposition* that I have seen, Persian and Arabic remain indispensable to the text's comprehension.[79] And, more importantly, God's disclosure of the alphabet is a revelation of *the alphabet* rather than the Pashto alphabet. The uniquely Pashto letters are not appendages to some other acknowledged and stable alphabet. The tools of language itself are (re)revealed. The letter *tseh*—an alveolar affricate not found in Persian, Arabic, or Hindawi—is given to Bayazid along with the *alif* and the *bā'*, the *cheh* and the *zheh*. The Arabic and Persian letters are enfolded into God's disclosure of the alphabet. These letters—including the Pashto ones—participate equally in the cosmogonic and revelatory power of language.

We have drifted far from discussions of ethnicity, vernacular language, and the local concerns of a movement remembered as "Pashtun" or "Afghan." Our drift is a risk worth taking, however, for it allows us to see the challenge that *The Best Exposition* poses to our historiographical and analytical categories.

The gap between what we have seen in *The Best Exposition* and what we might expect from a "vernacular manifesto" or an early utterance of Pashtun consciousness is immense.[80] The Roshaniyya sent Persian epistles to rulers in Badakhshan of present-day northern Afghanistan and in the Deccan in southern India. Participants in the Roshaniyya shed local identifiers and adopted new names such as *Aghazpuri* and *Roshani*. They composed familiar, recognizable Sufi texts in Arabic. Bayazid Ansari denied identification as an "Afghan" and rooted his genealogical distinction in descent from an Arab of Muhammad's community, Abu Ayyub Ansari. And *The Best Exposition*—the "first" text of a reportedly nativist movement—embeds Pashto into a larger semiotic repertoire of Persian, Arabic, Hindawi, wolves, livestock, water, mountains, and dreams. We simply cannot grasp this text according to our familiar habits of thought that would link this first Pashto text deterministically to a politics of Pashtun peoplehood.

So, what of "ethnicity" and "vernacular"? We face the proposition that these words offer little by way of explanation; rather, they are the weary scaffolding propping up narratives born of imperial and nationalist projects. We might follow Bruno Latour and identify such words as tools of "purification."[81] They assist us as we sort the world into distinct "ontological zones": the startling religious gestures of the Roshaniyya conveniently find a place as an expression of ethnic parochialism. Nations and peoples continue to look as we expect them. So too does Islam continue to look as we expect.

I am certainly not asking us to assent to the theological convictions of the Roshaniyya. There is no need for us to affirm that God revealed the alphabet to Bayazid. Rather, I am suggesting that *revelation* is a frame for approaching *The Best Exposition* that amplifies certain features of language and genre in *The Best Exposition.* These features—these gestures of revelation—evince a community that is stranger to our histories than words such as *Afghan, Sufi, heretic,* or *Muslim* allow. Here is a community defining itself through its inhabitation of multiple times at once, *becoming* multiple lives at once.

Moreover, this is a community that turned to the Qur'an as something to be imitated—or, better, "not imitation at all but a capture of code." As Deleuze and Guattari indicated, "code capturing" transforms both sides of the equation. As *The Best Exposition* "imitates" the Qur'an, there is a mirrored "becoming-*The Best Exposition*" on the part of the Qur'an. We can think back to a Qur'anic verse cited in *The Best Exposition*:

> Though all the trees in the earth were pens, and the sea ink, with seven seas after it to replenish it, yet would the Words of God not be spent. God is All-mighty, All-wise.[82]

As we saw, the Pashto "imitation" of this verse reaches beyond seven seas to invoke seventy thousand pens broken from use and drawing from countless empty inkwells the size of seas. Following both the Arabic and the Pashto, we find a statement that seems to be a Persian translation of that same Arabic Qur'anic verse:

> Though all that is on the earth became a type of pen, and the sea ink, and if beyond this there were seventy thousand other seas, yet would the writing of the attributes of Speech of God Most High not be spent. God is the All-Mighty, All-Wise.[83]

But this is not a precise translation of the Arabic Qur'an, is it? Something has shifted, and the seven seas of ink have become seventy thousand.

Could it be that *this* subtle shift models for us that "small door" through which alternative historical visions of Islam may enter?[84] The Roshaniyya do not come to us as just one more point on the vector of Islamic history. As pursuers of God's language and practitioners of *revelation*, their example reframes and transforms the past. Following the Roshaniyya, we see on the horizon a vision of the Qur'an—and Islam—as something to be grasped, renewed, and respoken through mimetic gestures and by new letters.

And this vision was a threatening one. Muslim and non-Muslim sovereigns and saints of the Persianate world bound their authority to claims of revelation and the manipulation of sacred letters. Revelation was dangerous, as was the larger semiotic ideology of the Roshaniyya from which *The Best Exposition* emerged. As we transition now to the works of Akhund Darweza and his heresiography of Bayazid Ansari, we will find that the castigations of the Roshaniyya cascade *not* upon doctrinal errors or theological failings. Akhund Darweza assaults their language.

4 / Vernacular Apocalypse: Poetic and Polemical Emergences of Pashto Literature

Arzani's Pashto bears the traits of the Creator of Night and Day.

—MULLA ARZANI, *Divan*

Bayazid's bones have their own story to tell. As the revelatory words of Bayazid's tongue drew the Roshaniyya into war with Mughal rulers and their local allies, our sources evaporate. There is a gap in our records between the messianic career of Bayazid that we find in Mukhlis's hagiographic *The Book of States* (considered for all its doppelgängers and dreams in chapter 1) and the events befalling the Roshaniyya at the time of and after Bayazid's death. How did he die? As a stray sentence in *The Book of States* suggests, did thirst and exhaustion finally catch him even as he eluded the Mughal horsemen?[1] Did dejected and angry residents in Tirah turn their horses on Bayazid and trample his body to dust, as the polemicist Akhund Darweza suggests?[2] Our sources hesitate, offering only slivers of an event—the death of Bayazid—that we could naturally expect to dominate the memories of the Roshaniyya that flit across the manuscripts in our hands.

With greater confidence, however, our sources tell us of Bayazid's bones. In 1876, Major Henry Raverty followed Akhund Darweza's account by relating that Bayazid's coffin was seized from his family in the midst of a battle between the Roshaniyya and Mughal forces. "The arch-heretic's coffin . . . was broken open. Some of his bones were burnt, and some cast into the Abáe-Sin [i.e., the Indus River]."[3]

Mukhlis provides an alternative story of Bayazid's bones in *The Book of States*. Though some enemies of Bayazid indeed seized his coffin and cast it into the Indus, according to our hagiographer of Bayazid, God preserved the coffin and guided it ashore. Friends of Bayazid found his coffin and informed Bayazid's son Jalala of its location. On Jalala's command, Roshani devotees brought the coffin to the environs of Peshawar and buried Bayazid near one of his dearest disciples, Muhammad Kamal. In Mukhlis's words, "It is now a site of pilgrimage where dreams are granted."[4]

This chapter and the next continue our story of the Roshaniyya pursuit of God's language by examining the traces and remains left by the Roshaniyya after the death of Bayazid, after the first wave of Roshani defeats dealt by the Mughal army, and after the millennium had begun without a Roshani ascension to power in the region. How did disciples, enemies, critics, and curious observers respond to the shattering of the Roshaniyya? As the bones of Bayazid attest, the responses were divergent, even contradictory. Perhaps his bones were broken and burnt, cast into the northern waters of the Indus so that the ashen remains of Bayazid could dissolve into a marker of the frontier—a marker of exclusion, isolation, and rejection. Or perhaps his bones were reclaimed, buried, and thus integrated into a larger Persianate tradition of humic sainthood and shrine visitation.[5] In this chapter and the next, we turn away from the sources associated with Bayazid's teaching and his effort to speak the language of God, and we focus on those remnants of the Roshaniyya left to later generations. Stories of Bayazid's bones are one trace left by the Roshaniyya, but the more substantial inheritance left in their wake lies in their innovative use of Pashto as a written language. The emergence of Pashto as a written language is a remnant of the Roshaniyya, however contested and contradictory the process of a vernacular's emergence as literature would be after the death of Bayazid.

The previous chapter asked: Why does the first use of Pashto as a written language occur in *The Best Exposition*? Why does Pashto find written form in the rhyming eclecticism of a text aiming not to represent but to make present—*to be*—God and God's language? My answer was admittedly evasive: *The Best Exposition* is hardly a "Pashto" text at all. The metalinguistic self-consciousness of *The Best Exposition* does not reflect on its nature as a composition *in Pashto*. Quite to the contrary, the point of *The Best Exposition* is that it is in "God's language," an anti-Babel language, a revelatory language—and *not* confined to Pashto or any other merely human language. Pashto is but one aspect of a larger literary effort to use rhetoric and multilingualism to break language away from its human provenance.

I am perhaps overcompensating in my efforts to break free of the categorical shackles that have bound the historiography of the Roshaniyya to a narrow range of interpretations. As noted throughout this book, the

Roshaniyya have typically been cast as nativist Afghans / Pashtuns who cared less for any deep connections with what we call "religion" and more for something we call "ethnic self-consciousness;" they have also been cast as parochial fanatics committed to vernacular language.[6] As convinced as I am that we must avoid those interpretations, if we are to understand how the Roshaniyya challenge our histories of religion, Islam, and South Asia, there is no point in avoiding the obvious: Bayazid's texts are remembered as the first instances of written Pashto. How did the men and women of the Mughal world respond to this new use of Pashto as a written language?

This chapter considers two responses to the "Pashto-ness" of the Roshani project—two agonistic and fundamentally opposed responses that nevertheless converge to render Pashto as the site of religious contest. One inheritor of Bayazid's linguistic efforts was Mulla Arzani Khweshgi. Arzani was a disciple to Bayazid who reportedly carried Bayazid's message and epistles south into "Hindustan"—that is, into northern India. He was also an accomplished poet who wrote ghazals in Pashto that sang and celebrated the divinity of Pashto. He will be the primary focus of this chapter, but we will contrast his sense of Pashto with that of a more polemical author: the Sunni theologian and heresiographer Akhund Darweza. In his own writings, Akhund Darweza positions himself as the arch-nemesis of Bayazid, and he relates his journeys back and forth across the Khyber in efforts to stamp out the heresies he sees among the Roshaniyya. He too uses Pashto, but unlike Arzani he insists that his Pashto is nothing but the instrument to reach a wide audience of misguided heretics. Language cannot—*should not, must not*—be hallowed and revered as an emblem of the divine. In the rift between Arzani's and Akhund Darweza's poetics, we find competing understandings of cosmology and competing understandings of belonging, identity, and history in the Afghan highlands.

These two responses represent a process that we might call "vernacularization": the development of Pashto as a written language that emerges in relationship to other languages (most prominently, Persian). We cannot assume, however, that the models of vernacularization we find elsewhere in South Asia—and elsewhere around the globe—can be used to understand the vernacularization of Pashto in the late sixteenth century along the Afghan frontier. The written Pashtos of Arzani and Akhund Darweza—the poet and the polemicist—emerge as the site of contest for different conceptualizations of God's presence in language. Pashto vernacularization served as one locus for the unfolding of a larger religio-cultural pattern we have been tracing in this book: theo-semiotic anxieties and imaginations storming over the possibility of speaking God, hearing God, finding God in the words of one's own tongue and in a word-saturated world ever on the cusp of apocalypse.

While Bayazid pursued God's language via an eclectic set of languages, practices, dreams, and bids for messianic authority, his death marks an important shift exemplified by the competing Pashtos of Mulla Arzani and Akhund Darweza. On the one hand, Arzani's liturgical Pashto ghazals abandon the anti-Babel universalism of Bayazid's project, opting for an intimate rhetoric of secrets between God and those with Pashto literary knowledge. Conversely, Akhund Darweza sought to stamp out the idolatrous fetishization of language and linguistic form that he witnessed among Bayazid and his Roshani followers. In both cases, however, we see that imaginations of Pashto and competing ideologies of inscribing Pashto—competing vernacularizations—intersect to open new possibilities of conceptualizing God and becoming Afghan in the early modern period.

Approaching the Vernacular

For those like me who were raised in a monolingual household and fed a diet consisting primarily of European and American history in early schooling, it is perhaps not a surprise at all that Pashtuns would use Pashto as a written language. So immersed are many in a particular brand of nationalism and a particular history of vernacularization (Think Dante! Think Martin Luther!) that there is something commonsensical—something natural—about a people using "their" language.[7] When we encounter, therefore, the common accounts of the Roshaniyya that attribute the Pashto of *The Best Exposition* to a burgeoning ethnic self-awareness or cast the use of written Pashto as an extension of nativist irredentism at the edges of an empire, we can likely nod along in agreement.

This sense that there is something *taken for granted* when a people possess their own vernacular literature, however, is not an accurate reading of the history of South Asia. The *taken-for-granted-ness* is, rather, a product of our own ideologies of language and peoplehood.[8] Our relationship to language is a relationship that both reflects and generates particular ideological stances toward the world. What we see in the linguistic diversity of the world—or, better, what we are *capable* of seeing—is a matter suffused with social, political, metaphysical, and ontological weight.[9] The tendency in English-language communities to view the world as marked by different instantiations of "one people with one language" is an assumption reflecting Euro-American notions of nationalism, race, and ethnicity—an assumption that Judith Irvine and Susan Gal name as "iconization."[10] As they elaborate, iconization suggests "a transformation of the sign relationship between linguistic features (or varieties) and the social images with which they are linked. Linguistic features that index social groups or activities appear to be iconic representations of them, as if a linguistic feature somehow depicted or displayed a social group's inherent nature or essence."[11] In other words, Irving and Gal's iconization articulates the *naturalization* of approaching language as inherently braided to the "essence" of a people, an ethnicity, or a society.

With Irvine and Gal having named this ideological, we can step outside this ideology—even if it is only a partial, temporary step—and observe how odd a thing it is to use a "new" language to write. As Babur passed through the Afghan highlands on either side of the Khyber Pass, he marveled at the multiplicity of languages spoken: Persian and Arabic, Chaghatai and other Turkic languages, "Afghan," and numerous "Indian" languages.[12] In the sixteenth and seventeenth centuries, the Pashto that we find in *The Best Exposition* is marked by the inclusion of words that scholars sometimes describe as Ormuri—a local language of communities in Waziristan.[13] It seems that Bayazid knew Ormuri, Pashto, Persian, Arabic, and Hindawi—and it is likely that multilingualism was the norm for those in the Afghan highlands. Persian had long been the preeminent language of poetry, hagiography, and court history.[14] Arabic retained its potency and value as the language of the Qur'an and many of the Islamic traditions of learning: theology, jurisprudence, exegesis, and so forth. Some three hundred years after the drama of the Roshaniyya, Christian missionaries in Peshawar complained of the need to learn Hindawi or Urdu for preaching in the bazaar, Persian for appearing well versed, Arabic for understanding rival religious texts, and a variety of different Pashtos in order to avoid sounding like a distant stranger when making home visits.[15] Different languages allowed different types of questions to be posed, different types of relationships to be created, and different spaces to be opened. The turn to Pashto writing was *not* the natural extension of literature into the unified tongue of a monolithic people.

The turn to Pashto, moreover, was a risk without a clear benefit. To break away from Arabic and Persian writing was to discard the well-honed lexicons of specific discourses. As Bayazid's Pashto was written in the Arabic / Persian alphabet, the first generation of Pashto literature is legible only to those who already knew either Arabic or Persian (and likely both). And for what end? So that one linguistic community among many in the Afghan highlands might have its "own" literature? Such an explanation—while partially true, perhaps—places an immense causal weight on ethnic self-determination and proto-nationalism. As noted throughout this book (and especially in chapter 1), the language of ethnic self-determination and ethnic self-consciousness is strikingly absent in the literature of the Roshaniyya. I have suggested that the introduction of written Pashto in *The Best Exposition* follows a Persianate messianic logic that valued the breadth and expanse of alphabets for their ability to fully contain God's presence.[16] Bayazid was aiming for God's language and not for the language of the Pashtuns.

Whether one accepts this aspect of my argument or not, the use of Pashto as a written language was by no means a natural development or taken-for-granted process. As with many of our well-worn approaches to the past, the perceived *naturalnness* of Pashto vernacularization tells us more about us in the twenty-first century—about our ideologies of language and ethnic identity—than it does about the Roshaniyya and their Pashto-writing inheritors.

So how else might we understand the "vernacularization" of Pashto?[17] If we reject the iconization of "ethnic vernaculars" described by Irvine and Gal, what alternatives can help us understand the emergence of a written language alongside Persian and Arabic models? Vernacularization has been a generative topic in histories of South Asia.[18] Our purpose in this section is not to survey the entirety of this thriving discussion; rather, I will only gesture to some exemplary works that may serve as beacons for our own assessment of Pashto.

The topic of the vernacular is a tangled one, and scholars find distinct threads to pull and examine, often approaching the question in starkly different ways: Is vernacularization a religious process or a political one? Is the vernacular about quotidian transformations or the result of decisions by the elite? When a language becomes a written language, does it mimic, resist, reify, or parasitically threaten the previous written languages of the region? Is vernacularization a slow, centuries-long social transformation, or is it a matter of individual choices made over the span of a generation? Cutting across the sprawl of this subject matter, Christian Novetzke's work, *The Quotidian Revolution*, weaves many of these threads together in its examination of the vernacularization of Marathi language in twelfth- and thirteenth-century India.

Among Novetzke's most forceful arguments is that vernacularization is not simply the "process of a language becoming written and literary"[19] but attests to a seismic remaking of culture. Vernacularization is the "indigenizing of a broad range of discursive mediums across a semiotic landscape" and the formation of new sorts of "publics" participating in new—and more accessible—conversations on the good, the true, and the desired direction of society.[20] While the development of a written

Marathi literature may appear sudden—the mere blink of two lifetimes—Novetzke insists that the appearance of written Marathi is but the visible sign of more profound social and intellectual shifts toward the power of common people and everyday life. Vernacularization, seen in the emergence of Marathi literature, makes visible a "quotidian revolution" and an increasing valorization of what is shared, what is common, and what is ordinary.

With his emphasis on vernacularization as an index of larger processes, Novetzke is building upon the foundational works of Sheldon Pollock. The very lexicon that we use in discussing the vernacular in South Asia betrays a debt to Pollock's work, but Novetzke's analysis offers some needed paths leading beyond certain elements of Pollock's argument. At its bluntest, Pollock's story of vernacularization is a story of power, a story of politics, and a story of courtly elites. In a magisterial survey of *literization* and *literarization* in the subcontinent, Pollock demonstrates how princes and local kings across India patronized the production of literature in new languages—Kannada, Assamese, Gujarati, and others.[21] In breaking the absolute dominance of Sanskrit and Persian in the written, literary sphere, these courtly elites sought to garner cultural capital and establish their distinctive place in the complex ecosystem of premodern Indian politics.

As Novetzke notes, however, Pollock's desire to break free of the Orientalist images of "mystical India" as a land of spiritual renewal, intuition, and religious possibility has resulted in an overcorrection.[22] Pollock argues that vernacularization is a political process rather than a religious one. This type of argument simultaneously reifies "religion" as a phenomenon possessing a distinct (nonpolitical?) essence and, as Novetzke suggests, requires the exclusion of multiple languages from Pollock's model: Marathi, Punjabi, and—we can add—Pashto. In contrast to Pollock's model of political patronage, Novetzke tells a story of vernacularization in which the inscription of indigenous languages reflects the efforts of religious teachers to meet the concerns of everyday Marathi speakers.[23] Out of ethical and religious concern for the lives and salvation of the common person, thirteenth-century Brahmanical figures such as Chakradhar and Jnandev not only used Marathi but infused their teachings, their anecdotes, and their translations of the *Bhagavad Gita* with the imagery and lexicon of the quotidian. Unlike Pollock's courtly elite playing a game of power consolidation, Novetzke's saints turn to the innovative use of Marathi as a written language to expand the public and leap across that gap between the elite and the common.

As we gaze back at the Pashto of *The Best Exposition*, we can immediately see that it does not follow the pattern suggested by Pollock. Bayazid Ansari's family received the respect of the local population for their religious leadership, but they were not exceptionally wealthy, nor were they patronized by courtly elites. Similarly, we have no evidence that Mulla Arzani and Akhund Darweza turned to Pashto for reasons of political patronage or political prestige, though Akhund Darweza certainly expressed his sympathies with the Mughal elite. The earliest instantiations we have of written Pashto fall outside the court, and the "Afghan" courts of the Suri and Lodhi dynasties sponsored Persian histories rather than Pashto poems.[24]

But what of Novetzke's model? As explored in chapter 2, Bayazid's earliest disciples included women, orphans, craftsmen and artisans, and nomadic herders. Mulla Arzani—whose poetry we will consider shortly—is one of the rare members of the Roshaniyya to have a vaunted social reputation as an accomplished poet and wordsmith. Until the conversion of entire communities and tribal groups, Bayazid's mission enveloped the nonelite. Could it be that the Pashto literature of the Roshaniyya is the literary manifestation of a growing concern among an emergent *public*, of a community rising from the everyday lives of the Afghan highlands?

Here we stumble again on the striking eclecticism and audacity of Roshani literature. Roshani written discourse is primarily a Persian one; the Pashto of Bayazid intimately threads into a multilingual effort to write God into language; and Arzani's Pashto, as we will soon see, is a Pashto of self-valorization and triumph that claims to baptize Arzani's verses in semiotic divinity. Whatever the quotidian composition of the Roshani disciples, the Roshani literature we have seeks the apotheosis of the spiritually elite, the reopening of Muhammad's prophetic moment *in this moment now*, and the scouring of human qualities from language so that their tongues might become organs angelic and divine. Akhund Darweza's Pashto polemics imagine an everyday audience of the nonelite, but the akhund sneers at the common Afghans' lack of education even as he orients his texts toward them (and we will revisit his works later in this chapter).[25] Novetzke points to the convergence of a growing everyday egalitarianism in Marathi communities, the use of Marathi as a written language, and a Marathi literature of charming stories and simple spiritual lessons accessible to a wide audience. Despite the notes of liberation that characterize the Roshaniyya's messianic and revelatory endeavors, we see no such convergence in their early Pashto literature.

Farina Mir's work on the development of a Punjabi *poetics of belonging*, however, offers us another avenue for understanding the development of Pashto.[26] Eschewing the tendency to see Punjabi literature as an early modern language of *resistance*, Mir emphasizes the *resiliency* of Punjabi vernacular literature during the colonial period. According to Mir's analysis of Punjabi *qiṣṣas* (stories), Punjabi literature did not serve primarily as a rebuke or rejection of imperial and colonial political powers, be they Mughal or British. Rather, Punjabi literature evoked a distinct "poetics of belonging." It beckoned to a sociality alternative to the logics of ethnicity and state: a sociality constituted by the inscription and circulation of Punjabi stories, a sociality marked by the consumption and circulation of these texts, and a sociality that resiliently persisted despite the transformations and traumas of imperial, colonial, and national movements.[27]

What all three of these approaches—Pollock's Kannada model (among other vernaculars), Novetzke's Marathi model, and Mir's Punjabi model—offer us is a chance to adjust our eyes to semiotic and linguistic ideologies far removed from those of common modern Euro-American thinking. So how can we tie our various threads together? I suggest this: as we approach the vernacularization of Pashto in the wake of Bayazid's messianic career, the center of our discussion must rest with the worlds and relationships constituted by the process of vernacularization as it manifests in the works of Mulla Arzani and Akhund Darweza. The questions cannot simply be *Who patronized this inscription of Pashto? Who read this work? Why Pashto at this moment?* As important as those questions are, they ignore the lessons of Pollock, Mir, and Novetzke that vernacularization is an index of social and intellectual change. Our question is not *Who is Pashto for?* It is rather *Who is created by Pashto?*

We find competing, agonistic answers to this question. After the apocalyptic and messianic experimentations of the Roshaniyya—after their attempt to speak God's very presence into the stuff of this world through the multilingual rhymes of *The Best Exposition*—it should be no surprise that the poetic and polemical heirs of the Roshaniyya disagreed on the nature of that soul born of Pashto's vernacularization.

The Poet Arzani

Apart from Bayazid Ansari and his family, there are few details on the individual members of the Roshaniyya. Bayazid's son Jalala met Emperor Akbar on the banks of the Indus;[28] one of Bayazid's grandsons, Ahdad, led the Roshaniyya in low-burning rebellion against Mughal control;[29] and another of Bayazid's grandsons, Ilahdad, was folded into the Mughal *mansabdar* system and anointed by Emperor Jahangir as a midlevel Mughal nobleman with the new name of Rashid Khan.[30] Mukhlis mentions certain beloved disciples such as Bibi Fatima (Bayazid's wife), Shir 'Ali,

Muhammad Kamal, and Shaykh Bayazid (the martyred double of Bayazid Ansari). Mukhlis claims to excerpt portions of a Persian spiritual-didactic text called *The Endeavor of the Seekers* ("Maqṣūd al-ṭālibīn") and attributes this to a disciple known as Khalifa Mawdud. Our record is sparse, and thus the records we have of the poet Mulla Arzani contrast notably with those of the other Roshani disciples.

As Mukhlis's *The Book of States* records, Mulla Arzani was Bayazid's intimate disciple and was deputized by Bayazid to initiate members into the Roshaniyya.[31] As discussed in chapter 1, Bayazid's method of deputizing his followers—of deeming them khalifas—marks an intriguing departure from the patterns of Sufi history. When Mulla Arzani received permission to initiate men and women as Roshaniyya, he received permission to do so in the name of Bayazid. These initiates became disciples of Bayazid, not of Mulla Arzani—and thus Mulla Arzani stood as "the Bayazid" for initiates who never met Bayazid Ansari.

The Book of States adds that Bayazid charged Mulla Arzani to go to "Hindustan" (loosely: "northern India") so that "the people of God may receive the knowledge of the essence and the learning of unity" from Arzani.[32] Mukhlis writes that Mulla Arzani was an esteemed poet in the "Afghan language."[33] Akhund Darweza, in his unceasing efforts to repudiate Bayazid and the rank heresies Akhund Darweza perceived among the Roshaniyya, uses Arzani's poetic reputation as a means of demeaning Bayazid and the Roshaniyya. It was not Bayazid who wrote *The Best Exposition*, let alone God; rather, it was Mulla Arzani, the one poet among that lot of reckless and impious fools.[34]

We do not know what transpired on Mulla Arzani's journey to the south, whom he met and persuaded, what Pashto songs he sang and what tetralingual revelations of God he shared. There are manuscripts of Roshani sources found in Rampur, Hyderabad, and Patna—are these the faint marks of Mulla Arzani's missions in northern India? We have but two material traces that bear the name Arzani: a collection of Pashto ghazal poems called *Divan-i Arzani*, available in manuscript form; and an elegant, if small, shrine in Patna devoted to a "Shah Arzani" who died in 1032 of the hijri calendar (1622–23 CE).[35] While the Shah Arzani who died in Patna is plausibly the Arzani Khweshgi of the Roshaniyya, I have not been able to confirm the connection.

In most copies, such as the one held in the British Library that serves as the basis of my analysis, the divan of Arzani is a modest collection of forty-eight poems ranging in length from eight to thirty verses. They are ghazals—that classic form of poetic composition that structures and molds poetry in Arabic, Persian, Turkish, Urdu, and dozens of other lan-

"The Shrine of Shah Arzani at Patna," watercolor by Sita Ram, 1814–15, Add. Or. 4705, by permission of the British Library.

guages throughout the worlds of Islam. Though the provenance of the manuscript of this divan is difficult to date, *The Book of States* suggests that these ghazals would have been composed after Mulla Arzani's initiation as a disciple of Bayazid (presumably in the 1570s) and before his death in 1632–33 CE. If that is correct, then these poems are the earliest examples of self-consciously Pashto literature that we have aside from *The Best Exposition*, discussed in the previous chapter, and the translations that follow are the first translations available from this crucial source. As will be demonstrated, the poems of Arzani encapsulate critical aspects of Roshani cosmology and theo-semiotics, but they also represent a consolidation and even an extension of Bayazid's eclectic efforts. We find in these poems declarations that the cosmos is saturated with communicative potential, that existence in its entirety is immersed in God and God's love, that language is not just a means of communication but the very stuff of the divine, and that humans (or at least Arzani) can elevate their tongues into organs of divinization when guided by a perfect master (*pīr-i kāmil*). The following ghazal is representative of many of these themes. Ghazals—including those of Arzani—do not have titles as many English poems do; however, I have given a title to the following translations for the sake of referencing them later.

The Strum of the Robab[36]

Let me describe my God anew,
let me give praise for prophets true.

A hidden treasure was my Lord
who lov'd His Being, so knew it too.

When love prevails, surrounds, and drowns,
a belov'd forsakes the known milieu.

From God's true light is born both worlds:
both here, now, and what shall ensue.

Behold: *Ahad* becomes *Ahmad*
as *mīm* alights and renews.

The seeker holds his heart in hand,
and pawns it for a fortune true.

The world's the strum of the robab—
all songs the same beatitude.

My Master beckons: *Nahnu aqrab!*[37]
So hear: the Qur'an calls to you.

God envelops all: an ocean
for beggar, king, and madman, too.

To speak the truth is to make alive.
So hear: this beggar speaks to you.

In God's hands, today's broken body
awaits resurrection, born anew.

O Strayer from the righteous path!
Go slow! Where are you running to?

On the dark way, the strayer's alone,
a wretch gone wild, without clue.

Arzani! Say it in Pashto
so that you do what you must do.[38]

Formally, this poem follows the conventions of the ghazal. With this particular translation, I have attempted to reproduce those stylistic conventions. Each couplet represents the two hemistiches of each Pashto verse. Each verse / couplet is discrete, and thus the perspective is constantly shifting from the implied personal "I" of the first verse to a cosmic perspective that describes the cosmogonic "separation" of God's light in the fourth verse, from the intimacy of "my Master" to the detachment of the final verse in which it is "Arzani" who receives the poetic command. As is common in ghazals, the last line of Arzani's ghazals embeds his *takhallus* (loosely: a pen name) in the verse as a signature or tag declaring that this is indeed the work of Arzani. As I've attempted to replicate with a rhyming *-oo* sound, the Pashto of this ghazal rhymes throughout as each verse concludes with a *-dā* sound (as does the first hemistich of the first verse). This is all to suggest that the ghazals of Arzani are profoundly conventional in poetic form; their innovation rests in the use of Pashto and in the exploration of Pashto's messianic and divine potential.

Conventional form does not mean that form is inconsequential, however, nor that the poetics of Arzani are separate from his theological project. As many scholars of Persian ghazal have argued, there are aspects of ghazal convention that render the ghazal an exceptional medium for Sufi ideas of self, love, God, and annihilation.[39] As each verse stands alone, each verse offers a chance to leap from one perspective to another and to leave the listener or reader unsure of whose voice we are hearing, whose love we are witnessing, and whose perspective we are adopting. The poetic voice of the ghazal is one in motion, and it is thus a vehicle for conveying and performing the instability (and ultimate falsity) of the annihilative self as conceptualized by Sufis.

As an example of the theological potential of poetic ambiguity, we can consider the tenth verse above. "To speak the truth is to make alive. / So hear: this beggar speaks to you." While I interpret the unstated object of "to make alive" to be the "reality of being," I am unsure whose speech we are considering. The subsequent reference to "this beggar" might ground the phrase "to speak the truth" in the persona of Arzani the poet. We could read the verse thus: "When Arzani the beggar speaks the truth, he makes the world come alive—and now he speaks to you." But isn't it also possible that the insistence that "this beggar speaks" asserts the poet's participation in "to speak the truth" that has its origins outside of the poet? Might we read this as "And hear this beggar speak so that he may join the divine and cosmic speaking of truth that reveals the world to us"?

As Ahoo Najafian has argued, ambiguity is the formal pivot of the ghazal and this renders the ghazal exceptionally capable of re-creating the Sufi theological fluidity of a God who both *is* and *is not* the stuff of this existence.[40] Arzani's poetry is no exception, demonstrating that the shape of language—its materiality, structure, rhetoric, rhyme, and so forth—is irrevocably braided to its religious imagination and ethical aims.

While aspects of this ghazal resonate with a common Sufi pursuit of a God who is ever-transforming (at least in our base human eyes), the themes of this ghazal are recognizably Roshani. The world we find in this poem is a world soaked in language and oriented toward praise of God. "The world's the strum of the robab" is to cast the world as potential sound. Its telos is music, but we find it in need of realization. It is a world on the cusp of strumming the robab, just as *The Best Exposition* declares the wolf, the ox, the sand, and the soil to ever be on the cusp of manifesting God via human perception and articulation. The metaphor of the robab's string suggests a similar metaphysics: all is potential theophany, all is a potential manifestation of God.

Like *The Best Exposition*, language is not the mere means to discuss the communicative nature of the cosmos; language is the stuff of creation. To borrow from Gilles Deleuze, we can say that letters and words circulate *in* the world and not as a transparent representation *of* the world.[41] In the fifth line, Arzani writes, "*Aḥad* becomes *Aḥmad* as *mīm* alights and renews." Arzani is suggesting that "the one" (*aḥad*) takes the form of "the most-praised one" (*Aḥmad*) with the descent of the letter *mīm* into *aḥad*. If Bayazid had not described himself as attaining a stage of *Aḥmad* (see chapter 3), we could confidently interpret *Aḥmad* as the prophet Muhammad, as Ahmad is a common name for him. Whether *Aḥmad* is Muhammad or Bayazid, Arzani is pointing to the linguistic manifestation of God's oneness in prophetic revelation—a process imitated in the alighting of the letter *mīm*. The attention to the "*mīm*" evinces a concern for letters as individually consequential and possessive of a gravity apart from their use in symbolic codes.

This aspect of Arzani's cosmological imagination is sharper in the following ghazal, that, for convenience, I have titled "The Alchemy of *Be!*":

The Alchemy of Be!

You are the first *alef* and the last *zee*.
Free this beggar from his hypocrisy!

I trace the letters, I make a record
in the name of the Most High Almighty.

If I were to seek to praise another,
I'd be tracing mud in futility.

My God is pure, My God is limitless:
as vast, as wide, as grand as the sea.

God created the cosmos and its end
by the life-giving alchemy of *Be!*[42]

Every atom praises God: dirt and flesh
and stardust of Heaven's bright Pleiades.

That is not silence. You are not silent!
All sing and praise God's power and glory.

To God belong the color'd silks of rainbows,
the sky's millstone orbit, turning gently.

. . . .

Endeavor, Arzani! Strive in Pashto
and render this poem a reality![43]

The poem begins with a self-conscious consideration of its linguistic nature: it is a matter of letters, traced by a pen, for the purpose of worship. Arzani's semiotic ideology—the way in which he imagines how language can and should function—does not cast language as the transparent conveyor of meaning. Rather, to invoke Robert Yelle's analysis of religion and language, these first verses display *semiotic density*: a persistent signaling of their own linguistic nature.[44] The poem transitions from the semiotic density of the opening to an evocation of a Qur'anic verse that serves as a guiding star for Islamic lettrist cosmologies: "And God says, 'Be!' and so it is."[45] As noted, the Roshaniyya possess a vision of the cosmos as constituted by letters, and this is a vision shared by Hurufis, Nuqtavis, and other Muslim movements that we may group under the larger canopy of "lettrism."[46] This verse is foundational to lettrist religious imaginations, suggesting that the entirety of existence is an act of language and that we are but spoken into being. God does not just communicate with humans through language; God creates humans through language.

"The Strum of the Robab" and "The Alchemy of *Be!*" repeat the theological language of existential oneness and divine immersion that we find in other texts of the Roshaniyya. In *The Endeavor of the Believers*, Bayazid Ansari cites the renowned Andalusian Sufi Ibn 'Arabi, and we can see in these poems the traces of Ibn 'Arabi's thought (which is often shorthanded as *waḥdat al-wujūd* or "unity of existence").[47] "The Alchemy of *Be!*" depicts God as a vast enveloping sea, and the poem declares that any human's presumption of self-possession—of sovereignty over one's existence and one's body—is but an illusion that will be cast aside by death, if not before. God is the creator of every atom and the possessor of the entirety of the cosmos. In the hemistich "A hidden treasure was my Lord," "The Strum of the Robab" alludes to a beloved *ḥadīth qudsī* (that is, a hadith that relates the word of God) that appears frequently in Ibn 'Arabi's texts and serves as a platform for Ibn 'Arabi's cosmogonic understanding: "I was a hidden treasure and I longed to be known, so I created a creation that I be known."[48] Creation and existence are thus the processes by which God comes to see, know, and love God. We have already noted that these poems adhere to a simple idea: all is theophany, all is a manifestation of God's presence. We can extend this: all is auto-theophany. And if we're feeling up for it, we might even say: all is semiotic auto-theophany.

Throughout these poems, we find more than an ontological description in which everything is part of God's self-revelation. This "semiotic auto-theophany" lies on the boundary between description and prescription. God's longing "to be known" bends creation—including the human being—toward the telos of revealing God's self-love to God. *That* is our project and our ethical burden, and so Arzani insists throughout his divan that the human being remember God, worship God, and give in to the gravitational force of God's love and the human's purpose. Even as the poems communicate this imperative, they assert that this teleology is complicated by the inherently doxological (that is: "worshipping") nature of creation. In simpler terms, we are already participating in the manifestation of God's presence. As Arzani assures the reader in "The Alchemy of *Be!*": "That is not silence. You are not silent! All sing and praise God's power and glory." These poems are an invitation to realize one's ongoing participation in God's process of self-love and self-disclosure.

But if the task, purpose, and reality of creation is to participate in this cosmic theophany, what does that mean for the human being? According to Arzani's poetry, the answer is simple: speak and write Pashto. In another poem that I have called "Become Ash" (the translation style of which will be discussed shortly), Arzani writes:

Become Ash

This beggar's Pashto poems are white pearls

that bear the traits of the Powerful and no other.

. . .

Do not whisper His hidden secrets as testament.

The fires of the innermost secret,

once loosed, once wild,

will consume us by their flames.

Come and burn!

Become ash until only pearl remains![49]

The poem maintains a paradoxical tension between secrecy and revelation. Secrets (asrar) are not to be offered forth as testament or proof (*barhana*), and the secret (or "inner heart," sirr) threatens to consume the human in fire. That annihilation, however, is precisely the point and the process through which the pearls of being are revealed. Though the poem urges its listener into the paradox of secret-keeping and revelatory self-annihilation, we already hold the result of such an annihilative process in our hands: the poem itself is a pearl. Arzani's Pashto, it would seem, is both the result and the contributing cause in the process of God's manifestation and the annihilation of the human self.

Before moving on to another poem that draws into relief Arzani's concern for Pashto *as Pashto*, I should offer a note on translation. As is obvious, my translation of the excerpt from "Become Ash" unfolds according to a different logic than my translations of "The Strum of the Robab" and "The Alchemy of *Be!*" This is a consequence of the multivalence that lends the ghazal such power in Sufi discourse, and yet each aspect of a translation—the words selected, the meter maintained or abandoned, the rhyme, the titles given for convenience—is a choice that *forecloses* the ghazal's ambiguity and, consequently, the dynamism of its theology. A better translator could maintain the formal markers of a ghazal without giving them a quaintness that strict rhyme and meter schemes possess in English. In Pashto (or Persian, Arabic, Turkish, Urdu, etc.), a ghazal does not appear quaint, as if it were a nursery rhyme. Ghazals can be sorrowful, aggressive, quiet, demanding, melancholic, violent; a ghazal can possess virtually any tone in the way that I cannot approach when attempting English rhyme and meter. Rather than pretend that any single form of ghazal translation I can offer would felicitously reproduce the work of these ghazals, my solution is simply to play with form and offer differing styles. By making this choice, my hope is that the reader will not assume that the experience of encountering these English rhymes and meters coincides with the experience of hearing or seeing these poems in Pashto. To be clear, however, all the original poems of Arzani translated in this chapter follow the conventions discussed above and partially reproduced in the translation of "The Strum of the Robab."

The translation's form, moreover, becomes a tool for amplifying aspects of the poem that I consider to be central. This is especially clear in the following translation, where I have attempted to draw attention to the frequent use of Arabic words within Arzani's Pashto. In the following translation, I have taken the greatest liberty in adding words and supplementing Arzani's poem so that the Arabic words of the poem are simultaneously comprehensible to an English-language audience and identifiable as Arabic words within a non-Arabic poem.

The Master of Nahnu Aqrab

Bismillah! In the name of the name of praise of the Lord of the

Nahnu aqrab, the master of "we are closer!" This

faqir is a beggar, but he brought to Pashto what he took from the

*'Arab*s, that he may sing of the One of

la sharīk, the One without partner and rival, the One who is your only

dhahb, your golden coin of true purchase. Remember that all four

madhhabs concur that love of gold is legally

haram and lures the seeker from the

talab-quest for a God who is already so near. But distractions abound: the pleasures of

lawb, of trifling games, of sinful debauchery. O! I seek refuge in the shelter of

a'udhu—the shelter of the *I seek refuge!* The shelter from the blackness of the

nafs, the blackness of the crawling and stinging scorpion

'aqrab that is the human's carnal self. The quest for God, the noble

talab demands the right habits of

adab for the Lord, the

rabb, who turns away from the brutish

bi-adab. A Muslim's tongue is gentle, his lips are

*labb*s of truth and beauty. Be a dashing rider, mounted and

> *murakkab*-ed on this steed and you'll never ride another. Be a fish, annihilated, in the
>
> *halik* sea, the sea that saves and swallows, creates and undoes.
>
> *Dhikr* is the cause for understanding this paradox, for gaining
>
> *ma'rifa*'s insight. For there is no deed nor action without
>
> *sabab* causes. And so Arzani's Pashto bears the traits of the
>
> *Khāliq*, the Creator of Day and Night.[50]

Here we begin to see the distinctions between Arzani's linguistic imagination and Bayazid's own. While Bayazid sought the language of God in the braiding together of four interpenetrating languages, Arzani repeatedly identifies Pashto throughout the divan as a language above other languages. The language of God does not exist as a universal language that is accessible only via Bayazid's acrobatic multilingualism; it rests here in the Pashto of Arzani. Pashto is sacred in the most elemental sense of being "set apart," of being the language of praising and singing for God. Arzani folds Arabic Qur'anic phrases into his Pashto verse, embedding "We are closer" (*nahnu aqrab*) and "I seek refuge" (*a'udhu*) as totems into the fabric of his Pashto. The oath that begins this poem extends beyond the common oath taken upon God's name in Islamic discourses. This is not the *basmalah*—the *In the name of God*—but is instead the *In name of the name of the praise of the Lord.* It is an oath sworn on the name of the name of God. Arzani's Pashto swears not by God but by God as made present in language.

Oaths are powerful acts and "events of language" that attempt to link "words and things."[51] Arzani's semiotic density is not the decadence of linguistic play but a claim to power. The bid for power, messianic authority, and linguistic preeminence found in the texts of the Roshaniyya—including Arzani's poetry—unfolds according to an imagination of language immanently saturated with God's presence. In the style of its linguistic self-consciousness, the language of Arzani and the Roshaniyya places a wager on the God of the oath: a God whose being causes a coincidence of word and thing, a God whose divinity spills over any putative existential boundaries and flows into those instances of human language that sing, remember, and participate in God. In seeking the presence of God in Pashto, the language of the Roshaniyya does not point to the *beyond* or the *above*. And so in the final verse, Arzani boldly proclaims that his Pashto is the language that "bears the traits" of God. The Pashto verb of this verse—*ṣifat kawal*—is typically translated from contemporary Pashto as "to worship" or "to praise." In this case, the final verse would read: "And so Arzani's Pashto praises the creator of day and night." Given the saturation of Roshani theology with late medieval Islamic lettrism and given the persistent Roshani experimentation with the divinity of letters and words, I believe a more literal translation of *ṣifat kawal* is appropriate.[52] In theological contexts, *ṣifat* from the Arabic *ṣifa* is a "trait," "attribute," or (less often) "description" of God. *Kawal* is a verb used in compound constructions but, at its base, means "to do" or "to perform." Thus, *sifat kawal* is "divine attribute + to do"—and the possible meanings stretch from "to describe [God]" to "to perform [God's] divine attributes." I attempt to split the difference with the phrase "bears the traits"—a translation that leans on the ambiguity of "bear" as meaning both "possess" and "carry forth."

We played with the concept of "semiotic auto-theophany" above; here Arzani positions his poetry as the medium of this auto-theophany: it bears the traits of God. We saw this same idea in "Become Ash," where Arzani writes that his Pashto verses "bear the traits of the Powerful and no other." Arzani's point is not merely that the cosmos is created of words spoken by God and that God's enveloping, immersing presence is a linguistic one—that we, as creatures, are anointed in the letters and names of God. More than this, Arzani seems to suggest that this cosmic language is *Pashto* and, specifically, Arzani's Pashto.

We can retrace the steps in this logic.

1. God created the world through language.
2. God envelops the world.
3. God should be revealed (a "should" compelled by God's self-love).
4. Language reveals God. Pashto (or Arzani's Pashto) most clearly reveals God as the language of language—the language that swears upon language.

If this is our progression, then we cannot turn away from the conclusion: Pashto (as written and practiced by Arzani) accomplishes the actions of God. If we can forgive the use of a decidedly Neo-Platonic term, we could describe Arzani's poetry as "theurgical"—it is language that "does the work of God" by mimicking divine action.[53] Pashto participates in God's loving revelation of God to God by continuously re-revealing and making present God through verse.

We can consider one additional selection from Arzani's divan that exemplifies many of these themes and notably emphasizes the human poet's capacity to stage the manifestation of God:

His Heart Is a Garden

I will beg the Glorious one,
for my words are so pitiful!
I will ask for aid from my Master,
for aid comes to the suffering.
I will knock upon the Lord's door,
for to knock on another's door is to lose the way.
You will dig among stones and soil, moss and meadow—
and will you find the Real?
Who will give her soul to the Lord?
For she is the traveler upon the way.
The traveler will circumambulate the heart,
and so become the true pilgrim.
Arzani will find these blossoming verses,
for his heart is a garden of Pashto.[54]

Arzani begins his poem by beseeching God to assist him linguistically, for it is language that fundamentally characterizes the relationship between created and Creator. The poet continues to witness the presence of God in all aspects of creation before imploring the reader or listener to begin upon her path. But as noted, this is a path that has already been walked, for our doxological task of worship is accomplished whether we will it or not. And so the path is one of circumambulation around the heart. In a verse that could have been lifted straight from Ibn 'Arabi's own mystical poetry, Arzani concludes by describing his heart as a verdant garden, the flowers of which are Pashto.[55] The theurgy of Arzani blossoms into a poem that participates in the divine (self-)disclosure that it describes; the verses imitate the story of creation, animated as it is by language, revelation, and love. Across his divan, the poet whispers just below the surface of his verses that his poems are not poems *about* God. No, they *are* God, they bear the traits of the Lord, and they grant God a chance to witness God.

The remainder of Arzani's divan maintains a focus on these revelatory and theurgical qualities of Pashto, even as it examines specific ethical tasks within this process, such as maintaining the shari'a, obeying the perfect master, and devoting oneself to the dhikr.

Though Arzani's Pashto literature extends the messianic semiotic imaginations of Bayazid and a longer history of Persianate religious experimentation, there are significant ruptures between Bayazid and Arzani. Drowned in the violence of the Roshani-Mughal conflict, the universal ambitions of Bayazid's multilingualism have vanished. Bayazid's revelatory language fired in fits, lurching across linguistic boundaries in an attempt to escape the baseness of human language. Arzani's ghazals conjure a different relationship between word and people. It is a relationship (or a "footing," to enlist Charles Taylor's language) in which Pashto speaker relates to Pashto speaker across a more exclusive exchange of verses that are presented as words simultaneously secret and revealed. There is no direct sense of "being Afghan" in these poems, but we see the beginning of an exclusive community whose conditions of belonging require Pashto. Vernacularization does not bubble up from an ethnic spirit but, rather, "being Afghan" is an elite status constituted by these new forms of Pashto. This is a process of *Afghan becoming* that we will explore in the next chapter.

What do Mulla Arzani's poems tell us about vernacularization and the literary cultures emerging at the turn of the seventeenth century? What people are created and beckoned into belonging by these ghazals and by the semiotic ideology that we can trace in Arzani's verse? We can answer these questions more precisely after we briefly examine another spark of Pashto literature catching in the Afghan highlands: the theological tracts and heresiographies of Akhund Darweza that sought to undo what the Roshaniyya had wrought.

The Polemicist Akhund Darweza

Throughout his itinerant career on both sides of the Khyber, Akhund Darweza surveyed the spiritual landscapes of the Indo-Afghan frontier and found a world on the precipice of ruin and unbelief. His parents had come from the regions of Lamghan and Balkh, and his mother's family claimed descent from Alexander the Great. He did not claim recognition, in other words, as an Afghan.[56] An eighteenth-century biographical dictionary of Sufi saints lists 1553 CE as the year of Akhund Darweza's birth, and this is certainly plausible enough, if difficult to corroborate.[57] As a young man, Akhund Darweza pledged himself to Sayyid 'Ali Tirmidhi, the only capable religious master he could find in the region.[58] Together they wandered the Afghan highlands in constant efforts to spare the Afghans the consequences of their own spiritual recklessness. Akhund Darweza and Sayyid ʿAli debated and disputed numerous pirs who claimed that they were God, or that they were the mahdi, or that they were a nabi (prophet), or that they had unveiled the Unseen realm. And, according to Akhund Darweza's own account, he and his master Sayyid ʿAli inevitably shamed these spiritual impostors and would-be saints, messiahs, and gods. No one, however, proved a sterner test or a greater source of Afghan spiritual depravation than the "illuminated master" (pir-i roshan), Bayazid Ansari—an opponent derisively referenced as the "dark master" (pir-i tarik) throughout Akhund Darweza's corpus.[59] Nevertheless, even this archheretic who led numerous Afghans over the edge of disbelief and spilled the blood of countless true Muslims—*may God Most High keep him in Hell for eternity!*—was eventually defeated, and Akhund Darweza successfully extinguished the heretical fires of the Roshaniyya wherever he encountered them.[60]

This, at least, is how Akhund Darweza represented his career. Our examination of Akhund Darweza will span two chapters. In this chapter, we extend a brief consideration to Akhund Darweza's role in the development of Pashto literature. He will receive considerably more attention in the next chapter. While Akhund Darweza's Persian texts on the genealogy of the Afghans are central to the formation of Afghan identity that occurred in the wake of the Roshaniyya (i.e., a process of "Afghan becoming"), the single most popular work of this polemicist is the one that bears on Pashto literature's emergence: "Makhzan al-Islām" (*The Treasure Chest of Islam*), composed circa 1605 CE. This work offered a "beginner's guide to Islam," and this was evidently a popular project, as there are more extant manuscripts of *The Treasure Chest* in the archives of Peshawar, Islamabad, Hyderabad, and London than of any other Pashto text apart from the beloved poetic divans of Khushhal Khan Khatak and Rahman Baba.[61] *The Treasure Chest of Islam* was, in short, a foundational work of Afghan religious cultures and Pashto literature of the early modern period.

Before opening *The Treasure Chest*, it is worth a moment to pause to recenter the driving question of this chapter: How did Pashto "vernacularize"? How did it become a written language and why did such a process unfold in the late sixteenth and early seventeenth centuries (as it seems to have done) in a context of seething imaginations of messianic semiotics and amid the violent clashes of competing millenarian expectations? Among the principal arguments of this chapter is that vernacularization did not occur as the effervescent product of a bubbling ethnic self-consciousness. Rather, we find more fruitful analytic ground by flipping the equation. Pashto literature interpellates—it calls and beckons into being—particular socialities and particular ways of acting, relating, and inhabiting in the world. Moreover, it is in the poetics and metapragmatics of the language of these nascent Pashtos that we find the models for these idealized communities: how these texts use rhymes, imagery, meter, intertextuality, ambiguity, mimesis, and so on offers us a glimpse of semiotic ideologies of these texts and, consequently, of the people these texts sought to birth from these words.

But perhaps the simplest version of my argument is merely this: the vernacularization of Pashto unfolded in different—even contradictory and agonistic—ways.

While there are divergences between the semiotic ideology of Arzani's Pashto poems and the tetralingual eclecticism of Bayazid's *The Best Exposition*, these differences pale in comparison to what we find in Akhund Darweza's *The Treasure Chest*. This work is not only a relentless critique of Roshani heresy (as the akhund sees it). It is an assault upon the imagination of language that the Roshaniyya cultivated in their works, and, consequently, upon the notions of the past, of repetition, and of belonging sustained by Roshani imaginations of language.

This section of the chapter, therefore, turns to Akhund Darweza's Pashto texts to find a conception of Pashto and its use as a language of writing that competes with what we have seen in Arzani's and Bayazid's works. Yet again, we will find the most fruitful points of analysis in the poetics of these sources. Specifically, we will consider three examples found in Akhund Darweza's polemics: his ideology of translation, his critique of Roshani linguistic sins, and what is unstated and absent in Akhund Darweza's "alphabet."

Even as this section serves as a necessary counterpoint to the theosemiotic experiments of Roshani messiahs and devotees, let us not miss the obvious convergence of the Roshaniyya and their feverish opponent, Akhund Darweza. The akhund spent his life castigating the Roshaniyya, but ultimately he met them on familiar ground. Pashto—in its capacities and incapacities, in the way it sutured the human to God or in the way it simply revealed the false promise of such a union—was the common ground for the debate on theology and belonging. These were the stakes of the competing poetics of Pashto vernacularization: what it meant to belong as Muslims in a history of God and God's prophets, what it meant to be blessed and to devote oneself to the blessed of the world, and what it meant to take seriously one's existence as the spoken syllables of a God of revelation and language.

Most manuscripts of *The Treasure Chest* consist of eight discrete sections (*bayāns*) that we might fruitfully approach as eight distinct texts.[62] Akhund Darweza's bayans have been copied and reproduced as individual texts for circulation, and so, for instance, his translation and commentary on a didactic poem known as "Qaṣīdat bad' al-amālī" is widely found as an independent text in numerous archives.[63] Furthermore, Akhund Darweza's family continued to reproduce and expand *The Treasure Chest*, and so Karimdad Darweza, for instance, added his own lengthier *Alphabet Book* ("Alif-nāma") to his father's original.[64] *The Treasure Chest* is not a stable book, but is rather a nexus of Persian, Arabic, and Pashto writings emerging from a religious family and representing a shared scholarly perspective and commitment to Maturidi-Hanafi Sunnism.[65]

According to Akhund Darweza's introduction, the Roshaniyya are the motivation behind the very existence of *The Treasure Chest*: he set about composing *The Treasure Chest* to undo the damage of Roshani messianism. Akhund Darweza makes a similar point in the beginning of most of his texts. Though only one of the eight sections of *The Treasure Chest* directly addresses the Roshaniyya, the vision of Sunni Islamic orthodoxy found in *The Treasure Chest* is glimpsed against the horizon of Roshani "heresies." This is a polemic, and the Roshaniyya are the target. How does the polemical nature of this anti-Roshani "beginner's guide" to Islam shape the process of vernacularization that we are tracing? This is a question most obviously answered in the poetics of Akhund Darweza's translations.

Four of the sections of *The Treasure Chest* are translations, paraphrases, or commentaries on previous Arabic works: the pious poems "Qaṣīdat bada' al-amālī" of al-Ushi (perhaps d. 1179–80 CE) and "Qaṣīdat al-burda" of al-Busiri (d. ca. 1292–98 CE), a theological summary known as the *Khulasah* of al-Kaydani and an epistle on sects and heretics by Najm al-Din Abu Hafs 'Umar ibn Muhammad al-Nasafi (d. 1142–43 CE) that draws upon al-Nasafi's work *Doctrines* ("'Aqa'id").[66] These sources reveal the orientation of Akhund Darweza's intellectual pedigree toward intellectual predecessors of Herat and Bukhara. "Qaṣīdat al-burda" and "Qaṣīdat bada' al-amālī" are among the most widely circulated and translated theological poems in eastern Sunni Islamic networks, and they—like al-Nasafi and al-Kaydani—are popular in Maturidi-Hanafi intellectual worlds.[67] They are, in other words, representative of "mainstream" Sunni Islam in the period.

While Akhund Darweza's influences reveal a concern for sharply drawn theological norms, so too does his approach to language and translation.

Let us consider just a few verses from his translation of "Qaṣīdat bada' al-amālī." This didactic poem includes the following verses in Arabic:

Wa ḥaqqun amru mi'rājin wa ṣidqun fa-fī-hi naṣṣu akhbārin 'awālī

Wa marjū shifā'ati ahli khayrin li-'aṣḥābi al-kabā'ira ka-'l-jibāli

Wa inna al-anbīyā' la-fī amānin 'an al-'aṣyāni 'amdan wa ini'zāli

Wa mā kānat nabīyan qaṭ unthā wa lā 'abda wa shakhṣa dhū ifti'āli[68]

In English, we might represent those verses as:

The matter of the mi'raj is true for there are excellent reports in its attestation.

Intercession is the only hope for the committer of mountain-like desecration.

And the prophets are safe from intentional disobedience and from God's isolation.

Never has a prophet been a woman—nor a slave nor a teller of fabrication!

However infelicitous, my translation preserves a sense of the rhyme and rhythm of al-Ushi's poem. Akhund Darweza translates these verses into a Pashto that loses these formal similarities and opts instead for lucid clarifications. In English, we might translate Akhund Darweza's Pashto translation of the poem as:

The Prophet's mi'raj is both true and it happened in a waking body.

It was not a dream, and it was not fancy. This report is apparent now.

Whoever does not attest to the Prophet's mi'raj in body is an infidel.

All prophets are kept safe from minor and major sins. They do not sin with intention.

The prophets in their prophethood—never has there been a woman . . . nor a slave. Whoever attests to this is in apostasy and is lying. . . .[69]

My interest in this section is not with its doctrinal content, though it certainly suggests an image of Akhund Darweza as concerned with consolidating a guarded and stable notion of who can claim prophetic inspiration and divine blessing. Rather, this passage warrants consideration for how its translation choices reveal a broader ideology of language and form in Akhund Darweza's thinking. He eliminates the polyvalence of the "truth" (haqq) of the mi'raj (the Prophet Muhammad's nighttime ascension to heaven), explaining that the mi'raj's truth refers specifically to its nature as a corporeal and conscious event. In his emendations, Akhund Darweza sacrifices any formal resonances between his translation and al-Ushi's Arabic poem in order to promote doctrinal clarity. His translation of "Qaṣīdat bad' al-amālī" and other Arabic works suggest, therefore, that he aims for a Pashto of transparency and self-denial. Pashto is a means to communicate Arabic ideas, nothing more. The formal qualities of Arabic remain stuck in the Arabic for, ultimately, those formal qualities do not matter to the Pashto that Akhund Darweza is creating. As his introduction in *The Treasure Chest* suggests, he has written in "Afghan" because "the master of darkness has written in Afghan."[70] This was simply a strategic decision, in other words, that Akhund Darweza made to counter the works of Bayazid Ansari.

If we think back to the relationship struck between Bayazid Ansari's *The Best Exposition* and the Qur'an, we can already see a radically divergent semiotic ideology. In Bayazid's texts, the *materiality* of language—its shape, its rhyme, its letters—effectively stitches together the linguistic capacity of a saint, his or her interior development, and a cosmos fully saturated with language and signs. Bayazid therefore crafts an appropriately intimate style of translation and imitation that emphasizes the aural and visual continuities of *The Best Exposition* and the Qur'an. In Arzani's ghazals, likewise, we saw Arzani's playful use of Arabic phrases as "totems" embedded among his Pashto words and among his declarations of Pashto's blessedness or even divinity. In both of these examples, Bayazid and Arzani approach the *meaning* of a word as—at most—a single aspect of the grander potency inherent in the word. Akhund Darweza, on the other hand, forgoes any literary games that might compromise the precision of his translation of the *meaning* and the *signified* content. The formal elements of the *signifier* are, if anything, a potential impediment to truth.

As the next chapter will explore, an epistemological anxiety strikes at Akhund Darweza. He fears the anarchy possible when knowledge can be gained from the Unseen realm, delivered through dreams, traced in the shape and form of letters, uncovered in the materiality of the world, and spoken by human tongues deemed angelic. His God is the God of oaths and guarantees who guides human knowledge by instructing humans to reject all knowledge that is not vouchsafed by traditions of learning and lineages of careful, disciplined knowing. Outside of Sufi or juridical initiatory lineages, how could a word be true in itself? Only the Qur'an is an exception; only its language bears the truth without authorization by the guardians of orthodoxy.

So it is that Akhund Darweza's critiques of the Roshaniyya drag a vision of Pashto in their wake. Akhund Darweza's Pashto clears away and empties that which language had accrued in the Roshani imagination. Akhund Darweza's Pashto is clear, blunt, and repetitive: it rejects any notion that language can undo or overturn what tradition (as he understands it) has taught. As he turns to specific critiques of the Roshaniyya, he rejects the possibility of a Pashto wahy-revelation, he rejects the reliability of inspired Pashto verses (ilham), he rejects the idea that dhikr phrases alone can purify the spirit of a human, he rejects that any insights from the Unseen realm can abrogate what the jurists have determined to be God's shari'a, and he rejects as absurd that *The Best Exposition* has any of the linguistic potency that is properly confined to the Qur'an. In another section of *The Treasure Chest*, Akhund Darweza instructs on the proper rules for *qirā'a*—the proper recitation and vocalization of the Qur'an—and he insists that Qur'anic reading without knowledge of proper pronunciation is an illicit activity ensuring a place in hell.[71] As this critique of the Roshaniyya unfolds, Akhund Darweza's Pashto is seen to be one that disavows the significance of its own form, shape, rhythm, and materiality. The grounds for truth in language are found in the preserved lineages of scholars and traditions. Language, in itself, is inconsequential unless we are discussing the Qur'an. The importance of *lineage* in securing linguistic truth will be a central theme in the following chapter on Afghan genealogies.

Despite his critiques of the Roshani linguistic errors, Akhund Darweza continues to meet his Roshani enemies on linguistic grounds. In Akhund Darweza's account of a debate with a Roshani disciple, the disciple argues that demonstration of God's immersive, participatory, and encompassing oneness finds proof in a Qur'anic verse quoted by Bayazid: "Innaka 'alá kulli shay'in muḥīṭun" (And truly You envelop all things). Akhund Darweza rejects Bayazid's ontological scheme in its entirety, but the means of his rejection bears notice. He contends that Bayazid has mistaken his citation. Akhund Darweza does *not* criticize Bayazid for the shift from *innahu* to *innaka* ("Truly, *He* envelops all things" vs. "Truly, *You* envelop all things"). Rather, Akhund Darweza decries Bayazid's replacement of the Arabic word *ma'* (with) with *'alá* (upon)—a blunder we might represent in English as the transformation of "God surrounds all things" into "God envelops all things." The shift is from an emphasis upon God's expansive omnipotence to an emphasis upon the immersion and participation of being in God. Curiously, Akhund Darweza's version of the verse ("Innahu maʿ kulli shay'in muḥīṭun"), like the version attributed to Bayazid's citation, is not found in the Qur'an as we have it standardized today. Rather, verse 54 of surah 41, *Fuṣṣilat*, reads: "Innahu bi-kulli shay'in muḥīṭun" (God surrounds all things). Regardless of whose Qur'anic citation more closely accords with the contemporary, standard edition of the Qur'an to which we often attribute a transhistorical prevalence, it is Akhund Darweza's representation of Bayazid's error that concerns us. Bayazid's fault does not solely lie in the theological distortion of this substitution of prepositions. Rather, Akhund Darweza notes that Bayazid's version of the verse includes an extra letter. *ʿAlá* is indeed one letter greater than *maʿ* in Arabic. Akhund Darweza writes that the Qur'an has 1,213,330 letters. The heresy of Bayazid's Qur'anic citation reveals itself through its violation of Qur'anic linguistics: it is simply a letter too far for Akhund Darweza.

An excerpt from a final section of *The Treasure Chest* confirms Akhund Darweza's concern for the linguistic sins of the Roshaniyya: the section called *The Alphabet Book* (Alif-nāma). In introducing his alphabet, the akhund decries those *hurufi*s who attribute to individual letters concealed meanings. Perhaps Akhund Darweza intends an oblique reference to Bayazid or perhaps he is generally criticizing lettrist thinkers following in the rich Islamic tradition exemplified by the Hurufis.[72] As a response to this abuse of letters, Akhund Darweza provides his own alphabet "that accords with shariʿa per the request of my friends" in which each letter of the alphabet serves as mnemonic for a single, standardized meaning.[73] The letter *alif* stands for *Allah*:

> The name of God is free of points. Whoever is engaged with the Name is wayfaring toward God. Every wayfarer who goes in accordance with the shariʿa [also goes] with Qur'an and the hadith. [The letter *alif*] is an exemplar for the world. Whosoever is in opposition to these two [i.e., Qur'an and hadith] lives in disbelief. Whoever is not straight upon the path is lost, no matter their miracles and unveilings.[74]

Were we to find this passage in the works of Bayazid, Arzani, or the numerous Hurufis, Nuqtavis, and lettrists of the premodern period, the visual straightness of the letter *alif* would be a compelling demonstration of the oneness of God and the necessity of a direct path to God. Written on a page, *alif* is a single, vertical line. In the linguistic imaginations we have explored, it beckons the viewer to witness its form and materiality as intimately, irrevocably, and essentially bound to its semantic meaning as the first letter of *Allah*. But such iconicity of interpretation is absent in Akhund Darweza's alphabet. The letters are but opportunities to reiterate conventional theological themes of God's absolute transcendence, the centrality of the shari'a, and so forth. The letters of his alphabet book, in other words, do not shimmer with a potency all their own—they are convenient and conventional mnemonic tools for Akhund Darweza's project of cultivating unambiguous theological norms, nothing more.

Conclusion

Pashto literature quickly moved beyond the Roshaniyya. New forms of Pashto verse, new genres of Pashto expression, and new imaginations of Pashto as a language of writing and literature eclipsed the theurgical hymns of Arzani and the shots, bursts, and flashes of Bayazid's revelatory Pashto that was grafted to three other languages in a quest for the anti-Babel language of God. In the wake of these early efforts, some poets continued to find inspiration in the Roshaniyya. Dawlat Lohani, for instance, wrote ghazals and quatrains that reverentially invoked Bayazid's teachings of God's immersive being.[75] Mirza Khan Ansari was a descendant of Bayazid who composed subtle ghazals on beloved Sufi themes.[76] The moth, for instance, that flies into the annihilating candle flame it so desires is a recurring image in Mirza's poetry. These works, however, possess neither the strangeness of Bayazid's revelatory language nor the commitment to Pashto's divinity that Arzani suggests. In fact, they represent a shift away from the radical messianism of the Roshaniyya to participation in the much more familiar and acceptable tradition of the unity of being (wahdat al-wujud) often associated with Ibn 'Arabi, among many others. Outside of these few inheritors of the Roshaniyya, we find some prominent poets who joined Akhund Darweza in rejecting the Roshani model. Most famous of all is Khushhal Khan Khatak: the Pashtun warrior whose rebellious actions landed him in a Mughal prison for decades. He composed anthems to the wild, relentless spirit of the "Afghans"—a spirit that had been compromised by their internecine rivalries and willingness to submit to the Mughal emperors. Like Akhund Darweza, he cast Bayazid and the Roshaniyya as heretics, and he lamented that their corrupt beliefs had rent any possibility of a unified resistance to Mughal control. This rejection, however, suggests that Pashto verse still bore the imprint of the Roshaniyya even as it sought to leave their memories.[77] The family of Khushhal Khan Khatak wrote histories and genealogies of the Afghans that expanded Pashto into genres that neither Akhund Darweza nor the

Roshaniyya had explored in Pashto.[78] After Khushhal, we find the ghazals of Rahman Baba—a Sufi poet whose lines still adorn tombs and shops of Peshawar or are written with a finger on a dusty truck window.[79]

While the literature of the Roshaniyya was spurned by all but a few curious individuals of the late seventeenth century, Akhund Darweza's texts continued to circulate throughout the Afghan diaspora of South Asia: from Kandahar and Kabul across the Khyber to Peshawar and then to Rampur, Tonk, and Patna in northern India and down to Hyderabad in the south. *The Treasure Chest* remained an anchor point for Afghan courts in their understanding of Sunni religiosity, and his Pashto prose served as a model and source for the composition of religious texts and genealogies throughout the eighteenth century.[80] Unsurprisingly, the section of Akhund Darweza's work that explicitly criticizes the Roshaniyya (in all their linguistic heresies of improper Qur'anic recitation and false claims to revelation) is frequently absent from later manuscript copies of *The Treasure Chest*. Though the work was penned as a polemic, the heretic under attack had been forgotten by later readers.

The argument of this chapter has not been that Arzani and Akhund Darweza are the progenitors of Pashto literature or the daring litterateurs who spurred the process of Pashto vernacularization. Almost certainly, the boundary between Pashto literature and Persian literature—and between written Pashto literature and oral Pashto recitations of poetry and didactic storytelling—was an exceedingly porous boundary. Almost certainly, there were numerous other examples of figures such as Arzani and Akhund Darweza who experimented with Pashto writing but whose manuscripts have been lost to us. Arzani and Akhund Darweza do not offer us a comprehensive grasp of Pashto's development as a written language; rather, the poet and the polemicist gesture toward the ideological breadth of early Pashto writing. Pashto writing was imagined in competing, agonistic ways and against violently different cosmological and semiotic horizons.

In attending to the imaginations and ideologies of Arzani's and Akhund Darweza's writing, we have found that some common assumptions on vernacular literatures do not assist our understanding of these early Pashto texts. There appears to be little evidence that their Pashto writing emerged from an instinct to inscribe a Pashto language for an Afghan people. The logic of ethnic monolingualism that animates many theories of the vernacular fails in this case. With the poems of Khushhal Khan Khatak, it is possible to find such a linguistic ideology, for he indeed clamors for *one* language for *one* people that could form a unified political community on *one* land.[81] Critically, however, Khushhal's imagination of Pashto is just one among many. As we tightly bind vernacular literature to a single ethnic community and *explain* vernacularization as an expression of ethnic self-consciousness, we lose sight of the splendid array of Pashtos that emerged in the wake of the Roshaniyya. Their devotees, inheritors, and critics explored—more than we have allowed—far stranger and more elusive ways of imagining Pashto and its capacity to stitch humans to their God.

I am not suggesting, however, that the Pashto texts of Arzani and Akhund Darweza existed apart from questions of identity, sociality, and the conditions of belonging as an *Afghan*. To the contrary, I urge that we follow the paths set by Farina Mir and Christian Novetzke in approaching vernacular and sociality as co-constitutive elements of our story. The audiences for these sources find their footing in the warp and woof of these linguistic imaginations. Arzani's ghazals and Akhund Darweza's polemics are beckoning particular communities and social relationships into being—communities and socialities that we can recognize in retrospect as *Afghan*. For Arzani, this was a community of the initiated, spiritual elite that could engage Pashto as a language of revelatory secret-sharing—all guarded by the ethics of Sufi master-disciple relationships. Akhund Darweza's unsparing Pashto prose became a tool for him to hollow out and collapse the exaggerated reverence the Roshaniyya had shown to the formal qualities of language. His was a Pashto that cast Pashto-readers and listeners as a marginalized, lesser people in need of paternalistic education and protection from common Hurufi heresies. The consolidation of these nascent, competing notions of *Afghan* identity is the focus of the next chapter, in which we begin to see the amorphous, fluid term *Afghan* gain increasing specificity in attempts to narrate the descent of the Afghans from "the Tall King"—*Malik Talut* of the Qur'an's second sura—who is typically identified as the Biblical King Saul.

So what of Pashto's emergence as a language of writing? I would like to conclude this chapter by urging us to see it as a risk—as a wager placed on certain formations of language, community, and conceptions of God. Arzani and Bayazid wagered on the breadth of the Pashto alphabet to contain and fulfill the presence of God that spilled over the limits of Arabic and Persian. Those languages abide in a Pashto that exceeds the limits of other languages; it is Pashto pearls that are left amid the ash after the fiery annihilation of God's secrets are loosed upon our language. Arzani and Bayazid wagered on the spiritual authority and revelation made possible by turning to a medium of communication that would *reduce* and limit their potential audience. They gave up the regional legibility of Persian in a bid for God's language.

Akhund Darweza, to the contrary, risked meeting the Roshaniyya on their chosen theological terrain. He severely rejected their linguistic imaginations, but he did so by acknowledging their first premise: how we use Pashto is how we position ourselves in the cosmos. Language is metaphysics—even for Akhund Darweza's Pashto that seeks to disavow its own formal significance.

5 / The Vanguard of Disbelief: Afghan Ethnicity and Temporality after the Roshaniyya

When Saul set out with his armies, he said,
"God will test you by a river.
Whoever drinks the water will not be one of mine."

—QUR'AN 2:249

In the mid-nineteenth century, Muhammad Hayat composed a genealogy of the Afghans that narrated the proliferation of different tribes and communities from a shared ancestor named Afghana, a son of Saul, the king of Israel and Judah.[1] As was common in the sixteenth to nineteenth centuries, Muhammad Hayat used the term *Afghan* to designate a people typically referred to as *Pashtun, Pathan*, or *Pukhtun* in contemporary discourse. Like the many other Afghan genealogies from the early seventeenth century through the late nineteenth century, Muhammad Hayat's account is *etiological*—it offers explanations for the putatively distinctive features of the Afghans by appealing to a distant past. Such etiological genealogies argue that Afghans owe their tall stature to their ancestor King Saul, renowned for his imposing height. It is their descent from King Saul (called *malik talut* in the Qur'an) that explains the Afghans' unusual custom of calling local leaders and elders by the title of *malik*, the Arabic word for "king." Their abilities in war are owing to their genealogical connection to the famous general of Muhammad's community, Khalid ibn Walid.[2] Their "tribal" fragmentation is attributable to a curse laid upon them by Muhammad himself.[3]

What distinguishes Hayat's account from other such genealogies, however, is that he also provides an etiology for these etiological genealogies themselves. Why did these texts begin to appear in the early seventeenth century with such frequency? According to Hayat, the genre of the "Afghan genealogy" emerged in response to an accusation that the blood of demons flowed in the Afghans.[4] As Hayat's story goes, a Safavid ambassador to the Mughal court sneered at the presence of an Afghan courtier. The ambassador declared the Afghans to be the children born of an unholy bargain: the wicked king Zuhak had offered a thousand virgin women to a "phantom of terrific aspect" so that the demon would ignore Zuhak's kingdom. A legendary and monstrous figure found in the Persian *Book of Kings* ("Shāh-nāmah"), Zuhak was feared both for his cruelty and for the two snakes that grew directly from his shoulders and fed on the brains of Zuhak's victims. Despite his own monstrosity, Zuhak was revolted by the demon's spawn and banished the infants and their mothers to "remote deserts and plains." And so the Afghans came to be.[5]

The Safavid diplomat's genealogy of the Afghans was, in short, unflattering. Hayat tells us that it was in response to this slander that Afghans began to inscribe and circulate the true history of their descent from King Saul through to the famed hero Qais, whose sons became the progenitors of the various Afghan tribes of Hayat's own time.

I have found no previous mention of the specific details of Hayat's story before the nineteenth century, but the intention behind his story resonates with the goals of this chapter: to examine the emergence of Afghan genealogies in the wake of the Roshaniyya's messianic challenge. As Hayat's own story suggests, these genealogies tethered notions of peoplehood to time in an environment of competitive genealogical narratives. They sought to map seventeenth-, eighteenth-, and nineteenth-century topographies of belonging by appealing to temporalities—to articulations and experience of time—that included prophets, kings, messiahs, recursive pasts, and anticipations of an eschatological moment yet to come. While the term *Afghan* was often a vague descriptor in the fifteenth and sixteenth centuries, out of these texts came notions of being Afghan that were more detailed, more reified, and more firmly anchored to temporal imaginations (however contested these imaginations may be).

We find in these texts an articulation of "the Afghans" that resembles what we might call an *ethnicity*. At the same time, we see that genealogies—and even the notion of peoplehood that they inscribe—elude the contemporary category of ethnicity. These genealogies are irrevocably techniques of temporality and its religious imagining. Like Bayazid's messianic language, these genealogies frame peoplehood as a means to play with the stuff of the past and future and as a way to think through God and knowledge of God. Can our contemporary appeal to the notion of ethnicity contain the imaginations of being and becoming Afghan that we find in these genealogies, so shot through as they are with temporal, semiotic, and theological contests?

Central to this exploration is the work of a polemicist we met in the previous chapter: Akhund Darweza's *Recollection of the Pious and the Wicked* ("Tadhkirat al-abrār wa-'l-ashrār," hereafter *The Pious and the Wicked*), composed circa 1611 CE, which includes one of the earliest extant Afghan genealogies. Akhund Darweza explicitly presents this text as a rejection of the Roshaniyya. But why? If an Afghan genealogy was the answer to the Roshaniyya, then what was the question? Why would a genealogy that traces Afghans back to King Saul serve as an effective response to the seething revelations of Bayazid's *The Best Exposition* and the Roshani community that coalesced around this vernacular messiah? Seen as texts that tether temporal imaginations to notions of belonging and identity, genealogies may be a more direct response to the messianic language of the Roshaniyya than we at first presume. Indeed, one of my arguments is that revelation and "ethnicity" are tightly bound together in these debates between the Roshaniyya and their critics.

While the focus of this chapter is on Akhund Darweza's genealogy of the Afghans, he was by no means alone in adopting the term *Afghan* as part of an agonistic rejection of Roshani messianism. The first part of this chapter will assess this term and how its use became an aspect of the Mughal suppression of the Roshaniyya. The term *Afghan* and the histories of the "Afghans" gained greater definition as a part of an imperial project of wrestling the Afghan highlands under control. Following this, we shift from the Mughal court and turn to Akhund Darweza's *The Pious and the Wicked*. How did he perceive the theological danger of the Roshaniyya such that a genealogy could serve as a response? The answer lies with the epistemological anxiety that motivates Akhund Darweza's writing. He fears the anarchic possibilities of knowledge unmoored from lineages that carefully preserve a linear temporality, whether those lineages be Sufi or ethnic. He fears, in other words, the chaos of knowledge that could emerge from Bayazid's messianic claims of repeating the prophetic moment of Muhammad. Finally, this chapter assesses Akhund Darweza's decision to pair an Afghan genealogy with an image of the Afghans on the Day of Resurrection. While previous scholars have approached the genealogies of the Afghans as a manifestation of the putative Afghan characteristic of valuing ethnic and tribal descent—as if these genealogies were the discursive equivalent of endogamous marriage—this chapter suggests that these genealogies are far more elusive to our contemporary habits of mind.[6] Descent, for Akhund Darweza, is as much an attempt to shape and understand the apocalyptic future as it is to explain the boundaries of Afghan blood and belonging. In Akhund Darweza's imagination, etiological explanations of peoplehood and eschatology resonate in profound ways.

This chapter seeks to tell the story of how a notion of Afghanness developed, and how quick we have been to pin this Afghanness as ethnicity, thus masking the theological, temporal, and semiotic stakes of something stranger and more elusive to our habits of thought.

A Brief History of the Afghans

In the introduction to this book, I recounted the story of the Roshaniyya as we usually find it: a story of some Afghans who drew upon marginal—or even "extreme"—Islamic mystical and eschatological traditions to mobilize other Afghans in a proto-nationalist insurrection against the political control of the Mughal Empire.[7] The work of the previous chapters was to find an approach that casts a different light upon the words and imaginations of the Roshani pursuit of God's language. The supposed Pashto / Afghan vernacular of these proto-nationalists is woven into seething multilingual hymns and offers forth these words as emblems of divine presence and messianic time. The words of the Roshaniyya do not seek to represent an ethnic people as much as they strive to create and constitute a community of light, of revelation, and of tongues touched by the divine. The dhikr could transform an individual, and the stories of the doubled saint could become the narrative grounds for staging a messianic community. We lose sight of these aspects of the Roshaniyya when the light we shine catches only the proto-nationalist, the ethnic, the *Afghan*.

But aside from what the "proto-nationalist" story obscures and erases, we face more elemental problems: What does "Afghan" even mean? As it circulates through our archives, is there a consistent usage that would allow us to plot the Roshaniyya in an "Afghan" history?

In a word: no. At the very least, we can identify three major periods in the history of the term *Afghan*.[8] The variance of the term's usage is revealing; Afghanness is not a thing but something that happened and continues to happen. It is always embedded in dynamic social contexts and shaped for divergent political purposes. In the earliest period (ca. 500–1525 CE), the term was a vague and amorphous Persian cypher to identify the inhabitants of the mountainous regions from Kabul to Swat, from Peshawar to Kandahar, and other neighboring regions. There are possible connections between the term *Afghan* and a third-century Sassanian inscription mentioning the *abgan*. A sixth-century Sanskrit astronomical text likewise notes the existence of the *avagana*. The tenth-century Persian geography *Boundaries of the World* ("Ḥudūd al-ʿālām") includes an early extant use of the term *afghan*, as do later Ghaznavid and Timurid histories.[9] What is important to note, however, is that these early uses suggest no specificity—no sense of who these people were and how they may have described themselves nor appreciation for possible internal differences despite the intriguing etymological connections between *afghan, abgan,* and *avagana*.[10] The term *Afghan* as used in this period aims not to represent a specific community living in the Afghan highlands. It is but an old shorthand: those who live over there, beyond the mountains' horizon.

In the Mughal era before British colonial encounters along the Afghan frontier (ca. 1525–1800 CE), the term undergoes a rapid transformation in usage—and it is this period which concerns us in this chapter. Initially, the term was used by Mughal chroniclers to refer to the Lodi and Suri enemies of the Mughals as well as to the rebellious people of the Afghan highlands.[11] By the early seventeenth century, self-identifying Afghan courtiers in the Mughal Empire began to reclaim this term through genealogies and ghazal poetic collections. For most of this period, the term *Afghan* operated as a Persian synonym for the term *Pashtun*. During the period of the Roshani movement (ca. 1575–1625 CE), however, the word held a number of competing ideological and theological valences that we will explore for the remainder of this chapter.

The third period in the use of the term *Afghan* corresponds to nationalist projects and their development in connection with British imperial discourses. During the latter half of the nineteenth century, as the British Empire fought a series of wars with Afghans under the leadership of the Barakzai family, *Afghanistan* emerged as an aspirationally independent and sovereign nation-state. Nationalist discourses during the time of Abdur Rahman Khan (the amir of Afghanistan from 1880 to 1901), Habibullah Khan (r. 1901–19), and Amanullah Khan (r. 1919–29), for example, developed a notion of the Afghan as fiercely independent—and this was a period in which the ruling Pashtun elite frequently conflated Afghan and Pashtun.[12] British imperial discourses, on the other hand, frequently reiterated the characteristics of Mughal descriptions of the Afghans: unruly, chaotic, and fanatical. The "frontier fanatic" developed into a stock character and the most consistent figure to represent "the Afghan" in the British imperial imagination.[13] Though many Pashtun leaders have continued to uphold a Pashtun social hegemony within Afghanistan throughout the nineteenth, twentieth, and twenty-first centuries (including the current Taliban government), the term *Afghan* has politically broadened to include, theoretically, all citizens of Afghanistan regardless of their ethnic identification. Hazara, Tajik, Pashtun, Uzbek, and others—all are legally "Afghan" within the state.[14]

So when we discuss the Roshaniyya as part of "Afghan history," what does that modifier suggest? Whose perspective is smuggled into this terminology without our realizing it? The usage of the term *Afghan* in the Mughal era—this chapter's primary concern—was entangled with imperial authority and the suppression of the Roshaniyya. Though Afghan genealogists and courtiers attempted to reclaim "Afghan" for their own political projects, the process of defining this term in the late sixteenth and early seventeenth centuries contributed to hegemonic systems of imperial control, as we will see.

We can begin exploring the Mughal-era meanings of "Afghan" with a denial. According to *The Book of States*, an infant Bayazid Ansari was escorted by his uncle Khudadad from Jalandhar in the Punjab to the mountains around Kaniguram in present-day Waziristan, Pakistan.[15] Bayazid and Khudadad's northwestern path crossed the army of Babur in 1525 as it invaded India from Kabul to establish what would become the Mughal Empire.[16] When Mughal soldiers stopped Khudadad and Bayazid, they questioned Khudadad, "Is the child Afghan?" "No, he is Ansari."[17] A revealing response: Khudadad feared the implications of identifying as Afghan.

Though *The Book of States* is possibly projecting a later anxiety about being Afghan back onto an early sixteenth-century event, this anecdote captures the connotations of "Afghan" during the reigns of Babur, Humayun, Akbar, and Jahangir. The armies of Babur wrested political control from the excesses of a failing "Afghan" Lodi dynasty—or so the story goes when retold in Mughal chronicles of the middle to late sixteenth century. As Raziuddin Aquil has argued, the Mughal historians were compelled to represent the Afghans with particular hostility, for Mughal rule was rooted in part in the appropriation of Lodi and Suri techniques and institutions of governance.[18] Babur's son and heir, Humayun, temporarily lost control over much of his father's domain. As Humayun's troubled reign attested, there was no guarantee of Mughal sovereignty, and the possibility of an Afghan revanche endured. The Mughal chroniclers did their part to address this concern by engaging in a process of discursive vulgarization of the so-called Afghans.[19] In place of cunning, magnanimity, or prudence, the irredentist Afghans of Mughal chronicles seized and held their power through the locust-like numbers of their wild warriors that spilled from the highlands under the command of fanatical warlords.

Though motivated by the Mughal court's rivalry with its Lodi and Suri enemies, the vulgarization of the Afghans is clearly evident in Mughal accounts of the Roshaniyya. While Mughal chronicles do not record details of the Mughal-Roshaniyya conflict during Bayazid's lifetime, there are substantial accounts of the conflict as it continued under the leadership of Bayazid's son Jalal al-Din.[20] Known widely as Jalala—and known by the Mughals as Jalala-yi tariki, or Jalala of the Dark—Bayazid's son did not initially continue his father's hostilities with the Mughals. Rather, our various sources agree that Jalala visited Emperor Akbar's court in supplication and friendship.[21] Akbar's court was a mobile one, and as it moved northwest in a 1581 effort to suppress a challenge to the throne from Akbar's brother Mirza Hakim (governing in Kabul), Akbar received Jalala and a host of Roshani devotees.[22] Echoing the incident of the infant Bayazid, the Roshaniyya in Akbar's court denied that they were Afghans at all and had no meaningful tribal affiliation: they were simply Roshani.[23]

However friendly this rapprochement between Jalala and Akbar was, hostilities reemerged in 1586—and the Roshaniyya became "Afghans" in the Mughal chronicles. In *The Generations of Akbar* ("Ṭabaqāt-i akbārī"), the Mughal chronicler Khwaja Nizam al-Din presents the conflict as one between the Mughals and "Afghans" under the leadership of Jalala.[24] The Mughals desired to secure the Khyber Pass after it had been plundered, and so Akbar dispatched Raja Birbal and other generals to address the "haughty" Afghans in the passes and to "uproot the thorn of turbulence."[25] The first attempt to control the Khyber ended in disaster for the Mughal armies. Raja Birbal recklessly advanced into the mountains and led the Mughals into a hellish trap. Raja Birbal's army stubbornly continued until dusk, when

> [the] army reached a defile, the heights of which on every side were covered with Afghans. Arrows and stones were showered down upon the troops in the narrow pass, and in the darkness and in the narrow defile men lost their path, and perished in recesses of the mountain. A terrible defeat and slaughter followed. Nearly eight thousand men were killed, and Raja Birbal, who fled for his life, was slain.[26]

Though Jalala eluded capture and killing until the year 1596 CE, Jalala's initial victory—stunning as it was—was the only significant loss for Akbar's campaign in the region. With new leadership, the military efforts against Jalala and the Roshaniyya were successful in opening the Khyber Pass. Apparently satisfied with the strengthened military presence and the security promised through the construction of numerous forts, Akbar returned his court to Lahore in April 1586, thirteen months after his arrival in Attock.[27] More significant than the military details is the emergence of a discursive transition in which the Roshaniyya *become Afghan* in the chronicles of the Mughals as the hostilities between the Roshaniyya and the Mughals intensify.

As noted, when Akbar's court wound north to repel Mirza Hakim's rebellion in 1581, the emperor welcomed Jalala. A third voice at this courtly encounter—the voice of Father Antonio Monserrate—confirms how the term *Afghan* functioned partially as a vague descriptor of the inhabitants of the Sulaiman Mountains and partially as an accusation of chaotic, anti-Mughal hostility.[28] Monserrate was a Portuguese Jesuit who joined Akbar's court, debated such topics as the signs of the End of the World with Akbar, and recorded his observations. His travelogue comments briefly on Jalala's visit (describing him as a son of a heretic), but it is his other comments on the Afghans that are most relevant.

When describing the diversity of Akbar's cavalry, Monserrate claims that there were fifty thousand riders, who included

> Mongols, some Persians, other Turquimanni, Chacattaei, Osbequii, Arachosii, Balochii, Patnanei, Indians and Gedrosii. There were Musalmans and also Hindus, in whom he put a great deal of confidence. Many Parthians, Arii and Paropanisadae also came to reinforce the royal army.[29]

Monserrate relies upon Greco-Roman geographical terms, but, whatever the provenance of his lexicon, Monserrate is recognizing and naming distinct identities. The Arachosii came from Arachosia around Kandahar; the Patnanei were Pathans, a term that Monserrate uses to refer to the onetime residents of Swat who migrated to India; the Parthians could refer to those who came from the northwestern regions of present-day Afghanistan; the Arii named those of Herat; and the Paropanisadae came from the region once known as Gandhara in the Peshawar Valley that would have been near Monserrate and Akbar's place of conversation by the Indus River near Attock. Later, Monserrate describes a peace brokered by Akbar between rival "Delazacquian chiefs," or Dilazak Pashtuns as they are typically named today.[30] In other texts for other purposes, these horsemen—Kandaharis, Pathans, Parthians, Heratis, Peshawaris, Dilazaks—might all be known as Afghan. The powerful gaze of the emperor casts a canopy of order, however, and thus these "ethnic" and regional differences proliferate with a careful, managerial precision. Incorporated into the court's military order, they have specificity and distinction. They are not Afghan, for that refers not to these soldiers of empire but rather to the recalcitrant ones in the highlands who walk the edges of order and chaos.

Though Monserrate describes the provenance of Akbar's cavalry as it gathered in Lahore and Peshawar, so-called Afghans only appear in Monserrate's recollections when the court of Akbar and his cavalry march across the Khyber. On this western vector, the Jesuit's recollections drift toward the uncanny and mysterious, and he describes various Afghan communities in ever-stranger ways. He first scoffs at a story that a stone bears the handprint of 'Ali, the son-in-law of the Prophet Muhammad.[31] He puzzles over the ruins of "a city of slaves," and then gazes upon the ruins of another city he calls Landighana. He comments on Landighana:

> Stories are told about its ancient inhabitants, resembling those which are told about the Amazons. It is said that the stronghold used to be occupied by women, who waged war on the surrounding tribes. In order to keep up their numbers they attacked and carried off travelers. Boy-babies were killed or exposed; girls were brought up and trained to arms. They were finally conquered and driven out, but they have left their name in these ruins. In reality, fables apart, a band of wicked women must have lived there and given their name to the place: as sometimes happens with fugitive slaves.[32]

It is during this journey through these traces of lost cities and legendary pasts that Monserrate uses the term *Afghan*—or "Aufgan," as we find it spelled in Monserrate's *Commentary*. The "Aufgans" are the desperate residents of this region around the Khyber who "live by agriculture" but are "miserably off for draught animals and ferry-boats."[33]

What analytical weight can we hoist upon the putative Afghan or Pashtun ethnic self-consciousness that previous scholars have identified as the explanation for the Roshaniyya's innovative use of Pashto and their violent conflict with Mughal armies? Issues of belonging, identity, and sociality are undeniably central to the Roshani pursuit of God's presence in language, but can those issues be named and understood as Afghan? Monserrate learned from his interlocutors that the Afghans were those who existed on the dangerous edges of the empire. They were an amorphous swarm of chaos and violence that required the order and substance that Akbar's presence gave to the realm. They belonged to the unknown and legendary. And so, in Mughal sources of the sixteenth and early seventeenth centuries, the Roshaniyya were *discredited* as Afghans. In this context, the term is not descriptive but polemical.

From roughly 1550 to 1620, therefore, the discursive record witnesses such invocations of the Afghans as swarming, as fissiparous, and as the masses outside of the ordering gaze of Emperor Akbar. The seventeenth century marks a change, however, and witnesses a reclamation project by Afghan courtiers in the Mughal Empire. As scholars such as Nile Green and Jos. J. L. Gommans have described, the courts of the Afghan diaspora throughout India sponsored the inscription of Afghan genealogies that traced Afghan origins to King Saul.[34] The most celebrated of these genealogies was Ni'mat Allah Harawi's *The Afghan Treasure Chest*

("Makhzan-i Afghānī"), but the King Saul narrative appears in nearly all narratives of Afghan ethnogenesis. Harawi's *The Afghan Treasure Chest* and Akhund Darweza's *The Pious and the Wicked* were both composed circa 1611 CE; Khushhal Khan Khatak composed *The Book of the Turban* ("Dastar-nāmah") in 1665 CE; and Afzal Khan Khatak and Hafiz Rahmat Khan sponsored mid-eighteenth-century works called *The Bejeweled History* ("Tārīkh-i muraṣṣaʿ") and *The Summary of Lineages* ("Khulāṣat al-ansāb").[35] All of these works contain the King Saul narrative, as do the works commissioned by the British in the nineteenth century, such as the aforementioned *The Afghan Life* ("Ḥāyat-i Afghān") of Muhammad Hayat and Ahmed Ali's *The Pleasure of Reflections* ("Nuzhat al-ḍamāʾir").[36] Over the course of the nineteenth and twentieth centuries, British sources began to develop their own logic of tribe and ethnicity that incorporated translated Persian and Pashto genealogies into a recognizably British discourse of Afghan tribalism.[37]

These texts aimed to valorize the Afghan present through a story of a prophetic past. Niʿmat Allah begins his story of the Afghans with the preeternal prophetic light of Muhammad as it descended into the loins of Adam to be passed down through the generations.[38] The prophetic spark eventually fell to Malik Talut, the "Tall King" of the Qur'an who was identified as King Saul of Israel and Judah by the medieval Muslim community of Qur'an scholars.[39] Just before his death, Saul impregnated his wife with twins: Asif and Afghana. They became the highest-ranking members of Solomon's court. As the Israelites fell into eventual idolatry, God used the tyrant Nebuchadnezzar (Bukhtnasar) to punish the Israelites and push them into exile. The descendants of Afghana went in two directions: some went south to Mecca and others went east to the *koh-i sulayaman*: the Sulaiman Mountains that form the border of present-day Afghanistan and Pakistan.[40] From the descendants of Afghana in the Sulaiman Mountains came Qais, a warrior who joined his distant cousins in Mecca to fight alongside Muhammad. Qais had four sons—Sarban, Bet, Ghurghasht, and Karlan—whose descendants formed the four major tribal networks of Niʿmat Allah's era.[41]

As Green and Gommans argue, these types of genealogical efforts by Niʿmat Allah served to justify and celebrate the place of Afghans in the Mughal court and to reclaim the identification and the inheritance of being Afghan.[42] In the process, these texts shifted the logic of belonging. Green argues, for instance, that Lodi and Suri nobles had stitched together diverse networks of courtiers and Sufis through patronage and discipleship. Works such as *The Afghan Treasure Chest* recast networks of belonging as a matter of shared communal origins and biological descent.[43]

Whatever success the Afghan courtiers of the seventeenth and eighteenth centuries such as Niʿmat Allah had in rescuing the term Afghan from the denigrations of previous generations, European imperial scholars of the nineteenth century once again used the term Afghan to suggest the wildness of the frontier and the eternal unpredictability of a people of vigor, passion, and inherent fragmentation. As the French ethnologist James Darmesteter concluded, "The Afghans do not have a history, because anarchy has none."[44]

Like the scholars of the Mughal Empire before him, Dr. John Leyden used his 1812 account of the Roshaniyya to reify the wild anarchy of the Afghans. In this report, he describes the followers of Bayazid Ansari as Afghans who "live[d] and die[d] like beasts" and were "bred" for insurrection.[45] Leyden directs his ire toward Bayazid Ansari as a religious insurrectionist who prefigures the Sufis of Leyden's own time: Sufis who often led the anticolonial resistances on both sides of the Khyber. Leyden insists that it is the pirs—and not the more traditional legal and theological scholars of the *ʿulamā'* class—that have continuously activated, organized, and abused the anarchic racial energy of the Afghans. And so Leyden laments, "All calamities of the Afghans are attributed to these pirs."[46]

Leyden's report was widely circulated and cited frequently in the subsequent hundred years. Carl Ernst has analyzed it as an influential exemplar of British Orientalist approaches to Sufism across the globe.[47] Perhaps Leyden's most important reader of the nineteenth century, however, was Mountstuart Elphinstone, the Scottish author of *An Account of the Kingdom of Caubul*, produced after his 1809 mission to Shir Shah's court on behalf of the British Empire. It was Elphinstone's imagination of Afghanistan that, more than any other, shaped the epistemological approach of the British colonial officials to the region.[48] Elphinstone's most notable contribution lies in his assertion of the primacy of the Afghan tribe in Afghan society as a patrimonial genealogical construct. In other words, Elphinstone understands membership in an Afghan tribe as primarily a matter of biological descent. Moreover, as Bernard Hopkins has argued, Elphinstone's description of the Afghans is at heart "a philosophical one" in which the tribal society of the Afghans finds its place in a unified history of civilizations.[49] The centrality of tribal membership—as a matter of blood and kin—converges with Elphinstone's conceptualization of social evolution. To be tribal—as the Afghans "naturally" were—is to be less evolved civilizationally.

It was only after the 1809 Elphinstone mission to Shir Shah that the British administrators fully directed the colonial apparatuses of information and intelligence toward the nascent nation-state of Afghanistan.

Elphinstone's account was influential enough, however, that it shaped the molds into which British colonial officials poured their collected information. Hopkins has identified critical decisions that can be traced to Elphinstone's conceptualization of Afghan society and Pashtun tribes. Most importantly, the British generally understood "political power [as] ultimately rest[ing] with the Pashtun."[50] The developing nation of Afghanistan was a diverse one, but the Pashtuns emerged as the predominant representatives of Afghanness in the British literature. Having accepted the centrality of lineage and genealogical membership in Pashtun logics of power and authority, the British assumed all nontribal social formations to be inherently destabilizing and external to the proper functioning of a nineteenth-century nation—an idea seen clearly in Leyden's distrust of pirs and their archetypal predecessor, Bayazid Ansari.

Finally, Elphinstone and his colonial readers strove to "territorialize" the Pashtuns and fix their belonging to a determined geographical region.[51] Elphinstone's description of Bayazid Ansari exemplifies this territorializing logic. Though Elphinstone echoes Leyden in condemning Bayazid as an eclectic Sufi whose experience with Hindus and yogis perverted any adherence to orthodox Islam, Elphinstone adds an evocative postscript to his account of Bayazid. By way of conclusion, Elphinstone writes:

> Bauyazeed was a man of great genius, and his religion spread rapidly among the Berdooraunees [Durranis] till he was able to assemble armies, and to enter on a regular contest with the government: he was, however, at length defeated by the royal troops, and died of fatigue and vexation. His sons attempted to support his sect, in which they were long successful, but most of them were cut off; and two black rocks in the Indus are pointed out as the transformed bodies of Jellalloodeen and Kemaloodeen, the sons of the Peeree Taureek, who were thrown into the river by command of Aukhoond Derwezeh. Those rocks are still called Jellalleea and Kemauleea; and being situated near the whirlpools made by the junction of the river Caubul, they furnish a figure to the orthodox, who say that it is natural that boats should be dashed to pieces against the bodies of those heretics, who had already caused the shipwreck of so many souls.[52]

In Elphinstone's brief description, therefore, we see a remarkable instance of the imagined territorialization of the Afghans at work. Slain by the refutations of a true Muslim such as Akhund Darweza, the sons of Bayazid have become the very landscape itself, transmuted from the genealogical heirs of an errant heretic into the topographic manifestations of treachery and destruction. Neither the polemicist Akhund Darweza nor the hagiographer Mukhlis attributed responsibility for the deaths of Jalal al-Din (Jalala) and Kamal al-Din to Akhund Darweza. The actual history matters little, however, since the shipwrecking rocks of "Jellalloodeen and Kemaloodeen" are critical to Elphinstone's vision of the Roshaniyya. It is Elphinstone's account—and the imaginative structures he uses to frame his account—that guided British efforts to stubbornly understand the Afghans as emerging autochthonously from the rocky crags of the Afghan highlands, fully formed in their tribal identities and committed to a brutish, aggressive, and ultimately anarchic egalitarianism. Bayazid Ansari and his traces become—again—the material to construct a more general image of the "Afghan" in service of an imperial project. With the Afghan and his tribe as an extension of the natural world, it is the pir, as prefigured by Bayazid and his sons, that haunts this imagined geography as a looming danger. The pir holds the power to fanatically organize men and women around nontribal lines, and, in so doing, threatens the British imperial order.

What we have seen unfolding in these accounts is the increasing calcification of a particular image of the "Afghan." Bayazid Ansari's life became the useful historical proof for the inherence of Afghan irredentism since, in these accounts, he came to prefigure the treacherousness of a "heterodox" and "fanatical" religious leader among the Afghans. This was a process of *Afghan becoming* and of the *racialization* of the Afghans as a people with a particular essence and role in the hierarchies of empire.[53] It is a process, moreover, that converges with a rejection of the revelatory and temporal imaginations of the Roshaniyya. We should not merely approach the history of the term Afghan by sorting *what* this term means in different contexts: a blessed descendant of Saul in one context or a racist caricature in another. Rather, we need to attend to *how* an "Afghan history" of the Roshaniyya is just as shot through with metaphysical and imperial commitments as is a "messianic" history of the Roshaniyya. Genealogy and ethnicity are the techniques to smother the challenges of Roshani visions of language, time, and belonging. Confined to the unruly Afghans, the messianic revelations of Bayazid stall on the borders of ethnic difference. Even Niʿmat Allah's celebratory account of Afghan descent delimits Afghan religion to Afghans. When presented in their own terms as the universal speech of God, the Roshani revelations encroach upon the same constructions of kingship, sainthood, and divine language that infuse the Mughal court's self-understanding.

This convergence of genealogy and anti-Roshani polemic—of ethnicity and particular ideologies and metaphysics of language and belonging—

becomes much clearer in a closer look at the genealogical work of Akhund Darweza.

Epistemological Anxiety on the Afghan Frontier

The preceding sections of this chapter are a preamble for the striking work of Akhund Darweza. We met Akhund Darweza in the last chapter as we considered his Pashto *Treasure Chest of Islam* and the semiotic ideology that shaped its innovative use of Pashto. *Treasure Chest* was among the most-copied manuscripts in Pashto (and in Persian translation) throughout the Afghan diaspora of South Asia.[54] In all his works, Akhund Darweza presents himself as the archenemy of the Roshaniyya, the polemical scourge of Afghan heretics, and the rare defender of Sunni Islam. This self-valorization extends to a Persian work attributed to Akhund Darweza titled *Remembrance of the Pious and the Wicked.* Composed circa 1611 CE, *The Pious and the Wicked* is among the earliest extant genealogies of the Afghans.

Like Niʿmat Allah's contemporaneous *Afghan Treasure Chest*, Akhund Darweza's *Pious and the Wicked* traces the origins of the Afghans to Afghana, son of King Saul, and then from Afghana to the four brothers who became the progenitors of the four major tribal networks of the Afghans: Bet, Sarban, Gharghusht, and Karlan. And like Niʿmat Allah's account, Akhund Darweza's genealogical narrative pivots on a prophecy delivered by Muhammad to the Afghan supporters of his cause. Niʿmat Allah centers this part of the story on the legendary figure of Qais—the champion and leader of those Afghans of the Sulaiman Mountains who returned west to aid Muhammad's movement. In Niʿmat Allah's account, Muhammad received word from the angel Gabriel that the hero Qais should be known as ʿAbd al-Rashid Qais Pathan. Gabriel explains that *pathan/pahtan* is the term for the wood used to build the keel of a boat, and just so the Afghans will be the keel of the Muslim community.[55] In short, Niʿmat Allah's history presents Afghans as ceaseless and devoted monotheists from the time of Afghana until the seventeenth century.

Grimmer is the account of Akhund Darweza. He makes no mention of the figure of Qais, though he indeed presents the Afghans as the itinerant sons of Saul who left the Sulaiman Mountains to join Muhammad in the spread of Islam. Rather than being met with celebratory titles from Gabriel, however, Muhammad delivers a curse:

> The pearl-speaking tongue of Muhammad (*peace be upon him!*) said, "All the Afghans will be in Hell on the Day of the Resurrection."

> When the Afghans heard this, they became dejected and grief-stricken. They scattered in order to disperse their collectivity.[56]

Why does Akhund Darweza include this episode in his account of the descent of the Afghans? And how does this account of Muhammad's Afghan curse serve as a rebuttal to the Roshaniyya, as Akhund Darweza suggests at the beginning of *The Pious and the Wicked*?

I argue that Akhund Darweza conceptualizes Afghanness as irrevocably shot through with theological and temporal stakes—and thus the nature of "being Afghan" is irrevocably shot through with the heretical temptations and possibilities exemplified by Bayazid Ansari. The history of the Afghans dooms them to a present and a future of uncertainty, fragmentation, and misplaced fervor for would-be messiahs and claims of revelation. They are incarnations of the fickle nature of belief and learning. Akhund Darweza fears that *Afghanness* itself threatens the durability of Islamic traditions of knowledge—and thus a current of epistemological anxiety connects Akhund Darweza's Afghan genealogy to his polemics against the Roshaniyya. In his imagination, being Afghan and imitating the Qur'an are both threats to the very possibility of trustworthy knowledge.

The Pious and the Wicked is not just a genealogy and history of the origins of the Afghans: it is a three-part "remembrance" (*tadhkira*) that brackets the genealogy of the Afghans between a hagiographical celebration of Akhund Darweza's own master Sayyid 'Ali and a searing polemic against the Roshaniyya. From this structural perspective, the text's argument is clear: Afghans are suspended between two giants of religion. On one side, there is the pious Sayyid 'Ali inviting the Afghans into right practice, right faith, and right reliance upon authoritative transmissions of tradition. On the other side, Bayazid Ansari—the wicked archheretic—threatens to extinguish the Afghans' dim hopes for God's mercy. The Afghans are on the precipice of damnation, and Bayazid threatens to lure them fully across the "edge of disbelief" (*hadd-i kufr*).[57]

We can begin with Akhund Darweza's polemics against the Roshaniyya before connecting them back with his genealogy of the Afghans. For the akhund, the Roshaniyya are not the singular threat to orthodoxy throughout the Afghan highlands; more troublingly, they merely exemplify the heresy of the land.

Shaykh Nani, for example, polluted the Muhammadzai with heresies from the yogis (*jogīyān*) such as metempsychosis (*tanāsukh*) and libertinism (*ibāḥat*).[58] Pir Tayyib opposed the shari'a while preaching among the Yusufzai.[59] Mulla Mir articulated a cosmological vision in which a tent (*khayma*) with seventy thousand entrances (*darvaza*) exists above the sublime cosmic position of God's throne (*'arsh*).[60] Khwaja Khizr Afghan of Bajwara falsely claimed to have completed the *hajj* pilgrimage seven times, while Sarmast ("drunk-head") deemed forbidden musical practices to be halal.[61] Ironically, Akhund Darweza's catalogue of these and other religious villains offers an intriguing revelation: the Afghan highlands were an area of considerable spiritual eclecticism that served as the stage for encounters between intellectual and religious traditions associated with Iran, Central Asia, and India. Akhund Darweza's attempt to flatten the spiritual landscape reveals the variations within its topography.

There is an anxiety coursing through Akhund Darweza's *The Pious and the Wicked*: religious books err, Shi'is lie, devils whisper, scholars lapse, pirs self-aggrandize, and walis and saints corrupt. Akhund Darweza lives in highlands haunted by such claims, but it is Bayazid Ansari who earns particular opprobrium. As Akhund Darweza summarizes:

> Bayazid Ansari . . . attributed to himself lordship [*rubūbiyya*]—meaning: he claimed that he is the Guide [*hādī*] of the Lost, with the character [*ṣifat*] of the Prophet of the End of Time. This is damnation. If he called himself the "leader-astray of the believers," that title would be more appropriate! He abolished commands of the shari'a such as fasting, prayer, pilgrimage, almsgiving, and so on for the masses.[62]

The claim to possess the "character of the Prophet" is the primary sin in the akhund's polemic. Undergirding all the colorful accusations that Akhund Darweza levies against the Roshaniyya (some of which we will explore) is a persistent horror at the Roshani claim to sacred language from unseen realms. Akhund Darweza's anxiety is fundamentally a semiotic and epistemological one: there is simply no way to verify truth claims and revelations such as Bayazid's pseudo-prophecies outside of carefully maintained lineages of masters and disciples.

This anxiety is especially apparent as Akhund Darweza describes a religious experience endured by his own master, Sayyid 'Ali. As Sayyid 'Ali recounts, "In this spiritual state, I could neither speak nor draw breath. After a while, I became aware of the differences among the states."[63] Sayyid 'Ali was rare in this ability to distinguish true and false religious visions and states. As Sayyid 'Ali continues:

> It is known that when innovators and false claimers see a dream or hear a voice, they consider that to be an unveiling [*kashf*] or a miracle [*karāmat*], and they take themselves to be a saint [*wālī*] or to be connected to God, and through this they seek out fame among

> the people until they may achieve some status. This is but pure error. We seek refuge in God from that! They do not know that this is from the host of encounters with Satan. And to follow Satan in any and all ways is disbelief.[64]

The danger is clear; disembodied voices and dreams come as frequently from the devils of these worlds as from the angels. Akhund Darweza then cites a hadith of Muhammad to explain the process of divine communication with the world:

> When God the Majestic World-Holder desires to accomplish something on earth, He informs the bearers of the throne. The bearers of the throne deliver this news to other angels, and so this commandment passes from mouth to mouth among the angels. The devils, however, take flight and reach the heavens. If the fire of starlight hits them, they are burned to ash and flee away. If they find some refuge from star-fire, they cast those stolen words in the ears of saints [*awlīyā'*], both sleeping and awake.[65]

This hadith is not suggesting that communication with the Unseen realm is impossible for human beings; the devils and jinn who escape the star-fire do indeed whisper into the ears of men and women. Even more intriguingly, he is not suggesting that the jinn and devils report *false* content—these are the commands of God. Rather, the problem rests in the unreliability of such lines of communication. The jinn are devious precisely because their whispers *could* be the truth. So how could we trust the whispers of the jinn?

As Akhund Darweza comments upon the hadith, even Muslims are tempted by these secrets stolen among the stars:

> This happens often with yogis and those who are the vanguard of disbelief [*pīshvāyān-i kufr*], but some ignorant Muslims are also taken by this error and arrive at the edge of disbelief. They accept the speech of the jinn and then consider themselves famous: *I have news from the unseen!* They become pleased and they claim: *I am one of the people who have access to the hidden world!* They are merely following the jinn, and to follow the jinn is to commit disbelief.[66]

Akhund Darweza rejects an imagination of language in which language has the expansive capacity to be a medium through which divinity and revelation may be touched, grasped, and spoken. Language is simply too fragile to bear the cosmological and revelatory weight that Bayazid attributes to it. Whereas Bayazid sees language as a durable, even rugged extension of the continuous revelation of the created world—in which language is plastic enough to survive its savvy manipulation and stable enough to concentrate power in particular words and phrases—Akhund Darweza sees language as a hollow lure tempting us away from the truth.

The only guarantee of revelatory language comes either from the authenticating (and disciplining) role of careful lineages of scholarly tradition *or* from the presence of the angel Gabriel. But here Bayazid fails as well. In Akhund Darweza's records of his debates with Roshani disciples, he takes it as a given that Bayazid claims to have wahy (revelation) without claiming to have met the angel Gabriel. If so, how could we know that Bayazid has received revelation from God if Gabriel does not deliver this revelation to Bayazid's ear on God's behalf? How could Bayazid even know? In contrast to the false revelations found in Bayazid's "weak mind," "Gabriel appeared in his own form" thirty-three times to Muhammad.[67] As Akhund Darweza badgers a Roshani disciple, "Did your pir attain this discourse [i.e., the wahy of *The Best Exposition*] through his own fancy [*wahm*] or through Gabriel? If it is through his own faculty, then it is not prophetic knowledge."[68] Bayazid's bid for direct communication with God reveals the fragility and unreliability of Roshani discourses informed by the Unseen realm.

Central to Akhund Darweza's revulsion to the Roshaniyya is Bayazid's insistence that language is a connective tissue between the realms of the seen and the unseen, the human and the angelic, the messianic and the material. As we saw in the previous chapter, Akhund Darweza's semiotic ideology is strikingly different from the semiotic ideology of Roshani language use; he seeks a Pashto that obliterates its own formal significance and conveys propositional truths of Islam without interferences such as rhyme, shape, and sound. Akhund Darweza's Pashto resonates with the theological suspicion of the Unseen that we find in these polemical passages. In his conceptualization of cosmology and language, the *ẓāhir* and *bāṭin* (the exoteric and esoteric) can never be clearly distinguished. Akhund Darweza suggests what consequences this dichotomy might have on ritual practice:

> The school of heretics [*madhhab-i mulḥidān*] says that one [of batin and zahir] can exist without the other and that shari'a obligations are lifted when the unveiling of Reality [*ḥaqīqat*] occurs. Damn this belief! For this school, . . . abrogation [of law and ritual] is possible. But one of batin and zahir cannot exist without the other![69]

Bayazid and Akhund Darweza both acknowledge the interpenetration of the apparent zahir and hidden batin realms, but they view that interaction from opposing angles. Bayazid sees the zahir through the batin. He sees the esoteric or hidden realm as enveloping the material and apparent realm. The manifest is saturated with the hidden. The shape of words, scraps of paper, and specific dhikr phrases—the stuff of zahir exteriority—can transform the entire cosmos, zahir or batin, precisely because these material objects shimmer with both hidden and manifest significance. Akhund Darweza, conversely, sees the hidden through the frame of the manifest. Whatever we know of the hidden can only be guaranteed by the reliability of what is manifest. Verifiability through the zahir is our only guide in understanding the batin.

From the frailty of new revelation and language born from the Unseen, other sins in behavior and action cascade forth. Akhund Darweza, for instance, lists the following iniquities of Bayazid:

> He committed all sorts of deeds prohibited in shariʿa, such as: eating haram food; spilling nonlegal blood [*na-ḥaqq*]; brigandry; pillaging Muslims; adultery; recognizing as halal the intercourse with foreign women [*vaṭi' kardan-i zanān-i bīgānagān*] who have not been legally married; wine drinking; beard shaving; claiming descent from ancient prophets; showing hostility to knowledge and scholars; killing pious scholars; and more.[70]

Akhund Darweza recounts a personal encounter with Bayazid's violation of shariʿa norms:

> One night in Hashtnaghar, I was a guest of this damned-one [Bayazid]. It was my habit from a young age to stay awake in the night with the intention of monitoring my spiritual states. There was only a light curtain between me and his bedroom.[71]

Those of us with challenging roommates in our past can predict where this story is going:

> I observed he was with his wife in bed during the entire night. At dawn, he arose from his bed dressed in pajamas, entered the mosque, and sat down without completing [ritual] bathing or ablutions. After all his followers arrived, they began their morning prayers. Out of everyone there that morning, only my prayers counted.[72]

Akhund Darweza's complaints illustrate his anxiety over Bayazid's messianic message: claims to new revelation are both the seeds of sin and heresy's fullest fruit.

So how do we connect Akhund Darweza's anti-Roshani polemics to the genealogy of the Afghans? As the very structure of *The Pious and the Wicked* suggests, Akhund Darweza positions Afghanness on a precipice. To be Afghan is to live ever-tempted by the disbelief exemplified by Bayazid, even as the possibility of Afghan redemption remains. In short, Akhund Darweza imagines Afghans as incarnations of the very epistemological anxiety provoked by Bayazid's messianic rhymes.

Muhammad's curse upon the Afghans, as quoted above, is worth revisiting in this light:

> The pearl-speaking tongue of Muhammad (*peace be upon him!*) said, "All the Afghans will be in Hell on the Day of the Resurrection." When the Afghans heard this, they became dejected and grief-stricken. They scattered in order to disperse their collectivity.[73]

In a striking example of a self-fulfilling prophecy, the Afghans become so dismayed at Muhammad's word that they attempt to dissolve the very identity that has been cursed, thereby guaranteeing their own fragmentation. They seek, in short, to cease being the "Afghans"—but Akhund Darweza's genealogy presents the Afghans as *defined* by this destructive fragmentation.

If we back up the story of the Afghans to the moment of their conversion to Islam, the peculiar style of their conversion to Islam foreshadows the fate Akhund Darweza envisions for them:

> All peoples of the world, Arab and Ajam, one by one, individual by individual came to the message of the prophet Muhammad and entered the faith. But the seventy leaders [*maliks*] of the Afghans grasped the message in one instance, and as a collective they entered faith. The seventy leaders then shared the reality of the prophecy of the Seal of the Messengers with their own tribal communities, and all at once the communities—along with wives and children—turned to faith.[74]

This collectivity is both the beginning and end of the Afghans in Akhund Darweza's account; their embrace of Islam and their cursed scattering and fragmentation emerge from the distinctively collective nature of being Afghan. The co-implicating features of Afghan egalitarianism and fragmentation have severe religious and political consequences. Akhund Darweza casts the Afghans as enthusiastic believers burdened by their ignorance and passion. To outpace the anxiety of Muhammad's curse, they respond with zeal:

> Regarding a person of learning—nay, any person who may recite a scrap of the Word of God—the Afghans exalt him and they accept

> his word in eye and in heart. Yet in their ignorance, they cannot recognize if a person is learned or not, and they cannot recognize a traditionalist from an innovator.[75]

The fervor of the Afghans—left unshaped outside the molds of proper religious tradition—manifests in misguided practices. Akhund Darweza appreciates their commitment to fasting, but he shows little sympathy, for example, for their inability to distinguish between suras of the Qur'an or for the Khatak women's belief that their turning of the millstone is a form of prayer.[76] Possessed by an ignorant enthusiasm for religious matters, the Afghans of Akhund Darweza's imagination emerge as particularly susceptible to the corruptions of a figure like Bayazid Ansari. The proliferation of heretical wali-saints and false mahdis is thus both cause and consequence of the Afghans' ethnic becoming. Their fragmentation has intensified their search for a salvational figure, but their willingness to follow all possible messiahs has merely increased their fragmentation.

Akhund Darweza's genealogy of the Afghans is thus an argument that the fissiparous nature of the Afghans is pressed into their very bones by the history of their predecessors. The heresies of Bayazid Ansari are the theological corollaries to the curses of Afghan descent that Akhund Darweza describes. The latter two parts of *The Pious and the Wicked*—that is, the genealogy of the Afghans and the critique of the Roshaniyya—are thus similar stories of the ever-present danger of fragmentation and disunity.

In many ways, the solution to the akhund's anxious imagination of Afghan becoming converges with the Mughals' vulgarization of the Afghans: they need an emperor to discipline them. To return a final time to Muhammad's curse, Akhund Darweza reports that Muhammad listened to the complaints of the hell-bound Afghans and responded: "I did not say that *you* will be in hell; rather, your descendants will be in hell. After you, there will be absolute ignorance because your descendants will only rarely accept a king."[77]

Temporality and Ethnicity

It is worth pausing to note the distance we have moved from the weary story of the Roshaniyya as an ethnic movement or proto-nationalist stirring. Previous scholars have leaned on the Roshaniyya's homogenous ethnic composition to explain their conflict with the Mughals, as if these appeals to Afghanness were obviously sturdier and more ontologically durable than appeals to revelatory language, Sufi saints, and visions of a messiah. The presumed stability of *Afghanness* has dissolved in our sources. For the Mughals and the British, "Afghan" functioned as an accusation and as part of a process of racializing a particular group as inherently unruly and threatening to imperial order. In Niʿmat Allah's stories of King Saul and Qais—or in sources such as Khushhal Khan Khatak's hymns to Afghan pride—the term *Afghan* indeed sought to rally a people into coherence and unify them around a story of origins.[78] And, yet, for Akhund Darweza, "Afghan" functioned as a paradox, a tragedy, and a question about a people whose bodies incarnate a theological temptation.

What these various accounts demonstrate—and Akhund Darweza's above all—is that thinking through ethnicity and peoplehood is irrevocably a *temporal* project. Much like the revelations and apocalyptic ghazals of the Roshaniyya, these genealogies and invocations of the term *Afghan* are ways of cultivating particular and competing relationships to the past, present, and future. For both Niʿmat Allah's celebration of the Afghans as sons of Saul and the Mughals' vulgarization of the Afghans, the Afghans are people eternally fixed by their past. For Akhund Darweza, the temporal relationship is more complex. There are cycles and patterns of temptation and redemption, but above all his story tells of the need for maintaining tradition and lineage. It is the lines that save us: the linear movements, the lineages, the passing from hand-to-hand of learning. The world—and even the heavens in their starlight—are shadowed by the tricks of jinn, the lies of false messiahs, and the fragility of language. For Akhund Darweza, the lineage of the Afghans reiterates the danger of messianic repetition and the need for linear temporality. Caught in agonistic opposition, the genealogical accounts of ethnicity and the poetics of messianism both represent efforts at beckoning particular communities into being and establishing competing relationships to time.

As the contemporary French theorist Bernard Stiegler has argued, "The unity of the ethnic group is governed by the relation to time, more precisely, the relation to a collective future sketching in its effects the reality of a common becoming."[79] *This* notion of ethnicity as future-looking—rather than one that hinges on shared biological origins—more accurately conveys the paradoxes of Akhund Darweza's approach. While his genealogy looks to the distant past and the time of biblical patriarchs such as Saul and Solomon, and while he insists that preserving and detailing the lines of descent and tradition are necessary for recognizing the challenge of heresy found incarnate in Afghan blood, his project is one of ever-becoming. There is *not* a stable identity in being Afghan, as Akhund Darweza constructs it; rather, that very identity is marked by its position of instability, of wavering on the edge between passionate orthodoxy and reckless heresy. As Rogers Brubaker has argued, ethnicity is an epistemological option—it is a "perspective on the world."[80] So it is with Akhund Darweza's genealogy. It is only *about* the Afghans in a cursory sense. The "Afghans," rather, are a "peopling" and incarnation of the fundamental semiotic and temporal concerns and anxieties of his theological imagination. The choice of Afghan becoming in Akhund Darweza's genealogy is between the fragile pseudo-revelations and temporalities of messianic repetition or the redemptive lineages of tradition guaranteed by imperial order.

Akhund Darweza's approach to Afghanness in his genealogy concludes with a vision of the coming end times—another sign that we are better off approaching ethnicity as a matter of temporality, becoming, and the future. In his remembrance of the heresies of the Roshaniyya, Akhund Darweza veers into a discussion of other heretics in the Afghan highlands. Aside from the aforementioned eclectic set of would-be messiahs roaming these mountains, Akhund Darweza harshly critiques the *rawāfiḍ*: the refuseniks, the renouncers, the ones who *reject* the truth. In other words: the Shiʿis. This is, of course, a derogatory term for Shiʿi Muslims, and it reflects Akhund Darweza's inheritance of fifteenth-century anti-Shiʿi polemics sponsored by Timurid courts.[81] Akhund Darweza's critique of Shiʿis focuses less on the concept of the imam as an authority figure and more squarely on the messianism that inflects many varieties of Shiʿi Islam. Notably, this stern polemicist connects the Roshaniyya to the Shiʿis because of their similarly messianic imaginations and the way they perforate the steady lines of a lineal tradition based on communally recognized authority. Once we push beyond the sardonic sneering and scoffing at the putative contradictions of Shiʿi messianism ("Does the mahdi come from the west as some say or from the east as others say?"), we find that Akhund Darweza offers an eschatological vision of his own.[82]

Akhund Darweza's story of the End begins with the appearance of the redeeming mahdi and his eschatological partner, Jesus the masih (messiah). We are given a common account of the success that will follow in the wake of the mahdi's Muslim armies. The enemies' fortress crumbles as the mahdi's armies shout *Allāh akbar*, and the mahdi reclaims the *tābūt* (the ark of the covenant) in which the staff of Moses rests. But then the different armies of the mahdi each covet the staff, and the staff fractures into four pieces.[83] The armies fall into disunion and hostility, and the vaunted armies of the mahdi destroy one another. Upon this intracommunal bloodshed, the trumpet sounds.[84] All of life ceases, and Akhund

Darweza writes that there is such a profound absence that no ants are left to devour the unharvested ripe fruits and heavy grains as they fall to the earth.[85]

Our story so far is recognizable within Islamic traditions, but the next scene is less familiar. After the trumpet's blast and the death of nearly all life, a cow bleats in thirst. Rain falls upon the land, and it is rain that is "pure and white like semen" (*āb-i safīd o khāliṣ hamchon āb-i manī*). At God's command, Gabriel gathers the white rain and gives it directly to the cow, but still the cow's thirst remains. And so the trumpet sounds again, and God resurrects all creatures, whether their death was caused by the first trumpet blast or occurred centuries in the past. The resurrected beings form an immense crowd, so congested that each person can only rest one foot on the ground at a time. All humans stand in a pool of boiling sweat, the depth of which is commensurate with the depravity of their sins. Only the righteous find relief in the shade of God's Throne. Upon their evaluation, men and women must cross the "bridge of the traverse" (*pul-i ṣirāṭ*). The inevitability of individual moral reckoning haunts the series of images. As Akhund Darweza concludes, "Why did you not side with the pious? . . . If you were displeased by the actions of others, why did you not flee from them?"[86]

Beginnings and ends coincide in Akhund Darweza's theological vision of Afghanness. How so? To begin with, there is a clear resonance between Saul's emergence as king and the eschatological invocation of the ark and the staff. In Akhund Darweza's story of King Saul—which echoes the stories of al-Tabari, al-Tha'labi, and other narrators of prophetic lives—Saul's ascension to the throne involves two material signs from God. Samuel identifies Saul with a God-given staff, and the return of the ark confirms for the Bani Isra'il that Saul is their true king. The staff of Moses is not Samuel's staff, but the Qur'an aurally links the figure of Saul (*Ṭālūt*) to the presence of God-given staffs and arks (*tābūt*) plundered by Goliath (*Jālūt*). After the mahdi's armies retake the ark for a final time, can we see the shattering of the ark-housed staff as a revocation of the kingship and unity granted by God to Saul? What God gave to kings, disunion among the Muslims has destroyed.

This, of course, has been Akhund Darweza's interpretation of the Afghans as a people. As descendants of Saul, they have inherited a mark of his kingship—the term *malik*—but their refusal to submit to divinely sanctioned hierarchies has produced a catastrophic fragmentation. Epistemologically, temporally, theologically, socially: the Afghans embody and model a dreadful promise of the end times when kingly inheritances fracture in the stubborn hands of those preferring messianic ruptures over union and submission to the empire.

Conclusion

As I was researching this book, I was fortunate to have friends, guides, colleagues, and hosts throughout Afghanistan, Pakistan, India, England, and the United States. I was welcomed, supported, encouraged, and challenged by many magnanimous people who identify as Afghan or Pashtun. One friend, Wali, took a day off from his work in Islamabad to drive me through the rolling hills of northwest Pakistan, while an acquaintance whom I had met for a mere five minutes, Yunus, insisted on my presence at his family's home for a lunch overlooking a magnificent valley near Swat. Sahar's family in Uttar Pradesh gave me a tour of their family's two-hundred-year-old mango grove. I am embarrassed by how much has been offered me and how inadequately I can express my gratitude or reciprocate. Yunus, Wali, Sahar, and many others sought to explain their generosity of spirit as a simple matter of *pashtunwali*. Being hospitable is simply part of being Pashtun / Afghan, they insisted. It's in our blood.

I mention these moments now because the argument of this chapter may be construed as a simple deconstruction of the term *Afghan* and its (occasional) synonym, *Pashtun*. Rather than bearing a stable meaning, this term *Afghan* populates premodern texts for diverse purposes: as a declaration of noble descent from King Saul, as a condemnation of anti-imperial fanaticism, as a meditation upon the ever-present temptation of fragmentation and schism among Muslims. At its crudest, my argument approaches a full rejection of the coherence and the meaning of this term, *Afghan*—and an implicit denial of my friends' understanding of themselves and their pasts.

That is not the aim of my argument, though I acknowledge the real tension between my approach and the confidence with which my friends express the salience of being Afghan. Rather, following Akhund Darweza, the effort of this chapter has been to reorient our perspectives on the putative *Afghan past* and the determinism that is smuggled in by this ethnonym. As I have attempted to demonstrate in this chapter and throughout this book, various actors have pressed the idea of Afghan identity and ethnicity into the service of imperial expansion, historical explanation, civilizing missions, and nationalist organizing. Mughal chroniclers depicted the Afghans as the unruly enemies of Mughal order. The British colonial epistemology of the nineteenth and early twentieth centuries relied upon the enduring tribal recalcitrance of the Afghans who resisted British military control throughout the Afghan highlands.[87] More recently, the American imaginary of Afghanistan has conjured an image of the Afghans as timeless and eternal—as if the mountains had blocked the very paths of time from passing among the Afghans.[88] These explanations have reified "Afghanness" as a means to explain the failures of a civilizing "order" despite the incredible violence imported by imperial militaries. When specific political, intellectual, and social movements are explained away as simply the product of being Afghan, we are left with Olaf Caroe's vision of the *absence* of history in the region:

> Rather are [the Afghans] like the waters of the sea; the storm-waves pass and disturb the surface, bringing flotsam and jetsam with the wind and sending the froth flying; the water, the essential element, mixes and turns around, but in itself remains the same.[89]

Caroe was the governor of Peshawar during the time of British India, and his 1958 book *The Pathans* was among the most influential English-language books on the peoples of the Afghan highlands. It is to *his* vision of *being Afghan* that I am attempting to propose an alternative.

In this way, I hope that I join my friends in Afghanistan and Pakistan who have sought to reclaim and redefine what Afghan / Pashtun ethnicity entails. They do so by celebrating the historical patterns of generosity, hospitality, independence, and creativity that they see in their families and ancestors despite the persistent media representations of the region as one of violence, chaos, and tragedy. In that way, they echo Niʿmat Allah's efforts to offer a vision of Afghan origins in a blessed past sanctified by Saul, Solomon, and Muhammad alike. They echo more recent efforts by Afghan and Pakistani scholars to portray Bayazid Ansari as an "philosopher, scientist, and logician" or "an enlightened thinker" and to represent the Roshaniyya as figures of an "authentically" Afghan / Pashtun form of Islam.[90] In a more dramatic act of defining Pashtun identity, the recent prime minister of Pakistan, Imran Khan, authored *Warrior Race* in 1993. As the dust-cover promotional material describes, Khan journeyed through "wild and hostile terrain, finding a proud and warlike people. . . . Every [Pashtun] male carries a gun and defends his independence and the honour of his family and his tribe, to the death."[91]

My strategy is different. If the efforts described above aim at redefining the *Afghan* part of "Afghan ethnicity," I am interested in taking aim at the category of *ethnicity* and how that might help explain the repetition of over-deterministic and false images of Afghans. Scholarship on the Roshaniyya—rare as it is—has tended to emphasize their place in an "Afghan history." This interpretation appears sound when filtered through the proliferation of Afghan genealogies inscribed in the decades following Bayazid Ansari's messianic career, oftentimes as a direct challenge to the putative heresies of the Roshaniyya. Coupled with Mulla Arzani's Pashto ghazals and a blossoming Pashto literature of the seventeenth century marked by Khushhal Khan Khatak's stirring cries for Afghan political unity, there is considerable evidence in favor of framing this entire story as a chapter in the history of the Afghans. This is a story of contest over what it means to be Afghan, and ethnicity is thus the thread that weaves these disparate actors together. Recent scholarship by no means adopts a deterministic approach to Afghan ethnicity, as if Afghans were *born* to be one way or another. Nevertheless, in describing the Roshaniyya, the field has approached religion as a veneer resting upon communal or ethnic motivations and has described Bayazid's theology as an expression of an Afghan desire for independence from the Mughals. Though Afghan may mean different things to different people, ethnicity abides as the grounds of our histories.

But I'm not so sure. I worry that the interpretative (and even ontological) priority granted to "Afghan ethnicity" over "messianism," for instance, simply reflects the continued dominance of (ethno)nationalist histories over those of class, culture, and religion. As we immerse ourselves in the rhythms of these texts—in the multilingual messianism of *The Best Exposition*, the intimate Pashto apotheosis of Arzani's rhymes, and the threats of epistemological anarchy in Akhund Darweza's *The Pious and the Wicked*—the story seems quite different from what we typically mean by "ethnicity." The Roshani religious imagination was one of transformation and of a possible ontological shift from devils to angels through the dhikr-based disciplining of one's tongue. Arzani's vision of being Afghan was tethered to his mystical Pashto verses, and so "being Afghan / Pashtun" seemed dependent upon grasping the theo-linguistic mysteries of which he sang. And though Akhund Darweza's genealogy of the Afghans fits at first blush with a "folk" understanding of ethnicity as a matter of collective descent and shared cultural traditions, a closer look suggests that his eschatological notion of the "Afghans" is not so familiar to our contemporary habits of thought.

As I have attempted to demonstrate, Akhund Darweza's conception of the *stuff* that binds Afghans together is not solely a matter of descent or the past. It is multitemporal and its mood subjunctive. The peoplehood of the Afghans is ever a becoming: a question, a temptation, a possibility of falling over the precipice into schism and heresy or uniting under a single sovereign and a single Sunni orthodoxy. Akhund Darweza links

Afghan descent from Saul to the curse of Muhammad and to the eschatological future in which the armies of the mahdi fracture. The peoplehood of the Afghans, moreover, is caught between the recollection of the damned heretic Bayazid and the blessed saint Sayyid ʿAli Tirmidhi, whose knowledge is vouchsafed by his initiation into four—yes, as the akhund proudly insists, *four!*—lineages of Sufi learning.[92] Caught between the pious and the wicked, Akhund Darweza's conception of the Afghans is not about whether they are the descendants of a demon or the sons of Saul; rather, Akhund Darweza places peoplehood on a vector of becoming.

Akhund Darweza's understanding of peoplehood is thus intricately bound up with his semiotic ideology and historical imagination. Contrary to Bayazid's seeming delight in repetition and complex chronoscapes that a Qur'anic imitation can produce, Akhund Darweza is fiercely antirepetition. He seeks refuge in a temporality that is extended and full—telescoped to its max through the linear passage of learning from one scholar to another. It is tradition and lineage in their fullness that guide us.

Consider a passage in which Akhund Darweza instructs his readers that Sufi "masters must teach disciples only to the extent of the disciples' spiritual capacity."[93] This is a conventional Sufi norm found in any number of treatises on the ethics of master-disciple relationships. What matters is not solely the message but the lineage in which this message is embedded. In *The Pious and the Wicked*, Akhund Darweza attributes this message to his master, Sayyid ʿAli Tirmidhi, but the akhund writes that Sayyid ʿAli learned this ethic from *his* master, Shaykh Salar Rumi of Ajmer. Still within the frame of *The Pious and the Wicked*, we learn that Shaykh Salar Rumi, in turn, instructed Sayyid ʿAli on this ethic by telling a story of another master in Shaykh Salar Rumi's lineage, ʿAbd Allah Shattar (d. 1485 CE), whose *own* master cancelled a spiritual lesson on uttering a powerful dhikr phrase because a horse had wandered near enough to overhear the lesson. ʿAbd Allah Shattar's master feared the ill effects of an untrained horse learning an advanced dhikr—neatly illustrating the ethic that masters teach disciples to their capacity.[94] All of these figures—Akhund Darweza, Sayyid ʿAli, Shaykh Salar Rumi, ʿAbd Allah Shattar—perform their mastery of Sufi ethics by ascribing their knowledge to a previous link in the chain.

In many ways, we find in this story of an over-dhikr'ed horse the central themes of Akhund Darweza's theology and its entwinement with semiotics, temporality, and peoplehood. Words are dangerous in their irreducible materiality and effective power; they must be tamed and channeled through master-disciple relationships; and proper sociality involves the linear fullness of tradition. The Afghans must remember the lines of their own descent to understand the question that propels Afghan becoming forward: the fullness of Sunni orthodoxy or the heretical anarchy of Bayazid's messianic timewarps and semiotic materiality?

We are left with our own question: Is this *ethnicity* in any way that we recognize it? Or do we find that the contours of identity, belonging, and peoplehood in the texts of Akhund Darweza, Bayazid Ansari, Mulla Arzani, and others offer us a different conceptual topography? I have argued that it is indeed different: that the vision of ethnicity that we find in these texts is one aimed at both pasts and futures and one that tethers the very substance of one's belonging to the words one says and the messianic potential one chases or rejects.

Ishmael's Daydream: A Conclusion

We have met many Bayazids, but there is space for one more: Bayazid the Ansari. In Mukhlis's hagiography, *The Book of States*, we find that Bayazid is a descendant of Abu Ayyub al-Ansari, the companion of the prophet who lent his home to Muhammad in Medina and who died fighting for the prophetic cause outside the walls of Constantinople.[1] Mukhlis relates a hadith in which Muhammad expresses the intimacy of these early companions (*anṣār*) to Muhammad, "The ansar are the hair on my chest while the rest of creation is my outer garment."[2] Ansari means "one of the ansar" or "like the ansar," and the very name Bayazid Ansari thus makes an argument for Bayazid's place in prophetic history: Bayazid is among those intimate companions of the prophet. Bayazid's abbreviated genealogy in *The Book of States* includes his father, 'Abd Allah, among ancestors such as Shaykh Bayazid the Bird and Shaykh Ibrahim Danishmand. Mukhlis does not, however, develop an image of Bayazid as an emblem of familial blessedness. It was in the breaking of family bonds that Bayazid's sainthood opened to the participation of his disciples, and it was in criticism of inherited religious authority that Bayazid staked his own spiritual authority. Bayazid's blessedness emerged, in part, from his hostile relationship with 'Abd Allah as both father and traditional scholar. Genealogical belonging, in Mukhlis's presentation, plays an ambiguous role—it sanctifies Bayazid as the heir to the "hair of Muhammad's chest" while simultaneously providing the social formation which Bayazid must reject as he becomes the luminous master, the revelatory wretch, and the guide at the End.

In 1710 CE, 'Ali Muhammad Walad Gul Ansari recorded Bayazid's genealogy again. 'Ali Muhammad Walad's work, *The Remembrance of the Ansaris* (or *The Remembrance of the Companions*, "Tadhkirat al-anṣār"), is a collection of twenty biographies detailing the lives of the Ansari family—or, more accurately, one of the numerous Ansari families of the Islamic world.[3] 'Ali Muhammad Walad begins with Abu Ayyub al-Ansari and then leaps in his second biography to Ibrahim Danishmand. Here we learn—as K. Hussan Zia has detailed—that Ibrahim Danishmand was a Turk from Anatolia who sought religious education first in Mecca and then in Iraq.[4] In Baghdad, he became a disciple of the renowned Sufi master Shahab al-Din Abu Hafs al-Suhrawardi.[5] Upon Suhrawardi's death in 1212 CE, Ibrahim Danishmand moved his family to Multan and then Jalandhar. In Jalandhar many Danishmands settled, but Ibrahim and his sons began to travel to Bengal and back.[6] 'Ali Muhammad Walad claims that Ibrahim died in the area of Jalandhar and was entombed there. Zia, however, observes that there is a tomb for Ibrahim Danishmand near Dhaka that remains a site of pilgrimage and celebration on the day of Ibrahim's *'urs*: his "wedding" with God when he left his mortal flesh to be with God in death.[7]

The biographical entry on Bayazid in *The Remembrance of the Ansaris* repeats many of the well-known points of his life that we explored in chapter 1: his dreams of Khidr, his repeated trials, and his composition of *The Best Exposition*, *The Endeavor of the Faithful*, *The Path of Oneness*, and the autobiography that putatively became *The Book of States* after Mukhlis's edits. His conflict with the Mughals is cast simply as a response to the rapacious and oppressive taxing of Afghan traders, and 'Ali Muhammad Walad recounts the divergent paths of Bayazid's ancestors. Some continued in violent struggle against the Mughals while others—notably Rashid Khan and his family—entered into the Mughal court as noble servants.[8]

There are at least two significant differences in the story of *The Remembrance of the Ansaris* from what we have previously considered, however. First, there is no sense that *The Best Exposition* is anything but a collection of Sufi teachings; there is no sense that it represented an effort to bring God into the ink of a multilingual revelation or that it drew upon the same messianic ideas that shaped Akbar's claims to cosmic sovereignty. Second, the source of Bayazid's spiritual insights came not from his shocking attempt at fratricide and subsequent repentance upon hearing the "calling voice." Rather, Bayazid gained his wisdom directly from the tomb of Shaykh Ibrahim Danishmand, the patriarch-pilgrim of this Suhrawardi-Ansari family who settled in South Asia.[9] Though Zia argues that there is no (currently known) tomb in Jalandhar and that Ibrahim died in present-day Bangladesh, it does not alter the literary logic of 'Ali

Muhammad Walad's account. As ʿAli Muhammad Walad attributes the insights of Bayazid to the tomb of Ibrahim Danishmand, he punctuates the larger argument of *The Remembrance of the Ansaris*: the lineage of the Danishmands is a blessed one that brings Suhrawardian Sufi knowledge to the soil of Kaniguram, Jalandhar, Dhaka, and other sites of Danishmand settlement. As for Bayazid, he is but one example of the capacity for a blessed, noble family with roots in Anatolia, Baghdad, and Medina to sanctify South Asia through their interred presence and weave the networks of Islamic learning and piety ever more densely across the globe.

The account of ʿAli Muhammad Ansari illustrates some of the central arguments of this book. Though the details that ʿAli Muhammad provides of Bayazid are nearly identical to other accounts of Bayazid, the placement of this account in a collection of Danishmand biographies suggests an important historical shift. Whatever sociality of participatory messianism Bayazid's texts struggled to articulate and constitute had been rejected by Mughal violence and the polemical efforts of Akhund Darweza. As argued in the previous chapter, the response to Bayazid involved the consolidation of "Afghan" identity as the descendants of King Saul and ʿAbd al-Rashid Qais Pathan. Becoming Afghan had coalesced as a matter of patrilineal descent from a shared ancestor and the consequent fragmentation into rival tribal formations, even if this notion of "descent" does not carry the same determinism that "ethnicity" has in some more recent accounts. The formulation of Afghan identity around lineage and descent coincided with imperial ideologies. As Akhund Darweza explicitly noted—and as Mughal, British, and American imperial observers persisted in repeating—the "inherent" anarchy of Afghan tribal formations required the presence of a strong empire to bring order, orthodoxy, and taxation. Snuffed were the possibilities of Roshani messianism, and they gave way to a firmer, more consolidated socio-religious vision in which the populations of the Afghan highlands belonged *as Afghans*. *The Remembrance of the Ansaris* provides more evidence of this transformation. Bayazid—the messiah, the heretic, the wretch, the one of the divine tongues—had become another attestation of the governing logic of lineage and descent. He was a Danishmand, an Ansari, a Turk; his followers were Afghans. Messianism had given way to ethnicity—or something like it.

The Bayazid that we meet in *The Remembrance of the Ansaris* is one that I find to be historically plausible. Despite contemporary claims that Bayazid was an Afghan hero (or villain), there is hardly any evidence in the texts of the Roshaniyya that Bayazid identified as an Afghan, nor is there any evidence that he was a "Hindustani" who brought yogic teachings to gullible Afghan Muslims, as later Mughal chronicles suggest. Neither an autochthonous proto-nationalist nor an outsider and polluter of some pure Afghan Sunni Islam, Bayazid emerges from larger patterns of mobility, exchange, and migration.[10] In short, it seems eminently plausible that he descended from a Turkic family that claimed the name of "Ansari" because of the connection between Anatolia and the narratives of Abu Ayyub al-Ansari. This family developed a multigenerational affiliation with Suhrawardi Sufi practices, and they later migrated into South Asia as so many other scholars, saints, poets, and warriors did.[11]

That Bayazid has been given so many labels and is remembered in such different ways attests to the remarkable possibilities of mobility in the Persianate world—a world influenced by Persian-language literary and cultural traditions of sainthood, poetry, sovereignty, and more. Furthermore, as Richard Eaton's recent work on India in the Persianate age attests with such clarity, the "Persianate world" was an eminently porous one that was open to exchange and translation with the cultural traditions informed by Sanskrit, Pali, and other languages of India.[12] And so we meet Bayazid: Afghan, Indian, Turk; Sufi saint, lettrist heretic, foreign yogi; messiah, teacher, nationalist; Muslim, damned, luminous.

And while this particular story of Bayazid—Bayazid the Ansari, descendant of Turkic Danishmands with Suhrawardi Sufi connections—is a highly plausible story and the one that best explains the strange story of a "failed" messiah by emphasizing the mobility and possibility of the Persianate world, this story is not enough. The stories of the Roshaniyya demand that we reflect on that very instinct to identify the real and the plausible in the life of Bayazid. What logics of language and history tempt us to drive a pin through Bayazid's heart and fix and display him in the shadowbox of this monograph?

The power of Bayazid rests in the fluidity of the stories about him and in how that fluidity offers us a chance to let our assumed categories of analysis shift. These are the "mountains" we explored in the introduction: a reliance upon determinative explanations of ethnicity, a taken-for-granted understanding of "real" Islam, and a continuous (if hidden) commitment to unfurling history as a calendrical line in accordance with the secularity of our time. Yet, in the thoroughly eschatological imagination of the Roshaniyya, mountains turn to dust.

Let us remember again a miracle attributed to Bayazid: he is the saint whose heart takes the shape of all that passes through it.[13]

In the opening of Herman Melville's *Moby Dick*, the restless Ishmael struggles to understand his attraction to the sea. He is opaque to himself, and he attributes his wanderlust to the "invisible police officer of the Fates."[14] Unlike Bayazid's experience, though, Ishmael's Fates exercise their control not through an angelic voice but as ink stamped on a handbill that advertises the theatrical performance of the future: "And, doubtless, my going on this whaling voyage, formed part of the grand programme of Providence that was drawn up a long time ago. It came in as a sort of brief interlude and solo between more extensive performances."[15] The handbill of Ishmael's daydreams reads:

> "Grand Contested Election for the Presidency of the United States.
>
> "WHALING VOYAGE BY ONE ISHMAEL.
>
> "BLOODY BATTLE IN AFFGHANISTAN."[16]

The United States invaded Afghanistan in October 2001. During the presidential election cycles since then, there has invariably been at least one American pundit who remembers this opening to *Moby Dick* and cites it for his public as an ironic commentary. In 2008, for instance, Jeffrey Goldberg wrote in the *Atlantic Monthly* that Ishmael's imagined handbill attests to "the timelessness of trouble in Afghanistan." In 2004, 2012, 2016, and 2020, we have heard the same message from such pundits: "The more things change, am I right?" There is a barely concealed prayer of gratitude or a sneer of disdain in these invocations of Ishmael's dreams. *Thank God we're not stuck in a cycle like that. Thank God we're not trapped in repetitions of violence. Thank God we move forward in time unlike them. There's no choice but to abandon this land of inherent chaos.*

The timelessness of Afghanistan is a myth, of course. As works by Faiz Ahmed, Shah Mahmoud Hanifi, Sana Haroon, Alla Ivanchikova, Nile Green, Robert Crews, Shahzad Bashir, and many others have demonstrated, the regions that are now known as Afghanistan have been thoroughly enmeshed in networks of global exchange and circulation.[17] We might even explain the current cycle of violence in Afghanistan as a product of how thoroughly enmeshed Afghanistan is in such a global context. As Crews and Bashir write, "Contrary to its stereotypical portrayal as a land forgotten by time . . . there is hardly any modern idea or weapon that has not had a significant impact on the region."[18] There is nothing timeless about these troubles: they represent specific actions made for contingent reasons, typically at the expense of Afghan lives and typically in pursuit of expanding some other nation's global power.

Beyond this, however, Goldberg and others who cite this passage from *Moby Dick* seem to miss Melville's larger point. Melville desires not the damnation of Afghanistan as a place of war; rather, he seeks to articulate Ishmael's relationship to the Fates. Melville reveals how Ishmael imagines "Affghanistan" in the process of self-formation. The imagined history of a distant, violent nation, anchored in timelessness, becomes a plotted point in Ishmael's own tracing of the frontier between self and world, of determining the line between his own choices and those of Providence, and of reflecting on how exposed he is to forces beyond his control. This is a declaration of Ishmael's self-obscurity, of his vulnerability, and of his ultimate passivity in the face of the mysterious workings of time. He does not know himself, and the fantasy of a handbill filled with contested elections and bloody battles is a desperate attempt to understand.

Goldberg's citation flips the meaning of Ishmael's handbill by using Melville's text as proof of Afghanistan's timelessness rather than as proof of an American's illusion of control. In doing so, Goldberg aims to numb Americans to their imperial crimes in Afghanistan and to absolve Americans of the violence exported across the world. After all, the troubles in Afghanistan are timeless, aren't they?

Ishmael's dreams of a timeless handbill press upon the repetitions of the American media as well. We can reject the crude notion of Afghan timelessness found in something like Goldberg's nod to Melville, but the theme of repetition is an important one for our story. As John Lardas Modern has noted, the handbill of Ishmael delivers the language of the Fates as an artifact of American print media.[19] Perhaps the greater irony is not that "Affghanistan" is still witnessing bloody battles but that the American discourse of Afghanistan is unchanged in the 150 years since Ishmael's daydream.

A different type of repetition characterizes the traces of the Roshaniyya. Rather than the mechanical reproduction of many American images of Afghanistan—a repetition that renders Afghanistan and its pasts something to be consumed and controlled—the repetitions of the Roshaniyya seek the wild openness of messianic repetition. We can recall the story that began this book: in a village of Roshani devotees, Second Jesus was born and Second Mary repeated her dhikr prayers and fasted for forty days until her death. These strange portents announced the presence of the mahdi, Bayazid Ansari. The stories of Bayazid's life were replete with repetition: doppelgängers intercepted his dreams, and his biography repeated the lives of past prophets. According to Roshani theology and practice, the repetition of dhikr phrases shaped the very stuff of the Roshani self and transformed human tongues into the tongues of angels and hallowed "wretches." The central revelation of the Roshaniyya—*The Best Exposition*—repeats the Qur'an while transforming it, imitating it, re-forming it, and re-presenting it. For the Roshaniyya, Islam did not emanate outward from seventh-century Mecca, and they do not find themselves on some frontier between the local and the Islamic. The phenomena of seventh-century Mecca *are* the phenomena of sixteenth-century Kaniguram—and they are rendered such through the dhikr remembrances and Qur'anic rhymes of the illuminated master. This is not a perspective that accords with the common histories of Islam, and, to borrow Shahzad Bashir's words, the case of the Roshaniyya thus asks that we understand Islam as "a matter forever in the process of being made and unmade through the agency of the authors who invoke it in specific sociohistorical circumstances."[20]

These are repetitions that do not fix and calcify the Roshaniyya through rote assault or predictability; rather, these repetitions elude our assumptions. As soon as we've pinned Bayazid as a butterfly for display, just then we find another repetition of him still there in the folds of Mukhlis's stories. By being repetitive, the words and worlds of the Roshaniyya are open to reinterpretation.

This book has argued for the analytical value of focusing on the language of the Roshaniyya—and an idea of repetition helps us see this worth again. I suggested that we can best understand the Roshaniyya by focusing on "semiotic ideology:" how the Roshaniyya implicitly and explicitly imagine the workings of letters, words, signs, and songs. In the semiotic ideology of the Roshaniyya, language matters. Language is heavy; it is thick; and we cannot easily see *through* language to the represented truth of the world. Rather, it is truth; it is part of the world. The form, shape, structure, and materiality of language and texts are more than the unfortunate preconditions of linguistic communication. These aspects shimmer with revelatory, messianic, divine, transformative, self-annihilating, and world-making capacities. As words repeat, the repetition is not merely conveying the same message again. Rather, given how thoroughly words sink into the world for the Roshaniyya, repetition is powerful. Repetition can be a reiteration and an immanent re-instantiation of the divine voice. Words do not symbolically point to something beyond themselves. In the Roshani imagination of language in which the very stuff of the cosmos is linguistic, words *work* their meaning by being a microcosmic part to the macrocosmic whole.

This is all to say: the repetitions of the words of the Roshaniyya are precisely what eludes our categories and challenges us to think through vernacular literatures, Islamic history, belonging, and the texture of temporality in new ways.

Bayazid's career was short. His texts were rejected. His sons and followers were slaughtered, enslaved, displaced, and at times incorporated into the Mughal empire. His ideas were condemned as heresy, and his messianic claims ridiculed as delusion. To pose a familiar question: What can a failed messiah teach us?

We are now in a place to reject this question. To begin with, there is no single messiah in Bayazid. The most explosive text attributed to him—*The Best Exposition*—is one that empties itself of any author. It is an attempt at speaking God's language and not Bayazid's. Even more importantly, just as *The Book of States* presents us with a Bayazid to grasp, it is a Bayazid that fragments in our very hands. He is the saint whose power comes from his dissolution, his doubling, and his constitution through the participation of others. The disciples of Bayazid dreamt his dreams and initiated new members into the Roshaniyya directly in his name. The messiah of this book is not Bayazid but the Roshaniyya participation in plural Bayazids.

The participatory messianism of the Roshaniyya involved both hierarchical master-disciple relationships as well as the inclusiveness of a dispersed sainthood and a "vernacularized" divine language. As women, orphans, dispossessed Afghan traders, struggling nomads, blacksmiths, and those on the religious margins heeded the call of Bayazid, they understood this process as a loss of previous family and tribal affiliations, a submission to the dhikr regimes of a perfect master, an annihilation of one's self, an immersion in God, and participation in the becoming of the saint-messiah. This participatory messianism marked a rupture in the patterns of tribal and religious relationships. On a broader level, perhaps the participatory messianism of the Roshaniyya generated precisely the type of epistemological and religious anarchy that Akhund Darweza feared. According to *The Book of States*, the Second Jesus and Second Mary inaugurated the eschatological end events in a village of Roshani disciples without Bayazid's authority. Was this village merely following Bayazid's own teachings to their logical conclusion? To the conclusion that the revelatory messianism of Bayazid was something to do, something to speak, and not something simply to follow? Rather than a failed messiah, we have a "weak" one, to borrow again from Walter Benjamin.[21] The tiny displacement of the messianic rests in an "imperceptible trembling of the finite" that makes the limits—the categories, frames, words that we hang upon our objects of study—indeterminate and mobile.[22] Disorientation, as Sara Ahmed tells us, may be the path to "sustain[ing] wonder."[23]

The messianic is an act of historical recognition and historiographical hesitation that questions the determinacy of our own tools of analysis; the messianic is an awareness of an interruptive and rapturous repetition that suspends the order of things through a finite trembling, however weakly. I have attempted to detail how the Roshaniyya understood the scraps of the past and brought them to the shimmering instantiation of divine language in their own disciplined tongue, just as Bayazid dreamt of a scrap of paper with the "greatest name" written upon it that spurred his own apotheosis. I have presented the Roshaniyya, therefore, as interested in a "weak messianism" not because Bayazid was (or was not) a failed messiah; rather theirs was a weak messianism that involved a historical and linguistic fulfillment of the past. The ostensibly fixed and singular moment of God's revelation to Muhammad became unmoored in time, repeatedly cracked away from the seventh century, and left open to reclamation through the ambiguity of its temporal limits.

Ishmael's handbill offers a final reminder. Ishmael has become one of the classic characters of the American imagination, but his name bequeaths him the legacy of the putative "other": the son less cherished in the Biblical tradition, the son cast into the desert, and the son whose prophetic status found reclamation by the Qur'an and its Muslim exegetes.[24] So here—in the very heart of the ostensible canon of American literature—we find the enduring constitutive presence of Islamic cultural words, and we find Ishmael has connected his efforts to wrestle fate and know himself anew to Afghanistan.

A Note on Sources

Singing with the Mountains seeks to bring the story of the Roshaniyya and their pursuit of revelation into dialogue with how we (the "we" who do not live in the sixteenth- and seventeenth-century Afghan highlands) imagine language, understand the history of religion in South Asia, and approach narratives of sainthood, apocalypticism, and the vernacular, among other topics. Given that the purpose of this book is thus more closely associated with "religious studies" as a field than with South Asia studies or even history, I have elected to avoid thorough discussions of the material manuscript record except where it directly bears on the quality of religious language and revelation. The manuscript record is undoubtedly important, however, and I would like to direct those interested in the Roshaniyya to the archives that could sustain a different approach than the one I have offered. To be clear, the following comments solely address those sources directly connected to the Roshaniyya and not the numerous other sources of the Mughal era that have shaped this book, such as the chronicles of the Lodi-Suri dynasties, the blessed genealogies of the Afghans, Persian Sufi texts, and so on.

While many of the sources associated with the Mughal court's representation of the Roshaniyya (such as *The Book of Akbar*) are readily available in print and in translation, the sources more immanent to the Roshaniyya and their critics remain in their language of composition and / or as manuscripts. There are numerous sources attributed to Bayazid Ansari, some of which we have considered: the revelations of *The Best Exposition* ("Khayr al-bayān"), the didactic counsel of *The Endeavor of the Believers*

("Maqṣūd al-mu'minīn"), and the evangelizing efforts of the *The Path of Oneness* ("Ṣirāṭ al-tawḥīd"). *The Best Exposition* was edited and published in 1988 by Muhammad 'Abd al-Quddus Qasimi, but for this book I have relied on three manuscript versions of *The Best Exposition*: the tetralingual Berlin and Hyderabad copies alongside the entirely Persian manuscript found at Rampur.[1] *The Endeavor of the Believers* was published in Arabic in 1976 by Mir Wali Khan Mas'udi, and an Arabic manuscript of *The Endeavor* can be found at the Raza Library in Rampur.[2] *The Path of Oneness* is only available as a manuscript—as far as I am aware, at least (a caveat that applies to this entire section). There are manuscripts of *The Path of Oneness* available at the Ganj Bakhsh Library in Islamabad and at the Raza Library in Rampur.[3] Recently, Zalmay Haywadmal edited a publication of *The Joy of the Chosen* ("Farḥat al-mujtabá") and 'Abdul Khaliq Rashid edited a publication of *The Mysteries Laid Bare* ("'Uryān al-ghayb").[4] Both of these texts are attributed to Bayazid Ansari, and they repeat in near-verbatim ways what we find in other sources of the Roshaniyya. Waleed Ziad has recently discussed a nineteenth-century collection of manuscripts (*majmū'a*) found in Tashkent that contains a "book of counsel" ("Naṣīḥat-nāmah") attributed to Bayazid Ansari.[5] I have not seen this text, but "naṣīḥat-nāmah" is how Persian-language sources have described Bayazid's *The Endeavor of the Believers*, so I assume that the Tashkent "Naṣīḥat-nāmah" is a translation of *The Endeavor*. Finally, *The Book of States*—the hagiography of Bayazid attributed to Mukhlis—was published in 2009 based on a manuscript held at Aligarh Muslim University (which is accessible as a microfilm at the Noor International Microfilm Center in Delhi).[6] In addition to those poems of Mulla Arzani which I have discussed in this book, I have recently published translations of other poems in the journal *Afghanistan*.[7] In that article, I include a brief note on the existence of other manuscripts attributed to Mulla Arzani.

The case of Akhund Darweza's texts is similar. There is a published edition of *The Treasure Chest of Islam* ("Makhzan al-Islām"), and there are dozens of manuscripts throughout Afghanistan, Pakistan, India, and the United Kingdom.[8] Other sources, however, are only available as manuscripts. *The Remembrance of the Pious and the Wicked* is found as a manuscript in London and in Islamabad.[9] As noted in chapter 4, *The Treasure Chest* is an amorphous, "open" text that included multiple sections that were often copied as individual texts. There are numerous manuscripts entitled "An Interpretation of Amali's Poem" ("Sharḥ qaṣādat āmālī"), for example.[10] In other manuscripts, this interpretation is merely one part of *The Treasure Chest*. Numerous texts—on legal issues, on "women's issues," on prayer, and so on—are found in South Asian archives and seem largely to be excerpts from *The Treasure Chest*. A text known as *The Guidance of the Seekers* ("Irshād al-ṭālibīn") is attributed to Akhund Darweza and is available as a published lithograph. It consists primarily of arguments similar to those found in *The Treasure Chest*.[11]

One of the challenges of these Roshani and anti-Roshani texts is their very repetition: *The Joy of the Chosen* and *The Mysteries Laid Bare* repeat in near-verbatim ways the arguments and teachings of *The Best Exposition* and *The Endeavor of the Believers*. I would insist, however, that the genre and form of these texts matters immensely. It is quite a different thing to offer a lesson on the nature of Sufi masters as a dialogue between a father and son (such as we find in *The Endeavor*), as a revelation from God (as we find in *The Best Exposition*), and as a song (as we find in *The Joy of the Chosen*). Given the significance of form and genre, I have chosen to focus on individual texts rather than attempting to compile a Roshani theology across multiple texts. The consequence, however, is that there has been little discussion in this book of Bayazid's *The Joy of the Chosen* and *The Mysteries Laid Bare* or of Akhund Darweza's *The Guidance of the Seekers*.

Notes

Preface

1. Walter Benjamin, "The Task of the Translator," in *Illuminations*, ed. Hannah Arendt (New York: Schocken Books, 1969), 80–81.

Mountains and Messiahs: An Introduction

1. This account is translated (and lightly adapted) from *The Book of States* ("Hal-Namah"), a hagiography of Bayazid Ansari. ʿAlī Muḥammad Mukhliṣ Kandahārī Shīnvārī, *Ḥāl-nāmah-yi Miyān Roshan* (Kabul: Vizārat-i Iṭṭilāʿāt va Farhang, 2009), 346–49.

2. Mukhliṣ, 346–49.

3. Mukhliṣ, 349 and following.

4. Scott Kugle, *Hajj to the Heart: Sufi Journeys across the Indian Ocean* (Chapel Hill: University of North Carolina Press, 2021), 24–27 and 155–62.

5. This is a common version of the story, and one recent iteration can be found in Jonathan L. Lee, *Afghanistan: A History from 1260 to the Present* (London: Reaktion Books, 2018), 57–60.

6. Sara Ahmed, *Queer Phenomenology: Orientations, Objects, Others* (Durham, NC: Duke University Press, 2006), 24; Maurice Merleau-Ponty, *Phenomenology of Perception* (London: Routledge, 2002), 296, cited in Ahmed, *Queer Phenomenology*, 24.

7. Sergei Andreyev, "The Rawshaniyya," in *The Heritage of Sufism: Late Classical Persianate Sufism (1501–1750)*, ed. Leonard Lewisohn (Oxford: Oneworld, 1999), 311.

8. Andreyev's brief characterization did note that the work was dialogic, but, despite his description, I was not prepared for how perplexing and intriguing this dialogue would be.

9. For descriptions of Safavid and Mughal monarchs such as Shah Ismail Safavi that similarly emphasize the centrality of messianism, Sufi sainthood, embodiment, and millenarianism, consider especially the following works: Shahzad Bashir, "Shah Ismaʿil

and the Qizilbash: Cannibalism in the Religious History of Early Safavid Iran," *History of Religions* 45 (2006): 234–56; Kathryn Babayan, *Mystics, Monarchs, and Messiahs: Cultural Landscapes of Early Modern Iran*, Harvard Middle Eastern Monographs (Cambridge, MA: Harvard University Press, 2002); A. Azfar Moin, *The Millennial Sovereign: Sacred Kingship and Sainthood in Islam* (New York: Columbia University Press, 2012).

10. Mukhliṣ, *Ḥāl-nāmah-yi Miyān Roshan*, 257.

11. We can consider Kerwin Klein's work on US historiography as a helpful comparative point that also demonstrates the intense ideological work performed by history writing about "frontiers." Kerwin Klein, *Frontiers of Historical Imagination: Narrating the European Conquest of Native America, 1890–1990* (Berkeley: University of California Press, 1997).

12. For examples of this impulse, see especially André Wink, "On the Road of Failure: The Afghans in Mughal India," *Cracow Indological Studies*, no. 11 (2009): 267–339; Andreyev, "The Rawshaniyya," 290–318; Joseph Theodore Arlinghaus, "The Transformation of Afghan Tribal Society: Tribal Expansion, Mughal Imperialism and the Roshaniyya Insurrection, 1450–1600" (PhD diss., Duke University, 1989), chap. 6.

13. Sana Haroon, *Frontier of Faith: Islam in the Indo-Afghan Borderland* (New York: Columbia University Press, 2007).

14. For the limitations of "belief" as a gravitational center of the academic study of religion, consider Manuel A. Vásquez, *More Than Belief: A Materialist Theory of Religion* (Oxford: Oxford University Press, 2010).

15. Bruno Latour has made a similar point (with much more elegance) in *Rejoicing: Or the Torments of Religious Speech*, trans. Julie Rose (Cambridge: Polity, 2013).

16. Carl Ernst's eminently readable discussion of this topic remains an excellent standard for the study of Orientalism and Sufism: Carl Ernst, *Sufism* (Boulder, CO: Shambhala, 2011), chap. 1. Also consider Rosemary Corbett, *Making Moderate Islam* (Stanford, CA: Stanford University Press, 2016); Richard King, *Orientalism and Religion: Post-colonial Theory, India, and "The Mystic East"* (London: Routledge, 1999).

17. For consideration of Islamic eschatology and the place of 'Isa/Jesus in these narratives, consider Abbas Amanat, *Apocalyptic Islam and Iranian Shi'ism* (London: I. B. Tauris, 2009); Zeki Saritoprak, *Islam's Jesus* (Gainesville: University Press of Florida, 2015).

18. For a useful survey of Pashto literature, consider Sergei Andreyev, "Pashto Literature: The Classical Period," in *Oral Literature of Iranian Languages: Kurdish, Pashto, Balochi, Ossetic, Persian and Tajik: Companion Volume II to A History of Persian Literature*, vol. 18, ed. Philip G. Kreyenbroek and Ulrich Marzolph (London: I. B. Tauris, 2010), 89–113.

19. Judith Butler has explored the ethical consequences of Western narratives of war (including in Afghanistan) in *Frames of War: When Is Life Grievable?* (New York: Verso, 2016). Important exceptions to this dominant American narrative of Afghanistan can be found in Nile Green and Nushin Arbabzadah, eds., *Afghanistan in Ink: Literature between Nation and Diaspora* (Oxford: Oxford University Press, 2012).

20. For a discussion of why and how this is possible, consider Noah Coburn, *Losing Afghanistan: An Obituary for the Intervention* (Stanford, CA: Stanford University Press, 2016).

21. I have used the term "Afghan" to describe the community at the heart of my historical investigation that resided in the Afghan highlands and spoke Pashto, among other languages. In writing on modern Afghanistan and Pakistan, I use the term

"Pashtun" to avoid equating citizens of Afghanistan with a single ethnic group. The historical sources of the sixteenth and seventeenth centuries, however, exclusively use the term "afghān," and I have followed suit.

22. See Mark Graham, *Afghanistan in the Cinema* (Champaign: University of Illinois Press, 2010).

23. Shahzad Bashir and Robert D. Crews, *Under the Drones: Modern Lives in the Afghanistan-Pakistan Borderlands* (Cambridge, MA: Harvard University Press, 2012), 2.

24. Bashir and Crews, 262.

25. Waleed Ziad, *Hidden Caliphate: Sufi Saints beyond the Oxus and Indus* (Cambridge, MA: Harvard University Press, 2021).

26. In this way, I seek to contribute to and expand on a project such as Robert Crews's in *Afghan Modern*. Robert D. Crews, *Afghan Modern: The History of a Global Nation* (Cambridge, MA: Belknap, 2015.

27. For a critique of the work performed by "tribe" in American discourses, consider Robert Crews, "The Taliban and Nationalist Militancy in Afghanistan," in *Contextualising Jihadi Thought*, ed. Jeevan Deol and Zaheer Kazmi (New York: Columbia University Press, 2011), 369–84; M. Jamil Hanifi, "Editing the Past: Colonial Production of Hegemony through the 'Loya Jerga' in Afghanistan," *Iranian Studies* 37, no. 2 (2004): 295–322. For a discussion of the emergence of "tribe" as a category of analysis in English-language sources on Afghanistan, consider the conclusion of this book as well as B. D. Hopkins, *The Making of Modern Afghanistan* (Basingstoke, UK: Palgrave Macmillan, 2012); Martin J. Bayly, *Taming the Imperial Imagination: Colonial Knowledge, International Relations, and the Anglo-Afghan Encounter, 1808–1878* (Cambridge: Cambridge University Press, 2016).

28. Olaf Caroe, *The Pathans: 550 B.C.–A.D. 1957* (London: Macmillan, 1958), 192.

29. Shahzad Bashir, "On Islamic Time: Rethinking Chronology in the Historiography of Muslim Societies," *History and Theory* 53, no. 4 (2014): 519–44; Anand Vivek Taneja, *Jinnealogy: Time, Islam, and Ecological Thought in the Medieval Ruins of Delhi* (Stanford, CA: Stanford University Press, 2017). The phrase "homogenous, empty time" is Walter Benjamin's. Walter Benjamin, *Illuminations*, trans. Harry Zohn (New York: Random House, 2007), 262.

30. Bashir, "On Islamic Time," 520.

31. Bashir cites Jonathan Berkey, Ira Lapidus, and Marshall Hodgson as historians who assume this type of linear temporality in their histories of Islam. Bashir, 523.

32. Bashir, 542–44.

33. This seems to be Andreyev's position on the matter. Sergei Andreyev, "The Rawshaniyya." More generally, Jay Trimingham was an influential proponent of a model of Sufi history in which the Sufis operated as a vanguard of Islamization due to the (seemingly unique) Sufi ability to adapt to local cultures, use vernacular languages, and synthesize other religions with the tenets of mystical Islam. More recent works on the history of Sufism have justifiably critiqued the rigidity of Trimingham's historical periodization and his reliance upon broad and determinative characterizations of Sufis. Though Trimingham's work has largely been rejected, there are some significant continuities between his model and contemporary analyses of Sufi history. Richard Eaton's work, for instance, significantly nuances the conclusions of Trimingham by offering a much more sophisticated description of the role played by Sufis in bridging "Islam" and indigenous non-Muslim populations. Consider Eaton's work and the work of Nile

Green for more discussion of this issue. Richard M. Eaton, *The Rise of Islam and the Bengal Frontier* (Berkeley: University of California Press, 1993); Nile Green, *Sufism: A Global History* (Oxford: Wiley-Blackwell, 2012).

34. Saba Mahmood, *Religious Difference in a Secular Age: A Minority Report* (Princeton, NJ: Princeton University Press, 2015), 195–207, esp. 197.

35. Qur'an 73:14. This is A. J. Arberry's translation with my own modification.

36. Benjamin, *Illuminations,* 255.

37. Benjamin, 255.

38. Giorgio Agamben, *Time That Remains.*

39. Giorgio Agamben introduces his discussion of messianic "tiny displacement" through reference to a "well- known parable" that was told by Walter Benjamin ("who heard it from Gershom Scholem") to Ernst Bloch, "who in turn transcribed it in *Spuren.*" Agamben *then* relates Benjamin's own version of the story, implicitly revealing the "tiny displacement" that occurs between Benjamin's and Bloch's versions of Scholem's Hassidic parable. Agamben presents Benjamin's story in this manner: "The *Hassidim* tell a story about the world to come that says everything there will be just as it is here. Just as our room is now, so it will be in the world to come; where our baby sleeps now, there too it will sleep in the other world. And the clothes we wear in this world, those too we will wear there. Everything will be as it is now, just a little different." Agamben, *Coming Community*, 53.

40. Agamben, *Coming Community*, 54.

41. Mayte Green-Mercado, *Visions of Deliverance: Moriscos and the Politics of Prophecy in the Early Modern Mediterranean* (Ithaca, NY: Cornell University Press, 2020).

42. For a recent discussion of how the conception of history as "change over time" serves expansionist, colonial, Christian purposes in the nineteenth-century United States (and thus how our history writing is always a religious project at some level), consider Kathryn Gin Lum, "The Historyless Heathen and the Stagnating Pagan: History as Non-Native Category?," *Religion and American Culture: A Journal of Interpretation* 28, no. 1 (2018): 73.

43. Shahzad Bashir, "Everlasting Doubt: Uncertainty in Islamic Representations of the Past," *Archiv für Religionsgeschichte* 20, no. 1 (2018): 26.

44. Andreyev, "Pashto Literature," 89–113. For another survey of Pashto literature, consider V. V. Kushev, "The Dawn of Pashtun Linguistics: Early Grammatical and Lexicographical Works and Their Manuscripts," *Manuscripta Orientalia* 7, no. 2 (2001): 3–9.

45. Farina Mir, *The Social Space of Language: Vernacular Culture in British Colonial Punjab* (Berkeley: University of California Press, 2010); Anne Murphy, "Writing Punjabi across Borders," in *South Asian History and Culture* 9, no. 1 (2018): 68–91; Sheldon Pollock, *The Language of the Gods in the World of Men: Sanskrit, Culture, and Power in Premodern India* (Berkeley: University of California Press, 2006); Christian Novetzke, *The Quotidian Revolution: Vernacularization, Religion, and the Premodern Public Sphere in India* (New York: Columbia University Press, 2016); Francesca Orsini, "The Multilingual Local in World Literature," *Comparative Literature* 67, no. 4 (2015): 345–74.

46. Andreyev, "Pashto Literature."

47. For an incisive discussion of the (assumed) link between ethnic identity and vernacularization, consider Judith T. Irvine and Susan Gal, "Language Ideology and

Linguistic Differentiation," in *Regimes of Language: Ideologies, Polities, and Identities*, ed. Paul V. Kroskrity (Santa Fe, NM: School of American Research Press, 2000).

48. The idea that those preaching on the apocalypse or claiming to be the messiah are mad is, surprisingly, a widely held hermeneutic assumption. For instance, consider the general approach taken by Landes (in an otherwise fascinating book) that we need to explain the appeal of the apocalyptically minded despite their apparent tendency to be consistently and stubbornly "wrong." Richard Landes, *Heaven on Earth: The Varieties of the Millennial Experience* (Oxford: Oxford University Press, 2011).

49. For further discussion of this, consider Giorgio Agamben, *The Fire and the Tale*, trans. Lorenzo Chiesa (Stanford, CA: Stanford, 2017), 107–8.

50. Webb Keane, *Christian Moderns: Freedom and Fetish in the Mission Encounter* (Berkeley: University of California Press, 2007).

51. Keane, 21.

52. Keane, 11.

53. For more on the enduring Protestantism of it all, consider Robert A. Orsi, *History and Presence* (Cambridge, MA: Harvard University Press, 2016).

54. As Ann Stoler has argued, cultures enact different function ontologies so that the heft of *being* is something witnessed, encountered, ascribed, and *spoken* according to particular regimes of knowing. Put differently, the naturalization of the Roshaniyya as Afghan is something that happened and something that was achieved. In the historical functional ontologies of Europe and American scholarship, ethnicity becomes a natural part of the world. Consider Ann Laura Stoler, *Along the Archival Grain: Epistemic Anxieties and Colonial Common Sense* (Princeton, NJ: Princeton University Press, 2010), 4ff.

55. For an excellent work that also adopts Keane's inquiry as a starting point of sorts, see Matthew Engelke, *A Problem of Presence: Beyond Scripture in an African Church* (Berkeley: University of California Press, 2007).

56. Saba Mahmood, "Religious Reason and Secular Affect," in *Is Critique Secular? Blasphemy, Injury, and Free Speech*, by Mahmood et al. (New York: Fordham University Press, 2013).

57. Karmen MacKendrick, *The Matter of Voice: Sensual Soundings* (Oxford: Oxford University Press, 2016).

58. Rowan Williams, *The Edge of Words: God and the Habits of Language* (London: Bloomsbury Continuum, 2014).

59. Noah Salomon, *For Love of the Prophet: An Ethnography of Sudan's Islamic State* (Princeton, NJ: Princeton University Press, 2016).

60. Charles Taylor, *The Language Animal* (Cambridge, MA: Harvard University Press, 2016), chap. 4.

61. Keane, *Christian Moderns*, 87ff.

62. Saba Mahmood, "Rehearsed Spontaneity and the Conventionality of Ritual: Disciplines of Salat," *American Ethnologist* 28, no. 4 (2001): 843.

63. Bruno Latour's analysis of the "modern" production of scientific regimes of knowledge is a necessary complement to Taylor and Keane's discussion of instrumentalist semiotics. To borrow Latour's terminology, we might say that an instrumentalist semiotic ideology "sorts" signifiers and that which is signified into distinct "ontological zones." Signifiers possess a hollowed-out, arbitrary ontology. This "sorting" of ontologies—or "purification," as Latour would say—is a central feature of the project

to convince ourselves that we are modern. Bruno Latour, *We Have Never Been Modern*, trans. Catherine Porter (Cambridge, MA: Harvard University Press, 1993), especially 10–11.

64. The analysis of the category of "religion"—and how this category is central to projects of modernity, secularism, capitalism, and white supremacy, among other phenomena—is a rich and growing line of inquiry within the academic study of religion. Some exceptional works in the field include Tomoko Masuzawa, *The Invention of World Religions: Or, How European Universalism Was Preserved in the Language of Pluralism* (Chicago: University of Chicago Press, 2005); Brent Nongbri, *Before Religion: A History of a Modern Concept* (New Haven, CT: Yale University Press, 2015); Tisa Wenger, *We Have a Religion: The 1920s Pueblo Indian Dance Controversy and American Religious Freedom* (Chapel Hill: University of North Carolina Press, 2009); John Lardas Modern, *Secularism in Antebellum America* (Chicago: University of Chicago Press, 2011). Less work has been conducted on this issue as it pertains to the study of Islam and religion in Central and South Asia, though some notable exceptions include Ilyse Morgenstein Fuerst, *Indian Muslim Minorities and the 1857 Rebellion: Religion, Rebels, and Jihad* (London: I. B. Tauris, 2017); Cemil Aydin, *The Idea of the Muslim World: A Global Intellectual History* (Cambridge, MA: Harvard University Press, 2017); and Shahab Ahmed, *What Is Islam? The Importance of Being Islamic* (Princeton, NJ: Princeton University Press, 2015).

65. For all the richness of Charles Taylor's recent work on the philosophy of language, this is an area of inquiry that is sorely missing in *The Language Animal*. For consideration of these issues, see (among many others) Toril Moi, *Sexual/Textual Politics* (London: Routledge, 1985); Judith T. Irvine and Susan Gal, "Language Ideology and Linguistic Differentiation," in *Regimes of Language: Ideologies, Polities, and Identities*, ed. Paul V. Kroskrity (Santa Fe, NM: School of American Research Press, 2000), 35–84. The essays in Alessandro Duranti's edited anthology, *A Companion to Linguistic Anthropology* (Malden, MA: Blackwell, 2004), are also excellent entry-points into this topic of language ideology and conceptions of ethnicity.

66. Keane, *Christian Moderns*, 41.

67. Or, as Stephan Palmié might put it, we are dealing with a "porous membrane" in which scholars and the "objects" of their study collectively interface to jointly contribute to "the cooking of history." Stephan Palmié, *The Cooking of History: How Not to Study Afro-Cuban Religion* (Chicago: University of Chicago Press, 2013), especially 259–62.

68. "Metapragmatics" is a term typically associated with the linguistic anthropology of Michael Silverstein. See Michael Silverstein, "Metapragmatic Discourse and Metapragmatic Function," in *Reflexive Language: Reported Speech and Metapragmatics*, ed. John Lucy et al. (Cambridge: Cambridge University Press, 1993), 33–58. The hermeneutic process being described is—as is likely clear—deeply resonant with the process described by Hans-Georg Gadamer. Hans-Georg Gadamer, *Truth and Method* (London: Bloomsbury Academic, 2013).

69. "Language does not abolish the all-important distance between bodies; on the contrary, by affirming the always unfinished character of converse or exchange, it acknowledges the non-negotiable diversity of bodies, and gives us a clue to the ethical basis of recognizing the other as never to be possessed." Williams, *Edge of Words*, 117.

70. Gerard Manley Hopkins, 'No worst, there is none' in *Gerard Manley Hopkins: The Major Works* (Oxford: Oxford University Press, 2009), 167.

71. Qur'an 6:60.

Chapter 1: Bayazid's Doubles

1. Eric Cross's book *The Tailor and Ansty* is an ethnography of sorts, recording the stories of a loquacious Irish tailor named Tim Buckley. The book is an interesting entry point into questions of identity and ethnicity that are relevant to our discussion, but I offer this quote for another reason. The quote is taken from Buckley's recounting of a common Irish folktale in which the king of the cats (Balgury) has died, and the new king of the cats (Balgeary) hears the news and assumes his throne. It is, as I understand it, a story similar to the messianic unveiling that we explore in this chapter—an unveiling that transpires through narratives of doubles, imitations, and mirrorings. Tell Bayazid that Bayazid is dead! For an illuminating discussion of the role played by *The Tailor and Ansty* in debates regarding Irish identity, consider Caleb Richardson, "'They Are Not Worthy of Themselves': The Tailor and Ansty Debates of 1942," *Éire-Ireland* 42, no. 3 (2007): 148–72.

2. ʿAlī Muḥammad Mukhliṣ Kandahārī Shīnvārī, *Ḥāl-nāmah-yi Miyān Roshan* (Kabul: Vizārat-i Iṭṭilāʿāt va Farhang, 2009), 255.

3. Mukhliṣ, 255.

4. The names of the host and rival—Payanda and Masum—are not mentioned in *The Book of States*, for instance.

5. Gabrielle M. Spiegel, "History, Historicism, and the Social Logic of the Text in the Middle Ages," *Speculum* 65 (1990): 59–86; Shahzad Bashir, *Sufi Bodies: Religion and Society in Medieval Islam* (New York: Columbia University Press, 2011).

6. Giorgio Agamben, *The Highest Poverty: Monastic Rules and Form-of-Life*, trans. Adam Kotsko (Stanford, CA: Stanford University Press, 2013), 16. Consider also Ingrid Nelson and Shannon Gayk, "Introduction: Genre as Form-of-Life," *Exemplaria* 27 (2015): 1–17.

7. Mukhliṣ, *Ḥāl-nāmah-yi Miyān Roshan*, 276.

8. Mukhliṣ 276.

9. Mukhliṣ, 274.

10. Mukhliṣ, 275.

11. Though hagiographies were long neglected in the academic study of Islam, the scholarship on these valuable sources has grown rapidly in the past decades. This is a welcome development. For exemplary approaches to hagiography, consider Bashir, *Sufi Bodies*; Amina Steinfels, *Knowledge before Action: Islamic Learning and Sufi Practice in the Life of Sayyid Jalāl al-dīn Bukhārī Makhdūm-i Jahāniyān* (Columbia: University of South Carolina Press, 2012); Noah Salomon, *For Love of the Prophet: An Ethnography of Sudan's Islamic State* (Princeton, NJ: Princeton University Press, 2016). For a wide-ranging discussion of the comparative study of hagiographies, consider the special edition of *Religions* devoted to "hagiology," beginning with this introduction: Massimo A. Rondolino, "Introduction: Comparative Hagiology, Issues in Theory and Method," *Religions* 11, no. 4 (2020).

12. For general considerations of the literary cultures at Mughal courts, consider Audrey Truschke, *Culture of Encounters: Sanskrit at the Mughal Court* (New York:

Columbia University Press, 2016); Richard Eaton, *India in the Persianate Age, 1000–1765* (Berkeley: University of California Press, 2019).

13. For a comparative analysis of hagiography, consider John Renard, *Friends of God: Islamic Images of Piety, Commitment, and Servanthood* (Berkeley: University of California Press, 2008).

14. Azfar Moin, *The Millennial Sovereign: Sacred Kingship and Sainthood in Islam* (New York: Columbia University Press, 2012).

15. Abū al-Faḍl ibn Mubārak, *Akbar-nāmah*, ed. and trans. Wheeler M. Thackston as *The History of Akbar* (Cambridge, MA: Harvard University Press, 2014–17), 1:13–15.

16. Abū al-Faḍl, 1:13–15.

17. Abū al-Faḍl, 1:17.

18. Joseph Theodore Arlinghaus, "The Transformation of Afghan Tribal Society: Tribal Expansion, Mughal Imperialism and the Roshaniyya Insurrection, 1450–1600" (PhD diss., Duke University, 1989), chap. 6.

19. For other valuable works on the study of hagiography outside the Islamic context, consider Nicolette Zeeman, "Imaginative Theory," *Middle English* (2007): 222–40; Anke Bernau and Eva von Contzen, eds., *Sanctity as Literature in Late Medieval Britain* (Manchester: Manchester University Press, 2015).

20. Kathryn Gin Lum, "The Historyless Heathen and the Stagnating Pagan: History as Non-Native Category?," *Religion and American Culture: A Journal of Interpretation* 28, no. 1 (2018): 73.

21. Saba Mahmood, *Religious Difference in a Secular Age: A Minority Report* (Princeton, NJ: Princeton University Press, 2015), 195–207, esp. 197.

22. S. A. A. Rizvi, "Rawshaniyya Movement," *Abr-Nahrain* 6 (June 1965): 63–91; Rizvi, "Rawshaniyya Movement (continued)," *Abr-Nahrain* 7 (August 1967): 62–98.

23. Mahmood, *Religious Difference in a Secular Age*, chap. 5.

24. Arlinghaus, "Transformation of Afghan Tribal Society," 282.

25. Felice Lifshitz, "Beyond Positivism and Genre: 'Hagiographical' Texts as Historical Narrative," *Viator* 25 (1994): 95–113.

26. Rizvi, "Rawshaniyya Movement," 71–74.

27. For a critique of a purely "symbolic" reading of hagiographies, consider Bashir's discussion of miraculous food in *Sufi Bodies*, chap. 6.

28. Gin Lum, "Historyless Heathen," 70–79.

29. Agamben, *Highest Poverty*.

30. Rizvi, "Rawshaniyya Movement," 63–91. Other examples of studies that pursue the historical Bayazid include Tariq Ahmed, *Religio-political Ferment in the N.W. Frontier during the Mughal Period: The Raushaniya Movement* (Delhi: Idarah-i Adabiyat-i Delli, 1982); Yār Muḥammad Maghmūm Khaṭṭak, *The Rowshanites and Pashto Literature* (Peshawar: Pashto Academy, University of Peshawar, 2005).

31. Mukhliṣ, *Ḥāl-nāmah-yi Miyān Roshan*, 5.

32. Mukhliṣ, 5–7.

33. Mukhliṣ, 11–33.

34. Mukhliṣ, 78–91.

35. Mukhliṣ, 90.

36. Mukhliṣ, 94–97.

37. Mukhliṣ, 251.

38. Mukhliṣ, 255.

39. Mukhliṣ, 346–49.

40. Mukhliṣ, 349–55.

41. Mukhliṣ, 355.

42. On Mirza Hakim, consider Munis Faruqui, "The Forgotten Prince: Mirza Hakim and the Formation of the Mughal Empire in India," *Journal of the Economic and Social History of the Orient* 48, no. 4 (2005): 487–523. For a discussion of the Roshaniyya and Mirza Hakim that does not explicate its sources, consider I'jāz al-Haqq Quddūsī, *Tazkirah-yi ṣūfiyā-yi sarḥad* (Lahore: Markazi Urdu Board, 1966), 83–145.

43. Mukhliṣ, *Ḥāl-nāmah-yi Miyān Roshan*, 355.

44. Jan-Peter Hartung, "Frontiers–Pieties–Resistance," in *Dynamics of Change in the Pakistan–Afghanistan Region: Politics on Borderland*, ed. Shahida Aman and Muhammad Zubair (Peshawar: University of Peshawar, 2017), 39–54.

45. For works that explore the stunning diversity of representations of Muhammad's life (or lives), consider Kecia Ali, *The Lives of Muhammad* (Cambridge, MA: Harvard University Press, 2014); Tarif Khalidi, *Images of Muhammad: Narratives of the Prophet in Islam across the Centuries* (New York: Doubleday, 2009).

46. Agamben, *Highest Poverty*, 60–62.

47. Dimitris Vardoulakis, *The Doppelgänger: Literature's Philosophy* (New York: Fordham University Press, 2010), 2.

48. For perspectives on dream cultures in Islamic society, consider the following works: Nile Green, "The Religious and Cultural Roles of Dreams and Visions in Islam," *Journal of the Royal Asiatic Society* 13 (2003): 287–313; Özgen Felek and Alexander D. Knysh, *Dreams and Visions in Islamic Societies* (Albany: State University of New York Press, 2012).

49. Mukhliṣ, *Ḥāl-nāmah-yi Miyān Roshan*, 5.

50. Mukhliṣ, 23–26.

51. Mukhliṣ, 41–43.

52. Mukhliṣ, 54–60.

53. Mukhliṣ, 61.

54. Mukhliṣ, 55.

55. Mukhliṣ, 32.

56. Mukhliṣ, 32–33.

57. Mukhliṣ, 33.

58. Bashir, *Sufi Bodies*, chaps. 5 and 7.

59. Mukhliṣ, *Ḥāl-nāmah-yi Miyān Roshan*, 57–66.

60. For a provocative account of dreams and imaginal realms in the philosophies of Ibn 'Arabi, consider Henry Corbin, *Creative Imagination in the Sufism of Ibn 'Arabi* (Princeton, NJ: Princeton University Press, 1969). Also consider William C. Chittick, *The Sufi Path of Knowledge: Ibn al-'Arabi's Metaphysics of Imagination* (Albany: State University of New York Press, 1989), chap. 3.

61. Mukhliṣ, *Ḥāl-nāmah-yi Miyān Roshan*, 42–43.

62. Elsewhere in *The Book of States*, Bayazid explicitly describes his Sufi initiation as done in the "Uvaysi" manner (190). For a discussion of the social function of claims to Uvaysi initiation, consider Devin DeWeese, "An 'Uvaysī Sufi in Timurid Mawarannahr: Notes on Hagiography and the Taxonomy of Sanctity in the Religious History of Central Asia," *Papers on Inner Asia* 22 (1993).

63. Mukhliṣ, *Ḥāl-nāmah-yi Miyān Roshan*, 25.

64. Mukhliṣ, 26–27.

65. Mukhliṣ, 27.

66. Mukhliṣ, 27–28.
67. Mukhliṣ, 28.
68. For excellent analyses of Islamic narratives on the prophet Ibrāhīm in a comparative context, consider Robert C. Gregg, *Shared Stories, Rival Tellings: Early Encounters of Jews, Christians, and Muslims* (Oxford; New York, NY: Oxford University Press, 2015), chap. 6; Carol Bakhos, *The Family of Abraham: Jewish, Christian, and Muslim Interpretations* (Cambridge, MA: Harvard University Press, 2014), chaps. 2–3.
69. Mukhliṣ, *Ḥāl-nāmah-yi Miyān Roshan*, 29.
70. Mukhliṣ, 29.
71. For these works, consult Muḥammad ibn al-Ḥusayn Sulamī, *Ṭabaqāt al-ṣūfīyah*, ed. Nur al-Din Shuraybah (Cairo: Maktabat al-Khanji, 1969); Farīd al-Din ʿAṭṭār, *Farīd ad-Din ʿAttār's Memorial of God's Friends: Lives and Sayings of Sufis*, trans. Paul Losensky (Mahwah, NJ: Paulist, 2009). For literary analyses of Sufi biographical traditions, consider Michael Cooperson, *Classical Arabic Biography: The Heirs of the Prophets in the Age of al-Ma'mūn* (Cambridge: Cambridge University Press, 2000), chap. 5; Jawid A. Mojaddedi, *The Biographical Tradition in Sufism: The Tabaqat Genre from al-Sulami to Jami* (Richmond, UK: Curzon, 2001).
72. ʿAṭṭār, *Farīd ad-Din ʿAttār's Memorial of God's Friends*, 114–26.
73. ʿAṭṭār, 154.
74. Shahzad Bashir, "Muhammad in Sufi Eyes: Prophetic Legitimacy in Medieval Iran and Central Asia," in *The Cambridge Companion to Muhammad*, ed. Jonathan E. Brockopp (Cambridge: Cambridge University Press, 2010), 219–20.
75. For works that explore the stunning diversity of representations of Muhammad's life (or lives), consider Ali, *Lives of Muhammad*; Tarif Khalidi, *Images of Muhammad: Narratives of the Prophet in Islam across the Centuries* (New York: Doubleday, 2009).
76. Mukhliṣ, *Ḥāl-nāmah-yi Miyān Roshan*, 29.
77. For a representative example of such an exchange, see Mukhliṣ, 175.
78. I have transliterated this rival shaykh's name as *Uriyā*, but its proper transliteration is unknown to me.
79. Mukhliṣ, *Ḥāl-nāmah-yi Miyān Roshan*, 226.
80. Mukhliṣ, 353.
81. Mukhliṣ, 354.
82. Bashir, "Muhammad in Sufi Eyes," 224.
83. For the foundational discussion of chronotopes, consider Mikhail Bakhtin, *The Dialogic Imagination: Four Essays* (Austin: University of Texas Press, 1983), 84ff.
84. Mukhliṣ, *Ḥāl-nāmah-yi Miyān Roshan*, 204.
85. Mukhliṣ, 219.
86. See chapter 5 for a discussion of the polemics of Akhund Darweza.
87. If we accept the narrative logic of *The Book of States*, this event suggests the hypocrisy of later Mughal persecution of the Roshaniyya. Mirza Hakim, the Mughal prince and rival of Akbar governing in Kabul, sanctioned (or perhaps "pardoned") Bayazid in a face-to-face meeting even as later Mughal governors would condemn him to heresy from a distance. Mukhliṣ, *Ḥāl-nāmah-yi Miyān Roshan*, 216. For more on Mirza Hakim, consider Faruqui, "Forgotten Prince."
88. Mukhliṣ, *Ḥāl-nāmah-yi Miyān Roshan*, 335–46.
89. Mukhliṣ, 1–4.

90. Bāyazīd Anṣārī, "Ṣirāṭ al-tawḥīd," n.d., MS 15978, Ganj Bakhsh Library, Iran-Pakistan Institute of Persian Studies, Islamabad, fol. 18; Bāyazīd Anṣārī, "Ṣirāṭ al-tawḥīd," n.d., MS 924, Raza Library, Rampur.

91. Mukhliṣ, *Ḥāl-nāmah-yi Miyān Roshan*, 256–57.

92. For more on Aḥmad Bashiri, consider Shahzad Bashir's *Sufi Bodies*. For the other sources, consider 'Alī ibn Ḥusayn Kāshifī Ṣāfi, *Rashaḥāt 'ayn al-ḥayāh* (Beirut: Dār al-Kutub al-'Ilmīyah, 2008); Jāmī, *Nafaḥāt al-uns min haẓarāt al-quds* (Tehran: Kitābfurūshī-i Mahmūdī, 1958); "Tuḥfa-yi qāsimī" (Kolkata, seventeenth century), Curzon Collection 261, Asiatic Society of Bengal; Muḥammad Hāshim ibn Muḥammad Qāsim Badakhshānī, *Zubdat al-maqāmāt* (Lahore: Būstān-i Adab, 1969).

93. Agamben, *Highest Poverty*, 57.

Chapter 2: The *Dhikr* of the Wretch

1. Bāyazīd Anṣārī, *Maqṣūd al-mu'minīn*, ed. Mīr Walī Khān Mas'ūdī (Islamabad: Majma' al-Buḥūth al-Islāmīya, 1976), 177–80.

2. Pierre Hadot, *Philosophy as a Way of Life: Spiritual Exercises from Socrates to Foucault*, ed. Arnold I. Davidson, trans. Michael Case (Malden, MA: Wiley-Blackwell, 1995), 82

3. For further discussion of self-formation through models of "being acted upon," consider Amira Mittermeier, *Dreams That Matter: Egyptian Landscapes of the Imagination* (Berkeley: University of California Press, 2011); Anand Vivek Taneja, *Jinnealogy* (Stanford, CA: Stanford University Press, 2018).

4. In *The Book of States*, we read that Bayazid ordered some faithful disciples to deliver epistles with Roshani teachings to a host of rulers, including Emperor Akbar. The manuscripts of *The Path of Unity* claim to reproduce just such an epistle, and the epistle is attributed to "Bayazid the Wretch" and frequently cites the sayings of Bayazid the Wretch without ever explaining the connection to *sukūna*. Bāyazīd Anṣārī, "Ṣirāṭ al-tawḥīd," MS 15978, Ganj Bakhsh Library, Iran-Pakistan Institute of Persian Studies, Islamabad.

5. Poverty (*faqr*) and other related concepts have been central to many traditions of Sufi practice. For an especially interesting manifestation of Sufi commitments to poverty and abasement, consider Ahmet Karamustafa, *God's Unruly Friends: Dervish Groups in the Islamic Middle Period, 1200–1550* (Oxford: Oneworld, 2006).

6. Careful mapping of the stages of the spiritual path has been an aspect of Sufi literature from the time of al-Sarraj and al-Qushayri in the tenth and eleventh centuries. For translated excerpts of these works, consider Michael Sells, *Early Islamic Mysticism: Sufi, Qur'an, Mir'aj, Poetic, and Theological Writing* (Mahwah, NJ: Paulist, 1996).

7. Bāyazīd Anṣārī, *Maqṣūd al-mu'minīn*, 346.

8. Bāyazīd Anṣārī, 348.

9. The hadith cited by Bayazid can be found in *Jami' at-Tirmidhī*, Book 36, Hadith 49, Vol. 4, Book 10, Hadith 2352, trans. Abu Khaliyl (Dar-es-Salaam, 2007.

10. Toufic Fahd, "Sakīna," in *Encyclopaedia of Islam*, ed. P. Bearman et al., 2nd ed., (Brill Online, 2012–), accessed April 26, 2017, http://referenceworks.brillonline.com/entries/encyclopaedia-of-islam-2/sakina-SIM_6505.

11. Bāyazīd Anṣārī, *Maqṣūd al-mu'minīn*, 347.

12. A. J. Arberry, *The Koran Interpreted: A Translation* (New York: Simon and Schuster, 1955).

13. Fahd, "Sakīna."

14. For elaboration upon *performance* in language, consider especially J. L. Austin, *How to Do Things with Words* (Cambridge, MA: Harvard University Press, 1962); Judith Butler, *Bodies That Matter: On the Discursive Limits of "Sex"* (New York: Routledge, 1993); Michael Sells, *Mystical Languages of Unsaying* (Chicago: University of Chicago Press, 1994).

15. Bāyazīd Anṣārī, *Maqṣūd al-mu'minīn*, 356.

16. Bāyazīd Anṣārī, 357.

17. Bruno Latour, *Rejoicing: Or the Torments of Religious Speech*, trans. Julie Rose (Cambridge: Polity, 2013), 32.

18. Ian R. Netton, *Sufi Ritual: The Parallel Universe* (London: Curzon, 2000), 11.

19. Consider Sufi presentations of "Sufism" as a project in Rosemary Corbett, *Making Moderate Islam* (Stanford, CA: Stanford University Press, 2016); Mark Sedgwick, *Western Sufism: From the Abbasids to the New Age* (Oxford: Oxford University Press, 2016).

20. Corbett, *Making Moderate Islam: Sufism, Service, and the "Ground Zero Mosque" Controversy*; Richard King, *Orientalism and Religion: Post-colonial Theory, India, and "The Mystic East"* (London: Routledge, 1999).

21. Mahmood Mamdani, *Good Muslim, Bad Muslim: America, the Cold War, and the Roots of Terror* (New York: Pantheon, 2004).

22. James Joyce, *Ulysses* (1922; Oxford: Oxford University Press, 2011), 186.

23. Qur'an 36:82.

24. Daniel Sheffield, "The Language of Paradise in Safavid Iran: Speech and Cosmology in the Thought of Āẕar Kayvān and His Followers," in *There's No Tapping around Philology*, ed. Alireza Korangy and Daniel Sheffield (Wiesbaden: Otto Harrassowitz Verlag, 2014), 161–83.

25. Sheffield, 169.

26. Orkhan Mir-Kasimov, *Words of Power: Ḥurūfī Teachings between Shi'ism and Sufism in Medieval Islam* (London: I. B. Tauris, 2015), 45.

27. Mir-Kasimov, 58–59.

28. For a common treatment of dhikr as a ritual technique for distinct Sufi networks, consider the use of the term in this concise but rich introduction: Nile Green, *Sufism: A Global History* (Oxford: Wiley-Blackwell, 2014), esp. 239.

29. For a general introduction to these varieties, consider Carl Ernst, *Sufism* (Boston: Shambhala, 2011), chap. 4.

30. Devin DeWeese has examined the considerable diversity and evolution of Naqshbandī dhikr practices. See especially Devin DeWeese, "The Eclipse of the Kubravīyah in Central Asia," *Iranian Studies* 21, no. 1/2 (1988): 45–83; Devin DeWeese, "The Mashā'ikh-i Turk and the Khojagān: Rethinking the Links between the Yasavī and Naqshbandī Sufi Traditions," *Journal of Islamic Studies* 7, no. 2 (1996): 180–207. In addition to the aforementioned works by DeWeese, consider the description of 'Abd al-Ghanī al-Nabulusī in Barbara von Schlegell, "Sufism in the Ottoman Arab World: Shaykh 'Abd al-Ghanī al-Nābulusī (d.1143/1731)" (PhD diss., University of California, Berkeley, 1997), 164.

31. For a wide-ranging consideration of Afghanistan as connected to global networks, consider Robert Crews, *Afghan Modern: The History of a Global Nation* (Cambridge, MA: Belknap, 2015). For a focused analysis of trading routes, consider Magnus Marsden, *Trading Worlds: Afghan Merchants across Modern Frontiers* (Oxford: Oxford University Press, 2016).

32. John F. Richards, *The Mughal Empire* (Cambridge: Cambridge University Press, 1996), 50. Also consider Stephen Dale's work on later mercantile connections throughout Central and South Asia. Stephen Frederic Dale, *Indian Merchants and Eurasian Trade, 1600–1750* (Cambridge: Cambridge University Press, 2002), esp. chap. 3.

33. Waleed Ziad, *Hidden Caliphate: Sufi Saints beyond the Oxus and Indus* (Cambridge, MA: Harvard University Press, 2021).

34. ʿAlī Muḥammad Mukhliṣ Kandahārī Shīnvārī, *Ḥāl-nāmah-yi Miyān Roshan* (Kabul: Vizārat-i Iṭṭilāʿāt va Farhang, 2009), 333–34.

35. Consider Talal Asad's classic comments on ritual: *Genealogies of Religion: Discipline and Reasons of Power in Christianity and Islam* (Baltimore: Johns Hopkins University Press, 1993), chap. 2.

36. Najm al-Dīn Kubrá, *Fawāʾiḥ al-jamāl wa fawātiḥ al-jalāl* (Kuwait: Dar Saʿād al-Subāḥ, 1993), 131.

37. Both Hadot and Foucault emphasized the importance of formation in the ancient philosophical schools and the transformation of interiorized spaces and levels in the self, but they differed starkly as to the understood purpose of such practices and spiritual exercises. In a work published shortly after Foucault's death, Hadot responded to Foucault by writing, "The description M. Foucault gives . . . is precisely too focused on the 'self.'" He goes on to explain that Foucault's presentation languishes in a narrow concern with the self's recognition of the self. The creative, liberating practices of self-cultivation and aesthetic self-formation lead ultimately back to a bondage in one's own boundaries of selfhood, even if Foucault is quick to celebrate the potential to perpetually devote one's self to changing these boundaries through disciplinary practices. What Foucault presents as the forging of an individual spiritual identity with the aim (*téléologie*) of perfect self-mastery, Hadot insists was rather the attempt to "change the level of the self" and "raise oneself up to universality." For Hadot's Greek philosophers, there is an ascension found within the depths of the disciplined self. "The movement of interiorization is inseparably linked to another movement, whereby one rises to a higher psychic level, at which one encounters another kind of exteriorization, another relationship with 'the exterior.'" As Hadot explains elsewhere, the spiritual exercises of the Greeks result in metamorphosis of the personality and a consequent conformation of one's perspective and existence to the perspective of "the Whole" or "the objective Spirit." Pierre Hadot, *Philosophy as a Way of Life: Spiritual Exercises from Socrates to Foucault* (Malden, MA: Wiley-Blackwell, 1995), 206–11.

38. Bāyazīd Anṣārī, *Maqṣūd al-muʾminīn*, 129.

39. Bāyazīd Anṣārī, 132; Qur'an 73:19.

40. For a stirring meditation on the complexities of citation and voice, consider Karmen MacKendrick, *The Matter of Voice: Sensual Soundings* (New York: Fordham University Press, 2016), 2–4.

41. Bāyazīd Anṣārī, *Maqṣūd al-muʾminīn*, 140–41.

42. Giorgio Agamben, *Language and Death: The Place of Negativity*, trans. Karen E. Pinkus with Michael Hardt (Minneapolis: University of Minnesota Press, 1991), 107. Also: Giorgio Agamben, *Infancy and History*, trans. Liz Heron (New York: Verso, 1993), 3–4.

43. Agamben, *Language and Death*, 107.

44. Giorgio Agamben, *The Man without Content*, trans. Georgia Albert (Stanford, CA: Stanford University Press, 1999), 68–70.

45. Agamben visits this concept across a number of works, and the most relevant for this discussion are *Language and Death*; *Infancy and History*; *The Man without*

Content; and *Potentialities* (Stanford, CA: Stanford University Press, 1999). For an effort that aims to synthesize these different writings, consider William Watkin, *The Literary Agamben* (London: Continuum, 2010), esp. 106–13 and 126–32.

46. Mukhliṣ, *Ḥāl-nāmah-yi Miyān Roshan*, 55–56.

47. Mukhliṣ, 70.

48. Saba Mahmood, "Rehearsed Spontaneity and the Conventionality of Ritual: Disciplines of Salat," *American Ethnologist* 28, no. 4 (2001): 843.

49. For an engaging discussion of the "limits of sincerity" in analyses of ritual, consider Adam Seligman et al., *Ritual and Its Consequences* (Oxford: Oxford University Press, 2008).

50. Bāyazīd Anṣārī, *Maqṣūd al-mu'minīn*, 326.

51. Bāyazīd Anṣārī, 299–300.

52. Bāyazīd Anṣārī, 202 and 345.

53. Sells, *Mystical Languages of Unsaying*, 1–12

54. Bāyazīd Anṣārī, *Maqṣūd al-mu'minīn*, 328–33.

55. Jean-Louis Chrétien, *The Call and the Response*, trans. Anne Davenport (New York: Fordham University Press, 2004), 78.

56. Jean-Luc Marion, *Being Given: Toward a Phenomenology of Givenness*, trans. Jeffrey Kosky (Stanford, CA: Stanford University Press, 2002).

57. Qur'an 39:86.

58. Bāyazīd Anṣārī, *Maqṣūd al-mu'minīn*, 176–78.

59. See Ernst's thoughtful introduction to this body of material in *Sufism*, chap. 1.

60. Some exemplary ethnographies of Sufi ritual include Joyce Flueckiger, *In Amma's Healing Room: Gender and Vernacular Islam in South India* (Bloomington: Indiana University Press, 2006; Robert Rozehnal, *Islamic Sufism Unbound* (New York: Palgrave Macmillan, 2009); Pnina Werbner, *Pilgrims of Love* (Bloomington: Indiana University Press, 2003).

61. For a truly beautiful account of a Sufi community that compellingly blends textual analysis with ethnographic observation, I cannot recommend highly enough the following work: Rian Thum, *Sacred Routes of Uyghur History* (Cambridge, MA: Harvard University Press, 2014).

62. As Talal Asad argued regarding ritual, we can allow "forgotten understanding[s]" of ritual to serve as a challenge to the symbolic approach of much anthropology, and thus: "The possibility is opened up of inquiring into the ways in which embodied practices (including language in use) form a precondition for varieties of religious experiences. . . . "Consciousness" becomes a dependent concept." Talal Asad, "Toward a Genealogy of the Concept of Ritual," in *Genealogies of Religion* (Baltimore: Johns Hopkins University Press, 1993), 76–77.

63. Webb Keane, *Christian Moderns: Freedom and Fetish in the Mission Encounter* (Berkeley: University of California Press, 2007), 87ff.

64. Rowan Williams, *The Edge of Words: God and the Habits of Language* (London: Bloomsbury Continuum, 2014), 93.

Chapter 3: Revelation through Repetition

1. In the following two chapters, we will consider the critics of the Roshaniyya who make such claims.

2. The works of William Chittick are excellent introductions to the theology of Ibn 'Arabi, which forms the basis for most Islamic expressions of "the unity of being": William Chittick, *The Sufi Path of Knowledge* (Albany: State University of New York Press, 1989). For consideration of the place of *wahdat al-wujud* in the Indian context among Naqshbandi Sufis, see Arthur Buehler, *Sufi Heirs of the Prophet* (Columbia: University of South Carolina Press, 1998).

3. Some of these works are truly excellent histories of Afghan religion, but they perseverate on notions of tribe and identity to the exclusion of the literary (and still stranger) aspects of *The Best Exposition*. Representative examples include Sergei Andreyev, "The Rawshaniyya," in *The Heritage of Sufism*, ed. Leonard Lewisohn (Oxford: Oneworld, 1999); Joseph Arlinghaus, "The Transformation of Afghan Tribal Society" (PhD diss., Duke University, 1989).

4. Aida Yared, "'In the Name of Annah': Islam and *Salam* in Joyce's *Finnegans Wake*," *James Joyce Quarterly* 35, no. 2/3 (1998): 401–38.

5. Some recent scholarship on the theoretical possibilities of *translation* have explored a similar idea: that translation necessarily involves a process of transformation. Consider Anand Vivek Taneja's chapter ("Translation") from his recent book, *Jinnealogy* (Stanford, CA: Stanford University Press, 2018), in which he discusses the work of Paul de Man and its value for translating Delhi's ruins.

6. Gilles Deleuze and Felix Guattari, *A Thousand Plateaus: Capitalism and Schizophrenia*, trans. Brian Massumi (Minneapolis: University of Minnesota Press, 1987), 10.

7. For a valuable consideration of the Prophet Muhammad's life and its (re)interpretations, consider Kecia Ali, *The Lives of Muhammad* (Cambridge, MA: Harvard University Press, 2014). On *i'jaz al-qur'an*, consider Margaret Larkin, "The Inimitability of the Qur'an: Two Perspectives," *Religion and Literature* 20, no. 1 (1988): 31–47; Sophia Vasalou, "The Miraculous Eloquence of the Qur'an: General Trajectories and Individual Approaches," *Journal of Qur'anic Studies* 4, no. 2 (2002): 23–53; Lara Harb, "Form, Content, and the Inimitability of the Qur'ān in 'Abd al-Qāhir al-Jurjānī's Works," *Middle Eastern Literatures* 18, no. 3 (2015): 301–21; Muhammad Khalaf-Allah Ahmad and Muhammad Zaghlul Sallam, eds., *Three Treatises on the I'jaz of the Qur'an*, trans. Issaa J. Boullata (Reading, UK: Garnet, 2015).

8. Some excellent exceptions to this neglect include Shawkat M. Toorawa, "Modern Arabic Literature and the Qur'an: Inimitability Creativity, . . . Incompatibility," in *Religious Perspectives in Modern Muslim and Jewish Literatures*, ed. Glenda Abramsom and Hilary Kilpatrick (London: Routledge, 2005), 25–40; Todd Lawson, *Gnostic Apocalypse and Islam: Qur'an, Exegesis, Messianism and the Literary Origins of the Babi Religion* (London: Routledge, 2012); Ayman A. El-Desouky, "Naẓm, I'jāz, Discontinuous Kerygma: Approaching Qur'anic Voice on the Other Side of the Poetic," *Journal of Qur'anic Studies* 15, no. 2 (2013): 1–21; Devin J. Stewart, "Rhythmical Anxiety: Notes on Abū'l-'Alā' al-Ma'arrī's (d. 449/1058) al-Fuṣūl Wa'l-Ghāyāt and Its Reception," in *The Qur'an and Adab: The Shaping of Literary Traditions in Classical Islam*, ed. Nuha Alshaar (Oxford: Oxford University Press in association with The Institute of Ismaili Studies, 2017), 239–72.

9. Shahzad Bashir, "On Islamic Time: Rethinking Chronology in the Historiography of Muslim Societies," *History and Theory* 53, no. 4 (December 2014): 519–44.

10. Daniel A. Madigan, *The Qur'ān's Self-Image: Writing and Authority in Islam's Scripture* (Princeton, NJ: Princeton University Press, 2001), 144.

11. Aziz al-Azmeh, *Islam and Modernities* (London: Verso, 2009), chap.6.

12. Qur'an 55:1–7.

13. The editors of *The Study Quran* have discussed these interpretations, noting especially al-Qurtubi and Ahmad ibn 'Ajibah as proponents of this view. Nasr et al., *The Study Quran* (New York: HarperOne, 2015), 1309–18.

14. Walid Saleh, *The Formation of the Classical Tafsīr Tradition: The Qur'ān Commentary of al-Tha'labī (d. 427/1035)* (Leiden: Brill, 2004), 19.

15. Saleh, 79–80.

16. See the following chapter for a specific discussion of this critique in the broader context of Akhund Darweza's work.

17. Diana Lobel, *A Sufi-Jewish Dialogue: Philosophy and Mysticism in Bahya ibn Paquda's "Duties of the Heart"* (Philadelphia: University of Pennsylvania Press, 2007), 122.

18. Lobel, 125.

19. For a helpful collection of *i'jāz* writings from a formative period of Sunni Islam, consider Ahmad and Sallam, eds., *Three Treatises on the I'jaz of the Qur'an.*

20. Qur'an 36:82.

21. Shahzad Bashir, "The Imam's Return: Messianic Leadership in Late Medieval Shi'ism," in *The Most Learned of the Shi'a: The Institution of the Marja' Taqlid*, ed. Linda S. Walbridge (Oxford: Oxford University Press, 2005), 21–33.

22. Shahzad Bashir, *Fazlallah Astarabadi and the Hurufis* (Oxford: Oneworld, 2005), 80–81.

23. Orkhan Mir-Kasimov, *Words of Power: Ḥurūfī Teachings between Shi'ism and Sufism in Medieval Islam* (London: I. B. Tauris, 2015), 45.

24. Mir-Kasimov, 58–59.

25. Vladmir Minorsky, "The Poetry of Shāh Ismā'īl I," *Bulletin of the School of Oriental and African Studies* 10, no. 4 (1942): 1010a and 1026a.

26. Ziba Mir-Hosseini, "Inner Truth and Outer History: The Two Worlds of the Ahl-i Haqq of Kurdistan," *International Journal of Middle East Studies* 26, no. 2 (1994): 267–69.

27. Artem Davydov, "On Souleymane Kanté's Translation of the Quran into the Maninka Language," *Mandenkan*, no. 48 (2012): 3–20; Dianne White Oyler, "Reinventing Oral Tradition: The Modern Epic of Souleymane Kanté," *Research in African Literatures* 33, no. 1 (2002): 75–93.

28. Konrad Tuchscherer and Paul E. H. Hair, "Cherokee and West Africa: Examining the Origins of the Vai Script," *History in Africa* 29 (2002): 427–86.

29. Louis E. Fenech, *The Sikh* Ẓafar-namah *of Guru Gobind Singh: A Discursive Blade in the Heart of the Mughal Empire* (Oxford: Oxford University Press, 2012); Daniel Sheffield, "The Language of Paradise in Safavid Iran: Speech and Cosmology in the Thought of Āẕar Kayvān and His Followers," in *There's No Tapping around Philology*, ed. Alireza Korangy and Daniel Sheffield (Wiesbaden: Otto Harrassowitz Verlag, 2014), 161–83.

30. Bāyazīd Anṣārī, "Ṣirāṭ al-tawḥīd," n.d., MS 15978, Ganj Bakhsh Library, Iran-Pakistan Institute of Persian Studies, Islamabad; Bāyazīd Anṣārī, "Ṣirāṭ al-tawḥīd," n.d., MS 924, Raza Library, Rampur, India.

31. Bāyazīd Anṣārī, "Ṣirāṭ al-tawḥīd" (Islamabad), 53. I use page numbers instead of folio numbers since each individual page is marked clearly with a number in the manuscript of *The Path of Oneness.*

32. Bāyazīd Anṣārī, "Ṣirāṭ al-tawḥīd" (Islamabad), 9.

33. By that, I mean that they are attributed to *bayazid al-miskin* in the introduction of the text.

34. *Subḥānu-ka al-mālik al-bārī, judā kard ʿālim-i nūrī āz nārī, bāyazīd ānṣārī*; J. Leyden, "On the Rosheniah Sect and Its Founder, Bayezid Ansari," *Asiatick Researches* 11 (1812): 380.

35. Leyden is quoting Akhund Darweza from a source that I have not seen. Leyden, "On the Rosheniah Sect," 380.

36. For discussion of vernacular literature and vernacularization, consider the following works: Alexander Beecroft, *An Ecology of World Literature: From Antiquity to the Present Day* (London: Verso Books, 2015), chap. 4.; Christian Lee Novetzke, *The Quotidian Revolution: Vernacularization, Religion, and the Premodern Public Sphere in India* (New York: Columbia University Press, 2016); Sheldon Pollock, *The Language of the Gods in the World of Men* (Berkeley: University of California Press, 2009).

37. The phrase emerges from Andreyev's chapter, which is an excellent survey of Pashto literature but gives brief expression to a deterministic approach to Pashto as a matter of Pashtun identity that is found throughout much English-language scholarship. Sergei Andreyev, "Pashto Literature: The Classical Period," in *Oral Literature of Iranian Languages: Kurdish, Pashto, Balochi, Ossetic, Persian and Tajik: Companion Volume II to A History of Persian Literature*, vol. 18, ed. Philip G. Kreyenbroek and Ulrich Marzolph (London: I. B. Tauris, 2010), 92.

38. I thank Eric Hoenes del Pinal for alerting me to the scholarship of Irvine and Gal. Judith T. Irvine and Susan Gal, "Language Ideology and Linguistic Differentiation," in *Regimes of Language: Ideologies, Polities, and Identities*, ed. Paul V. Kroskrity (Santa Fe, NM: School of American Research Press, 2000), 37.

39. Andreyev, "Pashto Literature: The Classical Period," 109.

40. Andreyev, 109.

41. Rowan Williams, *The Edge of Words: God and the Habits of Language* (London: Bloomsbury Continuum, 2014), 18.

42. Tyler Roberts, *Encountering Religion: Responsibility and Criticism after Secularism* (New York: Columbia University Press, 2013), 170. In this passage, Roberts is building upon Rowan Williams's *On Christian Theology* (Oxford: Wiley-Blackwell, 2000).

43. Agamben, *The Time That Remains: A Commentary on the Letter to the Romans*, trans. Patricia Dailey (Stanford, CA: Stanford University Press, 2005), 67–68.

44. Agamben, 74.

45. *Yā bāyazīd! Uktub ʿalā bidāyat al-kitāb bi-taʿẓīm al-ḥurūf bism allāh. Inna-nī lā uḍīʾ ʿajr al-ladhīna yaktabūn thumma yakhrajūn ḥarf-an ʿaw nuqṭa-tan thumma yaktabūn li-ʾl-ajl ṣaḥīḥ al-bayān*. Bāyazīd Anṣārī, *Khayr al-bayān*, ed. Muḥammad ʿAbd a-Quddūs Qāsimī (Peshawar: Pashto Academy at Peshawar University, 1988), 133; "Khayr al-bayān," 1650–51 CE / AH 1061, Ms. Or. Fol. 4093, Staatsbibliothek zu Berlin, fol. 3b. *Sūrat al-Tawbah* of the Qu'ran likewise begins without the *basmalah*, and Qur'anic commentators have offered various explanations for this peculiar absence. Many have emphasized the severity of *al-Tawbah*'s critique of hypocrites and the like—this is a revealed "severing of a covenant and a declaration of conflict" for which the *basmalah*'s blessing would be inappropriate. The thirteenth-century Andalusian *mufassir* al-Qurṭubī has noted that it was a custom dating to pre-Islamic times to omit the *basmalah* when delivering a message rupturing a treaty. Others consider the absence of the *basmalah* as evidence of the continuity between *Sūrat al-Anfal* and *Sūrat al-Tawbah* (sūras 8 and 9, respectively), suggesting that they should be considered as

one complete sūra. (For a discussion of these issues and al-Qurṭubī's commentary, see Seyyed Hossein Nasr et al., *The Study Quran: A New Translation and Commentary* [New York: HarperOne, 2015], 503–4.) However intriguing the absence of the *basmalah* from *Sūrat al-Tawbah* is, I would suggest that its absence from the Berlin copy of "Khayr al-bayān" serves a different purpose. The absence is an attempt to communicate the immediacy of this message—to rupture not a treaty but the distinction between God's voice and the medium for transcribing God's voice.

46. Bāyazīd Anṣārī, *Khayr al-bayān* (Peshawar),131; "Khayr al-bayān" (Berlin), fol. 1b.

47. Bāyazīd Anṣārī, *Khayr al-bayān* (Peshawar), 132–33; "Khayr al-bayān" (Berlin), fol. 3a–3b.

48. Bāyazīd Anṣārī, *Khayr al-bayān* (Peshawar), 133; "Khayr al-bayān" (Berlin), fol. 3b.

49. This is Morgenstierne's conclusion, for instance, in his study discussed below.

50. We could also call this *dialogic*, noting alongside Mikhail Bakhtin the generative possibilities of a work marked by dialogue. Mikhail M. Bakhtin, *The Dialogic Imagination*, ed. Michael Holquist (Austin: University of Texas Press, 1981).

51. Bāyazīd Anṣārī, *Khayr al-bayān* (Peshawar), 131–32; "Khayr al-bayān" (Berlin), fol. 1b–3a; Qur'an 96:3–5.

52. Bāyazīd Anṣārī, *Khayr al-bayān* (Peshawar), 171–72.

53. For more discussion of the possible purposes of chiasmus in religious communication, consider Robert Yelle, *Semiotics of Religion: Signs of the Sacred in History* (London: Bloomsbury Academic, 2012), 48–50.

54. Qur'an 31:27.

55. Bāyazīd Anṣārī, *Khayr al-bayān* (Peshawar), 141–42; "Khayr al-bayān" (Berlin), fol. 10a–11a.

56. For an argument that drama and narrative transform the "content" of their communication in irreducible ways, consider Charles Taylor's recent work, in which he argues that the content or ideas of a drama / novel cannot be summarized without significant loss. Charles Taylor, *The Language Animal: The Full Shape of the Human Linguistic Capacity* (Cambridge, MA: Harvard University Press, 2016), esp. 291–319.

57. Interestingly, in Qur'anic contexts, *laḥn* (pl. *alḥān*) typically refers to mispronunciations and errors of recitation rather than to "tune" or "melody." Bāyazīd Anṣārī, *Khayr al-bayān* (Peshawar), 143; "Khayr al-bayān" (Berlin), 11b.

58. The translation of *bayān* used here ("explanation") and in the fifth verse of Surat al-Rahman will be discussed below.

59. Bāyazīd Anṣārī, *Khayr al-bayān* (Peshawar), 140; "Khayr al-bayān" (Berlin), fol. 9b.

60. Consider David Neil MacKenzie, "The Qasida in Pashto," in *Qasida Poetry in Islamic Asia and Africa: Classical Traditions and Modern Meanings*, ed. Stefan Sperl and Christopher Shackle (Leiden: Brill, 1996), 1:340–50; David Neil MacKenzie, "A Standard Pashto," *Bulletin of the School of Oriental and African Studies* 22, no. 1/3 (1959): 231–35.

61. This is a rhyme scheme, moreover, that extends across all the languages used in this revelatory performance. Even when *The Best Exposition* incorporates the nonrhyming words of the Qur'an, the prophet, and the *hādī* in Arabic—and offers translations in Persian and Hindawi—the text wraps these Arabic, Persian, and Hindawi statements with concluding phrases such as "In this there is a sign." By way

of an example, we can continue along with the passage excerpted above. Following the Pashto statement "May you believe this explanation," God (or the narrator) cites the Qur'an, "All that is in the heavens and the earth praises God." Though this citation ends with the Arabic word *al-arḍ* ("the earth"), the narrator concludes in Pashto with, "Pah qurān kaṣh dī 'ay**ān**." ("In the Qur'an there is a witnessing.") We then read an Arabic aphorism of the *hādī* ("All things speak the praise of the Merciful") before the section concludes in Pashto, "Hādī waylī dī raḥmat da khodā'ī pah dā kal**ām**." ("The guide—*may the mercy of God be upon him!*—said these words.") Even in its eclectic selection of languages, the sentences of *The Best Exposition* all conclude in **-ān** and **-ām** syllables. Bāyazīd Anṣārī, *Khayr al-bayān* (Peshawar), 140; "Khayr al-bayān" (Berlin) fol. 9b.

62. M. Bakhtin, "Forms of Time and of the Chronotope in the Novel," in *The Dialogic Imagination*, 84–85.

63. Williams, *Edge of Words*, 133–34.

64. For engaging discussions of the life of Muhammad and how Sufis model themselves after (and even "become") Muhammad, consider Kecia Ali, *Lives of Muhammad*; Shahzad Bashir, "Muhammad in Sufi Eyes: Prophetic Legitimacy in Medieval Iran and Central Asia," in *The Cambridge Companion to Muhammad*, ed. Jonathan E. Brockopp (Cambridge: Cambridge University Press, 2010).

65. Bruno Latour, *Rejoicing: Or the Torments of Religious Speech*, trans. Julie Rose (Cambridge: Polity, 2013), 168.

66. Karmen MacKendrick, *The Matter of Voice: Sensual Soundings* (Oxford: Oxford University Press, 2016); Paolo Virno, *When the Word Becomes Flesh: Language and Human Nature*, trans. Giuseppina Mecchia (South Pasadena, CA: Semiotext, 2015); Jean-Louis Chrétien, *The Call and the Response*, trans. Anne Davenport (New York: Fordham University Press, 2004).

67. Bāyazīd Anṣārī, *Khayr al-bayān* (Peshawar), 228–30.

68. "If you are sick or on a journey, or if any of you comes from the privy, or you have touched women, and you can find no water, then have recourse to wholesome dust and wipe your faces and your hands with it." Qur'an 5:6.

69. Bāyazīd Anṣārī, *Khayr al-bayān* (Peshawar), 230.

70. Citation reproduced as seen in context. Morgenstierne, "Notes on an Old Pashto Manuscript," *New Indian Antiquary* 2, no. 8 (November 1939): 573; Bāyazīd Anṣārī, "Khayr al-bayān" (Berlin), fol. 145a; *Khayr al-bayān* (Peshawar), 385.

71. "Signature" is a favored term of Giorgio Agamben's to describe a type of communicative sign whose meaning is *not* dependent on context and difference in the way that arbitrary symbols are. Rather, signatures "move and displace concepts and signs from one field to another" without a redefinition of semantic meaning. There is certainly something enchanted, even primordial, about Agamben's use of "signature." When I translate *nakhsha* as "signature," I do not intend all the abundant implications of Agamben's term; in this case, it is a felicitous coincidence that *nakhsha*—like Agamben's signature—is a type of sign that communicates a brute, enduring meaning that continues to *mean* similar things across a spectrum of cosmic, spiritual, and anthropological contexts. This definition of *signature* is drawn from *The Kingdom and the Glory* (p. 4), but his fullest discussion is found in *The Signature of All Things*. Giorgio Agamben, *The Kingdom and the Glory: For a Theological Genealogy of Economy and Government* (Stanford, CA: Stanford University Press, 2011); Giorgio Agamben, *The Signature of All Things: On Method* (Cambridge, MA: MIT Press, 2009).

72. Bāyazīd Anṣārī, *Khayr al-bayān* (Peshawar), 384–86; "Khayr al-bayān" (Berlin), fol. 144b–146a.

73. Qur'an 55:1–13. This is Arberry's translation with spelling modifications: A. J. Arberry, *The Koran Interpreted: A Translation* (New York: Simon and Schuster, 1955).

74. In this way, *The Best Exposition* resonates with a point made by Rowan Williams about Christian theology: the distinction between "natural theology" and "revealed theology" begins to collapse as language becomes recognized an extension of the cosmos. Williams, *Edge of Words.*

75. Bāyazīd Anṣārī, *Khayr al-bayān* (Peshawar), 132–33; "Khayr al-bayān" (Berlin), fol. 1b–2a.

76. Bāyazīd Anṣārī, *Khayr al-bayān* (Peshawar), 132–34; "Khayr al-bayān" (Berlin), fol. 2a–3b.

77. Hanifi, Andreyev, D. N. MacKenzie, Yar Muhammad Maghmoon Khattak, and Hafiz Muhammad Qasimi have all commented upon the subtle differences between Bayazid's orthography and alternative graphemes of the same phonemes in other early Pashto texts such as Khushhal Khan Khatak's divan.

78. Mukhliṣ tells us that Bayazid preached and taught in the language of the Afghans. Later Roshani authors such as Mullā Arzānī excavated the power of a specifically Pashto discourse: "Arzānī's Pashto verse has the characteristic of the Creator of day and night." Pashto excerpts from "Khayr al-bayān," moreover, circulated in the wider Roshani community as short, poetic fragments easily memorized and possibly sung: "Death comes suddenly upon a man. There is nothing in this world for a man." And yet we must hesitate before labeling "Khayr al-bayān" as a Pashto text. As Rozi Khan Burki argues, "Khayr al-bayān" includes distinctively "Ormuri" or "Baraki" words such as *nallatti* (pigs), *teshtan* (owner), and *haramunai* (ill-born). Given the reported locations of Bayazid's childhood in Ḥāl-Nāmah, it is likely that Bayazid spoke Ormuri in his household in Kaniguram and learned Persian, Arabic, and Pashto as part of his education. While any distinction between Ormuri and Pashto is certainly a porous one, Burki's point is important and reminds us of the fluid and unconsolidated nature of Pashto in the time of Bayazid's career.

79. More important than the inclusion of some stray Ormuri words is the persistent presence of Persian, Arabic, and Hindawi alongside the text we identify as Pashto or Ormuri. In the Berlin manuscript, approximately the first 20 percent of "Khayr al-bayān" includes translated repetitions of what is said in any one of the languages. As the work transitions away from a metalinguistic reflection on divine communication and toward explication of the Roshani spiritual path, Pashto becomes the dominant language of "Khayr al-bayān" for this variant. Nevertheless, the reader finds the Qur'an in Arabic and translated into Persian—and not Pashto. The quotations of the hādī are in Arabic with only the rare translation into Persian. Though the Hindawi portion of the text falls aside after the initial sections of "Khayr al-bayān," Persian and Arabic remain indispensable to comprehension. In the Hyderabad copy, the content of the entire text appears in all four languages—and they are similarly enmeshed as a few sentences of Arabic gives way to a few sentences of Persian, Pashto, and Hindawi. Finally, in the Rampur copy, we find a predominantly Persian text with untranslated Arabic citations of the hādī and the Qur'an. My point is simple: to identify "Khayr al-bayān" as a Pashto text is to fundamentally obscure the irrevocable multilingualism of this central Roshani work—a multilingualism of inscription and circulation.

80. For a discussion of the nature of a "vernacular manifesto," consider Alexander Beecroft, *An Ecology of World Literature: From Antiquity to the Present Day* (London: Verso Books, 2015), chap. 4.

81. Bruno Latour, *We Have Never Been Modern*, trans. Catherine Porter (Cambridge, MA: Harvard University Press, 1993), 10–11.

82. Quran 31:27.

83. Bāyazīd Anṣārī, *Khayr al-bayān* (Peshawar), 141–42; "Khayr al-bayān" (Berlin), fol. 10a–11a.

84. "For this reason, each instant may be, to use [Walter] Benjamin's words, the "small door through which the Messiah enters." The Messiah always already had his time, meaning he simultaneously makes time his and brings it to fulfillment." Agamben, *Time That Remains*, 115, quoting Walter Benjamin, *Illuminations*, trans. Harry Zohn (New York: Random House, 2007), 256.

Chapter 4: Vernacular Apocalypse

1. For efforts at reconstructing Bayazid's biography, consider chapter 1of this book as well as the following sources: André Wink, "On the Road of Failure: The Afghans in Mughal India," *Cracow Indological Studies*, no. 11 (2009): 267–339; Sergei Andreyev, "The Rawshaniyya," in *The Heritage of Sufism: Late Classical Persianate Sufism (1501–1750)*, ed. Leonard Lewisohn (Oxford: Oneworld, 1999), 290–318; Joseph Theodore Arlinghaus, "The Transformation of Afghan Tribal Society: Tribal Expansion, Mughal Imperialism and the Roshaniyya Insurrection, 1450–1600" (PhD diss., Duke University, 1989), chap. 6.

2. Akhūnd Darweza, "Tadhkirat al-abrār wa-'l-ashrār," MS Or. 222, fol. 125b, British Library, London (hereafter: "Tadhkirat al-abrār wa-'l-ashrār" (British Library).

3. H. G. Raverty, *Notes on Afghanistan and Baluchistan* (1880; reprint, Quetta: Gosha-e-Adab, 1976), 272.

4. 'Alī Muḥammad Mukhliṣ Kandahārī Shīnvārī, *Ḥāl-nāmah-yi Miyān Roshan* (Kabul: Vizārat-i Iṭṭilā'āt va Farhang, 2009), 390.

5. For various perspectives on pilgrimage and shrine-based piety in Muslim societies, consider Christopher S. Taylor, *In the Vicinity of the Righteous: Ziyāra and the Veneration of Muslim Saints in Late Medieval Egypt* (Leiden: Brill, 1999); Devin DeWeese, "Sacred History for a Central Asian Town: Saints, Shrines, and Legends of Origin in Histories of Sayrām, 18th–19th Centuries," in *Figures mythiques des mondes musulmans*, ed. Denise Aigle (Aix-en-Provence: Édisud, 2000); Pnina Werbner, *Pilgrims of Love: The Anthropology of a Global Sufi Cult* (Bloomington: Indiana University Press, 2003); Robert McChesney, *Waqf in Central Asia: Four Hundred Years in the History of a Muslim Shrine, 1480–1889* (Princeton, NJ: Princeton University Press, 1991); Engseng Ho, *The Graves of Tarim: Genealogy and Mobility across the Indian Ocean* (Berkeley: University of California Press, 2006).

6. For modern rereadings of the Roshaniyya, see the conclusion. Representative examples include Wink, "On the Road of Failure"; Allah Bux Yusufi, *Yusufzai Pathan* (Karachi: Muhammad Ali Education Society, 1973); Ali Khan Mahsood, *La Pīr Rokhan Tar Bacha Khana: Da Pukhtano Milli Mubarizi Ta Katana* (Peshawar: n.p., n.d.), 61; Bahadar Shah Zafar Kaka Khel, *Pukhtana: Da Tarikh pa Ranra ke* (Peshawar: Pashto Academy, n.d.); Yār Muḥammad Maghmūm Khaṭṭak, *The Rowshanites and Pashto Literature* (Peshawar: Pashto Academy, University of Peshawar, 2005), 8.

7. For a discussion of vernacularization on a global scale that is largely informed by European experiences, consider Alexander Beecroft, *An Ecology of World Literature: From Antiquity to the Present Day* (London: Verso Books, 2015).

8. See especially Webb Keane, *Christian Moderns: Freedom and Fetish in the Mission Encounter* (Berkeley: University of California Press, 2007).

9. Consider Charles Taylor, *The Language Animal* (Cambridge, MA: Harvard University Press, 2016), chap. 4.

10. Judith T. Irvine and Susan Gal, "Language Ideology and Linguistic Differentiation," in *Regimes of Language: Ideologies, Polities, and Identities*, ed. Paul V. Kroskrity (Santa Fe, NM: School of American Research Press, 2000).

11. Irvine and Gal, 37.

12. Bābur, *The Baburnama: Memoirs of Babur, Prince and Emperor*, ed. and trans. Wheeler M. Thackston (Washington, DC: Freer Gallery of Art and Arthur M. Sackler Gallery, Smithsonian Institution, 1996), 152–72.

13. Rozi Khan Burki, "Dying Languages with Special Focus on Ormuri," *Pakistan Journal of Public Administration* 6, no. 2 (2001): 6.

14. Consider Muzaffar Alam, *The Languages of Political Islam: India, 1200–1800* (Chicago: University of Chicago Press, 2004).

15. Thomas Patrick Hughes, "Twenty Years on the Afghan Frontier," *The Independent* 45 (1893): 455–56, 529–30, 637–38, 845–46, 1075–76.

16. This is elaborated upon in the previous chapter, but consider the following sources for analysis of letters and lettrism in Islamicate discourses: Orkhan Mir-Kasimov, *Words of Power: Hurūfī Teachings between Shiʿism and Sufism in Medieval Islam* (London: I. B. Tauris in association with the Institute of Ismaili Studies, 2015); Shahzad Bashir, *Fazlallah Astarabadi and the Hurufis* (Oxford: Oneworld, 2005).

17. Aside from the proto-nationalist vernacularization models of ethnic self-awareness mentioned above (and seen in the works of Andreyev and Arlinghaus), there are remarkably few discussions of Pashto vernacularization and, indeed, Pashto literature in general. Some notable exceptions: Walter N. Hakala, "Locating 'Pashto' in Afghanistan: A Survey of Secondary Sources," in *Language Policy and Language Conflict in Afghanistan and Its Neighbors*, ed. Harold Schiffman (Leiden: Brill, 2011), 53–88; Shah Mahmoud Hanifi, "A History of Linguistic Boundary Crossing within and around Pashto," in *Beyond Swat: History, Society and Economy along the Afghanistan-Pakistan Frontier*, ed. Benjamin Hopkins and Magnus Marsden (New York: Columbia University Press, 2013), 63–76; Anders Widmark, "Voices at the Borders, Prose on the Margins: Exploring the Contemporary Pashto Short Story in a Context of War and Crisis" (PhD diss., Uppsala University, Sweden, 2011).

18. Some representative examples of literature on the "vernacular" aside from those discussed in this chapter: Allison Busch, *Poetry of Kings: The Classical Hindi Literature of Mughal India* (2011); Daniel, *Fluid Signs* (1987); Leila Prasad, *Poetics of Conduct: Oral Narrative and Moral Being in a South Indian Town* (2007); Mitchell, *Language, Emotions, and Politics in South India: The Making of a Mother Tongue* (2009); DeNapoli, *Real Sadhus Sing to God: Gender, Asceticism, and Vernacular Religion in Rajasthan* (2014); Joyce Fleukiger, *In Amma's Healing Room* (2006); Anne Murphy, "Writing Punjabi across Borders," *South Asian History and Culture* 9, no. 1 (2018): 68–91.

19. Christian Lee Novetzke, *The Quotidian Revolution: Vernacularization, Religion, and the Premodern Public Sphere in India* (New York: Columbia University Press, 2016), 6.

20. Novetzke, 6.

21. Sheldon Pollock, *The Language of the Gods in the World of Men: Sanskrit, Culture, and Power in Premodern India* (Berkeley: University of California Press, 2006).

22. Novetzke, *Quotidian Revolution*, 7–9.

23. Novetzke, 13.

24. On the cultures of the Lodhi and Suri courts, consider Raziuddin Aquil, *Sufism, Culture, and Politics: Afghans and Islam in Medieval North India* (Oxford: Oxford University Press, 2007).

25. See especially Akhūnd Darweza, "Tadhkirat al-abrār wa-'l-ashrār" (British Library), fol. 74b.

26. Farina Mir, *The Social Space of Language: Vernacular Culture in British Colonial Punjab* (Berkeley: University of California Press, 2010). Novetzke's own work builds upon Farina Mir's—and both of their works build upon Pollock's. Nevertheless, Mir's emphases provide us with a better platform for understanding Pashto than those of Novetzke or Pollock.

27. Mir, 6 and 92–100.

28. Niẓām al-Dīn Aḥmad ibn Muḥammad Muqīm, *Tabakat-i-Akbari of Nizam-ud-Din Ahmad Bakhshi*, trans. and ed. H. M. Elliot and John Dowson (Lahore: Sang-e-Meel, 2006), 284–85.

29. Rizvi has compiled a sequence of the political events following Bayazid's death. S. A. A. Rizvi, "Rawshaniyya Movement (continued)," *Abr-Nahrain* 7 (August 1967): 62–98.

30. Jahāngīr, *The Jahangirnama: Memoirs of Jahangir, Emperor of India*, ed. and trans. Wheeler M. Thackston (New York: Freer Gallery of Art and Arthur M. Sackler Gallery in association with Oxford University Press, 1999), 124, 300–321, 353, 369, 386, 396, and 453–54. See also Muḥammad Ṣāliḥ Kambūh, *'Amal-i Ṣāliḥ, al-mawsūm bi Shāh Jahān Nāmah* (Lahore: Majlis-i Taraqqi-i Adab, 1958); Shaykh Farīd Bhakkarī, *Dhakhīrat al-Khawānīn of Shaykh Farīd Bhakkarī (Persian text)*, ed. S. Moinul Haq (Karachi: Pakistan Historical Society, 1961), 223; Shāh Navāz Khān Awrangābādī, *Ma'āthir al-Umarā'*, 3 vols. (Kolkata: Asiatic Society of Bengal, 1888–91), 595–602; consider also the translation by Beni Prasad and Henry Beveridge: *The Maāthir-ul-Umarā: Being Biographies of the Muhammādan and Hindu Officers of the Timurid Sovereigns of India from 1500 to about 1780 A.D.* (Calcutta: Asiatic Society, 1941).

31. Mukhliṣ, *Ḥāl-nāmah-yi Miyān Roshan*, XX.

32. Mukhliṣ, 345.

33. Mukhliṣ, 345.

34. Akhūnd Darweza, "Tadhkirat al-abrār wa-'l-ashrār" (British Library), fol. 124a.

35. According to a brief description available on the British Library's online gallery, this watercolor image "was produced for the Lord Moira, afterwards the Marquess of Hastings, by Sita Ram between 1814–15. Marquess of Hastings, the Governor-General of Bengal and the Commander-in-Chief (r. 1813–23), was accompanied by artist Sita Ram (flourished c.1810–22) to illustrate his journey from Calcutta to Delhi between 1814–15." The image can be viewed online here: https://www.bl.uk/onlinegallery/onlineex/apac/addorimss/t/019addor0004705u00000000.html.

36. All titles are my own, added solely for convenience.

37. This is the Arabic for "We are closer." This a reference to the sixteenth verse of the fiftieth sura of the Quran, which concludes: "We are closer to the human than his jugular vein" (*Naḥnu aqrab ilay-hi min ḥabl al-warīd*).

38. Mullā Arzānī, "Dīvān-i Arzānī," fol. 2b.

39. Consider, for instance, Ahoo Najafian's recent dissertation on ghazal in modern Iran: Ahoo Najafian, "Poetic Nation: Iranian Soul and Historical Continuity" (PhD diss., Stanford University, 2018). Dick Davis offers an alternative interpretation of ghazal form in which he considers the convergence of Sufi ideas and poetic form to be, generally, a "marriage of convenience." Dick Davis, "Sufism and Poetry: A Marriage of Convenience?," *Edebiyat* 10 (1999): 279–92.

40. Najafian, "Poetic Nation," esp. chaps. 1 and 2.

41. See a fuller discussion of this Deleuzean point in Lars Iyer, "Impersonal Speech: Blanchot, Virno, Messianism," in *The Messianic Now*, ed. Arthur Bradley and Paul Fletcher (London: Routledge, 2011), 101–16.

42. *Kun!*

43. Mullā Arzānī, "Dīvān-i Arzānī," fols. 1b–2a.

44. For Peircean semiotic schemes in the study of religion, consider Robert Yelle's work, especially Robert Yelle, *Semiotics of Religion: Signs of the Sacred in History* (London: Bloomsbury Academic, 2012), chaps. 1–2.

45. Qur'an 3:59.

46. As discussed in previous chapters, illuminating works on this subject include Orkhan Mir-Kasimov, *Words of Power: Ḥurūfī Teachings between Shi'ism and Sufism in Medieval Islam* (London: I. B. Tauris in association with the Institute of Ismaili Studies, 2015); Shahzad Bashir, *Fazlallah Astarabadi and the Hurufis* (Oxford: Oneworld, 2005).

47. For a provocative yet problematic account of dreams and imaginal realms in the philosophies of Ibn 'Arabī, consider Henry Corbin, *Creative Imagination in the Sūfism of Ibn 'Arabī*, trans. Ralph Manheim (Princeton, NJ: Princeton University Press, 1969). Also consider William C. Chittick, *The Sufi Path of Knowledge: Ibn al-'Arabi's Metaphysics of Imagination* (Albany: State University of New York Press, 1989), chap. 3.

48. For more on this verse, see William Chittick, *The Self-Disclosure of God: Principles of Ibn al-'Arabi's Cosmology* (Albany: State University of New York Press, 1997), chap. 1.

49. Mullā Arzānī, "Dīvān-i Arzānī," fols. 6b–7a.

50. Mullā Arzānī, fols. 4a–4b.

51. Giorgio Agamben, *The Sacrament of Language: An Archaeology of the Oath*, trans. Adam Kotsko (Stanford, CA: Stanford University Press, 2010), 46–50.

52. *Kawal* is also transliterated as *kawel*.

53. I draw upon the term "theurgy" as it is found in Gregory Shaw's description of Iamblichus: Gregory Shaw, *Theurgy and the Soul: The Neoplatonism of Iamblichus* (Brooklyn, NY: Angelico, 2014)

54. Mullā Arzānī, "Dīvān-i Arzānī," fols. 6a–6b.

55. See Michael Sells, *Mystical Languages of Unsaying* (Chicago: University of Chicago Press, 1994), chap. 4.

56. Akhūnd Darweza, "Tadhkirat al-abrār wa-'l-ashrār" (British Library), fols. 3b–5a.

57. The details of Akhund Darweza's own life are scattered throughout *The Pious and the Wicked*, but I'jāz al-Ḥaqq Quddūsī has performed the valuable task of compiling the various anecdotes of Akhund Darweza and Sayyid 'Ali Tirmidhī from *Al-Abrār wa-'l-Ashrār* into discrete biographies. Also see Quddūsī, *Tadhkirah-yi ṣūfiyyā-yi sarḥad* (Lahore: Markazi Urdu Board, 1966), 229–31. Quddūsī does not explicitly

identify the manuscript of *The Pious and the Wicked* he consults, so it is possible that he found Akhund Darweza's year of birth noted in a different manuscript than the ones I have consulted.

58. Akhūnd Darweza, "Tadhkirat al-abrār wa-'l-ashrār" (British Library), fol. 99a ff.

59. Akhund Darweza introduces the epithet early in his work, but the full description of Bayazid Ansari begins on fol. 113a.

60. *Khallada-hu Allāh Taʿālā fī al-nār*! Akhūnd Darweza, "Tadhkirat al-abrār wa-'l-ashrār" (British Library), fol. 113b. The death of Bayazid is described on fol. 116a.

61. Consider James Fuller Blumhardt and David Neil MacKenzie, *Catalogue of Pashto Manuscripts in the Libraries of the British Isles* (London: Trustees of the British Museum, 1965); Arif Naseem and Abdul Hameed, *Descriptive Catalogue of Manuscripts Pashto Academy, Library* (Peshawar: Pashto Academy, University of Peshawar, 2009).

62. Sayyid Taqwīm al-Ḥaqq Kākākhayl makes a similar point in his introduction to a printed edition of the text. This comment appears in the preface (in Pashto) on page "*sīn-waw*." Akhūnd Darweza, *Makhzan al-Islām*, ed. Muhammad Taqwīm al-Ḥaqq Kākākhayl (Peshawar: Pashto Academy, University of Peshawar, 1969), سو.

63. The Ganj Bakhsh Library in particular holds a number of texts associated with Akhund Darweza and his family, most of which are simply retitled excerpts from *Makhzan al-Islām*. As an example: Akhūnd Darweza, "Sharḥ Qaṣīdat Āmālī," MS 8356, Ganj Bakhsh Library, Iran-Pakistan Institute of Persian Studies, Islamabad.

64. Akhūnd Darweza, *Makhzan al-Islām*, ed. Kākākhayl, 158ff.

65. For the purposes of this analysis, I will primarily reference the British Library's manuscripts of *Remembrance of the Pious and the Wicked* and *The Treasure Chest of Islam*. Akhūnd Darweza, "Tadhkirat al-abrār wa-'l-ashrār," 1768, MS Or. 222; Akhūnd Darweza, "Makhzan al-Islām," n.d., India Office Islamic MS 2393; both, British Library, London.

66. Wilfred Madelung, "Al-Ūshī," in *Encyclopaedia of Islam*, ed. P. Bearman et al., 2nd ed. (Brill Online, 2012), http://dx.doi.org/10.1163/1573-3912_islam_SIM_7744; Stefan Sperl, "Muḥammad B. Sa'īd Al-Būṣīrī (d. c. 1296): The Burda in Praise of the Prophet Muhammad," in *Qasida Poetry in Islamic Asia and Africa*, vol. 2, *Eulogy's Bounty, Meaning's Abundance: An Anthology*, ed. Stefan Sperl and Christopher Shackle (Leiden: Brill, n.d.), 388–411 and 470–76; Kaydānī, *Khulaṣat al-Kaydānī* (Bombay: n.p., 1886); I. Poonawala, A. J. Wensinck, and W. Heffening, "Al-Nasafī," in *Encyclopaedia of Islam*, ed. P. Bearman et al., 2nd ed. (Brill Online, 2012), http://dx.doi.org/10.1163/1573-3912_islam_COM_0847. In *Remembrance of the Pious and the Wicked*, Akhund Darweza cites al-Nasafī frequently, but his most common source is Yaʿqūb Charkhī's *tafsīr* of the Qur'an. Yaʿqūb Charkhī, *Tafsīr-i Yaʿqūb Charkhī*, ed. Nūr Muḥammad Ṣaḥib (Istanbul: Yıldız, 1991).

67. For the emergence of Maturidism in Central Asia, see Wilfred Madelung, "The Spread of Maturidism and the Turks," *Biblos* 46 (1970): 109–68. For the appearance of *Bada' al-Amālī* and the works of al-Nasafī among others in the education of Maturidi-Hanafi scholars of Central Asia, consider Shahab Ahmed, "Mapping the World of a Scholar in Sixth / Twelfth Century Bukhāra: Regional Tradition in Medieval Islamic Scholarship as Reflected in a Bibliography," *Journal of the American Oriental Society* 120, no. 1 (2000): 24–43; Maria Subtelny and Anas B. Khalidov, "The Curriculum of Islamic Higher Learning in Timurid Iran in the Light of the Sunni Revival under Shāh-Rukh," *Journal of the American Oriental Society* 115 (1995): 210–36.

68. The text of "Bada' al-amālī" can be found on numerous websites, blogs, YouTube videos, and so forth, but it is rarely published in a book form independent of any

commentary. The poem, it would seem, serves as a vehicle for commentary and not as a "complete" work in and of itself. For the sake of convenience, I used the following digitized source: A.S.M.Q. al-Harawī, *Sharḥ al-Amālī*, Princeton University Arabic Collection (Maṭba'at al-'Ālam, 1901), 20–21, https://books.google.com/books?id=2msZAAAAYAAJ.

69. *Da nabī mi'rāj ham ḥaqq dī pah tan bīdārī dī. Nah pah khwab dī na pah wahm ūs dagha khabar bāhar dī. Har chi da nabah mi'rāj pah tan ḥaqq na ganẓīnah sikka hagha saṛey kāfir dī. 'Anbīya wāṛa pah amān wawala ṣaghīrah lah kabīrah gunāhūnawī sātalī. Na pah qaṣd wa gunāh kaṛī. Nah haytskalla anbīyā la nabūtah wū watalī. Hayts 'awratah paghambar nah wah har chi du'ī paydā shawī mastūrī dī. Nah bandah wū chi gawāhī bah ye wa rad na durūgh ye wū chi da durūghguy dūrī dī.* Akhūnd Darweza, "Makhzan al-Islām," fols. 5b–6a.

70. Akhūnd Darweza, *Makhzan al-Islām*, ed. Kākākhayl, 1–2.

71. "The third *bayān* on the reading (*qirā'a*) of the Qur'an explains that reading (*khwāndan*) the Qur'an in ignorance and without the practice of *'irāb*-pronunciation is considered an illicit activity (*āz munhīyāt*). In this regard has come the promise (*wa'īd*) [of Muhammad]—peace be upon him!—that *whoever reads the Qur'ān by his own opinion* (*ra'y*) *will make his abode in hell* (*al-nār*)." Akhūnd Darweza, "Makhzan al-Islām," fol. 55a; Akhūnd Darweza, *Makhzan al-Islām*, ed. Kākākhayl, 65.

72. "These days, some heretics have reported on letters and spelling. They've interpreted them so that in whatever-letter there is a concealed meaning. Whatever they say, however, is just disbelief." Akhūnd Darweza, "Makhzan al-Islām," fol. 61b; Akhūnd Darweza, *Makhzan al-Islām*, ed. Kākākhayl, 75.

73. Akhūnd Darweza, "Makhzan al-Islām," fol. 61b; Akhūnd Darweza, *Makhzan al-Islām*, ed. Kākākhayl, 75.

74. Akhūnd Darweza, "Makhzan al-Islām," fol. 61b; Akhūnd Darweza, *Makhzan al-Islām*, ed. Kākākhayl, 75.

75. Dawlat Lohani is also known as Dawlat Lawani. Consider Yār Muḥammad Maghmūm Khaṭṭak, *The Rowshanites and Pashto Literature*, 226–39.

76. H. G. Raverty, *Selections from the Poetry of the Afghans* (London: Williams and Norgate, 1862), 51–84. A manuscript in the Raza Library contains poetry attributed to both Dawlat Lohani and Mirza Khan Ansari, and the cataloguer makes two interesting suggestions: first, that the manuscript dates to the sixteenth century; and second, that Dawlat and Mirza are the same person using two pen names. While the composition of the poems could have occurred in the sixteenth century, I find it likely that the manuscript itself was inscribed at a later date. Mirza Dawlat Khan Ansari, "Dīwān-i Dawlat," sixteenth century, #3462, Raza Library, Rampur.

77. On Khushhal Khan Khattak, consider *Khushal Khan Khattak: The Great Warrior/Poet of Afghanistan: Selected Poems*, trans. Paul Smith (CreateSpace Independent Publishing Platform, 2012); *Dastar nama of Khushhal Khan Khattak*, ed. and trans. Arif Naseem (Peshawar: Pashto Academy, University of Peshawar, 2007); Raván Farhadi, "Khushḥāl Khān Khaṭak," in *Encyclopaedia of Islam*, ed. P. Bearman et al., 2nd ed. (Brill Online, 2012); Raverty, *Selections from the Poetry of the Afghans*.

78. Mikhail Pelevin, "The Khataks' Tribal Chronicle (XVII–XVIII): Extraliterary Text Functions," *Iran and the Caucasus* 18, no. 3 (2014): 201–12.

79. For translated selections of Rahman Baba, consider 'Abd al-Raḥmān Raḥmān Bābā, *The Nightingale of Peshawar: Selections from Rahman Baba*, ed. and trans. Jens Enevoldsen (Peshawar: Interlit Foundation, 1993); *The Complete Works of Rahman*

Baba: Poet of the Pukhtuns, ed. and trans. Momin Khan and Robert Sampson (self-published, 2012). Kindle ed.

80. Jos J. L. Gommans, *The Rise of the Indo-Afghan Empire, c.1710–1780* (Delhi: Oxford University Press, 1999), 111.

81. Raverty explicitly compares Khushhal to the "patriotic" Scottish highlanders who fought for independence from English rule. Raverty, *Selections from the Poetry of the Afghans*, 142ff. For a rigorous analysis of sources that *do* attempt to forge a strong connection between Pashto literature, Pashtun peoplehood, and Pashtun land, consider Pelevin's articles on the Khatak family's histories: Mikhail Pelevin, "The Beginnings of Pashto Narrative Prose," *Iran and the Caucasus* 21, no. 2 (2017): 132–49; Pelevin, "The Inception of Literary Criticism in Early Modern Pashto Writings," *Iranian Studies* (2020): 1–30; Pelevin, "The Khataks' Tribal Chronicle."

Chapter 5: The Vanguard of Disbelief

1. Muḥammad Ḥayāt Khān, *Afghanistan and Its Inhabitants*, ed. and trans. Henry Priestley (1874; Lahore: Sang-e-Meel, 1981), preface. Ḥayāt Khān's work, composed in Persian, was commissioned for British soldiers and is most widely (perhaps exclusively) available in English translation.

2. Ni'mat Allāh Harawī, *Tarikh-i-Khān Jahāni wa Makhzan-i Afghānī: A Complete History of the Afghans in Indo-Pak Sub-Continent, Edited on the Basis of Its Earliest and Six Other Manuscripts Accompanied with a Critical Introduction in English, Annotations, Geographical and Historical Notes in Persian*, ed. S. M. Imam al-Dīn (Dacca: Asiatic Society of Pakistan, 1960), 76–125.

3. Akhūnd Darweza, "Tadhkirat al-abrār wa-'l-ashrār," MS Or. 222, fol. 73b, British Library, London (hereafter: "Tadhkirat al-abrār wa-'l-ashrār" (British Library).

4. Muḥammad Ḥayāt Khān, *Afghanistan and Its Inhabitants*, 53. This story is referenced in Robert Nichols, *Settling the Frontier: Land, Law and Society in the Peshawar Valley, 1500–1900* (Karachi: Oxford University Press, 2001), 30; Jos. J. L. Gommans, *The Rise of the Indo-Afghan Empire, c. 1710–1780* (London: Oxford University Press, 1999), 167.

5. Muḥammad Ḥayāt Khān, *Afghanistan and Its Inhabitants*, 53.

6. For example, consider Thomas J. Barfield, *Afghanistan: A Cultural and Political History* (Princeton, NJ: Princeton University Press, 2010), 20–25. There is an extensive academic conversation on Pashtun ethnicity, most of which provides little or no discussion of the precolonial era. Consider, among others, Fredrik Barth, *Ethnic Groups and Boundaries* (Prospect Heights, IL: Waveland, 1998); Talal Asad, "Market Model, Class Structure and Consent: A Reconsideration of Swat Political Organisation," *Man* 7, no. 1 (1972): 74–94; Akbar S. Ahmed, *Millennium and Charisma among Pathans: A Critical Essay in Social Anthropology* (London: Routledge and Kegan Paul, 1976). For a general evaluation of Barth's influence in the study of Swat and Afghan / Pashtun society, consider David B. Edwards, "Learning from the Swat Pathans: Political Leadership in Afghanistan, 1978–97," *American Ethnologist* 25, no. 4 (1998): 712–28.

7. Consider André Wink, "On the Road of Failure: The Afghans in Mughal India," *Cracow Indological Studies*, no. 11 (2009): 267–339; Himayatullah Yaqubi, "Bayazid Ansari and Roushaniya Movement: A Conservative Cult or a Nationalist Endeavor?," *Journal of the Research Society of Pakistan* 50, no. 1 (2013): 149–70; Allah Bux Yusufi, *Yusufzai Pathan* (Karachi: Muhammad Ali Education Society, 1973); Ali Khan

Mahsood, *La Pīr Rokhan tar Bacha Khana: Da Pukhtano Milli Mubarizi ta Katana* (Peshawar: n.p., n.d.), 61; Bahadar Shah Zafar Kaka Khel, *Pukhtana: Da Tarikh pa Ranra ke* (Peshawar: Pashto Academy, University of Peshawar, n.d.).

8. Compare Willem Vogelsang, "The Ethnogenesis of the Pashtuns," in *Cairo to Kabul: Afghan and Islamic Studies Presented to Ralph Pinder-Wilson*, ed. Warwick Ball and Leonard Harrow (London: Melisende, 2002), 230.

9. Syed Jabir Raza, "The Afghans and Their Relations with the Ghaznavids and the Ghurids," *Proceedings of the Indian History Congress* 55 (1994): 784–91.

10. Ch. M. Kieffer, "AFGHAN," Encyclopaedia Iranica, Online Edition, 1982, accessed 14 February 2020, https://www.iranicaonline.org/articles/afgan-in-current-political-usage-any-citizen-of-afghanistan-whatever-his-ethnic-tribal-or-religious-affiliation.

11. Raziuddin Aquil, *Sufism, Culture, and Politics: Afghans and Islam in Medieval North India* (Oxford: Oxford University Press, 2012), 29–31.

12. Robert D. Crews, *Afghan Modern: The History of a Global Nation* (Cambridge, MA: Belknap, 2015), chap. 3.

13. Bernard D. Hopkins, *The Making of Modern Afghanistan* (Basingstoke, UK: Palgrave Macmillan, 2012), 1–31. Also consider Shah Mahmoud Hanifi, *Connecting Histories in Afghanistan Market Relations and State Formation on a Colonial Frontier* (Stanford, CA: Stanford University Press, 2011), chap. 1; Martin J. Bayly, *Taming the Imperial Imagination: Colonial Knowledge, International Relations, and the Anglo-Afghan Encounter, 1808–1878* (Cambridge: Cambridge University Press, 2016).

14. Kieffer, "AFGHAN." Consider also Crews, *Afghan Modern*, chaps. 4 and 5.

15. ʿAlī Muḥammad Mukhliṣ Kandahārī Shīnvārī, *Ḥāl-nāmah-yi Miyān Roshan* (Kabul: Vizārat-i Iṭṭilāʿāt va Farhang, 2009), 5–7.

16. For a brief consideration of Babur's place in the making of "Persianate India," see Richard Eaton's recent work: Richard Eaton, *Persianate India, 1000–1765* (Berkeley: University of California Press, 2019), 195–206. For a fuller treatment of Babur, consider Stephen Frederic Dale, *Babur: Timurid Prince and Mughal Emperor, 1483–1530* (Cambridge: Cambridge University Press, 2018).

17. Mukhliṣ, *Ḥāl-nāmah-yi Miyān Roshan*, 8–9.

18. Aquil, *Sufism, Culture, and Politics*, 29–31.

19. Aquil, 29–31.

20. Examples include Niẓām al-Dīn Aḥmad ibn Muḥammad Muqīm, *Tabakat-i-Akbari of Nizam-ud-Din Ahmad Bakhshi*, trans. and ed. H. M. Elliot and John Dowson (Lahore: Sang-e-Meel, 2006); Jahāngīr, *The Jahangirnama: Memoirs of Jahangir, Emperor of India*, ed. and trans. Wheeler M. Thackston (New York: Freer Gallery of Art, Arthur M. Sackler Gallery in association with Oxford University Press, 1999); Muḥammad Ṣāliḥ Kambūh, *ʿAmal-i Ṣāliḥ, al-mawsūm bi Shāh Jahān Nāmah* (Lahore: Majlis-i Taraqqī-i Adab, 1958).

21. Mukhliṣ, *Ḥāl-nāmah-yi Miyān Roshan*, 393–95; ʿAbd al-Qādir ibn Mulūk Shāh Badāʾūnī, *Muntakhab al-tawārīkh*, ed. and trans. as *Muntakhab ut-Tawarikh* by George S. A. Ranking, W. H. Lowe, and Wolseley Haig (Karachi: Karimsons, 1976), 361.

22. Munis D. Faruqui, "The Forgotten Prince: Mirza Ḥakīm and the Formation of the Mughal Empire in India," *Journal of the Economic and Social History of the Orient* 48, no. 4 (2005): 494–501.

23. Mukhliṣ, *Ḥāl-nāmah-yi Miyān Roshan*, 393–95.

24. Niẓām al-Dīn Aḥmad ibn Muḥammad Muqīm, *Tabakat-i-Akbari of Nizam-ud-Din Ahmad Bakhshi*, 284–85.

25. Cf. Abū al-Faḍl ibn Mubārak, *Akbar-nāmah*, ed. and trans. Henry Beveridge as *The Akbarnama of Abu-l-Fazl: The History of the Reign of the Emperor Akbar down to A.D. 1602* (Kolkata: Asiatic Society, 1897), 3:733.

26. Niẓām al-Dīn Aḥmad ibn Muḥammad Muqīm, *Tabakat-i-Akbari of Nizam-ud-Din Ahmad Bakhshi*, 285–86.

27. Abū al-Faḍl, *Akbar-nāmah* (1897), 3:780–84.

28. Antonio Monserrate, *The Commentary of Father Monserrate, S.J., on His Journey to the Court of Akbar*, ed. and trans. John S. Hoyland and S. N. Banerjee (London: Oxford University Press, 1922).

29. Monserrate, 83.

30. Monserrate, 141–42.

31. Monserrate, 144–45.

32. Monserrate, 146.

33. Monserrate, 149.

34. Nile Green, "Tribe, Diaspora, and Sainthood in Afghan History," *Journal of Asian Studies* 67 (2008): 171–211; Nichols, *Settling the Frontier*; Gommans, *Rise of the Indo-Afghan Empire c. 1710–1780*; Vogelsang, "The Ethnogenesis of the Pashtuns"; Mikhail Pelevin, "The Khataks' Tribal Chronicle (XVII–XVIII): Extraliterary Text Functions," *Iran and the Caucasus* 18, no. 3 (2014): 201–12.

35. Khūshḥāl Khān Khaṭak, *Dastar nama of Khūshḥāl Khan Khaṭak*, ed. and trans. Arif Naseem (Peshawar: Pashto Academy, University of Peshawar, 2007); Ḥāfiẓ Raḥmat Khān, *Khulāṣat al-ansāb: Sarah da Puṣhto tarjume*, trans. to Pashto by Muḥammad Navāz Ṭ̤ā'ir (Peshawar: Pashto Academy, University of Peshawar, 1973); Afḍal Khān Khaṭak, *Tārikh-i muraṣṣa'*, ed. Mohammad Khān Kamil Mumand (Peshawar: University Book Agency, 1974).

36. Aḥmad 'Alī, "Nuzhat Al-Ḍamā'ir," 1781, CUL Oo.6.58, Cambridge University Library, Cambridge, UK; Muḥammad Ḥayāt Khān, *Afghanistan and Its Inhabitants*.

37. Sana Haroon, *Frontier of Faith: Islam in the Indo-Afghan Borderland* (New York: Columbia University Press, 2007), 27–29.

38. Ni'mat Allāh Harawī, *Tārīkh-i Khān Jahānī wa Makhzan-i Afghānī*, 10–11.

39. The relevant verses on Saul/*malik talut* are Qur'an 2:247–51. For an insightful analysis on the theme of "order and chaos" operative in Islamic stories of Saul, consider Marianna Klar, *Interpreting Tha'labi's Tales of the Prophet: Temptation, Responsibility and Loss* (London: Routledge, 2006), 81–93.

40. Ni'mat Allāh Harawī, *Tārīkh-i Khān Jahānī wa Makhzan-i Afghānī*, 73–75.

41. Ni'mat Allāh Harawī, 116ff.

42. Green, "Tribe, Diaspora, and Sainthood in Afghan History," 172. In addition to Green's work, consider also Robert Nichols, *Settling the Frontier: Land, Law and Society in the Peshawar Valley, 1500–1900* (Karachi: Oxford University Press, 2001); Gommans, *The Rise of the Indo-Afghan Empire, c. 1710–1780*.

43. Green, "Tribe, Diaspora, and Sainthood in Afghan History," 172–90.

44. James Darmesteter, *Chants populaires des Afghans* (Paris: Imprimerie nationale, E. Leroux, 1888), quoted in Crews, *Afghan Modern*, 3.

45. John Leyden, "On the Rosheniah Sect and Its Founder, Bayezid Ansari," *Asiatick Researches* 11 (1812): 363–88.

46. Leyden, 398.

47. Carl W. Ernst, *Sufism: An Introduction to the Mystical Tradition of Islam* (Boulder, CO: Shambhala, 2011), 8–18.

48. Mountstuart Elphinstone, *An Account of the Kingdom of Caubul* (1815; Karachi: Oxford University Press, 1972). On Elphinstone, consider Hopkins, *Making of Modern Afghanistan.*

49. Hopkins, *Making of Modern Afghanistan*, 14.

50. Hopkins, 23–25.

51. Gilles Deleuze and Felix Guattari reference the notion of territorialization in a number of works. Consider, for example, Deleuze and Guattari, *A Thousand Plateaus: Capitalism and Schizophrenia*, trans. Brian Massumi (Minneapolis: University of Minnesota Press, 1987), 508–10. For a clear explication of Deleuzean "territorialization," consider Manuel DeLanda's recent work: Manuel DeLanda, *Assemblage Theory* (Edinburgh: Edinburgh University Press, 2016), 22–23.

52. Elphinstone, *An Account of the Kingdom of Caubul*, 274–75.

53. For a recent, insightful consideration of colonial processes of racialization in British India, consider Ilyse R. Morgenstein Fuerst, *Indian Muslim Minorities and the 1857 Rebellion: Religion, Rebels and Jihad* (London: Bloomsbury, 2017), chap. 1. For more on the notion of "racialization" and religion, consider Sylvester A. Johnson, *African American Religions, 1500–2000* (Cambridge: Cambridge University Press, 2015), chap. 8; Juliette Galonnier, "Choosing Faith and Facing Race: Converting to Islam in France and the United States" (PhD diss., Northwestern University, 2017), 16–79.

54. If we consider the catalogue of the Pashto Academy in Peshawar and the unified catalogue of Pashto manuscripts in the British Isles as representative samples, then Akhund Darweza's *Makhzan al-Islam* is quite clearly the most copied Pashto manuscript of this period. The Pashto Academy has forty-seven copies of *Makhzan al-Islam*, while the libraries of the British Isles hold an additional twenty-one copies. For comparison's sake, there are nine copies of *Yūsuf wa Zulaykhā*, five copies of *Ta'rīkh-i Muraṣṣa'*, and four copies of *Dīvān-i Khushḥāl* in the libraries of the British Isles. Arif Naseem and Abdul Hameed, eds., *Descriptive Catalogue of Manuscripts Pashto Academy, Library* (Peshawar: Pashto Academy, University of Peshawar, 2009); James Fuller Blumhardt and David Neil MacKenzie, *Catalogue of Pashto Manuscripts in the Libraries of the British Isles* (London: Trustees of the British Museum, 1965).

55. Ni'mat Allāh Harawī, *Tārīkh-i Khān Jahānī wa Makhzan-i Afghānī*, 110–11.

56. Akhūnd Darweza, "Tadhkirat al-abrār wa-'l-ashrār" (British Library), fol. 74a.

57. This is a favorite phrase of Akhund Darweza's, and it appears throughout the work. Consider as an example "Tadhkirat al-abrār wa-'l-ashrār" (British Library), fol. 15b.

58. Akhūnd Darweza, fol. 144b.

59. Akhūnd Darweza, fol. 28a.

60. Akhūnd Darweza, fols. 142b–143a.

61. Akhūnd Darweza, fols. 145a–146b.

62. Akhūnd Darweza, fol. 121b.

63. Akhūnd Darweza, fols. 15a–15b.

64. Akhūnd Darweza, fols. 15a–15b.

65. Akhūnd Darweza, fols. 15a–15b. This explanation of unseen communication—and its susceptibility to theft—is found in early accounts of the prophet Muhammad's life as well. Ibn Hishām, 'Abd al-Malik, and Muḥammad ibn Isḥāq, *The Life of*

Muhammad, ed. and trans. Alfred Guillaume (London: Oxford University Press, 1955), 90–93.

66. Akhūnd Darweza, "Tadhkirat al-abrār wa-'l-ashrār" (British Library), fols. 15a–15b.

67. Akhūnd Darweza, fol. 117b.

68. Akhūnd Darweza, fol. 117b.

69. Akhūnd Darweza, fol. 33a.

70. Akhūnd Darweza, fol. 121b.

71. Akhūnd Darweza, fol. 125b.

72. Akhūnd Darweza, fol. 125b.

73. Akhūnd Darweza, fol. 74a.

74. Akhūnd Darweza, fol. 73b.

75. Akhūnd Darweza, fol. 74b.

76. Akhūnd Darweza, fol. 74b.

77. Akhūnd Darweza, fol. 74a.

78. For a selection of translations from Khūshḥāl Khān's vast corpus, consider Khūshḥāl Khān Khaṭak, *Poems from the Divan of Khushal Khan Khatak*, trans. D. N. Mackenzie (London: George Allen and Unwin, 1965); Khūshḥāl Khān Khaṭṭak, *Khushal Khan Khaṭṭak: The Great Warrior/Poet of Afghanistan: Selected Poems*, trans. Paul Smith (CreateSpace Independent Publishing Platform, 2012).

79. Bernard Stiegler, *Technics and Time, 1: The Fault of Epimetheus*, trans. Richard Bearsworth and George Collins (Stanford, CA: Stanford University Press, 1998), 55.

80. Rogers Brubaker, *Ethnicity without Groups* (Cambridge, MA: Harvard University Press, 2010), 9; Rogers Brubaker, *Grounds for Difference* (Cambridge, MA: Harvard University Press, 2015), 104.

81. For the Timurid ruler Shāh Rukh's efforts to reject Islamic ideologies alternative to Māturīdī-Ḥanafī Sunnism, consider Maria Subtelny and Anas B. Khalidov, "The Curriculum of Islamic Higher Learning in Timurid Iran in the Light of the Sunni Revival under Shāh-Rukh," *Journal of the American Oriental Society* 115 (1995): 210–36.

82. Akhūnd Darweza, "Tadhkirat al-abrār wa-'l-ashrār" (British Library), fol. 167a.

83. Akhūnd Darweza, fol. 168a.

84. Akhūnd Darweza, fols. 168a–168b.

85. Akhūnd Darweza, fols. 168a–168b.

86. Akhūnd Darweza, fol. 169b.

87. Haroon, *Frontiers of Faith*.

88. William E. B. Sherman, "The Lost Tribes of the Afghans: Religious Mobility and Entanglement in Narratives of Afghan Origins," in *American and Muslim Worlds before 1900*, ed. John Ghazvinian and Arthur Mitch Fraas (London: Bloomsbury, 2020), 85–97.

89. Olaf Caroe, *The Pathans: 550 B.C.–A.D. 1957* (London: Macmillan, 1958), 192.

90. Abubakar Siddique, *The Pashtun Question: The Unresolved Key to the Future of Pakistan and Afghanistan* (London: Hurst, 2014), 28–29; "Scholars Analyse Peere Roashan's Philosophy," *Kabul Times*, January 12, 1975, vol. 13, no. 239. I am thankful to Mejgan Massoumi for directing my attention to this newspaper article.

91. Imran Khan, *Warrior Race: A Journey through the Land of the Tribal Pathans* (London: Chatto and Windus, 1993).

92. Akhūnd Darweza, "Tadhkirat al-abrār wa-'l-ashrār" (British Library), fols. 107b–108b; I'jāz al-Ḥaqq Quddūsī, *Tadhkirah-yi ṣūfiyyā-yi sarḥad* (Lahore: Markazi Urdu Board, 1966), 64–67.

93. Akhūnd Darweza, "Tadhkirat al-abrār wa-'l-ashrār" (British Library), fol. 19a.

94. Akhūnd Darweza, fol. 19a.

Ishmael's Daydream: A Conclusion

1. 'Alī Muḥammad Mukhliṣ Kandahārī Shīnvārī, *Ḥāl-nāmah-yi Miyān Roshan* (Kabul: Vizārat-i Iṭṭilā'āt va Farhang, 2009), 5. According to a well-known hadith quoted in *Ḥāl-nāmah*, the Prophet Muhammad arrived in Yathrib and left the choice for his abode to his (divinely guided) camel's volition. The camel bore Muhammad to the abode of Abu Ayyub al-Ansari, and Abu Ayyub's home was blessed as Muhammad's temporary residence. Upon his death, Abu Ayyub al-Ansari was reportedly buried at the walls of Constantinople, and the Ottoman sultans transformed his "rediscovered" burial place into a popular shrine lying in the heart of the Eyüp district of Istanbul. For a consideration of the role played by the Ebu Eyüb Ensari shrine in the sixteenth-century transformations of Ottoman Istanbul, consider the following article: Nuray Ozaslan, "From the Shrine of Cosmidion to the Shrine of Eyup Ensari," *Greek, Roman, and Byzantine Studies* 40, no. 4 (1999): 379–99.

2. Mukhliṣ, *Ḥāl-nāmah-yi Miyān Roshan*, 2.

3. 'Alī Muḥammad Walad Gul Anṣārī, "Tadhkirat al-anṣār," AH 1268 / 1852 CE, Shirani Collection MS 352/6202, University of the Punjab Library, Lahore, Pakistan.

4. K. Hussan Zia, *The Pathans of Jullunder* (Lahore: Maktaba-tul-Ilmiya, 1996), 10–14. Unfortunately, K. Hussan Zia does not provide clear bibliographical details or citations. I assume that he consulted the same manuscript of "Tadhkirat al-anṣār" (located in the Shirani Collection at the University of the Punjab) as I have, given that I have not found additional copies of this manuscript. The association of the family of Ibrāhīm Dānishmand with the lineage of Abū Ayyūb al-Anṣārī likely has its origins in the hallowed place that Abū Ayyūb has for Muslims of the Anatolian peninsula. Consider Ozaslan, "From the Shrine of Cosmidion to the Shrine of Eyup Ensari."

5. For more on the life of Suhrawardī, consult Erik S. Ohlander, *Sufism in an Age of Transition: 'Umar al-Suhrawardī and the Rise of the Islamic Mystical Brotherhoods* (Leiden: Brill, 2008).

6. According to most sources (including Ohlander's *Sufism in an Age of Transition*), Suhrawardī died in 1234 CE—not in 1212 CE as 'Alī Muhammad Walad writes in "Tadhkirat al-anṣār."

7. Zia, *The Pathans of Jullunder*, 14.

8. 'Alī Muḥammad Walad Gul Anṣārī, "Tadhkirat al-anṣār," fols. 76–81.

9. 'Alī Muḥammad Walad Gul Anṣārī, fols. 76–81.

10. For a stunning account of the long pattern of exchange across South and Central Asia, consider Finbarr Barry Flood, *Objects of Translation: Material Culture and Medieval "Hindu-Muslim" Encounter* (Princeton, NJ: Princeton University Press, 2009).

11. Consider Muzaffar Alam and Sanjay Subrahmanyam, *Indo-Persian Travels in the Age of Discoveries, 1400–1800* (Cambridge: Cambridge University Press, 2007).

12. Richard Eaton, *Persianate India, 1000–1765* (Berkeley: University of California Press, 2019).

13. Mukhliṣ, *Ḥāl-nāmah-yi Miyān Roshan*, 257.

14. Herman Melville, *Moby Dick* (1851; London: Random House UK, 2008), 6.

15. Melville, 6.

16. Jeffrey Goldberg, "Herman Melville on the Situation in Afghanistan," *The Atlantic*, August 5, 2008, https://www.theatlantic.com/international/archive/2008/08/herman-melville-on-the-situation-in-afghanistan/8633/.

17. This is, of course, only a partial list of recent writings on the history of Afghanistan. Faiz Ahmed, *Afghanistan Rising: Islamic Law and Statecraft between the Ottoman and British Empires* (Cambridge, MA: Harvard University Press, 2017); Shah Mahmoud Hanifi, *Connecting Histories in Afghanistan Market Relations and State Formation on a Colonial Frontier* (Stanford, CA: Stanford University Press, 2011); Sana Haroon, *Frontier of Faith: Islam in the Indo-Afghan Borderland* (New York: Columbia University Press, 2007); Alla Ivanchikova, *Imagining Afghanistan: Global Fiction and Film of the 9/11 Wars* (West Lafayette, IN: Purdue University Press, 2019); Nile Green, ed., *Afghanistan's Islam: From Conversion to the Taliban* (Berkeley: University of California Press, 2016); Robert Crews, *Afghan Modern: The History of a Global Nation* (Cambridge, MA: Belknap, 2015).

18. Shahzad Bashir and Robert D. Crews, *Under the Drones: Modern Lives in the Afghanistan-Pakistan Borderlands* (Cambridge, MA: Harvard University Press, 2012), 262.

19. John Lardas Modern, *Secularism in Antebellum America: With Reference to Ghosts, Protestant Subcultures, Machines, and Their Metaphors; Featuring Discussions of Mass Media, Moby-Dick, Spirituality, Phrenology, Anthropology, Sing Sing State Penitentiary, and Sex with the New Motive Power* (Chicago: University of Chicago Press, 2011), xxi.

20. Shahzad Bashir, "Everlasting Doubt: Uncertainty in Islamic Representations of the Past," *Archiv für Religionsgeschichte* 20, no. 1 (2018): 28.

21. Walter Benjamin, *Illuminations*, trans. Harry Zohn (New York: Random House, 2007), 254.

22. Consider note 39 of the introduction for elaboration on the "tiny displacement" of the messianic.

23. Sara Ahmed, *Queer Phenomenology: Orientations, Objects, Others* (Durham, NC: Duke University Press, 2006), 24.

24. For excellent analyses of Islamic narratives on the prophet Isma'il / Ishmael in a comparative context, consider Robert C. Gregg, *Shared Stories, Rival Tellings: Early Encounters of Jews, Christians, and Muslims* (Oxford: Oxford University Press, 2015), chap. 6; Carol Bakhos, *The Family of Abraham: Jewish, Christian, and Muslim Interpretations* (Cambridge, MA: Harvard University Press, 2014), chaps. 2–3.

A Note on Sources

1. Bāyazīd Anṣārī, *Khayr al-bayān*, ed. Muḥammad 'Abd a-Quddūs Qāsimī (Peshawar: Pashto Academy at Peshawar University, 1988); "Khayr al-bayān," 1650–51 CE / AH 1061, Ms. Or. Fol. 4093, Staatsbibliothek zu Berlin; "Khayr al-bayān," 1668 CE / AH 1079, Tas. 60, Cat. MS 3346, Salar Jung Museum, Hyderabad, India; "Khayr al-bayān," 1852–53 CE / AH 1269, MS 1070, Raza Library, Rampur, India.

2. Bāyazīd Anṣārī, *Maqṣūd al-mu'minīn*, ed. Mīr Walī Khān Mas'ūdī (Islamabad: Majma' al-Buḥūth al-Islāmīya, 1976); the edition found in the Raza Library in Rampur,

India, was shown to me by an archivist, but it was as yet uncatalogued and lacking an identifying number.

3. Bāyazīd Anṣārī, "Ṣirāṭ al-tawḥīd," n.d., MS 15978, Ganj Bakhsh Library, Iran-Pakistan Institute of Persian Studies, Islamabad, Pakistan; "Ṣirāṭ al-tawḥīd," n.d., MS 924, Raza Library, Rampur, India.

4. Bāyazīd Anṣārī, *Farḥat al-Mujtabá*, ed. Zalmay Haywādmal (Kabul: Da Afghānistān da 'Ulūmo Akāḍamī da Zhabo aw Adabiyāto Markaz [Academy of Language and Literary Sciences of Afghanistan], 2006); Bāyazīd Anṣārī, *'Uryān al-ghayb* (Delhi: India-Afghanistan Foundation, 2018).

5. Bāyazīd Anṣārī, "Nazihatnama," found in Shihab al-Din Dawlatabadi and others, Majmu'a-i Ras'ail (Khoqand, 1283/1866), MSS 9310, IVANRUz, Tashkent; Waleed Ziad, "Transporting Knowledge in the Durrani Empire: Two Manuals of Naqshbandi-Mujaddidi Sufi Practice," in *Afghanistan's Islam: From Conversion to the Taliban*, ed. Nile Green (Berkeley: University of California Press), 105–26.

6. 'Alī Muḥammad Mukhliṣ Kandahārī Shīnvārī, *Ḥāl-nāmah-yi Miyān Roshan* (Kābul: Vizārat-i Iṭṭilā'āt va Farhang, 2009).

7. William E. B. Sherman, "In the Garden of Language: Religion, Vernacularization, and the Pashto Poetry of Arzani in the Sixteenth and Seventeenth Centuries," *Afghanistan* 5, no. 1 (April 2022): 122–47.

8. Consider especially the collections at the University of Peshawar and the British Library. Arif Naseem and Abdul Hameed, *Descriptive Catalogue of Manuscripts Pashto Academy, Library* (Peshawar: Pashto Academy, University of Peshawar, 2009); Akhūnd Darweza, "Makhzan al-Islām," India Office Islamic MS 2393, British Library, London. The published edition is Akhūnd Darweza, *Makhzan al-Islām*, ed. Sayyid Taqwīm al-Ḥaqq Kākākhayl (Peshawar: Pashto Academy, University of Peshawar, 1969).

9. Akhūnd Darweza, "Tadhkirat al-abrār wa-'l-ashrār," 1768, MS Or. 222, British Library, London; "Tadhkirat al-abrār wa-'l-ashrār," eighteenth century, MS 562, Ganj Bakhsh Library, Iran-Pakistan Institute of Persian Studies, Islamabad.

10. Akhūnd Darweza, "Sharḥ qaṣīdat āmālī," eighteenth century, MS 8356, Ganj Bakhsh Library, Iran-Pakistan Institute of Persian Studies, Islamabad.

11. Akhūnd Darweza, *Irshād al-ṭālibīn* (Lucknow: Anvār-i Muḥammadī, 1883).

Bibliography

'Abbās Khān Sarwānī. *The Tārīkh-i-Shīr Shāhī of 'Abbās Khān Sarwānī*. Dacca: Dacca University Publication, 1964.

Abū al-Faḍl ibn Mubārak. *Ā'īn-i Akbarī*. Edited and translated by H. Blochmann and H. S. Jarrett. Frankfurt am Main: Institut für Geschichte der Arabisch-Islamischen Wissenschaften, 1993.

———. *Akbar-nāmah*. Edited and translated by Wheeler M. Thackston as *The History of Akbar*. 3 vols. Cambridge, MA: Harvard University Press, 2014–17. Edited and translated by Henry Beveridge as *The Akbarnama of Abu-l-Fazl: The History of the Reign of the Emperor Akbar down to A.D. 1602*. Kolkata: Asiatic Society, 1897. Page references are to the Thackston edition unless otherwise noted.

Afḍal Khān Khaṭak. *Tārḵh-i muraṣṣaʿ*. Edited by Mohammad Khān Kamil Mumand. Peshawar: University Book Agency, 1974.

Agamben, Giorgio. *The Coming Community*. Translated by Michael Hardt. Minneapolis: University of Minnesota Press, 1993.

———. *The Fire and the Tale*. Translated by Lorenzo Chiesa. Stanford, CA: Stanford, 2017.

———. *The Highest Poverty: Monastic Rules and Form-of-Life*. Translated by Adam Kotsko. Stanford, CA: Stanford University Press, 2013.

———. *The Kingdom and the Glory: For a Theological Genealogy of Economy and Government*. Translated by Lorenzo Chiesa. Stanford, CA: Stanford University Press, 2011.

———. *The Man without Content*. Translated by Georgia Albert. Stanford, CA: Stanford University Press, 1999.

———. *Means without End: Notes on Politics*. Translated by Vincenzo Binetti and Cesare Casarino. Minneapolis: University of Minnesota Press, 2000.

———. *The Sacrament of Language: An Archaeology of the Oath*. Translated by Adam Kotsko. Stanford, CA: Stanford University Press, 2010.

———. *The Signature of All Things: On Method*. Translated by Luca di Santo and Kevin Attell. Cambridge, MA: MIT Press, 2009.

———. *The Time That Remains: A Commentary on the Letter to the Romans*. Translated by Patricia Dailey. Stanford, CA: Stanford University Press, 2005.

Agha, Asif. *Language and Social Relations*. Cambridge: Cambridge University Press, 2007

Ahmad, Muhammad Khalaf-Allah, and Muhammad Zaghlul Sallam. *Three Treatises on the I'jaz of the Qur'an*. Translated by Issa Boullata. Reading, UK: Garnet, 2015.

Aḥmad 'Alī. "Nuzhat Al-Ḍamā'ir." 1781. CUL Oo.6.58. Cambridge University Library, Cambridge, UK.

Ahmed, Akbar S. *Millennium and Charisma among Pathans: A Critical Essay in Social Anthropology*. London: Routledge and Kegan Paul, 1976.

Ahmed, Faiz. *Afghanistan Rising: Islamic Law and Statecraft between the Ottoman and British Empires*. Cambridge, MA: Harvard University Press, 2017.

Ahmed, Sara. *Queer Phenomenology: Orientations, Objects, Others*. Durham, NC: Duke University Press, 2006.

Ahmed, Shahab. "Mapping the World of a Scholar in Sixth / Twelfth Century Bukhāra: Regional Tradition in Medieval Islamic Scholarship as Reflected in a Bibliography." *Journal of the American Oriental Society* 120, no. 1 (2000): 24–43.

———. *What Is Islam? The Importance of Being Islamic*. Princeton, NJ: Princeton University Press, 2015.

Ahmed, Tariq. *Religio-political Ferment in the N.W. Frontier during the Mughal Period: The Raushaniya Movement*. Delhi: Idarah-i Adabiyat-i Delli, 1982.

Akhūnd Darweza. *Irshād al-ṭālibīn*. Lucknow: Anvār-i Muḥammadī, 1883.

———. *Makhzan al-Islām*. Edited with notes by Muhammad Taqwīm al-Ḥaqq Kākākhayl. Peshawar: Pashto Academy, University of Peshawar, 1969.

———. "Makhzan al-Islām." India Office Islamic MS 2393. British Library, London.

———. "Sharḥ qaṣīdat āmālī." Eighteenth century. MS 8356. Ganj Bakhsh Library, Iran-Pakistan Institute of Persian Studies, Islamabad.

———. "Tadhkirat al-abrār wa-'l-ashrār." 1768. MS Or. 222. British Library, London.

———. "Tadhkirat al-abrār wa-'l-ashrār." Eighteenth century. MS 562. Ganj Bakhsh Library, Iran-Pakistan Institute of Persian Studies, Islamabad.

Alam, Muzaffar. *The Crisis of Empire in Mughal North India: Awadh and the Punjab, 1707–48*. Delhi: Oxford University Press, 1986.

———. *The Languages of Political Islam: India, 1200–1800*. Chicago: University of Chicago Press, 2004.

Alam, Muzaffar, Françoise Delvoye Nalini, and Marc Gaborieau, eds. *The Making of Indo-Persian Culture: Indian and French Studies*. New Delhi: Manohar, 2000.

Alam, Muzaffar, and Sanjay Subrahmanyam. *Indo-Persian Travels in the Age of Discoveries, 1400–1800*. Cambridge: Cambridge University Press, 2007.

———. *The Mughal State, 1526–1750*. Delhi: Oxford University Press, 1998.

———. *Writing the Mughal World: Studies on Culture and Politics*. New York: Columbia University Press, 2012.

Al-Azmeh, Aziz. *Islam and Modernities*. London: Verso, 2009.

Ali, Kecia. *The Lives of Muhammad*. Cambridge, MA: Harvard University Press, 2014.

ʿAlī ibn Ḥusayn Kāshifī Ṣafī. *Rashaḥāt ʿayn al-ḥayāh: Fī manāqib mashāyikh al-ṭarīqah al-Naqshabandīyah wa-ādābihim al-nabawīyah wa-asrārihim al-rabbānīyah*. Beirut: Dār al-Kutub al-ʿIlmīyah, 2008.

ʿAlī Muḥammad Walad Gul Anṣārī. "Tadhkirat al-anṣār." AH 1268 / 1852 CE 1268. Shirani Collection MS 352 / 6202. University of the Punjab Library, Lahore, Pakistan.

Amanat, Abbas. *Apocalyptic Islam and Iranian Shi'ism*. London: I. B. Tauris, 2009.

Amanat, Abbas, and Magnus Bernhardsson. *Imagining the End: Visions of Apocalypse from the Ancient Middle East to Modern America*. London: I. B. Tauris, 2002.

Andreyev, Sergei. "Pashto Literature: The Classical Period." In *Oral Literature of Iranian Languages: Kurdish, Pashto, Balochi, Ossetic, Persian and Tajik, Companion Volume II to A History of Persian Literature*, vol. 18, edited by Philip G. Kreyenbroek and Ulrich Marzolph, 89–113. London: I. B. Tauris, 2010.

———. "The Rawshaniyya." In *The Heritage of Sufism: Late Classical Persianate Sufism (1501–1750)*, edited by Leonard Lewisohn, 290–318. Oxford: Oneworld, 1999.

Anooshahr, Ali. "Mughal Historians and the Memory of the Islamic Conquest of India." *Indian Economic and Social History Review* 43, no. 3 (2006): 275–300.

Ansari, Sarah F. D. *Sufi Saints and State Power: The Pirs of Sind, 1843–1947*. Cambridge: Cambridge University Press, 1992.

Anzali, Ata. "Safavid Shi'ism, the Eclipse of Sufism and the Emergence of 'Irfan." PhD diss., Rice University, 2012.

Aquil, Raziuddin. *Sufism, Culture, and Politics: Afghans and Islam in Medieval North India*. Oxford: Oxford University Press, 2007.

Arberry, A. J. *The Koran Interpreted: A Translation*. New York: Simon and Schuster, 1955.

Arlinghaus, Joseph Theodore. "The Transformation of Afghan Tribal Society: Tribal Expansion, Mughal Imperialism and the Roshaniyya Insurrection, 1450–1600." PhD diss., Duke University, 1989.

Asad, Talal. *Genealogies of Religion: Discipline and Reasons of Power in Christianity and Islam*. Baltimore: Johns Hopkins University Press, 1993.
———. "Market Model, Class Structure and Consent: A Reconsideration of Swat Political Organisation." *Man* 7, no. 1 (1972): 74–94.
Aslam, Nadeem. *The Blind Man's Garden*. New York: Vintage, 2014.
Atkin, Albert. "Peirce's Theory of Signs." In *Stanford Encyclopedia of Philosophy*, edited by Edward N. Zalta. Stanford University, 2006–. Modified November 15, 2010. Summer 2013. http://plato.stanford.edu/archives/sum2013/entries/peirce-semiotics/.
'Aṭṭār, Farīd al-Dīn. *Farīd ad-Din 'Attār's Memorial of God's Friends: Lives and Sayings of Sufis*. Edited and translated by Paul Losensky. Mahwah, NJ: Paulist, 2009.
Austin, John Langshaw. *How to Do Things with Words*. Cambridge, MA: Harvard University Press, 1962.
Aydin, Cemil. *The Idea of the Muslim World: A Global Intellectual History*. Cambridge, MA: Harvard University Press, 2017.
Babayan, Kathryn. *Mystics, Monarchs, and Messiahs: Cultural Landscapes of Early Modern Iran*. Cambridge, MA: Harvard University Press, 2002.
Bābur. *The Baburnama: Memoirs of Babur, Prince and Emperor*. Edited and translated by Wheeler M. Thackston. Washington, DC: Freer Gallery of Art and Arthur M. Sackler Gallery, Smithsonian Institution, 1996.
Badakhshānī, Muḥammad Hāshim ibn Muḥammad Qāsim. *Zubdat al-maqāmāt*. Lahore: Būstān-i Adab, 1969.
Badā'ūnī, 'Abd al-Qādir ibn Mulūk Shāh. *Muntakhab al-Tawārīkh*. Edited and translated as *Muntakhab ut-Tawarikh* by George S. A. Ranking, W. H. Lowe, and Wolseley Haig. Karachi: Karimsons, 1976.
Bakhos, Carol. *The Family of Abraham: Jewish, Christian, and Muslim Interpretations*. Cambridge, MA: Harvard University Press, 2014.
Bakhtin, Mikhail M. *The Dialogic Imagination*. Edited by Michael Holquist. Austin: University of Texas Press, 1981.
Balabanlilar, Lisa. *Imperial Identity in the Mughal Empire: Memory and Dynastic Politics in Early Modern South and Central Asia*. London: I. B. Tauris, 2012.
Barfield, Thomas J. *Afghanistan: A Cultural and Political History*. Princeton, NJ: Princeton University Press, 2010.
Barth, Fredrik. *Ethnic Groups and Boundaries*. Prospect Heights, IL: Waveland, 1998.
———. *Features of Person and Society in Swat: Collected Essays on Pathans*. London: Routledge, 1981.
———. *Indus and Swat Kohistan: An Ethnographic Survey*. Oslo: Forenede Trykkerier, 1956.
———. *Political Leadership among Swat Pathans*. London: Athlone, 1965.
Bashir, Shahzad. "Everlasting Doubt: Uncertainty in Islamic Representations of the Past." *Archiv für Religionsgeschichte* 20, no. 1 (2018): 25–44.
———. *Fazlallah Astarabadi and the Hurufis*. Oxford: Oneworld, 2005.

———. "The Imam's Return: Messianic Leadership in Late Medieval Shi'ism." In *The Most Learned of the Shi'a: The Institution of the Marja' Taqlid*, edited by Linda S. Walbridge, 21–33. Oxford: Oxford University Press, 2005.

———. *Messianic Hopes and Mystical Visions: The Nūrbakhshīya between Medieval and Modern Islam*. Columbia: University of South Carolina Press, 2003.

———. "Muhammad in Sufi Eyes: Prophetic Legitimacy in Medieval Iran and Central Asia." In *The Cambridge Companion to Muhammad*, edited by Jonathan E. Brockopp. Cambridge: Cambridge University Press, 2010.

———. "On Islamic Time: Rethinking Chronology in the Historiography of Muslim Societies." *History and Theory* 53, no. 4 (2014): 519–44.

———. "Shah Isma'il and the Qizilbash: Cannibalism in the Religious History of Early Safavid Iran." *History of Religions* 45 (2006): 234–56.

———. *Sufi Bodies: Religion and Society in Medieval Islam*. New York: Columbia University Press, 2011.

Bashir, Shahzad, and Robert D. Crews. *Under the Drones: Modern Lives in the Afghanistan-Pakistan Borderlands*. Cambridge, MA: Harvard University Press, 2012.

Bāyazīd Anṣārī. *Farḥat al-Mujtabá*. Edited by Zalmay Haywādmal. Kabul: Da Afghānistān da 'Ulūmo Akāḍamī da Zhabo aw Adabiyāto Markaz [Academy of Language and Literary Sciences of Afghanistan], 2006.

———. *Khayr al-bayān*. Edited by Muḥammad 'Abd a-Quddūs Qāsimī. Peshawar: Pashto Academy at Peshawar University, 1988.

———. "Khayr al-bayān." 1650–51 CE / AH 1061. Ms. Or. Fol. 4093. Staatsbibliothek zu Berlin, Berlin.

———. "Khayr al-bayān." 1668 CE / AH 1079. Tas. 60, Cat. MS 3346. Salar Jung Museum, Hyderabad, India.

———. "Khayr al-bayān." 1852–1853 CE / AH 1269. MS 1070. Raza Library, Rampur, India.

———. *Maqṣūd al-mu'minīn*. Edited by Mīr Walī Khān Mas'ūdī. Islamabad: Majma' al-Buḥūth al-Islāmīya, 1976.

———. "Ṣirāṭ al-tawḥīd." N.d. MS 15978. Ganj Bakhsh Library. Iran-Pakistan Institute of Persian Studies, Islamabad, Pakistan.

———. "Ṣirāṭ al-tawḥīd." N.d. MS 924. Raza Library, Rampur, India.

———. *'Uryān al-ghayb*. Delhi: India-Afghanistan Foundation, 2018.

Bayly, Martin J. *Taming the Imperial Imagination: Colonial Knowledge, International Relations, and the Anglo-Afghan Encounter, 1808–1878*. Cambridge: Cambridge University Press, 2016.

Beecroft, Alexander. *An Ecology of World Literature: From Antiquity to the Present Day*. London: Verso Books, 2015.

Bellew, Henry Walter. *A General Report on the Yusufzais*. 1864; Lahore: Sang-e-Meel, 1977. Page references are to the 1977 edition.

Ben-Dor Benite, Zvi. *The Ten Lost Tribes: A World History*. Oxford: Oxford University Press, 2009.

Benjamin, Walter. *Illuminations*. Translated by Harry Zohn. New York: Random House, 2007.

Bernau, Anke, and Eva von Contzen, eds. *Sanctity as Literature in Late Medieval Britain*. Manchester: Manchester University Press, 2015.

Black, Antony. *History of Islamic Political Thought: From the Prophet to the Present*. Edinburgh: Edinburgh University Press, 2001.

Blake, Stephen P. *Time in Early Modern Islam: Calendar, Ceremony, and Chronology in the Safavid, Mughal, and Ottoman Empires*. Cambridge: Cambridge University Press, 2013.

Blumhardt, James Fuller, and David Neil MacKenzie. *Catalogue of Pashto Manuscripts in the Libraries of the British Isles: Bodleian Library, the British Museum, Cambridge University Library, India Office Library, John Rylands Library, School of Oriental and African Studies, [and] Trinity College, Dublin*. London: Trustees of the British Museum, 1965.

Bowen, John Richard. *A New Anthropology of Islam*. Cambridge: Cambridge University Press, 2012.

———. "Salat in Indonesia: The Social Meanings of an Islamic Ritual." *Man* 24, no. 4 (1989): 600–619.

Bradley, Arthur, and Paul Fletcher. *The Messianic Now: Philosophy, Religion, Culture*. London: Routledge, 2011.

Brown, Norman Oliver. *Apocalypse and/or Metamorphosis*. Berkeley: University of California Press, 1991.

Brown, Peter. *The Cult of the Saints: Its Rise and Function in Latin Christianity*. Chicago: University of Chicago Press, 1981.

Brubaker, Rogers. *Ethnicity without Groups*. Cambridge, MA: Harvard University Press, 2010.

———. *Grounds for Difference*. Cambridge, MA: Harvard University Press, 2015.

Buc, Philippe. *The Dangers of Ritual: Between Early Medieval Texts and Social Scientific Theory*. Princeton, NJ: Princeton University Press, 2001.

Buehler, Arthur F. *Sufi Heirs of the Prophet: The Indian Naqshbandiyya and the Rise of the Mediating Sufi Shaykh*. Columbia: University of South Carolina Press, 1998.

Burki, Rozi Khan. "Dying Languages with Special Focus on Ormuri." *Pakistan Journal of Public Administration* 6, no. 2 (2001). http://citeseerx.ist.psu.edu/viewdoc/download?doi=10.1.1.621.2975&rep=rep1&type= pdf.

Butler, Judith. *Bodies That Matter: On the Discursive Limits of "Sex."* New York: Routledge, 1993.

———. *Frames of War: When Is Life Grievable?* New York: Verso, 2016.

Caine, William Sproston. *Picturesque India: A Handbook for European Travellers*. London: Routledge, 1891.

Caroe, Olaf. *The Pathans: 550 B.C.–A.D. 1957*. London: Macmillan, 1958.

Charkhī, Ya'qūb. *Tafsīr-i Ya'qūb Charkhī*. Edited by Nūr Muḥammad Ṣāḥib. Istanbul: Yıldız, 1991.

Chatterjee, Kumkum. *The Cultures of History in Early Modern India: Persianization and Mughal Culture in Bengal*. New Delhi: Oxford University Press, 2009.

Chittick, William C. "Notes on Ibn al-'Arabī's Influence in the Subcontinent." *Muslim World* 82, no. 3–4 (1992): 218–41.

———. *The Self-Disclosure of God: Principles of Ibn al-'Arabi's Cosmology*. Albany: State University of New York Press, 1997.

———. *The Sufi Path of Knowledge: Ibn al-'Arabi's Metaphysics of Imagination*. Albany: State University of New York Press, 1989.

Chrétien, Jean-Louis. *The Call and the Response*. Translated by Anne Davenport. New York: Fordham University Press, 2004.

Coburn, Noah. *Losing Afghanistan: An Obituary for the Intervention*. Stanford, CA: Stanford University Press, 2016.

Cohn, Bernard S. *Colonialism and Its Forms of Knowledge*. Princeton, NJ: Princeton University Press, 1996.

Cohn, Norman. *The Pursuit of the Millennium: Revolutionary Millenarians and Mystical Anarchists of the Middle Ages*. New York: Oxford University Press, 1970.

Cook, David. *Contemporary Muslim Apocalyptic Literature*. Syracuse, NY: Syracuse University Press, 2005.

———. *Studies in Muslim Apocalyptic*. Princeton, NJ: Darwin, 2002.

Cooperson, Michael. "'Arabs' and 'Iranians': The Uses of Ethnicity in the Early Abbasid Period." In *Islamic Cultures, Islamic Contexts: Essays in Honor of Professor Patricia Crone*, edited by Behnam Sadeghi, Asad Q. Ahmed, Adam Silverstein, and Robert Hoyland. Leiden: Brill, 2015.

———. *Classical Arabic Biography: The Heirs of the Prophets in the Age of al-Ma'mūn*. Cambridge: Cambridge University Press, 2000.

Corbett, Rosemary. *Making Moderate Islam: Sufism, Service, and the "Ground Zero Mosque" Controversy*. Stanford, CA: Stanford University Press, 2016.

Corbin, Henry. *Creative Imagination in the Sufism of Ibn 'Arabi*. Translated by Ralph Manheim. Princeton, NJ: Princeton University Press, 2014.

Cornell, Vincent J. *Realm of the Saint: Power and Authority in Moroccan Sufism*. Austin: University of Texas Press, 1998.

Crews, Robert D. *Afghan Modern: The History of a Global Nation*. Cambridge, MA: Belknap, 2015.

———. "The Taliban and Nationalist Militancy in Afghanistan." In *Contextualising Jihadi Thought*, edited by Jeevan Deol and Zaheer Kazmi, 369–84. New York: Columbia University Press, 2011.

Crone, Patricia. "Atheism (pre-Modern)." In *Encyclopaedia of Islam, Three*, edited by Kate Fleet, Gudrun Krämer, Denis Matringe, John Nawas, and Everett Rowson. Brill Online, 2009–. Accessed April 26, 2017.

———. *God's Rule: Government and Islam*. New York: Columbia University Press, 2005.

Cross, Eric. *The Tailor and Ansty*. 1942; Cork, Ireland: Mercier, 1999. Page references are to the 1999 edition.

Currie, P. M. *The Shrine and Cult of Mu'īn al-dīn Chishtī of Ajmer*. Delhi: Oxford University Press, 1989.

Dale, Stephen Frederic. *Babur: Timurid Prince and Mughal Emperor, 1483–1530*. Cambridge: Cambridge University Press, 2018.

———. *Indian Merchants and Eurasian Trade, 1600–1750*. Cambridge: Cambridge University Press, 2002.

Dale, Stephen Frederic, and Alam Payind. "The Ahrāri *Waqf* in Kābul in the Year 1546 and the Mughul Naqshbandiyyah." *Journal of the American Oriental Society* 119 (1999): 218–33.

Damrel, David W. "The 'Naqshbandi Reaction' Reconsidered." In *Beyond Turk and Hindu: Rethinking Religious Identities in Islamicate South Asia*, edited by David Gilmartin and Bruce Lawrence. Gainesville: University Press of Florida, 2000.

Darmesteter, James. *Chants populaires des Afghans*. Paris: Imprimerie nationale, E. Leroux, 1888.

Darrow, William R. "Zoroaster Amalgamated: Notes on Iranian Prophetology." *History of Religions* 27, no. 2 (1987): 109–32.

Davis, Dick. "Sufism and Poetry: A Marriage of Convenience?" *Edebiyat* 10 (1999): 279–92.

Davydov, Artem. "On Souleymane Kanté's Translation of the Quran into the Maninka Language." *Mandenkan*, no. 48 (2012): 3–20. http://llacan.vjf.cnrs.fr/PDF/Mandenkan48/48Davydov.pdf.

Deeb, Lara. *An Enchanted Modern: Gender and Public Piety in Shi'i Lebanon*. Princeton, NJ: Princeton University Press, 2011.

———. "Piety Politics and the Role of a Transnational Feminist Analysis." *Journal of the Royal Anthropological Institute* 15, no. 1 (2009): 112–26.

DeLanda, Manuel. *Assemblage Theory*. Edinburgh: Edinburgh University Press, 2016.

———. *A New Philosophy of Society: Assemblage Theory and Social Complexity*. London: Bloomsbury Academic, 2006.

Deleuze, Gilles. *Kafka: Toward a Minor Literature*. Translated by Terry Cochran. Minneapolis: University of Minnesota Press, 1986.

Deleuze, Gilles, and Felix Guattari. *A Thousand Plateaus: Capitalism and Schizophrenia*. Translated by Brian Massumi. Minneapolis: University of Minnesota Press, 1987.

DeWeese, Devin. "The Eclipse of the Kubravīyah in Central Asia." *Iranian Studies* 21, no. 1/2 (1988): 45–83.

———. *Islamization and Native Religion in the Golden Horde: Baba Tükles and Conversion to Islam in Historical and Epic Tradition*. University Park: Pennsylvania State University Press, 1994.

———. "The Mashā'ikh-i Turk and the Khojagān: Rethinking the Links between the Yasavī and Naqshbandī Sufi Traditions." *Journal of Islamic Studies* 7, no. 2 (1996): 180–207.

———. "Sacred History for a Central Asian Town: Saints, Shrines, and Legends of Origin in Histories of Sayrām, 18th–19th Centuries." In *Figures mythiques des mondes musulmans*, edited by Denise Aigle. Aix-en-Provence: Édisud, 2000.

———. "An 'Uvaysī' Sufi in Timurid Mawarannahr: Notes on Hagiography and the Taxonomy of Sanctity in the Religious History of Central Asia." *Papers on Inner Asia*, no. 22 (1993).

Digby, Simon. "The Sufi Shaykh and the Sultan: A Conflict of Claims to Authority in Medieval India." *Iran* 28 (1990): 71–81.

———. "Tabarrukāt and Succession among the Great Chishtī Shaykhs of the Dehli Sultanate." In *Delhi through the Ages: Essays in Urban History, Culture and Society*, edited by R. E. Frykenberg, 63–103. Delhi: Oxford University Press, 1986.

Douglas, Mary. *Leviticus as Literature*. Oxford: Oxford University Press, 1999.

Durantaye, Leland de la. *Giorgio Agamben: A Critical Introduction*. Stanford, CA: Stanford University Press, 2009.

Duranti, Alessandro, ed. *A Companion to Linguistic Anthropology*. Malden, MA: Blackwell, 2004.

Eaton, Richard M. "Akbar-Nāma." In *Encyclopaedia Iranica*, edited by Ehsan Yarshater, vol. 1, fasc. 7, pp. 714–15. London: Routledge and Kegan Paul, 1985–. Originally published in 1984; last updated online July 29, 2011. Accessed April 26, 2017. http://www.iranicaonline.org/articles/akbar-nama.

———. *India in the Persianate Age, 1000–1765*. Berkeley: University of California Press, 2019.

———. *The Rise of Islam and the Bengal Frontier*. Berkeley: University of California Press, 1993.

Ebenezer, Matthew. "American Presbyterians and Islam in India 1855–1923: A Critical Evaluation of the Contributions of Isidor Loewenthal (1826–1864) and Elwood Morris Wherry (1843–1927)." PhD diss., Westminster Theological Seminary, Philadelphia, 1998.

Edwards, David B. "Learning from the Swat Pathans: Political Leadership in Afghanistan, 1978–97." *American Ethnologist* 25, no. 4 (1998): 712–28.

El-Desouky, Ayman A. "Naẓm, I'jāz, Discontinuous Kerygma: Approaching Qur'anic Voice on the Other Side of the Poetic." *Journal of Qur'anic Studies* 15, no. 2 (2013): 1–21.

Elias, Jamal. *Aisha's Cushion: Religious Art, Perception, and Practice in Islam*. Cambridge, MA: Harvard University Press, 2012.

———. "A Second 'Alī: The Making of Sayyid 'Alī Hamadānī in Popular Imagination." *Muslim World* 90, no. 3–4 (2000): 395–419.

Elphinstone, Mountstuart. *An Account of the Kingdom of Caubul*. 1815. Reprinted with notes by Olaf Caroe. Karachi: Oxford University Press, 1972. Page references are to the 1972 edition.

Engelke, Matthew. *A Problem of Presence: Beyond Scripture in an African Church*. Berkeley: University of California Press, 2007.

Eriksen, Thomas Hylland. *Fredrik Barth: An Intellectual Biography*. London: Pluto, 2015.

Ernst, Carl W. *Eternal Garden: Mysticism, History, and Politics at a South Asian Sufi Center*. Albany: State University of New York Press, 1992.

———. *Sufism*. Boulder, CO: Shambhala, 2011.

Ernst, Carl W., and Bruce Lawrence. *Sufi Martyrs of Love: The Chishti Order in South Asia and Beyond*. New York: Palgrave Macmillan, 2002.

Fahd, T. "Sakīna." In *Encyclopaedia of Islam*, edited by P. Bearman, Th. Bianquis, C. E. Bosworth, E. van Dozel, and W. Heinrichs, 2nd ed. Brill Online, 2012–. Accessed April 26, 2017. http://referenceworks.brillonline.com/entries/encyclopaedia-of-islam-2/sakina- SIM_6505.

Farīd Bhakkarī. *Dhakhīrat al-Khawānīn of Shaykh Farīd Bhakkarī (Persian text)*. Edited by S. Moinul Haq. Karachi: Pakistan Historical Society, 1961.

Farrin, Raymond. *Structure and Qur'anic Interpretation: A Study of Symmetry and Coherence in Islam's Holy Text*. Ashland, OR: White Cloud, 2014.

Faruqui, Munis D. "The Forgotten Prince: Mirza Hakīm and the Formation of the Mughal Empire in India." *Journal of the Economic and Social History of the Orient* 48, no. 4 (2005): 487–523.

———. *Princes of the Mughal Empire, 1504–1719*. Cambridge: Cambridge University Press, 2012.

Felek, Özgen, and Alexander D Knysh. *Dreams and Visions in Islamic Societies*. Albany: State University of New York Press, 2012.

Fenech, Louis E. *The Sikh* Ẓafar-Namah *of Guru Gobind Singh: A Discursive Blade in the Heart of the Mughal Empire*. Oxford: Oxford University Press, 2012.

Flood, Finbarr Barry. *Objects of Translation: Material Culture and Medieval "Hindu-Muslim" Encounter*. Princeton, NJ: Princeton University Press, 2009.

Flueckiger, Joyce. *In Amma's Healing Room: Gender and Vernacular Islam in South India*. Bloomington: Indiana University Press, 2006.

Foucault, Michel. *The Essential Foucault: Selections from the Essential Works of Foucault, 1954–1984*. Edited by Paul Rabinow. New York: New Press, 2003.

———. *Ethics: Subjectivity and Truth*. Edited by Paul Rabinow. New York: New Press, 1998.

———. *The History of Sexuality*. Vol. 3, *The Care of the Self*. Translated by Robert Hurley. Vintage Books edition. New York: Random House, 1988.

Gadamer, Hans-Georg. *Truth and Method*. London: Bloomsbury Academic, 2013.

Galonnier, Juliette. "Choosing Faith and Facing Race: Converting to Islam in France and the United States." PhD diss., Northwestern University, 2017.

Gazetteer of the Rawalpindi District. Rev. ed., 1893–94. Lahore: Civil and Military Gazette Press, 1895. Digitized edition. https://books.google.com.pk/

books/about/GAZETTEER_OF_THE_RAWALPINDI_DISTRICT_REV.html?id=PxsUAAAAYAAJ.

Geertz, Clifford. *Islam Observed: Religious Development in Morocco and Indonesia.* Chicago: University of Chicago Press, 1971.

Gellner, Ernest. *Saints of the Atlas.* London: ACLS Humanities E-Book, 2008.

Ghazali, Abū Hamid al-. *Al-Ghazalī on the Remembrance of Death and the Afterlife.* Translated by Timothy J. Winter. Cambridge: Islamic Texts Society, 2016.

Gilmartin, David. *Empire and Islam: Punjab and the Making of Pakistan.* Berkeley: University of California Press, 1988.

Gin Lum, Kathryn. "The Historyless Heathen and the Stagnating Pagan: History as Non-Native Category?" *Religion and American Culture: A Journal of Interpretation* 28, no. 1 (2018): 52–91.

Goldberg, Jeffrey. "Herman Melville on the Situation in Afghanistan." *The Atlantic*, August 5, 2008. http://www.theatlantic.com/international/archive/2008/08/herman-melville-on- the-situation-in-afghanistan/8633/.

Gommans, Jos J. L. *The Rise of the Indo-Afghan Empire, c. 1710–1780.* Delhi: Oxford University Press, 1999.

González, Roberto J. *American Counterinsurgency: Human Science and the Human Terrain.* Chicago: Prickly Paradigm, 2009.

———. "Going 'Tribal': Notes on Pacification in the 21st Century." *Anthropology Today* 25, no. 2 (2009): 15–19.

———. "The Rise and Fall of the Human Terrain System." *Counterpunch.* Accessed June 29, 2015. http://www.counterpunch.org/2015/06/29/the-rise-and-fall-of-the-human- terrain-system/.

Graham, Mark. *Afghanistan in the Cinema.* Champaign, IL: University of Illinois Press, 2010.

Great Britain Institution of Civil Engineers. *Minutes of Proceedings of the Institution of Civil Engineers.* 1902.

Green, Nile, ed. *Afghanistan's Islam: From Conversion to the Taliban.* Berkeley: University of California Press.

———. "Idiom, Genre and the Politics of Self-Description on the Peripheries of Persian." In *Religion, Language and Power*, edited by Nile Green and Mary Searle Chatterjee. New York: Routledge, 2008.

———. *Indian Sufism since the Seventeenth Century: Saints, Books and Empires in the Muslim Deccan.* London: Routledge, 2006.

———. *Making Space: Sufis and Settlers in Early Modern India.* New Delhi: Oxford University Press, 2012.

———. "The Religious and Cultural Roles of Dreams and Visions in Islam." *Journal of the Royal Asiatic Society* 13 (2003): 287–313.

———. *Sufism: A Global History.* Oxford: Wiley-Blackwell, 2012.

———. "Tribe, Diaspora, and Sainthood in Afghan History." *Journal of Asian Studies* 67 (2008): 171–211.

Green, Nile, and Nushin Arbabzadah, eds. *Afghanistan in Ink: Literature between Nation and Diaspora*. Oxford: Oxford University Press, 2012.

Green-Mercado, Mayte. *Visions of Deliverance: Moriscos and the Politics of Prophecy in the Early Modern Mediterranean*. Ithaca, NY: Cornell University Press, 2020.

Gregg, Robert C. *Shared Stories, Rival Tellings: Early Encounters of Jews, Christians, and Muslims*. Oxford: Oxford University Press, 2015.

Griffel, Frank. "Apostasy." In *Enyclopaedia of Islam, Three*, edited by Kate Fleet, Gudrun Krämer, Denis Matringe, John Nawas, and Everett Rowson. Brill Online, 2007–. Accessed April 26, 2017. http://dx.doi.org/10.1163/1573-3912_ei3_SIM_0044..

Gross, Jo-Ann. "Authority and Miraculous Behavior: Reflections on Karāmāt Stories of Khwāja 'Ubaydullāh Aḥrār." In *The Heritage of Sufism*, vol. 2, edited by Leonard Lewisohn. Oxford: One World, 1999.

———. "The Economic Status of a Timurid Sufi Shaykh: A Matter of Conflict or Perception?" *Iranian Studies* 21 (1988): 84–104.

Hadot, Pierre. *Philosophy as a Way of Life: Spiritual Exercises from Socrates to Foucault*. Edited and with an introduction by Arnold I. Davidson. Translated by Michael Case. Malden, MA: Wiley-Blackwell, 1995.

Ḥāfiẓ Raḥmat Khān. *Khulāṣat al-ansāb: Sarah da Puṣhto tarjume*. Translated into Pashto by Muḥammad Navāz Ṭā'ir. Peshawar: Pashto Academy, University of Peshawar, 1973.

Hakala, Walter N. "Locating 'Pashto' in Afghanistan: A Survey of Secondary Sources." In *Language Policy and Language Conflict in Afghanistan and Its Neighbors*, edited by Harold Schiffman, 53–88. Leiden: Brill, 2011.

Hanifi, M. Jamil. "Editing the Past: Colonial Production of Hegemony through the 'Loya Jerga' in Afghanistan." *Iranian Studies* 37, no. 2 (2004): 295–322.

Hanifi, Shah Mahmoud. *Connecting Histories in Afghanistan Market Relations and State Formation on a Colonial Frontier*. Stanford, CA: Stanford University Press, 2011.

———. "A History of Linguistic Boundary Crossing within and around Pashto." In *Beyond Swat: History, Society and Economy along the Afghanistan-Pakistan Frontier*, edited by Benjamin Hopkins and Magnus Marsden, 63–76. New York: Columbia University Press, 2013.

Harawī, A.S.M.Q. al-. *Sharḥ al-Amālī*. [Unknown location]. Maṭba'at al-'Ālam, 1901. Digitized by Princeton University Arabic Collection. https://books.google.com/books?id=2msZAAAAYAAJ.

Harb, Lara. "Form, Content, and the Inimitability of the Qur'ān in 'Abd al-Qāhir al-Jurjānī's Works." *Middle Eastern Literatures* 18, no. 3 (2015): 301–21.

Haroon, Sana. *Frontier of Faith: Islam in the Indo-Afghan Borderland*. New York: Columbia University Press, 2007.

Hartung, Jan-Peter. "Frontiers–Pieties–Resistance." In *Dynamics of Change in the Pakistan–Afghanistan Region: Politics on Borderland*, edited by Shahida

Aman and Muhammad Zubair, 39–54. Peshawar: University of Peshawar, 2017.

Haywādmal, Zalmay. *Da Puṣhto adabiyāto tārīkh*. Kabul: Dānish Khparandūyah, 2014.

Hirschkind, Charles. *The Ethical Soundscape: Cassette Sermons and Islamic Counterpublics*. New York: Columbia University Press, 2006.

Ho, Engseng. *The Graves of Tarim: Genealogy and Mobility across the Indian Ocean*. Berkeley: University of California Press, 2006.

Hopkins, B. D. *The Making of Modern Afghanistan*. Basingstoke, UK: Palgrave Macmillan, 2008.

Hughes, Thomas Patrick. *The Kalid-i-Afghani, Being Selections of Pushto Prose and Poetry for the Use of Students*. Lahore: Munshi Culab Singh and Sons, 1893.

Ibn Hishām, ʿAbd al-Malik, and Muḥammad ibn Isḥāq. *The Life of Muhammad*. Edited and translated by Alfred Guillaume. London: Oxford University Press, 1955.

Irvine, Judith T., and Susan Gal. "Language Ideology and Linguistic Differentiation." In *Regimes of Language: Ideologies, Polities, and Identities*, edited by Paul V. Kroskrity, 35–84. Santa Fe, NM: School of American Research Press, 2000.

Irvine, William. "The Bangash Nawabs of Farrukhabad—A Chronicle (1713–1857), Part 1." *Journal of the Asiatic Society of Bengal* 47 (1879): 277–358.

———. "The Bangash Nawabs of Farrukhabad—A Chronicle (1713–1857), Part 2." *Journal of the Asiatic Society of Bengal* 48 (1879): 41–174.

Ivanchikova, Alla. *Imagining Afghanistan: Global Fiction and Film of the 9/11 Wars*. West Lafayette, IN: Purdue University Press, 2019.

Iyer, Lars. "Impersonal Speech: Blanchot, Virno, Messianism." In *The Messianic Now*, edited by Arthur Bradley and Paul Fletcher, 101–16. London: Routledge, 2011.

Jackson, Bernard. *Studies in the Semiotics of Biblical Law*. Sheffield: Sheffield Academic Press, 2000.

Jahāngīr. *The Jahangirnama: Memoirs of Jahangir, Emperor of India*. Edited and translated by Wheeler M. Thackston. New York: Freer Gallery of Art and Arthur M. Sackler Gallery in association with Oxford University Press, 1999.

Jamālī, Ḥāmid ibn Faḍl Allāh. *The Mirror of Meanings, Mirʾāt al-Maʿānī: A Parallel English-Persian Text*. Edited and translated by A. A Seyed-Gohrab and Naṣr Allāh Pūrjavādī. Costa Mesa, CA: Mazda, 2002.

———. *Siyar al-ʿārifīn*. Edited by Muḥammad Ayyūb Qādirī. Chicago: University of Chicago Library, 1993.

James, William. *William James: Writings 1902–1910: The Varieties of Religious Experience, Pragmatism, A Pluralistic Universe, The Meaning of Truth, Some Problems of Philosophy and Essays*. New York: Library of America, 1988.

Jāmī. *Nafaḥāt al-uns min haẓarāt al-quds*. Edited by Mahdī Tawḥīdīpūr. Tehran: Kitābfurūshī-i Maḥmūdī, 1958.

Jenkins, Richard. *Rethinking Ethnicity*. Thousand Oaks, CA: Sage, 2008.

Johnson, Sylvester A. *African American Religions, 1500–2000*. Cambridge: Cambridge University Press, 2015.

Joshi, Rita. *The Afghan Nobility and the Mughals: 1526–1707*. New Delhi: Vikas, 1985.

Joyce, James. *A Portrait of the Artist as a Young Man*. Centennial Edition. New York: Penguin, 2016.

———. *Ulysses*. Edited with notes by Jeri Johnson. 1922. Oxford: Oxford University Press, 2011.

Karamustafa, Ahmet. *God's Unruly Friends: Dervish Groups in the Islamic Middle Period, 1200–1550*. Oxford: Oneworld, 2006.

Kaydānī. *Khulaṣat al-Kaydānī*. Mumbai: n.p., 1886. http://tinyurl.galegroup.com/tinyurl/tsdi7.

Kaykhusraw Isfadiyār. *Dabistān-i Madhāhib*. Edited with notes by Rahim Rizazadeh Malik. Tehran: Ṭahūrī, 1362 [1983].

Keane, Webb. *Christian Moderns: Freedom and Fetish in the Mission Encounter*. Berkeley: University of California Press, 2007.

Khalidi, Tarif. *Images of Muhammad: Narratives of the Prophet in Islam across the Centuries*. New York: Doubleday, 2009.

Khan, Imran. *Warrior Race: A Journey through the Land of the Tribal Pathans*. London: Chatto and Windus, 1993.

Khaṭak, Khūshḥāl Khān. *Dastar nama of Khūshḥāl Khān Khaṭak*. Edited and translated by Arif Naseem. Peshawar: Pashto Academy, University of Peshawar, 2007.

———. *Khushal Khan Khattak: The Great Warrior/Poet of Afghanistan: Selected Poems*. Translated by Paul Smith. CreateSpace Independent Publishing Platform, 2012.

———. *Poems from the Divan of Khushal Khan Khatak*. Translated by D. N. Mackenzie. London: George Allen and Unwin, 1965.

Khaṭṭak, Yār Muḥammad Maghmūm. *The Rowshanites and Pashto Literature*. Peshawar: Pashto Academy, University of Peshawar, 2005.

Kierkegaard, Søren. *Fear and Trembling/Repetition: Kierkegaard's Writings*, vol. 6. Translated by Edna H. Hong and Howard V. Hong. Princeton, NJ: Princeton University Press, 1983.

King, Richard. *Orientalism and Religion: Post-colonial Theory, India, and "The Mystic East."* London: Routledge, 1999.

Kishik, David. *The Power of Life: Agamben and the Coming Politics*. Stanford, CA: Stanford University Press, 2012.

Klar, Marianna. *Interpreting al-Tha'labī's Tales of the Prophet: Temptation, Responsibility and Loss*. London: Routledge, 2006.

Klein, Kerwin. *Frontiers of Historical Imagination: Narrating the European Conquest of Native America, 1890–1990*. Berkeley: University of California Press, 1997.

Kohn, Eduardo. *How Forests Think: Toward an Anthropology beyond the Human*. Berkeley: University of California Press, 2013.

Koopman, Colin. *Genealogy as Critique: Foucault and the Problems of Modernity*. Bloomington: Indiana University Press, 2013.

Kreyenbroek, Philip G., and Ulrich Marzolph, eds. *Oral Literature of Iranian Languages: Kurdish, Pashto, Balochi, Ossetic, Persian and Tajik, Companion Volume II to A History of Persian Literature,* vol. 18. London: I. B. Tauris, 2010.

Kugle, Scott. "ʿAbdallāh Shaṭṭār." In *Enyclopaedia of Islam, Three,* edited by Kate Fleet, Gudrun Krämer, Denis Matringe, John Nawas, and Everett Rowson. Brill Online, 2007–. First published online in 2013. Accessed April 26, 2017. http://dx.doi.org/10.1163/1573-3912_ei3_COM_23912.

———. *Hajj to the Heart: Sufi Journeys across the Indian Ocean*. Chapel Hill: University of North Carolina Press, 2021.

———. *Sufis and Saints' Bodies: Mysticism, Corporeality, and Sacred Power in Islam*. Chapel Hill: University of North Carolina Press, 2007.

Kushev, V. V. "The Dawn of Pashtun Linguistics: Early Grammatical and Lexicographical Works and Their Manuscripts." *Manuscripta Orientalia* 7, no. 2 (2001): 3–9.

Landes, Richard. *Heaven on Earth: The Varieties of the Millennial Experience*. Oxford: Oxford University Press, 2011.

Larkin, Margaret. "The Inimitability of the Qur'an: Two Perspectives." *Religion and Literature* 20, no. 1 (1988): 31–47.

Latour, Bruno. *Rejoicing: Or the Torments of Religious Speech*. Translated by Julie Rose. Cambridge: Polity, 2013.

———. *We Have Never Been Modern*. Translated by Catherine Porter. Cambridge, MA: Harvard University Press, 1993.

Lawson, Todd. *Gnostic Apocalypse and Islam: Qur'an, Exegesis, Messianism and the Literary Origins of the Babi Religion*. London: Routledge, 2012.

Leake, Elisabeth. *The Defiant Border: The Afghan-Pakistan Borderlands in the Era of Decolonization, 1936–65*. Cambridge: Cambridge University Press, 2016.

Lecercle, Jean-Jacques. *Deleuze and Language*. New York: Palgrave Macmillan, 2002.

Lee, Jonathan L. *Afghanistan: A History from 1260 to the Present*. London: Reaktion Books, 2018.

Leyden, J. "On the Rosheniah Sect and Its Founder, Bayezid Ansari." *Asiatick Researches* 11 (1812): 363–428.

Lifshitz, Felice. "Beyond Positivism and Genre: 'Hagiographical' Texts as Historical Narrative." *Viator* 25 (1994): 95–113.

Lingwood, Chad G. *Politics, Poetry, and Sufism in Medieval Iran: New Perspectives on Jāmī's Salāmān va Absāl*. Leiden: Brill, 2013.

Lobel, Diana. *A Sufi-Jewish Dialogue: Philosophy and Mysticism in Bahya ibn Paquda's "Duties of the Heart."* Philadelphia: University of Pennsylvania Press, 2007.

Loewenthal, Isidor. "Is the Pushto a Semitic Language?" *Journal of the Asiatic Society* 29, no. 4 (1860): 323–45.

Losensky, Paul E. *Welcoming Fighānī: Imitation and Poetic Individuality in the Safavid-Mughal Ghazal.* Costa Mesa, CA: Mazda, 1998.

MacKendrick, Karmen. *The Matter of Voice: Sensual Soundings.* Oxford: Oxford University Press, 2016.

MacKenzie, David Neil. "The Qasida in Pashto." In *Qasida Poetry in Islamic Asia and Africa: Classical Traditions and Modern Meanings*, edited by Stefan Sperl and Christopher Shackle, 1:340–50. Leiden: Brill, 1996.

———. "A Standard Pashto." *Bulletin of the School of Oriental and African Studies* 22, no. 1/3 (1959): 231–35.

———. "The Xayr ul-bayān." In *Indo-Iranica: Mélanges présentés à Georg Morgenstierne a L'occasion de son soixante-dixième anniversaire.* Wiesbaden: Harrassowitz, 1964.

Madelung, Wilfred. "Al-Ūshī." In *Encyclopaedia of Islam*, edited by P. Bearman, Th. Bianquis, C. E. Bosworth, E. van Dozel, and W. Heinrichs. 2nd ed. Brill Online, 2012. Accessed April 26, 2017. http://dx.doi.org/10.1163/1573- 3912_islam_SIM_7744.

———. "The Spread of Maturidism and the Turks." *Biblos* 46 (1970): 109–68.

Madigan, Daniel A. *The Qur'ān's Self-Image: Writing and Authority in Islam's Scripture.* Princeton, NJ: Princeton University Press, 2001.

Maffly-Kipp, Laurie F. *Setting Down the Sacred Past: African-American Race Histories.* Cambridge, MA: Belknap, 2010.

Mahmood, Saba. *Politics of Piety: The Islamic Revival and the Feminist Subject.* Princeton, NJ: Princeton University Press, 2012.

———. "Rehearsed Spontaneity and the Conventionality of Ritual: Disciplines of Ṣalat." *American Ethnologist* 28, no. 4 (2001): 827–53.

———. *Religious Difference in a Secular Age: A Minority Report.* Princeton, NJ: Princeton University Press, 2015.

———. "Religious Reason and Secular Affect." In *Is Critique Secular? Blasphemy, Injury, and Free Speech*, by Talal Asad, Wendy Brown, Judith Butler, and Saba Mahmood. New York: Fordham University Press, 2013.

Mahsood, Ali Khan. *La Pīr Rokhan tar Bacha Khana: Da Pukhtano Milli Mubarizi ta Katana.* Peshawar: n.p., [1990s?].

Malešević, Siniša. *The Sociology of Ethnicity.* London: Sage, 2004.

Mamdani, Mahmood. *Good Muslim, Bad Muslim: America, the Cold War, and the Roots of Terror.* New York: Pantheon, 2004.

Marion, Jean-Luc. *Being Given: Toward a Phenomenology of Givenness.* Translated by Jeffrey Kosky. Stanford, CA: Stanford University Press, 2002.

———. *Givenness and Revelation.* Translated by Stephen E. Lewis. New York: Oxford University Press, 2016.

Marsden, Magnus. *Trading Worlds: Afghan Merchants across Modern Frontiers.* Oxford: Oxford University Press, 2016.

Masud, Saifur Rahman. *Pir Roshan aur Roshani Inqilab.* Peshawar: Peshawar University Book Agency, [2000s?].

Masuzawa, Tomoko. *The Invention of World Religions: Or, How European Universalism Was Preserved in the Language of Pluralism.* Chicago: University of Chicago Press, 2005.

Mazzaoui, Michel. *The Origins of the Safawids: Šīʾism, Ṣūfism and the Gulāt.* Wiesbaden: F. Steiner, 1972.

McChesney, Robert. *Waqf in Central Asia: Four Hundred Years in the History of a Muslim Shrine, 1480–1889.* Princeton, NJ: Princeton University Press, 1991.

Melville, Herman. *Moby Dick.* 1851; London: Random House UK, 2008.

Melvin-Koushki, Matthew S. "The Quest for a Universal Science: The Occult Philosophy of Ṣāʾin Al-Dīn Turka Iṣfahānī (1369–1432) and Intellectual Millenarianism in Early Timurid Iran." PhD diss., Yale University, 2012.

Merleau-Ponty, Maurice. *Phenomenology of Perception.* London: Routledge, 2002.

Minorsky, Vladimir. "The Poetry of Shāh Ismāʿīl I." *Bulletin of the School of Oriental and African Studies* 10, no. 4 (1942): 1006a–1053a.

Mir, Farina. *The Social Space of Language: Vernacular Culture in British Colonial Punjab.* Berkeley: University of California Press, 2010.

Mir-Hosseini, Ziba. "Inner Truth and Outer History: The Two Worlds of the Ahl-i Haqq of Kurdistan." *International Journal of Middle East Studies* 26, no. 2 (1994): 267–85.

Mir-Kasimov, Orkhan. *Words of Power: Ḥurūfī Teachings between Shiʿism and Sufism in Medieval Islam.* London: I. B. Tauris in association with the Institute of Ismaili Studies, 2015.

Mitchell, Colin Paul. *The Practice of Politics in Safavid Iran: Power, Religion and Rhetoric.* London: I. B. Tauris, 2012.

Mittermaier, Amira. *Dreams That Matter: Egyptian Landscapes of the Imagination.* Berkeley: University of California Press, 2011.

Modern, John Lardas. *Secularism in Antebellum America: With Reference to Ghosts, Protestant Subcultures, Machines, and Their Metaphors; Featuring Discussions of Mass Media, Moby-Dick, Spirituality, Phrenology, Anthropology, Sing Sing State Penitentiary, and Sex with the New Motive Power.* Chicago: University of Chicago Press, 2011.

Moi, Toril. *Sexual/Textual Politics: Feminist Literary Theory.* London: Routledge, 2002.

Moin, A. Azfar. "Challenging the Mughal Empire: The Islamic Millennium according to ʿAbd al-Qadir Badayuni." In *Islam in South Asia in Practice*, edited by Barbara Daly Metcalf. Princeton, NJ: Princeton University Press, 2009.

———. "Messianism, Heresy and Historical Narrative in Mughal India." In *Unity in Diversity*, edited by Orkhan Mir-Kasimov, 393–413. Leiden: Brill, 2013.

———. *The Millennial Sovereign: Sacred Kingship and Sainthood in Islam.* New York: Columbia University Press, 2012.

Mojaddedi, Jawid A. *The Biographical Tradition in Sufism: The Tabaqat Genre from al-Sulami to Jami*. Richmond, UK: Curzon, 2001.

Mojtabai, Fath-allah. "Dabestān-e Madāheb." In *Encyclopaedia Iranica*, edited by Ehsan Yarshater, vol. 6, fasc. 5, pp. 532–34. London: Routledge and Kegan Paul, 1985–. Originally published December 15, 1993, and last updated November 10, 2011. Accessed April 26, 2017. https://www.iranicaonline.org/articles/dabestan-e- madaheb.

Monserrate, Antonio. *The Commentary of Father Monserrate, S.J., on His Journey to the Court of Akbar*. Edited and translated by John S. Hoyland and S. N. Banerjee. London: Oxford University Press, 1922.

Morgenstein Fuerst, Ilyse R. *Indian Muslim Minorities and the 1857 Rebellion: Religion, Rebels, and Jihad*. London: I. B. Tauris, 2017.

Morgenstierne, Georg. "Notes on an Old Pashto Manuscript." *New Indian Antiquary* 2, no. 8 (November 1939): 566–74.

Muʿazzam Shāh. *Tavārīkh-i Ḥāfiẓ Raḥmat Khānī: Afghān qabāʾil aur un kī tārīkh*. Peshawar: Pushto Academy of Peshawar University, 1977.

Muḥammad Ḥayāt Khān. *Afghanistan and Its Inhabitants*. Edited and translated by Henry Priestley. Lahore, 1874. Reprint, Lahore: Sang-e-Meel, 1981. Page references are to the 1981 edition.

Muḥammad Kabīr ibn Ismāʿīl. *Afsānah-i shāhān*. London: [unknown], 1775.

Muḥammad Mustajāb ibn Ḥāfiẓ Raḥmat Khān. *Gulistān-i raḥmat*. 1814. Reprinted as *The Life of Hafiz ool-Moolk, Hafiz Rehmut Khan*. Edited and translated by Charles Boileau Elliott. London: Oriental Translation Fund, 1831.

Muḥammad Ṣāliḥ Kambūh. *ʿAmal-i Ṣāliḥ, al-mawsūm bi Shāh Jahān Nāmah*. Lahore: Majlis-i Taraqqī-i Adab, 1958.

"Mukhliṣ," ʿAlī Muḥammad Kandahārī Shīnvārī. *Ḥāl-nāmah-yi Miyān Roshan* [Transliterated by publisher as Ḥālnāmah-ʿi Mya Rūṣhān]. Kabul: Vizārat-i Iṭṭilāʿāt va Farhang, 2009.

Mullā Arzānī. "Dīvān-i Arzānī." MS Or. 4496. British Library, London.

Murphy, Anne. "Writing Punjabi across Borders." *South Asian History and Culture* 9, no. 1 (2018): 68–91.

Mushtāqī, Shaykh Rizq Allāh. *Wāqiʿāt-i Mushtāqī*. Edited by Iqtidār Ḥusain Ṣiddīqī and Waqqār al-Ḥasan Ṣiddīqī. Rampur, Uttar Pradesh: Intishārāt-i Rāmpūr Reza Library, 2002. Also printed and translated as *Waqiʿat-e-Mushtaqui of Shaikh Rizq Ullah Mushtaqui*. Edited and translated by Iqtidar Husain Siddiqi. New Delhi: Indian Council of Historical Research and Northern Book Centre, 1993.

Najafian, Ahoo. "Poetic Nation: Iranian Soul and Historical Continuity." PhD diss., Stanford University, 2018.

Najm al-Din Kubra. *Fawāʾiḥ al-jamāl wa fawātiḥ al-jalāl*. Kuwait: Dar Saʿād al-Subāḥ, 1993.

Naseem, Arif, and Abdul Hameed. *Descriptive Catalogue of Manuscripts Pashto Academy, Library*. Peshawar: Pashto Academy, University of Peshawar, 2009.

Nasr, Seyyed Hossein, Caner Karacay Dagli, Maria Massi Dakake, Joseph E. B. Lumbard, and Mohammed Rustom. *The Study Quran: A New Translation and Commentary*. New York: HarperOne, 2015.

Nelson, Ingrid, and Shannon Gayk. "Introduction: Genre as Form-of-Life." *Exemplaria* 27 (2015): 1–17.

Netton, Ian R. *Sufi Ritual: The Parallel Universe*. London: Curzon, 2000.

Nichols, Robert. "Pashto Language Policy and Practice in the North West Frontier Province." In *Language Policy and Language Conflict in Afghanistan and Its Neighbors: The Changing Politics of Language Choice*, edited by Harold Schiffman, 263–81. Leiden: Brill, 2011

———. *Settling the Frontier: Land, Law and Society in the Peshawar Valley, 1500–1900*. Karachi: Oxford University Press, 2001.

Niʿmat Allāh Harawī. *Tarikh-i-Khān Jahāni wa Makhzan-i Afghānī: A Complete History of the Afghans in Indo-Pak Sub-Continent, Edited on the Basis of Its Earliest and Six Other Manuscripts Accompanied with a Critical Introduction in English, Annotations, Geographical and Historical Notes in Persian*. Edited by S. M. Imam al-Dīn. Dacca: Asiatic Society of Pakistan, 1960. Reprinted with Bernhard Dorn's English translation as *History of the Afghans: Translated from the Persian of Neamet Ullah*. Translated and introduced by Bernhard Dorn. Cambridge: Cambridge University Press, 2013. Page references are to the 1960 edition unless otherwise noted.

Niẓām al-Dīn Aḥmad ibn Muḥammad Muqīm. *Tabakat-i-Akbari of Nizam-ud-Din Ahmad Bakhshi*. Translated and edited by H. M. Elliot and John Dowson. Lahore: Sang-e-Meel, 2006.

Nongbri, Brent. *Before Religion: A History of a Modern Concept*. New Haven, CT: Yale University Press, 2015.

Novetzke, Christian. *The Quotidian Revolution: Vernacularization, Religion, and the Premodern Public Sphere in India*. New York: Columbia University Press, 2016.

Ohlander, Erik S. *Sufism in an Age of Transition: ʿUmar al-Suhrawardī and the Rise of the Islamic Mystical Brotherhoods*. Leiden: Brill, 2008.

Oliver, Edward Emmerson. *Across the Border: Or Pathan and Biloch*. London: Chapman and Hall, 1890. Digitally available at https://books.google.com/books?hl=en&lr=&id=pYpCAAAAIAAJ&oi=fnd&pg=PA1&dq=edward+oliver+across+the+border&ots=sGTsvkmmBZ&sig=jg1_Y4uUoKoeliCJMkG3SRh4hjs.

Orsi, Robert A. *History and Presence*. Cambridge, MA: Harvard University Press, 2016.

———. *The Madonna of 115th Street: Faith and Community in Italian Harlem, 1880–1950*. New Haven, CT: Yale University Press, 2010.

Orsini, Francesca. "The Multilingual Local in World Literature." *Comparative Literature* 67, no. 4 (2015): 345–74.

Oyler, Dianne White. "Re-inventing Oral Tradition: The Modern Epic of Souleymane Kanté." *Research in African Literatures* 33, no. 1 (2002): 75–93.

Ozaslan, Nuray. "From the Shrine of Cosmidion to the Shrine of Eyup Ensari." *Greek, Roman, and Byzantine Studies* 40, no. 4 (1999): 379–99.

Palmié, Stephan. *The Cooking of History: How Not to Study Afro-Cuban Religion*. Chicago: University of Chicago Press, 2013.

Pastner, Stephen L. "Power and Pirs among the Pakistani Baluch." In *Pakistan: The Social Sciences' Perspective*, edited by Akbar S. Ahmed. Karachi: Oxford University Press, 1990.

Paul, Jurgen. "Forming a Faction: The Ḥimāyāt System of Khwaja Ahrar." *International Journal of Middle East Studies* 23 (1991): 533–48.

Peirce, Charles S. *Writings of Charles S. Peirce: A Chronological Edition*, vol. 2: *1867–1871*. Bloomington: Indiana University Press, 1984.

Pelevin, Mikhail. "The Beginnings of Pashto Narrative Prose." *Iran and the Caucasus* 21, no. 2 (2017): 132–49.

———."The Inception of Literary Criticism in Early Modern Pashto Writings." *Iranian Studies* (2020): 1–30.

———. "The Khataks' Tribal Chronicle (XVII–XVIII): Extraliterary Text Functions." *Iran and the Caucasus* 18, no. 3 (2014): 201–12.

Pemberton, Kelly. *Women Mystics and Sufi Shrines in India*. Columbia: University of South Carolina Press, 2010.

Pennell, Theodore Leighton. *Among the Wild Tribes of the Afghan Frontier: A Record of Sixteen Years' Close Intercourse with the Natives of the Indian Marches*. Philadelphia: J. B. Lippincott, 1909.

Pollock, Sheldon. "The Cosmopolitan Vernacular." *Journal of Asian Studies* 57 (1998): 6–37.

———. *Forms of Knowledge in Early Modern Asia: Explorations in the Intellectual History of India and Tibet, 1500–1800*. Durham, NC: Duke University Press, 2011.

———. *The Language of the Gods in the World of Men: Sanskrit, Culture, and Power in Premodern India*. Berkeley: University of California Press, 2006.

———. *Literary Cultures in History Reconstructions from South Asia*. Berkeley: University of California Press, 2003.

Poonawala, I., A. J. Wensinck, and W. Heffening. "Al-Nasafi." In *Encyclopaedia of Islam*, edited by P. Bearman, Th. Bianquis, C. E. Bosworth, E. van Dozel, and W. Heinrichs, 2nd ed. Brill Online, 2012. Accessed April 26, 2017. http://dx.doi.org/10.1163/1573-3912_islam_COM_0847.

Puar, Jasbir. *Terrorist Assemblages: Homonationalism in Queer Times*. Durham, NC: Duke University Press, 2007.

Qamaruddin. *The Mahdawi Movement in India*. Delhi: Idarah-i Asabiyat-i Delhi, 1985.

Quddūsī, I'jāz al-Ḥaqq. *Tadhkirah-yi ṣūfiyyā-yi sarḥad*. Lahore: Markazi Urdu Board, 1966.

Rahman, Tariq. *Language and Politics in Pakistan*. Karachi: Oxford University Press, 1996.

———. *Language, Ideology and Power: Language Learning among the Muslims of Pakistan and North India*. Karachi: Oxford University Press, 2002.
———. "The Learning of Pashto in North India and Pakistan: An Historical Account." *Journal of Asian History* 35, no. 2 (2001): 158–87.
Raḥmān Bābā. *The Complete Works of Rahman Baba: Poet of the Pukhtuns*. Edited and translated by Momin Khan and Robert Sampson. Self-published, 2012. Kindle edition.
———. *The Nightingale of Peshawar: Selections from Rahman Baba*. Edited and translated by Jens Enevoldsen. Peshawar: Interlit Foundation, 1993.
Raverty, Henry George. *Notes on Afghanistan and Baluchistan*. 1880. Reprint, Quetta: Gosha-e-Adab, 1976.
———. *Selections from the Poetry of the Afghans, from the Sixteenth to the Nineteenth Century*. London: Williams and Norgate, 1862.
Raza, Syed Jabir. "The Afghans and Their Relations with the Ghaznavids and the Ghurids." *Proceedings of the Indian History Congress* 55 (1994): 784–91.
Renard, John. *Friends of God: Islamic Images of Piety, Commitment, and Servanthood*. Berkeley: University of California Press, 2008.
Richards, John F. *The Mughal Empire*. Cambridge: Cambridge University Press, 1996.
Richardson, Caleb. "'They Are Not Worthy of Themselves': The Tailor and Ansty Debates of 1942." *Éire-Ireland* 42, no. 3 (2007): 148–72.
Ricoeur, Paul. *Figuring the Sacred: Religion, Narrative and Imagination*. Edited by Mark I. Wallace. Minneapolis: Fortress, 1995.
Rizvi, S. A. A. "Rawshaniyya Movement." *Abr-Nahrain* 6 (June 1965): 63–91.
———. "Rawshaniyya Movement (continued)." *Abr-Nahrain* 7 (August 1967): 62–98.
Robbins, Vernon Kay. *The Tapestry of Early Christian Discourse: Rhetoric, Society, and Ideology*. London: Routledge, 1996.
Roberts, Tyler. *Encountering Religion: Responsibility and Criticism after Secularism*. New York: Columbia University Press, 2013.
Rondolino, Massimo A. "Introduction: Comparative Hagiology, Issues in Theory and Method." *Religions* 11, no. 4 (2020).
Rose, H. A. *A Glossary of the Tribes and Castes of the Punjab and North-West Frontier Province*. 1883. Reprint, Delhi: Low Price Publications, 1999.
Ross, David. *The Land of the Five Rivers and Sindh: Sketches Historical and Descriptive*. London: Chapman and Hall, 1883.
Rozehnal, Robert. *Islamic Sufism Unbound: Politics and Piety in Twenty-First Century Pakistan*. New York: Palgrave Macmillan, 2009.
Said, Edward W. *Orientalism*. New York: Vintage, 1979; London: Penguin, 2003.
Saleh, Walid. *The Formation of the Classical Tafsīr Tradition: The Qur'ān Commentary of al-Tha'labī (d. 427/1035)*. Leiden: Brill, 2004.
Salomon, Noah. *For Love of the Prophet: An Ethnography of Sudan's Islamic State*. Princeton, NJ: Princeton University Press, 2016.
Saritoprak, Zeki. *Islam's Jesus*. Gainesville: University Press of Florida, 2015.

Schlegell, Barbara von. "Sufism in the Ottoman Arab World: Shaykh ʿAbd Al-Ghanī Al- Nābulusī (d.1143 / 1731)." PhD diss., University of California, Berkeley, 1997.

"Scholars Analyse Peere Roashan's Philosophy." *Kabul Times*, January 12, 1975, vol. 13, no. 239 edition.

Sedgwick, Mark. *Against the Modern World: Traditionalism and the Secret Intellectual History of the Twentieth Century.* Oxford: Oxford University Press, 2004.

———. *Western Sufism: From the Abbasids to the New Age.* Oxford: Oxford University Press, 2016.

Sells, Michael. *Early Islamic Mysticism: Sufi, Qur'an, Mir'aj, Poetic, and Theological Writings.* Mahwah, NJ: Paulist, 1996.

———. *Mystical Languages of Unsaying.* Chicago: University of Chicago Press, 1994.

Shāh Navāz Khān Awrangābādī. *Ma'āthir al-umarā'*. 3 vols. Kolkata: Asiatic Society of Bengal, 1888–91. Reprinted as *The Maāthir-ul-Umarā: Being Biographies of the Muhammādan and Hindu Officers of the Timurid Sovereigns of India from 1500 to about 1780 A.D.* Translated and edited by Bani Prasad and Henry Beveridge. Calcutta: Asiatic Society, 1941. Page references are to the 1941 edition.

Shaw, Gregory. *Theurgy and the Soul: The Neoplatonism of Iamblichus*. Brooklyn: Angelico, 2014.

Sheffield, Daniel. "The Language of Paradise in Safavid Iran: Speech and Cosmology in the Thought of Āẕar Kayvān and His Followers." In *There's No Tapping around Philology*, edited by Alireza Korangy and Daniel Sheffield, 161–83. Wiesbaden: Otto Harrassowitz Verlag, 2014.

Sherman, Jacob Holsinger. "No Werewolves in Theology? Transcendence, Immanence, and Becoming-Divine in Gilles Deleuze." *Modern Theology* 25, no. 1 (2009): 1–20.

———. *Partakers of the Divine: Contemplation and the Practice of Philosophy.* Minneapolis: Fortress, 2014.

Sherman, William E. B. "In the Garden of Language: Religion, Vernacularization, and the Pashto Poetry of Arzani in the Sixteenth and Seventeenth Centuries." *Afghanistan* 5, no. 1 (April 2022): 122–47.

———. "The Lost Tribes of the Afghans: Religious Mobility and Entanglement in Narratives of Afghan Origins." In *American and Muslim Worlds before 1900*, edited by John Ghazvinian and Arthur Mitchell Fraas, 85–97. London: Bloomsbury, 2020.

———. "Qur'ānic Imaginations in the Making: New Religious Movements in Mughal-Era Islam." *Religion Compass* 15, no. 1 (January 2021): 1–10.

———. "Romance on the Afghan Frontier: Desire in the Literature of the Church Missionary Society in Peshawar." *Journal of Imperial and Commonwealth History* 49, no. 6 (2021): 1021–46. https://doi.org/10.1080/03086534.2021.1950325.

Siddique, Abubakar. *The Pashtun Question: The Unresolved Key to the Future of Pakistan and Afghanistan*. London: Hurst, 2014.

Silverstein, Michael. "Metapragmatic Discourse and Metapragmatic Function." In *Reflexive Language: Reported Speech and Metapragmatics*, edited by John A. Lucy, 33–58. Cambridge: Cambridge University Press, 1993.

Singh, David Emmanuel. "Sainthood and Revelatory Discourse." PhD diss., Oxford Centre for Mission Studies, Oxford, 2006.

Smith, George. *The Geography of British India, Political and Physical*. London: J. Murray, 1882.

Sperl, Stefan, trans. "Muḥammad B. Saʿīd al-Būṣīrī (d. c. 1296): The Burda in Praise of the Prophet Muhammad." In *Qasida Poetry in Islamic Asia and Africa*, vol. 2, *Eulogy's Bounty, Meaning's Abundance: An Anthology*, edited by Stefan Sperl and Christopher Shackle, 388–411 and 470–76. Leiden: Brill, 1996.

Spiegel, Gabrielle M. "History, Historicism, and the Social Logic of the Text in the Middle Ages." *Speculum* 65 (1990): 59–86.

Starrett, Gregory. "The Hexis of Interpretation: Islam and the Body in the Egyptian Popular School." *American Ethnologist* 22, no. 4 (1995): 953–69.

Steiner, George. *Real Presences*. Chicago: University of Chicago Press, 1989.

Steinfels, Amina. *Knowledge before Action: Islamic Learning and Sufi Practice in the Life of Sayyid Jalāl al-dīn Bukhārī Makhdūm-i Jahāniyān*. Columbia: University of South Carolina Press, 2012.

Stewart, Devin J. "Rhythmical Anxiety: Notes on Abū'l-ʿAlā' al-Maʿarrī's (d. 449 / 1058) al-Fuṣūl Wa'l-Ghāyāt and Its Reception." In *The Qur'an and Adab: The Shaping of Literary Traditions in Classical Islam,* edited by Nuha Alshaar, 239–72. Oxford: Oxford University Press in association with The Institute of Ismaili Studies, 2017.

Stiegler, Bernard. *Technics and Time, 1: The Fault of Epimetheus*. Translated by Richard Bearsworth and George Collins. Stanford, CA: Stanford University Press, 1998.

Stoler, Ann Laura. *Along the Archival Grain: Epistemic Anxieties and Colonial Common Sense*. Princeton, NJ: Princeton University Press, 2010.

Stowasser, Barbara Freyer. *Women in the Qur'an, Traditions, and Interpretation*. New York: Oxford University Press, 1994.

Subtelny, Maria, and Anas B. Khalidov. "The Curriculum of Islamic Higher Learning in Timurid Iran in the Light of the Sunni Revival under Shāh-Rukh." *Journal of the American Oriental Society* 115 (1995): 210–36.

Sulamī, Muḥammad ibn al-Ḥusayn. *Ṭabaqāt al-ṣūfiyah*. Edited by Nur al-Din Shuraybah. Cairo: Maktabat al-Khanji, 1969.

Sultan-i-Rome. "Origin of Pukhtuns: The Banī Israelite Theory." *Journal of the Pakistan Historical Society* 54, no. 4 (2006): 73–104.

Suvorova, Anna. *Muslim Saints of South Asia: The Eleventh to Fifteenth Centuries*. London: Routledge Curzon, 2004.

Ṭabarī, Abū Jaʿfar Muḥammad ibn Jarīr al-. *The Children of Israel*. Edited and translated by William M Brinner. Albany: State University of New York Press, 1991.

Taneja, Anand Vivek. *Jinnealogy: Time, Islam, and Ecological Thought in the Medieval Ruins of Delhi*. Stanford, CA: Stanford University Press, 2017.

Taylor, Charles. *The Language Animal: The Full Shape of the Human Linguistic Capacity*. Cambridge, MA: Harvard University Press, 2016.

Taylor, Christopher S. *In the Vicinity of the Righteous: Ziyāra and the Veneration of Muslim Saints in Late Medieval Egypt*. Leiden: Brill, 1999.

Thakur, A. K. *India and the Afghans: A Study of a Neglected Region, 1370–1576 A.D.* Patna: Janaki Prakashan, 1992.

Thaʿlabī, Aḥmad ibn Muḥammad al-. *ʿArāʾis al-Majālis fī Qiṣaṣ al-Anbiyā, or: Lives of the Prophets*. Edited by William M. Brinner. Leiden: Brill, 2002.

Thum, Rian. *Sacred Routes of Uyghur History*. Cambridge, MA: Harvard University Press, 2014.

Toorawa, Shawkat M. "Modern Arabic Literature and the Qur'an: Inimitability Creativity, . . . Incompatibility." In *Religious Perspectives in Modern Muslim and Jewish Literatures*, edited by Glenda Abramsom and Hilary Kilpatrick, 25–40. London: Routledge, 2005.

Toscano, Alberto. *Fanaticism: On the Uses of an Idea*. London: Verso, 2010.

Trimingham, John Spencer. *The Sufi Orders in Islam*. Oxford: Oxford University Press, 1971.

Truschke, Audrey. *Culture of Encounters: Sanskrit at the Mughal Court*. New York: Columbia University Press, 2016.

Tuchscherer, Konrad, and Paul E. H. Hair. "Cherokee and West Africa: Examining the Origins of the Vai Script." *History in Africa* 29 (2002): 427–86.

"Tuḥfah-yi Qāsimī." Anonymous, seventeenth century. Curzon Collection MS 261. Asiatic Society of Bengal, Kolkata.

Vanden Brook, Tom. "$725M Program Army 'Killed' Found Alive, Growing." *USA Today*, accessed March 10, 2016. http://www.usatoday.com/story/news/nation/2016/03/09/army-misled-congress-and-public-program/81531280/.

Vardoulakis, Dimitris. *The Doppelgänger: Literature's Philosophy*. New York: Fordham University Press, 2010.

Varisco, Daniel. *Islam Obscured*. New York: Palgrave Macmillan, 2000.

Vasalou, Sophia. "The Miraculous Eloquence of the Qur'an: General Trajectories and Individual Approaches." *Journal of Qur'anic Studies* 4, no. 2 (2002): 23–53.

Vásquez, Manuel A. *More Than Belief: A Materialist Theory of Religion*. Oxford: Oxford University Press, 2010.

Virno, Paolo. *When the Word Becomes Flesh: Language and Human Nature*. Translated by Giuseppina Mecchia. South Pasadena, CA: Semiotext, 2015.

Vogelsang, Willem. *The Afghans*. Oxford: Blackwell, 2002.

———. "The Ethnogenesis of the Pashtuns." In *Cairo to Kabul: Afghan and Islamic Studies Presented to Ralph Pinder-Wilson*, edited by Warwick Ball and Leonard Harrow, 228–35. London: Melisende, 2002.

Wenger, Tisa. *We Have a Religion: The 1920s Pueblo Indian Dance Controversy and American Religious Freedom*. Chapel Hill: University of North Carolina Press, 2009.

Werbner, Pnina. *Pilgrims of Love: The Anthropology of a Global Sufi Cult*. Bloomington: Indiana University Press, 2003.

Widmark, Anders. "Voices at the Borders, Prose on the Margins: Exploring the Contemporary Pashto Short Story in a Context of War and Crisis." PhD diss., Uppsala University, Sweden, 2011. Available online at http://www.diva-portal .org/smash/record.jsf?pid=diva2:454429.

Williams, Rowan. *The Edge of Words: God and the Habits of Language*. London: Bloomsbury Continuum, 2014.

———. *On Christian Theology*. Oxford: Wiley-Blackwell, 2000.

Windfuhr, Gernot, ed. *The Iranian Languages*. London: Routledge, 2009.

Wink, André. "On the Road of Failure: The Afghans in Mughal India." *Cracow Indological Studies*, no. 11 (2009): 267–339.

Yādgār, Ahmad. *Tārīkh-i shāhī, ma'rūf bah tārīkh-i salāṭīn fāghina*. Edited by Muhammad Hidayat Hosain. Tehran: Intishārāt-i Asāṭīr, 1390 [2011 or 2012].

Yaqubi, Himayatullah. "Bayazid Ansari and Roushaniya Movement: A Conservative Cult or a Nationalist Endeavor?" *Journal of the Research Society of Pakistan* 50, no. 1 (2013): 149–70.

———. "Conservative Sufism in the Pakhtun Borderland: Bayazid Ansari and Roushaniya Movement." *Journal of South Asian and Middle Eastern Studies* 33, no. 4 (2010): 61.

Yared, Aida. "'In the Name of Annah': Islam and *Salam* in Joyce's *Finnegans Wake*." *James Joyce Quarterly* 35, no. 2/3 (1998): 401–38.

Yelle, Robert. *Semiotics of Religion: Signs of the Sacred in History*. London: Bloomsbury Academic, 2012.

Yusufi, Allah Bux. *Yusufzai Pathan*. Karachi: Muhammad Ali Education Society, 1973.

Zafar Kaka Khel, Bahadar Shah. *Pukhtana: Da Tarikh pa Ranra ke*. Peshawar: Pashto Academy, University of Peshawar, n.d.

Zeeman, Nicolette. "Imaginative Theory." *Middle English* (2007): 222–40.

Zia, K. Hussan. *The Pathans of Jullunder*. Lahore: Maktaba-tul-Ilmiya, 1996.

Ziad, Waleed. *Hidden Caliphate: Sufi Saints beyond the Oxus and Indus*. Cambridge, MA: Harvard University Press, 2021.

———. "Transporting Knowledge in the Durrani Empire: Two Manuals of Naqshbandi-Mujaddidi Sufi Practice." In *Afghanistan's Islam: From Conversion to the Taliban*, edited by Nile Green, 105–26. Berkeley: University of California Press, 2016.

Index

Note: Page numbers in *italics* refer to illustrative matter.

basmalah, 101–2
batin, 168–69
Battle of Aghazpur, 39, 51
Bayazid, Shaykh, 127
Bayazid Ansari, vii–viii; about, 1, 4–5, 8, 10–12, 176, 187; assassination of, 29–30; death and remains of, 118–19; doubling of, 41, 55–61; dreaming, 41–47; Elphinstone on, 162–63; hagiography of, 30–37; of inquisition and initiation, 53–56; on language, 167–68; life of, 37–41; as miskin, 97; as prophet repeated, 47–53; sainthood of, 25, 30, 37, 44, 52–53, 56–57, 61, 180. See also *Endeavor of the Believers, The* ("Maqṣūd al-mu'minīn"); *Best Exposition, The* ("Khayr al-bayān"); *Book of States, The* (*Ḥāl-nāmah*; Mukhlis); *Path of Oneness, The* ("Ṣirāṭ al-tawḥīd"); Roshaniyya
"Become Ash" (Arzani), 133–34, 137
becoming, 138–39, 140–44, 157–64
Bejeweled History, The ("Tārīkh-i muraṣṣa"), 160
Benjamin, Walter, viii, 16, 187, 196n39
Best Exposition, The ("Khayr al-bayān"): authorship of, 102–4, 127; basmalah in, 101–2; chiasmus in, 103–6, 110; as imitation, 90–92, 103–4, 116, 186; about publication, 7, 19, 27, 90–92, 212nn78–79; revelation in, 95–101; rhyme and, 106–10
Bibi Fatima, 126
Birbal, Raja, 157
Bishr al-Hafi, 50
Book of Akbar, The (Akbar-Namah; Abu Fazl), 33–34, 58
Book of States, The (*Ḥāl-nāmah*; Mukhlis), viii, 26–27; on Bayazid as prophet, 47–53; Bayazid's assassination in, 29–30; on Bayazid's death, 118–19; Bayazid's hagiography and, 32–37; on Bayazid's inquisition and initiation, 54–56; on Bayazid's revelation, 21; dhikr narratives in, 80–82; dream narrative in, 41–47; on Mulla Arzani, 127; about publication, 190; story on Afghan ethnicity in, 156. *See also* Bayazid Ansari
Book of the Turban, The ("Dastar-nāmah"), 160
Boundaries of the World ("Hudud al-'alam"), 154
Breaths of Intimacy ("Nafaḥāt al-'uns"), 58
British colonialism, 3, 126, 155, 160, 161–62, 175–76
Brubaker, Rogers, 173
Calvanist missionaries, 23
Caroe, Olaf, 15, 176
chiasmus, 24, 103–6, 110
chillas, 4
Chiragh al-Din Ansari, 48–49
Chishti Sufis, 72–73
Chrétien, Jean-Louis, 110
Commentary (Monserrate), 158–59
Corbett, Rosemary, 69
cosmologies, 70–74, 85–86, 95, 98, 107, 111, 120, 165–68
Crews, Robert, 13

Danishmands, 182, 183
Darmesteter, James, 161
Darweza, Akhund: about, 11–12; epistemological anxiety of, 164–71; on lettrism, 70; polemics of, 27, 54–55, 94, 125, 139–47. *See also Pious and the Wicked* ("Tadhkirat al-abrār wa-'l-ashrār"); *Treasure Chest of Islam, The* ("Makhzan al-Islām")
Darweza, Karimdad, 142
Deleuze, Gilles, 92
descent, ethnic and tribal, 153
devils, 166–67, 177
dhikr, 2; givenness of, 84–89; meaning of, 72–75; practices of, 4, 27, 62–63, 69; weight of, 80–84. *See also* Sufism
Dilazak Pashtuns, 158
disorientation, 6
Distinguishing Gift, The ("Tuḥfa-yi qāsimī"), 58
divan, 137–39
Doctrines (Al-Nasafi), 142
doubling, 41, 55–57, 60–61. *See also* Bayazid Ansari
dream narrative, 41–47
Drops from the Fountain of Life ("Rashaḥāt 'ayn al-ḥāya"), 58
Durand Line, 7

Eaton, Richard, 183
Eight Gardens, The (Bashiri), 50
Elphinstone, Mountstuart, 161–63
End, The, 62–63
Endeavor of the Believers, The ("Maqṣūd al-mu'minīn"): on dhikr, 62, 72–75, 84–85; Ibn 'Arabi in, 132; language of, 58, 59, 88; about publication, viii, 189–91; Qur'anic verses and hadith in, 75–78; as record of Bayazid's thoughts, 101; wretches in, 63–72, 86, 87

Endeavor of the Seekers, The ("Maqṣūd al-ṭālibīn"), 127
epistemological anxiety, 144, 153, 164–71
Ernst, Carl, 161
ethnicity, as category, 9, 26, 91, 152, 176–77. *See also* Afghan ethnicity
etiological genealogies, 151–52

Final Words, The (Pir Musi), 96
Finest Waystations, The ("Zubdat al-maqāmāt"), 58
Finnegans Wake (Joyce), 90, 91
footing, 139
Foucault, Michel, 205n37
Fragrances of Beauty and the Openings of Majesty, The ("Fawā'iḥ al-jamāl wa fawātiḥ al-jalāl") by Najm al-Din Kubra, 73
fratricide, 49–50

Gabriel (angel), 164–65, 168
Gal, Susan, 98, 121–22
Generations of Akbar, The ("Ṭabaqāt-i akbārī"), 157
Al-Ghazali, 94
ghazals, 120, 121, 126–39, 144, 147–49, 155, 172, 177. *See also* apocalypticism
giddiness, 6
Gin Lum, Kathryn, 18, 35
Goldberg, Jeffrey, 184, 185
Gommans, Jos. J. L., 159, 160
grazing animal trope, 112–13
Great Book of Eternity, The (Fazlallah), 71, 95, 98
Greater Resurrection, 2
Green, Nile, 159, 160
Green-Mercado, Mayte, 18
Guattari, Felix, 92
Guidance of the Seekers, The ("Irshād al-ṭālibīn"), 191

Habibullah Khan, 155
hadith, 65–67, 75–78, 102, 133, 146, 167, 180, 224n1. *See also* Qur'an
Hadot, Pierre, 205n37
hagiography, 30–37, 199n11. See also *Book of States, The* (*Ḥāl-nāmah*; Mukhlis)
Ḥāl-nāmah. See *Book of States, The* (*Ḥāl-nāmah*; Mukhlis)
Hayat, Muhammad, 151–52, 160
Heavenly Regulations, The, 71
Heratis, 158
Hindawi, 7, 25, 59, 97, 101, 103, 114–15, 121, 122
"His Heart Is a Garden" (Arzani), 138
history, defined, 35
Hopkins, Bernard, 161, 162
Hopkins, Gerard Manley, 1, 27–28
human beings, realms of, 67–68
Hurufis, 71, 146
hybridity, 16

Ibn 'Arabi, 45, 132, 147
Ibn Sina, 45, 94
Ibrahim, 48–49, 50
iconization, 121–22
identity. *See* Afghan ethnicity
Ilahdad, 126
ilhām, 94
imitation, 90–92, 103–4, 106, 110, 116
India, 123–24
inimitability doctrine, 92
inquisition and initiation, 53–56
Irvine, Judith, 98, 121–22
Ishmael (character in *Moby Dick*), 183–85, 188

Jalal al-Din Ansari (Jalala and Jalala-yi Tariki), 40, 118–19, 126, 156–57, 158, 163
Jesus. *See* Second Jesus ('Īsá-yi thānī)
jinn, 38, 67–68, 75, 87, 88, 167, 172
jofor texts, 18
Joy of the Chosen, The ("Farḥat al-mujtabá"), 190, 191

Kamal, Muhammad, 119, 127
Kamal al-Din Ansari, 163
Kandaharis, 158
Kanté, Soulaymane, 96
Keane, Webb, 22–23, 24
Khan, Hafiz Rahmat, 160
Khatak, Afzal Khan, 160
Khatak, Khushhal Khan, 12, 99, 108, 140, 147–48, 160, 172, 177, 212n77
"Khayr al-bayān." See *Best Exposition, The* ("Khayr al-bayān")
Khidr, 42, 45–47, 57
Khwaja Khizr Afghan, 166
Khwaja Nizam al-Din, 157
Khyber Pakhutnkhwa region, 4
King, Richard, 69
Kugle, Scott, 5

Landighana, 159
language, power of, 25, 64, 71, 78–80, 121–23, 167–68. *See also* dhikr
Latour, Bruno, 69, 197n63

lettrism, 90, 146
Leyden, John, 9, 161, 162
Lifshitz, Felice, 36
Lobel, Diana, 94
Lodi-Suri dynasties, 4, 125, 155, 156, 160
Lohani, Dawlat, 147

MacKendrick, Karmen, 23, 110
Madigan, Daniel, 93
madness, 53–54
mahdī, vii, viii, 2, 4–5, 15. *See also* Bayazid Ansari
Mahmood, Saba, 15, 16, 23, 24, 35–36, 59, 69, 82
majnūn shudan, 53–54
Malik Ṭālūt. *See* Saul (king)
Mamdani, Mahmood, 69
Maqṣūd al-mu'minīn. See *Endeavor of the Believers, The* (*Maqṣūd al-mu'minīn*; Bayazid)
Marathi language, 123–24, 125
Mary. *See* Second Mary (Maryam-i thānī)
masīḥ, 4
"The Master of Nahnu Aqrab" (Arzani), 135–36
Mawdud, Khalifa, 127
Mecca, 18
Melville, Herman, 183–85
Merleau-Ponty, Maurice, 6
messianism, 16–18, 100–1, 187–88, 193n9. *See also* sainthood; Sufism
Mevlevi Sufis, 72–73
millenarianism, 5, 17, 140, 193n9
Mir, Farina, 125–26, 149
Mir, Mulla, 165–66
Mir-Kasimov, Orkhan, 71, 95
Mirza Hakim, 157
Mirza Khan Ansari, 147
miskin. *See* wretches
Moby Dick (Melville), 183–85
Modern, John Lardas, 185
Monserrate, Antonio, 158–59
Morgenstierne, Georg, 111
Moriscos, 18
Mughal Empire: depictions of Afghans by, 4, 152, 155–57, 175–76; *mansabdar* system, 126–27; Roshaniyya violence, vii, 1, 3, 156–58; textual chronicles on, 19
Muhammad (prophet): Abu Ayyub al-Ansari and, 37–38, 224n1; Bayazid and, 50–51, 109; curse on Afghans by, 164–65, 170–71; Islam's emergence and, 15–16, 17. *See also* Qur'an
Mujaddidi-Naqshbandis, 73
Mukhlis. *See* 'Ali Muhammad Qandahari (Mukhlis)
Musha'sha'iyya, 95
Mysteries Laid Bare, The ("'Uryān al-ghayb"), 190, 191

Najafian, Ahoo, 130
nakhṣha, 111–12
Nani, Shaykh, 165
Naqshbandi-Mujaddidis, 13–14, 69
Al-Nasafi, Najm al-Din Abu Hafs 'Umar ibn Muḥammad, 142
nausea, 6
Netton, Ian, 69
Ni'mat Allah Harawi, 159–61, 163, 164, 176
Novetzke, Christian, 123–24, 149
Nuqtavis, 18, 72, 132, 146

oaths, 136, 144
Ormuri, 122

Paropanisadae, 158
Parthians, 158
Pashto language, 5, 11, 12, 19–21, 58–59, 92, 101, 119–23, 212nn78–79. *See also* language, power of
Pashto literature, vii, 7, 98–101, 108, 140–44. *See also* ghazals
Pashtun, as term, 155. *See also* Afghan, as term
Pashtuns, 20, 98–99, 161–62. *See also under* Afghan
Pathans, 158
Pathans, The (Caroe), 176
Path of Oneness, The ("Ṣirāṭ al-tawḥīd"), 55, 58, 59, 96–98, 190
Persianate, as term, 14
Persian language, 33, 101, 183. *See also* language, power of
Peshawaris, 158
Pious and the Wicked ("Tadhkirat al-abrār wa-'l-ashrār"), 152–53, 160, 164–71. *See also* Darweza, Akhund
pir-i roshan, as term, vii, 2. *See also* Bayazid Ansari
Pir Tayyib, 165–66
Pleasure of Reflections, The ("Nuzhat al-ḍamā'ir"), 160

poetry. *See* Arzani, Mulla; ghazals
Pollock, Sheldon, 124, 125, 126
Prophet Muhammad. *See* Muhammad (prophet)
Punjabi literature, 125–26

Qabil and Habil, 50
Qais, 160, 164
"Qaṣīdat al-burda" (al-Busiri), 142
"Qaṣīdat bada' al-amālī" (al-Ushi), 142, 143–44
qirā'a, 145, 218n71
qiyāma, 71
Quotidian Revolution, The, 123
Qur'an: *The Best Exposition* as imitation of, 90–92, 103–4, 116, 186; Darweza on, 144–46; in *The Endeavor*, 75–78; *qirā'a* of, 145, 218n71; self-image of, 93; Surat al-Fussilat (Sura 41), 146; Surat al-Rahman (Sura 55), 7, 93, 107, 108–9, 113, 210n58; Sūrat Luqmān (Sura 31), 105. *See also* Muhammad (prophet)

Rahman Baba, 148
Raverty, Henry, 118
rawfid, 173
Recollection of the Pious and the Wicked. See Pious and the Wicked ("Tadhkirat al-abrār wa-'l-ashrār")
regional geography, 4, 15, 37
Remembrance of the Ansaris, The, 182
Remembrance of the Saints, The ('Attar), 50
revelation, vii–ix; of Bayazid, 12–13; *The Best Exposition* on, 91–100; as common literary practice, 19–21, 95
rhyme, 106–10, 210n61
Rizvi, S. A. A., 36, 37, 40
Roshaniyya, overview, vii–ix, 1–14, 187–88. *See also under* Afghan; Bayazid Ansari

Safavi, Isma'il, 96
saint, as term, viii–ix
sainthood: of Bayazid, 25, 30, 37, 44, 52–53, 56–57, 61, 180; narratives and tradition of, 27, 31, 119, 163, 183, 187. *See also* messianism; Sufism
Saleh, Walid, 93–94
Salomon, Noah, 23
Saul (king), 12, 151, 159, 160, 163, 174, 175
Sayyid 'Ali Mutaqqi, 5
Sayyid 'Ali Tirmidhi, 139–40, 165, 166–67
Second Jesus ('Īsá-yi thānī), 2, 3, 25, 39
Second Mary (Maryam-i thānī), 2, 3, 6, 10, 20, 25, 39, 185
self-image of the Qur'an, 93. *See also* Qur'an
semiotic ideology, 22–23, 24–25
shari'a, 112–13, 139, 145–47, 165–69
Sheffield, Daniel, 71
Shi'i Muslims, 5, 166, 173
Shir 'Ali, 126
Shir Shah, 161
"The Shrine of Shah Arzani at Patna" (Sita Ram), *128*, 215n35
ṣifat kawal, 137
signature, as term, 112, 113, 130, 211n71
Sikhs, 18, 72, 96
Siraj al-Din Ansari, 48
Sita Ram, *128*, 215n35
"The Strum of the Robab" (Arzani), 129–31, 132, 134
Sufi Generations (al-Sulami), 50
Sufism: Bashir on, 52; Bayazid Ansari and, 112–13, 115, 127; Darweza on, 178, 181; dream narrative in, 41–47; ghazals on, 130–34, 147; Leyden on, 9, 161, 162; Persian, 67–69; Suhrawardian, 182, 183; Trimingham on, 195n33; vision of, 88, 111. *See also* dhikr; messianism; Roshaniyya, overview; sainthood
Suhrawardi Sufism, 182, 183
Summary of Lineages, The ("Khulāṣat al-ansāb"), 160
Sunni Islam, 1–2, 11, 27, 54, 92, 120, 142, 148, 164, 177, 179
Surat al-Fussilat (Sura 41), 146
Surat al-Rahman (Sura 55), 7, 93, 107, 108–9, 113, 210n58
Sūrat Luqmān (Sura 31), 105

Tailor and Antsy, The (Cross), 29, 199n1
Taliban, 13
Taneja, Anand Vivek, 15
Taylor, Charles, 23, 139
temporality, 2, 17–18, 153, 171–75. *See also* timelessness
thabt al-lisān, 84
Al-Tha'labi, 94
theophanic stillness, 97
timelessness, viii, 12–14, 26, 59, 176, 184–85. *See also* temporality

Treasure Chest of Islam, The ("Makhzan al-Islām"), 140–42, 144, 145, 146, 148, 164, 190–91. *See also* Darweza, Akhund
Tu'i Afghans, 2–3

Urdu, 101, 122, 127. *See also* Hindawi
US war in Afghanistan, 13, 184. *See also* American imperialism

Vardoulakis, Dimitris, 41
vernacular literature, 19–21, 98–101, 115–16, 121–26. *See also* Pashto language; Pashto literature
Virno, Paolo, 110

waḥy, 94
Walad, 'Ali Muhammad, 182
walī, viii
"water of life" dream narrative, 45–47
Williams, Rowan, 23, 89, 99
wretches, 63–72, 86, 87, 97, 186

year 1000 (hijri calendar), 2, 17
Yelle, Robert, 132

zahir, 168–69
Al-Zamakhshari, 94
Ziad, Waleed, 13–14, 73
Zoroastrian community, 18, 70–72, 96
Zuhak (king), 152

William E. B. Sherman is an assistant professor of Islamic Studies in the Department of Religious Studies at the University of North Carolina at Charlotte.

www.ingramcontent.com/pod-product-compliance
Lightning Source LLC
Chambersburg PA
CBHW020400080526
44584CB00014B/1107
* 9 7 8 1 5 3 1 5 0 5 6 8 4 *